Economic Justice
and Democracy

Paths for the 21st Century
edited by Marcus Raskin

The Business of America: How Consumers Have Replaced Citizens and How We Can Reverse the Trend
Saul Landau

The American Ideology: A Critique
Andrew Levine

Economic Justice and Democracy

FROM COMPETITION TO COOPERATION

Robin Hahnel

Routledge
Taylor & Francis Group

NEW YORK AND LONDON

Published in 2005 by
Routledge
Taylor & Francis Group
270 Madison Avenue
New York, NY 10016

Published in Great Britain by
Routledge
Taylor & Francis Group
2 Park Square
Milton Park, Abingdon
Oxon OX14 4RN

Printed in the United States of America on acid-free paper
10 9 8 7 6 5 4 3 2 1

International Standard Book Number-10: 0-415-93344-7 (hardcover) 0-415-93345-5 (softcover)
International Standard Book Number-13: 978-0-415-93344-5 (hardcover) 978-0-415-93345-2 (softcover)

Library of Congress Cataloging-in-Publication Data

Catalog record is available from the Library of Congress

Taylor &Francis Group
is the Academic Division of T&F Informa plc.

Visit the Taylor &Francis Web site at
http://www.taylorandfrancis.com

and the Routledge Web site at
http://www.routledge-ny.com

This book is dedicated to my children:
Jesse, Ilana, Sara, Tanya, Dylan, and Aidan

Contents

Part IV. From Competition and Greed to Equitable Cooperation

Series Editor's Preface

The aim of the *Paths for the 21st Century* series is to encourage new ways of looking at problems, to foster practical approaches to longstanding problems, and to promote the knowledge capable of positively influencing people's everyday lives. The books in this series are intended to give the powerless a greater role in the discourse that strengthens communities without creating barriers between these communities. Toward this end, the "Paths" Project seeks out new ways for future generations to evade the pitfalls of the twentieth century while fostering a spirit of liberation that focuses on dignity and decency for all people.

The Paths Project acknowledges three contending approaches to the use and function of knowledge. The first views knowledge and inquiry as primarily in the service of domination, control, and manipulation of others. This form of knowledge most often results in blind, unquestioning, and dogmatic faith. The second approach focuses on knowledge as merely utilitarian with an ever increasing focus on technical specializations and subspecialization. It assumes a specific cause and solution to a given problem, and pays insufficient attention to the aims and values to which knowledge is ultimately subservient.

It is the third approach that I take as the basis for the Paths Projects. This approach assumes that knowledge and inquiry are directed toward liberation rather than control, seeking to understand the relationships between institutions, systems, problems, and, most importantly, values. This approach ultimately fosters greater democratic discourse and a more progressive social reconstruction. The Paths Project presumes that this third approach affords us the insight and wisdom necessary for creating dignity and equality and to end the exploitation of one group by another.

Paths for the 21st Century will draw together scholars and activists to create an invisible college, working together and trading ideas to stimulate thinking and discussion about issues affecting us domestically and internationally. It will present radical alternatives concerning what should be changed, and how these changes can be accomplished. In the end, the aim of the Paths Project is to lay the foundation for a new progressivism chastened by the lessons of the twentieth century and reconstructed for the twenty-first century. This is no small goal; it is one that, ultimately, in a democracy, can only be achieved through discussion and a community of inquiry and deliberation. It is my hope that the books in this series will help to begin and contribute to that dialogue without which social justice, personal freedom, and a progressive twenty-first century will never come about.

Marcus Raskin
Institute for Policy Studies and *George Washington University*

Acknowledgments

This book is the product of working for progressive social change as an economist and activist for almost 40 years. It bears the stamp of more people and more organizations than I could hope to mention, much less do justice to. In particular I want to thank Marcus Raskin for inviting me almost a decade ago to write a book on progressive economics for the *Paths for the 21st Century* series. He encouraged me to examine the thinking of those who fought to replace the economics of competition and greed with the economics of equitable cooperation during the twentieth century for lessons that would help those in the century ahead to achieve what we could not. Without him this book would never have happened. I also thank my editors at Taylor & Francis—Robert Tempio, Angela Chnapko, Tao Woolfe, and Eric Nelson—who sponsored such an ambitious adventure, and who tolerated every delay gracefully. Finally, I thank my graduate assistant at American University, Susan Bush, who offered invaluable suggestions after a careful reading of an early draft of the manuscript.

But mostly I wish to acknowledge the debt we owe to those who have gone before. We must be merciless in our criticisms of our predecessors if we are ever to do better, but while those who come after must learn how to go about things differently to accomplish what we could not, the sacrifices made by tens of millions of people in countless attempts to advance the cause of economic justice and democracy during the twentieth century should never be gainsaid. Those who prove themselves our betters will always owe those who went before a tremendous debt of gratitude.

Introduction

At the dawn of the twentieth century most critics of capitalism believed it would be capitalism's last. If they agreed on little else, socialists of all stripes expected democracy and economic justice to advance in tandem, replacing a wasteful system based on competition and greed with a more efficient, equitable economy in which workers and consumers planned how to cooperate through democratic procedures. But the more successful heirs to nineteenth-century socialism—twentieth-century communism and social democracy—both failed to advance the cause of economic justice and democracy, and libertarian socialism all but disappeared a third of the way through the century. So instead of hearing its last hurrah, capitalism beat back all challengers in the twentieth century, leaving us with an economy at the beginning of the twenty-first century that is far more technologically advanced and environmentally destructive—but no more equitable or democratic—than it was a hundred years ago.

Communist parties sacrificed economic and political democracy in the name of an economic justice they never delivered. Social democratic parties avoided the totalitarian errors of communism only to water down their commitment to economic justice and worker self-management, and become handmaidens to capitalism. In the end, neither delivered on their promises of economic justice or economic democracy, and both became unwitting accomplices to environmental destruction. As a result, communism had both feet, and social democracy had one foot in the dust bin of history as the door closed on the century each presumed would bear its name.

Criticism of both communism and social democracy from the left was by no means absent during the twentieth century. But no political movement suffered greater decline during the last century than libertarian socialism, which all but disappeared after 1939. No matter how prescient their criticisms of communist and social democratic rivals, libertarian socialists suffered defeat after defeat and became increasingly marginalized and irrelevant. The rise of the new left in the late 1960s and the appearance of "new social movements" in the 1970s and 1980s resurrected some old libertarian socialist themes, but not a new libertarian socialist movement. The collapse of communism and decline of social democracy at the century's end have stimulated renewed interest in libertarian socialism, but have not led to a full-blown revival of the movement.

Conservatives interpret the demise of communism, social democracy, and libertarian socialism as evidence that critics of capitalism underestimate its virtues and have no better alternative. Conservatives argue that critics misunderstand economic justice and economic democracy, and therefore fail to appreciate how capitalism delivers both while promoting economic efficiency. Conservatives cite the demise of communist and social democratic economies as proof that egalitarian notions of economic justice are incompatible with economic freedom and efficiency. They argue that redistributive demands by the less fortunate violate the economic freedoms of others and kill the geese who lay the golden eggs. Finally, conservatives argue that twentieth-century economic history proves that egalitarian outcomes can only be imposed by totalitarian means, explaining why, in their view, libertarian socialism can never get anywhere.

Economic Justice and Democracy: From Competition to Cooperation provides a different explanation for why things turned out as they have, and offers new ideas about what must be done differently in the century ahead to achieve better results. This book argues that capitalism triumphed in the twentieth century despite the fact that it is grossly unfair, undermines economic democracy, is terribly inefficient, and is destined to destroy the natural environment. This book argues that communism and social democracy failed because they failed to deliver economic justice and democracy, not because economic justice and democracy are utopian dreams in conflict with one another and with economic efficiency. This book argues that libertarian socialists fell into eclipse because they clung to debilitating myths, never learned how to work effectively in campaigns to reform capitalism, and failed to provide a compelling explanation of how workers can manage themselves and coordinate their division of labor without resort to either markets or central planning, not because human beings are incapable of equitable cooperation. Obviously this interpretation of twentieth-century economic history is at odds with better-known theories. It is certainly at odds with the procapitalist "victor's history." That is why there are many chapters to follow, and why there will have to be more books by many others to make the case complete. But before describing the central concern of the book—clarifying what equitable cooperation means, and developing an effective program for achieving it—two disclaimers are in order:

1. While most of *Economic Justice and Democracy* focuses on how to better promote the economics of equitable cooperation, some chapters explore why critics failed to overcome the economics of competition and greed in the twentieth century. However, it is the future, not the past, that primarily interests me. I am no historian. In my professional life I am an economist who specializes in analyzing the predictable effects of different economic institutions and systems. In my political life I am an activist who fights the pernicious effects of competition and greed and promotes the economics of equitable cooperation at every opportunity. I trespass on the turf of professional historians with a great deal of trepidation, and only because my economic analysis led me to a conclusion that begged for an historical explanation: Why were palpably inferior economic systems like capitalism and communism so much more successful in the twentieth century than clearly superior systems of democratic socialism? My excuse for trespassing is I could find no answer in the historical literature that satisfied me.[1]

2. Victories can be due to intrinsic strengths, good implementation, or fortuitous external circumstances. Similarly, defeats can be due to intrinsic weaknesses, poor implementation, or inhospitable circumstances. Therefore, proponents of any alternative capitalism defeated in the twentieth century—communism, social democracy, or libertarian socialism—can always blame defeat on poor implementation or unfavorable external factors rather than on intrinsic weaknesses in their program. While I recognize that all three reasons for defeat deserve serious consideration when trying to explain history, I do not afford them equal attention because I am primarily concerned with the future. I focus foremost on intrinsic strengths and weaknesses of communism, social democracy, and libertarian socialism because these are the most important to future

opponents of capitalism. In the case of communism, I ignore not only negative external factors but also misguided practice—both of which contributed to the historical defeat of communism—because I find the intrinsic weaknesses of command planning sufficient to prevent it from ever again playing a central role on history's stage.[2] In the case of social democracy and libertarian socialism, I pay little attention to the role played by inhospitable external factors, not because they were unimportant, but because there was little twentieth-century activists could do about them, and because many limiting external factors will be different in the century ahead. On the other hand, the role played by poor leadership and practice in the decline of social democracy and libertarian socialism during the twentieth century is of great interest to me. I believe social democracy will continue to play an important role well into the twenty-first century, and I believe libertarian socialist ideas will play an increasingly important role in the century ahead. Therefore, besides intrinsic weaknesses, I focus on poor implementation on the part of social democrats and libertarian socialists in the last century because I foresee a lengthy period during which the two will coexist and collaborate closely in the century ahead.

The Main Argument

The central argument of this book is that progressives need to go back to the drawing board and rethink how we conceive of economic justice and economic democracy. Until we face this intellectual challenge squarely it will continue to sabotage our best efforts to combat the economics of competition and greed. Conservative conceptions of economic justice and democracy are criticized because otherwise it is difficult to dispel popular myths about capitalism. But more importantly, this book argues that liberal notions of economic justice and democracy are flawed, and that continued confusion among liberal and radical reformers about economic justice and democracy will continue to undermine attempts to promote equitable cooperation. After carefully examining competing notions, this book concludes that economic justice should be defined as reward commensurate with sacrifice, and economic democracy should be defined as decision-making power in proportion to the degree affected.

After demonstrating why capitalism, central planning, and market socialism are all incapable of providing economic justice and democracy, a coherent set of economic institutions and procedures that can deliver economic justice and democracy while protecting the environment and promoting efficiency is spelled out. This participatory economy distinguishes between user rights and income rights to overcome defects in traditional conceptions of private and public ownership of productive assets. It forswears labor markets in order to compensate people fairly for their work, while still providing strong material incentives. And participatory planning avoids the pitfalls of central planning and markets by allocating goods and resources efficiently through a procedure that gives workers and consumers decision-making power in proportion to the degree they are affected by different economic choices.

However a participatory economy is only a guiding vision. After carefully examining legitimate concerns critics have raised about participatory economics as a long-run goal, the final part of the book explores how to promote the economics of equitable cooperation in the here and now through economic reform campaigns and movements that already exist, and through alternative experiments that grow in the cracks where capitalism fails to meet human needs and aspirations. There are suggestions about how to work in numerous pragmatic reform campaigns while remaining true to full economic justice and democracy. There are suggestions about how to broaden the base of existing economic reform movements while deepening their commitment to more far-reaching change. And finally, ideas for how to learn from and expand living experiments in equitable cooperation and better integrate reform work with prefigurative experiments are discussed.

Part I: Economic Justice and Democracy

Chapter 1, "Economic Justice," compares competing notions of economic justice both inside and outside progressive circles. It is pointed out that conservative and liberal conceptions of economic justice share a common basis—they are both "contribution-based" theories that justify how much people should receive on the basis of how much they contribute. In the conservative view, people should consume according to the contribution of their labor and their productive assets. In the liberal view consumption should depend only on personal contribution, and property income is seen as the source of inequities. It is argued that both views are incompatible with progressive values since contribution is determined by a host of factors over which individuals have little or no control. Consequently, any contribution-based theory of economic justice will prove contradictory and unsatisfactory, ultimately misleading movements seeking to make economic cooperation equitable.

Instead, after considering crucial issues raised by the conservative libertarian philosopher, Robert Nozick, and the famous liberal philosopher, John Rawls, a radical "sacrifice-based" theory of economic justice is defended: to each according to his or her effort, interpreted as any sacrifice an individual incurs in carrying out his or her economic duties.

Chapter 2, "Economic Democracy," argues that formal democracy does not guarantee real democracy. Just as universal suffrage does not guarantee that everyone has an equal opportunity to influence political decisions, being "free" to become an employer if one doesn't like being someone else's employee, or "free" to apply for a job elsewhere if one doesn't like the one s/he has, does not guarantee meaningful economic democracy. But neither does giving everyone one vote concerning an economic choice when some people are more affected than others by a decision. Economic democracy is more complicated than either economic freedom or majority rule. Moreover, appeals to property rights do not solve, but merely postpone, difficult issues regarding economic democracy.

This chapter argues for conceptualizing the idea that people should control their economic destinies as "economic self-management," defined as decision-making input in proportion to the degree one is affected by the outcome. According to this criterion, if an economic decision affects some people more than others, those with more at stake should have a greater say than those with less at stake. This criterion provides a way to resolve conflicts between different economic freedoms and the economic freedoms of different people when they inevitably arise, at least theoretically, without resort to arbitrary rules. While it does not resolve debates over how much different people are affected, it does provide a coherent basis for adjudication.

Chapter 3, "Debilitating Myths," shows how many twentieth-century progressives sustained themselves with false beliefs that capitalism's dynamism and technological creativity would prove to be its weakness as well as its strength. Grandiose Marxist crisis theories buoyed the hopes of the faithful in the face of setbacks for progressive organizations and causes, and even less ideological reformers were influenced by the myth that capitalism organized its own replacement. This chapter argues that what is true instead is that free-market capitalism cannot keep itself from devouring the environment, and will not provide even minimal economic security for most of the Third World and a growing underclass in the advanced economies. And even when capitalism is thoroughly reformed it cannot give people control over their economic lives or reward people fairly for the sacrifices they make. It is argued that, unfortunately, capitalism does not nurture the seeds of its own replacement in the way many of its twentieth-century critics hoped it would. Instead, capitalism fosters commercial values and behaviors, rationalizes exploitation, and teaches myths about its own desirability and inevitability, all of which must be successfully challenged if we are to achieve equitable cooperation. The chapter also argues that for much of the twentieth century the left was plagued by a false belief that economic dynamics and classes were always the dominant forces governing social stability and change. Unfortunately, their mistaken "economism" prevented them from recognizing the nature and power of nationalism, racism, and sexism, and also led to misguided approaches to building coalitions of different progressive social movements.

Part II: Rethinking Our Past

Starting from a clear understanding about what economic justice and economic democracy mean, chapter 4, "Neither Capitalism nor Communism," highlights the intrinsic flaws in the major economic institutions that dominated the twentieth century: private enterprise, markets, and hierarchical management in capitalist economies, and public ownership, central planning, and hierarchical management in communist economies.

The chapter argues that private ownership under more competitive conditions did stimulate the economic creativity of many of the fortunate, lucky, and able during the twentieth century, but it always failed to tap the creative potentials of the majority and led to inefficient conflicts between employers and employees. The chapter explains why public ownership reduced inequities but did nothing to solve the problem of democratic management and created a new problem: how to monitor the performance of managers appointed by the state. The chapter concludes that under central planning neither planners, managers, nor workers had incentives to promote the social economic interest. Nor did appending markets for final goods to the planning system enfranchise consumers in meaningful ways, as both workers and consumers were systematically deprived of self-management opportunities in centrally planned economies. On the other hand, the chapter explains how capitalist markets were guided by an "invisible foot" as well as an "invisible hand" rewarding those who externalized costs and rode for free, not only those who built better mouse traps and reduced production costs.

Chapter 5, "Social Democracy: Losing the Faith," describes how social democrats attempted to respond to the failures of capitalism without succumbing to the errors of communism. Particularly during the middle of the century social democrats enjoyed much success winning reforms that significantly reduced the inequities and inefficiencies of free market capitalism. However, while diluting the meaning of economic justice and economic democracy allowed social democracy to expand its electoral appeal into the middle class, it eventually cost them support among the most exploited. Social democrats' explicit acceptance of a system driven by greed and competition after World War II, combined with decades of backsliding on economic justice and democracy, also undermined their moral authority. Without moral authority or a solid base of political support, social democratic efforts to build a movement for equitable cooperation stalled, and when resurgent capitalism launched an all-out offensive at the end of the century they found themselves unable to defend gains they had worked decades to win. The chapter examines the strengths as well as the weaknesses of social democracy through the writings of two farsighted social democrats, Michael Harrington and Magnus Ryner, focusing on the Mitterrand socialist government in France during the early 1980s and the Swedish model of social democracy in the 1990s.

Chapter 6, "Libertarian Socialism: What Went Wrong?" takes up the story of libertatian socialists. While prominent in the first few decades of the twentieth century, libertarian socialists enjoyed little success in the last two thirds of the century largely because they failed miserably at reform work in advanced capitalist economies. A review of their considerable successes in Russia prior to 1920 and in Spain during the 1930s reveals that libertarian socialists were able organizers who lost their ability to reach out to large segments of the population after their defeat in Spain for reasons that are important to understand, but have been widely misinterpreted by latter-day libertarian socialists. Libertarian socialists also failed to provide a compelling case that a libertarian socialist economy was a realistic possibility. Social democrats and communists had easy answers to the important question: If not capitalism, then what? They could simply point to Sweden or to the Soviet Union. Having no living example to point to, other than a few short-lived experiments in wartime situations, the failure of libertarian socialists to make their vision of equitable cooperation more coherent and concrete inevitably increased popular skepticism that libertarian socialists offered a workable alternative as the "capitalist century" marched on.

Part III: What Do We Want?

In the aftermath of the collapse of communism, those who propose alternatives to capitalism fall into three camps: market socialism, community-based economics, and democratic planning. After explaining why economic vision is important, chapter 7, "Postcapitalist Visions," offers a critical examination of different versions of market socialism, explaining how they would improve significantly on capitalism, but also how they fail to provide an institutional framework capable of securing the economics of equitable cooperation. The motivations of proponents of community-based economics are praised, but the chapter points out that no vision of community-based economics has been elaborated into a rigorous model, and all versions leave crucial questions unanswered, including how economic relations between separate economic communities that are not entirely self-sufficient would be handled. The chapter concludes with a brief introduction to different models of democratic planning as a prelude to discussions of participatory economics in the two chapters that follow.

Chapter 8, "Participatory Economics," describes a system of democratic planning known as a participatory economy that can be subjected to rigorous analysis because it has been formalized as a coherent economic model. A participatory economy is a viable set of economic institutions that promote economic justice and democracy without sacrificing efficiency. It is proposed as a long-term goal for those fighting to advance the economics of equitable cooperation. The chapter describes how, in this libertarian version of democratic planning, production can be organized through worker councils, jobs can be balanced for empowerment and desirability, consumption can be based on sacrifices made at work and organized through consumer councils and federations, and self-managed worker and consumer councils can coordinate their activities through a participatory planning procedure in which they propose and revise their own activities in a way that generates equity and efficiency simultaneously. The model of a participatory economy is elaborated in sufficient detail so readers can see concretely why its proponents believe it promotes economic justice and democracy without sacrificing efficiency, but also so skeptics have something specific to criticize rather than only a rhetorical marshmallow to punch at.

This chapter also covers two subjects that were not broached in earlier presentations of participatory economics. It explains how pollution and environmental protection would be handled in both the annual and long-term participatory planning procedures, and why other features of a participatory economy would dampen excessive consumerism and avoid unproductive growth. The chapter also explains how a participatory economy could trade with, borrow from, or lend to other economies in ways that benefit the participatory economy but do not undermine its core principles, no matter whether international economic partners are poorer or richer, or what kind of economic system they may have.

While participatory economics is virtually unknown in mainstream circles, it has received considerable attention over the past twelve years from progressive economists and anticapitalist activists both inside and outside the United States, and therefore has been subjected to intense scrutiny and criticism. Moreover, many of the objections that have been raised to a participatory economy are similar to objections raised to any kind of worker self-management or democratic planning. Chapter 9, "Legitimate Concerns," considers whether a participatory economy lacks sufficient incentives for creative people to develop and deploy their talents, tolerates laziness, would devolve into a "dictatorship of the sociable," requires too many meetings, would fail to develop new technologies and products, or is incompatible with human nature.

Part IV: From Competition and Greed to Equitable Cooperation

Whereas Part 3 was concerned with clarifying what a full system of equitable cooperation might look like, Part 4 tackles the issue of a transition program. A participatory economy may be feasible and attractive, but it is only of academic interest if there is no way to get there from where we are today. A participatory economy is a long-term goal in most countries today, not a program that can be successfully fought for in the near future. So the crucial question is what can be done to promote the economics of equitable cooperation in the here and now amid the ravages of early twenty-first century Robber Baron capitalism? Chapter 10, "From Here to There: Taking Stock," takes a sober look at the formidable obstacles that confront us at the beginning of the new century and at the forces of resistance that have already begun to form.

Chapter 11, "Economic Reform Campaigns," discusses how activists can combat the adverse consequences of the economics of competition and greed in ways that promote the economics of equitable cooperation by working in a number of ongoing reform campaigns. The chapter discusses the importance of campaigns for various Keynesian reforms, campaigns for welfare and tax reform, living wage campaigns, campaigns to strengthen the public sector and curb market forces, and local campaigns to replace gentrification and sprawl with community development and smart growth.

Chapter 12, "Economic Reform Movements," explains why activists must help build powerful economic reform movements, and explores ways to do so without succumbing to pressures to weaken our commitment to economic justice and economic democracy or to abandon our long-run goal of replacing capitalism with a full system of equitable cooperation. The chapter contains concrete suggestions about how to work more effectively in the labor movement, the anticorporate movement, the environmental movement, the consumer movement, the poor people's movement, and the antiglobalization movement.

Besides building more powerful reform movements and working on campaigns to win meaningful reforms in ways that overcome weaknesses in the practice of both social democrats and libertarian socialists in the past, twenty-first century activists will have to create opportunities for growing numbers of people to enter into equitable cooperation with one another even while capitalism continues to survive for many decades into the future. This is the only way to develop the new habits necessary for people to transcend the culture of competition and greed that capitalism breeds. This is the only way to test and adjust our ideas about how to better organize our economic affairs. This is the only way to convince a majority of the population that a better world is possible. And this is the only way to prevent activist burnout and sellout over the long march.

Living examples of equitable cooperation already exist in different contexts and places. Chapter 13, "Experiments in Equitable Cooperation," provides a critical review of alternative currency systems, employee stock-ownership plans, worker and consumer-owned cooperatives, intentional egalitarian and sustainable living communities, and small experiments in participatory economics in the United States and Canada. Important international experiments in equitable cooperation like the Mondragon cooperatives in Spain, participatory budgeting in Kerala, India, and Porto Alegre, Brazil, and worker takeovers and neighborhood assemblies in Argentina are also examined. Finally, the chapter argues for the importance of elaborating new ways people working for extended periods in reform movements can personally commit to partial systems of equitable cooperation to counter the debilitating effects of capitalist culture.

The final chapter highlights the major challenges economic progressives must overcome in the decades ahead. It reiterates why we must abandon futile attempts to harness fear and greed, and instead work to replace the logic of competition and greed with systems of equitable cooperation. It explains the importance of remaining true to our principles of economic justice and democracy even when we are forced to settle for compromise outcomes. It explains why we must combine reform campaigns with prefigurative experiments, since neither alone is sufficient to defeat capitalism. And finally, the chapter explores how activists working to replace the economics of competition and greed with the economics of equitable cooperation can forge more productive relationships with other progressive movements like the civil rights, antiracist, women's, gay, environmental, and peace movements.

Part I

Economic Justice and Democracy

1

Economic Justice

When economic historians look back on the last fifth of the twentieth century what will stand out above all else will be the dramatic increase in inequality of wealth and income, both within and between countries. During the 1980s and 1990s inequality increased at unprecedented rates within the United States and most other advanced economies, and the gap between rich and poor countries widened sensationally. This spectacular rise in inequality came on the heels of a more measured trend toward greater equality during the previous half century. During the middle part of the twentieth century, social democratic and New Deal reforms in advanced capitalist economies greatly expanded the ranks of their middle classes and thereby reduced wealth and income inequalities inside their economies. At the same time communist governments, for all their faults, reduced internal income and wealth inequalities compared to their capitalist predecessors and made dramatic strides toward closing the gap in GDP per capita between their less developed economies and the more advanced capitalist countries. Finally, after World War II the postcolonial international economy guided by the Bretton Woods system managed to reduce the gap between rich and poor capitalist countries, even if only slightly. Unfortunately, these equalizing trends came screeching to a halt at the beginning of the 1980s, to be replaced by arguably the most dramatic redistribution of wealth and income from poor to rich the world has ever seen, as well as the disappearance of middle classes—scarcely older than a single generation—in large parts of the global economy.

Reverse Robin Hood

In a study published in 1995 by the Twentieth Century Fund, Edward Wolff concluded:

> Many people are aware that income inequality has increased over the past twenty years. Upper-income groups have continued to do well while others, particularly those without a college degree and the young have seen their real income decline. The 1994 *Economic Report of the President* refers to the 1979–1990 fall in real income of men with only four years of high school—a 21% decline—as stunning. But the growing divergence evident in income distribution is even starker in wealth distribution. Equalizing trends of the 1930s–1970s reversed sharply in the 1980s. The gap between haves and have-nots is greater now than at any time since 1929.[1]

Chuck Collins and Felice Yeskel report: "In 1976, the wealthiest one percent of the population owned just under 20% of all the private wealth. By 1999, the richest one percent's share had increased to over 40 percent of all wealth." And they calculate that in the twenty-one years between 1976 and 1997 while the top 1 percent of wealthholders doubled their share of the wealth pie, the bottom 90 percent saw their share cut almost in half.[2] Between 1983 and 1989 the average financial wealth of households in the United States grew at an annual rate of 4.3 percent after being adjusted for inflation. But the top 1 percent of wealthholders captured an astounding 66.2 percent of the growth in financial wealth, the next 19 percent of wealthholders captured 36.8 percent, and the bottom 80 percent of wealthholders in the United States lost 3 percent of their financial wealth. As a result the top 1 percent increased their share of total wealth in the United States from 31 to 37 percent in those six years alone, and by 1989 the richest 1 percent of families held 45 percent of all non-residential real estate, 62 percent of all business assets, 49 percent of all publicly held stock, and 78 percent of all bonds.[3] Moreover, "most wealth growth arose from the appreciation (or capital gains) of preexisting wealth and not savings out of income. Over the 1962 to 1989 period, roughly three-fourths of new wealth was generated by increasing the value of initial wealth—much of it inherited."[4] When we look to see who benefited from the stock market boom between 1989 and 1997 the same pattern emerges. The top 1 percent of wealthholders captured an astonishing 42.5 percent of the stock market gains over those years, the next 9 percent of wealthholders captured an additional 43.3 percent of the gains, the next 10 percent captured 3.1 percent, while the bottom 80 percent of wealth-holders captured only 11 percent of the stock market gains.[5]

While growing wealth inequality was more dramatic, income inequal-ity has been growing as well. Real wages fell in the United States after the mid-1970s to where the average hourly wage adjusted for inflation was lower in 1994 than it had been in 1968. Moreover, this decline in real hourly wages occurred despite continual increases in labor produc-tivity. Between 1973 and 1998 labor productivity grew 33 percent. Collins and Yeskel calculate that if hourly wages had grown at the same rate as labor productivity the average hourly wage in 1998 would have been $18.10 rather than $12.77, a difference of $5.33 an hour, or more than eleven thousand dollars per year for a full-time worker.[6] Moreover, the failure of real wages to keep up with labor productivity growth was worse for those in lower wage brackets. Between 1973 and 1993 workers earn-ing in the 80th percentile gained 2.7 percent in real wages while workers in the 60th percentile lost 4.9 percent, workers in the 40th percentile lost 9 percent, and workers in the 20th percentile lost 11.7 percent—creating much greater inequality of wage income.[7]

In contrast, U.S. corporate profit rates in 1996 reached their highest level since these data were first collected in 1959. The Bureau of Eco-nomic Analysis reported that the before-tax profit rate rose to 11.4 per-cent and the after-tax rate rose to 7.6 percent in 1996, capping an eight-year period of dramatic, sustained increases in corporate profits the Bureau called "unparalleled in U.S. history." Moreover, whereas previ-ous periods of high profits accompanied high rates of investment and eco-nomic growth, the average rate of economic growth over these eight years was just 1.9 percent Whatever was good for corporate profits was clearly *not* so good for the rest of us.

While there are a number of different ways to measure inequality, the most widely used by economists is a statistic called the Gini coefficient. A value of 0 corresponds to perfect equality and a value of 1 corresponds to perfect inequality. The Gini coefficient for household income in the United States rose steadily from 0.405 in 1966 to 0.479 in 1993, a remarkable 18.3 percent increase in income inequality among U.S. house-holds over the time period.[8]

Trends in global inequality are even more disturbing. Walter Park and David Brat report in a study of gross domestic product per capita in ninety-one countries that the value of the Gini rose steadily from 0.442 in 1960 to 0.499 in 1988, a 13 percent increase in the economic inequality between countries in less than twenty years.[9] The *Human Development Report 2000* published by the United Nations reported that between 1975 and 1990 GDP per capita in countries with a high human development index grew at a 2.1 percent average annual rate, while GDP per capita in countries with a low human development index *fell* at a 1 percent average annual rate (p. 205). The report also reveals that between 1990 and 1998 the average annual rate of growth of GDP per capita was more than twice as high in countries with a high human development index (1.7 percent) than in countries with a low human development index (0.8 percent). The gap between rich and poor countries has increased dramatically, and all evidence available so far indicates that this trend toward greater global inequality has continued into the new millennium as neoliberal globalization continues despite growing popular dissent.

The facts are clear: we are experiencing increases in economic inequality inside the United States reminiscent of the robber baron era of U.S. capitalism over a hundred years ago, and the acceleration of global inequality has reached unprecedented levels. But how should we interpret the facts? When are unequal outcomes inequitable and when are they not? Is it necessarily unfair when some consume more, or work less than others? Do those with more productive property deserve to work less or consume more? Do those who are more talented or more educated deserve greater rewards? Do those who contribute more, or those who make greater sacrifices, or those who have greater needs deserve more? There is no denying that economic inequality is increasing dramatically, both inside and between countries, but by what logic are unequal outcomes fair or unfair? A central argument of this book is that increasing confusion—and opportunism—among critics of capitalism about economic injustice contributed substantially to our failure to advance the cause of equitable cooperation in the twentieth century, and will continue to plague our efforts in the twenty-first century if we do not sharpen our understanding of economic justice and commitment to fighting for economic justice in any and all circumstances.

Different Conceptions of Economic Justice

Equity takes a backseat to efficiency for most mainstream economists, while the issue of economic justice has long been a passion of critics of capitalism. From Proudhon's provocative quip that "property is theft," to Marx's three-volume indictment of capitalism as a system based on the "exploitation of labor," economic justice has been a major theme in political economy. But as much as economic justice is still a passion of radical political economists today, we seem to have a difficult time saying clearly what it is. Instead, many radical economists find themselves in the position in which the late U.S. Supreme Court Justice Potter Stewart found himself when required to make a ruling on pornography. In his immortal words: "I shall not today attempt further to define pornography, but I know it when I see it." It seems few radical economists can define economic justice, but almost all believe they know economic *in*justice when they see it. Unfortunately this approach is an invitation to inconsistencies and opportunism that undermine the movement fighting for economic justice in the long run.

What is an equitable distribution of the burdens and benefits of economic activity? What reasons for differential compensation are morally compelling, and what reasons carry no moral weight? Four distributive maxims span the range of possible answers to the question how people *should* be compensated for their part in economic cooperation.

Maxim 1: To Each According to the Value of the Contribution of Her Physical and Human Capital

The rationale behind maxim 1 is that people should get out of an economy what they and their productive possessions contribute to the economy. If we think of economic goods and services as a giant pot of stew, the idea is that individuals contribute to how plentiful and rich the stew will be by their labor and by the nonhuman productive assets they bring to the economy kitchen. If my labor and productive assets make the stew bigger or richer than your labor and assets, then according to maxim 1 it is only fair that I eat more stew, or richer morsels, than you do.

While this rationale has obvious appeal, it has a major problem I call the *Rockefeller grandson problem*. According to maxim 1, the grandson of a Rockefeller with a large inheritance of productive property *should* eat a thousand times as much stew as a highly trained, highly productive, hardworking son of a pauper—even if Rockefeller's grandson doesn't work a day in his life and the pauper's son works for fifty years producing goods or providing services of great benefit to others. This will inevitably occur if we count the contribution of productive property people own, and if people own different amounts of machinery and land, or what is the same thing, different amounts of stocks in corporations that own the machinery and land, since bringing a stirring spoon, cooking pot, or stove to the economy kitchen increases the size and quality of the stew we can make just as surely as peeling potatoes and stirring the pot does. So it seems that anyone who considers it *unfair* when the idle grandson of a Rockefeller consumes more than a hardworking, productive son of a pauper cannot accept maxim 1 as their definition of economic justice.

A second line of defense for maxim 1, which can be thought of as the *conservative* conception of economic justice, is based on a vision of "free and independent" people, each with her own property, who, it is argued, would refuse to voluntarily enter a social contract on any other terms. This view is commonly associated with the writings of John Locke. But while it is clear why those with a great deal of productive property in Locke's "state of nature" would have reason to hold out for a social contract along the lines of maxim 1, why would not those who wander the state of nature with little or no productive property in their backpacks hold out for a very different arrangement? If those with considerable wherewithal can do quite well for themselves in the state of nature, whereas those without cannot, it is not difficult to see how requiring unanimity would drive the bargain in the direction of maxim 1. But then maxim 1 is the result of an unfair bargaining situation in which the rich are better able to tolerate failure to reach an agreement over a fair way to assign the burdens and benefits of economic cooperation than the poor, giving the rich the upper hand in negotiations over the terms of the social contract. In this case the social contract rationale for maxim 1 loses moral force because it results from an unfair bargain.

In *A Theory of Justice* (1971), John Rawls corrected this weakness in social contract theories of justice through the ingenious device of an "original position." Rawls explicitly acknowledged that no negotiation over a social contract had actually ever taken place at any point in history, and we were therefore talking about a hypothetical negotiation. More importantly, his idea of an original position also focused attention explicitly on the crucial issue of what constitutes a *fair* negotiating situation. Not surprisingly Rawls's argues that in his "original position"—where none know how much productive property they will have in their backpacks, and all must fear they will have little or none—rational people would *not* agree to maxim 1. We will consider below Rawls's own conclusion that what rational people in his original position would agree to is what he calls the difference, or maximin principle. However, for now we can draw a minimal conclusion: *Unless those with more productive property acquired it through some greater merit on their part, the income they accrue from this property is unjustifiable and therefore unfair*, in which case maxim 1 must be rejected as an acceptable definition of economic justice if we find that those who own more productive property did not come by it through greater merit.

One way people acquire productive property is through inheritance. But it is difficult to see how those who inherit wealth are more deserving than those who don't. It is possible the person *making* a bequest worked harder or consumed less than others in her generation, and in one of these ways sacrificed more than others. Or it is possible the person *making* the bequest was more productive than others. And we might decide that greater sacrifice or greater contribution *merits* greater reward. But in these scenarios it is not the heir who made the greater sacrifice or contribution, it is the person who made the bequest, so the heir would not deserve greater wealth on those grounds. So if we decide rewards are earned by sacrifice or personal contribution, income from inherited wealth violates both norms since *inheriting* wealth is neither a sacrifice nor a personal contribution.

A more compelling argument for inheritance is that banning inheritance is unfair to those wishing to *make* bequests than that it is unfair to those who would *receive* them.[10] To frame the dilemma in its starkest form, suppose those who wish to make bequests came by the productive property in a manner consistent with our conception of economic justice—whatever that might be—and rather than eat prodigious portions of caviar in the twilight of their lives, they prefer to pass on productive assets to their children or grandchildren. To deny them the right to do so would seem to be an unwarranted violation of their legitimate right to dispose of their economic wherewithal as they wish. One could argue (as Robert Nozick does) that if wealth is justly acquired it is unfair to prevent anyone from disposing of it as they wish, including bequeathing it to their descendants.

But what of the right of members of the younger generation to equal economic opportunities? If we permit inheritance of productive assets some will start out with significant advantages and others will be unfairly handicapped. I do not believe there is any way around this dilemma, which can be stated as follows: Do members of an older generation, when exercising their right to use their wealth as they wish, have the right to create unequal economic opportunities for a younger generation?

My answer is *no*. If we pose the issue in terms of rights, this is a case of conflicting rights, and I would argue that the right to an equal economic opportunity in life outweighs the right to bequeath significant wealth to one's offspring. In other words, while some freedom of consumption for the older generation is sacrificed by outlawing inheritance, this minor restriction of a right is necessary to protect a more fundamental right of the younger generation to equal economic opportunities.

However, I argue in the next chapter that to conceptualize economic democracy in terms of property rights is a problematic approach precisely because conflicting rights, or freedoms, are commonplace, and settling these conflicts by awarding a right to one party or the other is ultimately arbitrary. I suggest that instead of attempting to maximize economic freedom—a logically impossible task when people's economic freedoms conflict with one another and we consider the freedoms of different people incommensurable—the goal should be to award everyone decision-making power in proportion to the degree they are affected by the outcome. What if we consider conflicting interests over bequests in these terms? Since the younger generation is much more seriously affected by unequal economic opportunities than the older generation would be affected by limiting their freedom of consumption in this one respect, it would be justifiable to limit inheritance to bequests that do not generate significant differences in economic opportunities.

While the conflict between the right of bequest for an older generation and the right to an equal economic opportunity of a younger generation is only one of many conflicting freedoms, or rights in capitalist economies, it is a particularly important one. Awarding the property right in favor of inheritance permits those who are little affected—those making significant bequests—to make decisions with far-reaching consequences for many others—those who must start their economic lives with serious handicaps relative to some of their peers. It is also one mean by which economic injustice is perpetuated from generation to generation. In any case, no matter how the conflict between right of bequest and right to equal economic opportunity is settled, it is clear that those who *receive* income from inherited wealth benefit from an unfair advantage.

A second way people acquire more productive property than others is through good luck. Working or investing in a rising or declining company or industry constitutes good luck or bad luck. But unequal distributions of productive property that result from differences in luck are not the result of unequal sacrifices, unequal contributions, or any difference in merit between people. Good luck—by definition—is precisely *not* deserved, and therefore the unequal incomes that result from unequal distributions of productive property due to differences in luck must be inequitable as well.

A third way people come to have more productive property is through unfair advantage. Those who are stronger, better connected, have insider information, or are more willing to prey on the misery of others can acquire more productive property through a variety of legal and illegal means. Obviously if unequal wealth is the result of someone taking unfair advantage of another it is inequitable.

The last way people might come to have more productive property than others is by using some income they earned fairly to purchase more productive property than others. But there is a difficult moral issue regarding income from productive property even if the productive property was purchased with income we stipulate was fairly earned in the first place. Labor and credit markets allow people with productive wealth to capture part of the increase in productivity of *other people* that results when other people work with the productive wealth. To what extent the profit or rent owners of productive wealth receive initially is merited when they use their wealth to become employers or lenders we will have to consider very carefully. But even if we stipulate that some compensation is justified by a meritorious action that occurred *once* in the past, it turns out that labor and credit markets allow those who own productive wealth to parlay it into *permanently* higher incomes that *increase* over time without further meritorious behavior on their parts. This creates the dilemma that ownership of productive property *even if justly acquired* may well give rise to additional income that becomes greater than what is required to compensate its owner for her greater initial merit.[11]

In sum, if unequal accumulations of productive property were the result only of meritorious actions, and if compensation ceased when the meritorious action was fully compensated, using words like "exploitation" to describe payments to owners of productive property would seem harsh and misleading. On the other hand, if those who own more productive property acquired it through inheritance, luck, unfair advantage—or because once they have more productive property than others they can accumulate even more with no further meritorious behavior by using labor or credit markets—then calling the unequal outcomes that result from differences in wealth "unfair" or "exploitation" seems perfectly appropriate.

A compelling case can be made that differences in ownership of productive property that accumulate within a single generation due to
unequal sacrifices, unequal contributions people make themselves, or both
are small compared to the differences in wealth that develop due to inheritance, luck, unfair advantage, and accumulation. Edward Bellamy put
it this way in *Equality*, written in 1897:

> You may set it down as a rule that the rich, the possessors of great
> wealth, had no moral right to it as based upon desert, for either their
> fortunes belonged to the class of inherited wealth, or else, when accu-
> mulated in a lifetime, necessarily represented chiefly the product of
> others, more or less forcibly or fraudulently obtained.

At the end of the twentieth century, Lester Thurow estimated that
between 50 and 70 percent of all wealth in the United States is inherited.
Daphne Greenwood and Edward Wolff estimated that 50 to 70 percent
of the wealth of households under age fifty was inherited. Laurence Kotlikoff and Lawrence Summers estimated that as much as 80 percent of
personal wealth came either from direct inheritance or the income on
inherited wealth.[12] A study published in 1997 by United for a Fair Economy titled "Born on Third Base" found that of the four hundred on the
1997 Forbes list of wealthiest individuals and families in the United States,
42 percent inherited their way onto the list, another 6 percent inherited
wealth in excess of $50 million, and another 7 percent started life with
at least $1 million. In any case, presumably what Proudhon was think-
ing when he coined the phrase "property is theft" was that most large
wealthholders acquire their wealth through inheritance, luck, unfair
advantage, or unfair accumulation. A less flamboyant radical might have
stipulated that he was referring to productive, not personal property, and
added the qualification "property is theft—more often than not."

In closing, a TV commercial for the brokerage house of Salomon Smith
Barney provided a delicious example of the kind of ethical doublespeak
that is commonplace regarding income from property or wealth: in the
commercial a man of obvious taste and distinction solemnly informs us
that brokers at Salomon Smith Barney believe in "making money the old
fashioned way—earning it." What he means, of course, is that brokers
at Salomon Smith Barney discourage clients from giving in to the temptation of high gain, high risk strategies, and recommend instead a conservative strategy of expanding wealth more slowly but with greater
certainty, precisely *without earning* a penny of it.

Maxim 2: To Each According to the Value of the Contribution of only *Her Human Capital*

While those who support maxim 2 find most property income unjustifiable, advocates of maxim 2 hold that all have a right to the "fruits of their own labor." The rationale for this has a powerful appeal: if my labor contributes more to the social endeavor it is only right that I receive more. Not only am I not exploiting others, they would be exploiting me by paying me less than the value of my personal contribution. Maxim 2 can be thought of as the *liberal* conception of economic justice, but ironically, the same reason for rejecting maxim 1 applies to maxim 2 as well.

Economists define the value of the contribution of any input as the "marginal revenue product" of that input. In other words, if we add one more unit of the input in question to all of the inputs currently used in a production process, how much would the value of output increase? The answer is defined as the marginal revenue product of the input in question. But mainstream economics teaches us that the marginal productivity, or contribution of an input, depends as much on the number of units of that input already in use, and on the quantity and quality of other, complimentary inputs, as on any intrinsic quality of the additional input itself. This fact undermines the moral imperative behind any "contribution-based" maxim—that is, maxim 2 as well as maxim 1. But besides the fact that the marginal productivity of different kinds of labor depends largely on the number of people in each labor category in the first place, and on the quantity and quality of nonlabor inputs available for use, most differences in people's personal productivities are due to intrinsic qualities of people themselves over which they have no control. No amount of eating and weightlifting will give an average individual a 6-foot-11-inch frame with 380 pounds of muscle. Yet professional football players in the United States receive hundreds of times more than an average salary because those attributes make their contribution outrageously high in the context of U.S. sports culture. The famous British economist, Joan Robinson, pointed out long ago that however "productive" a machine or piece of land may be, its productivity hardly constitutes a moral argument for paying anything to its owner. In a similar vein one could argue that however "productive" a 380-pound physique—or a high IQ—may be, that doesn't mean the owner of this trait deserves more income than someone less gifted who works as hard and sacrifices as much. The bottom line is that the "genetic lottery" greatly influences how valuable a person's contribution will be. Yet the genetic lottery is no more fair than the inheritance lottery, and therefore maxim 2 suffers from the same flaw as maxim 1.[13]

In defense of maxim 2 it is frequently argued that while talent may not deserve reward, talent requires training, and herein lies the sacrifice that merits reward. For example, it is often argued that doctors' high salaries are compensation for all the extra years of education. But longer training does not necessarily mean greater personal sacrifice. It is important not to confuse the cost of someone's training to society—which consists mostly of the *trainer's* time and energy, and scarce social resources like books, computers, libraries, and classrooms—with the personal sacrifice of the *trainee*. If teachers and educational facilities were paid for at public expense—that is, if we had a universal public education system—and if students were paid a living stipend—so they forgo no income while in school—then the personal sacrifice of the student would consist only of her discomfort from time spent in school. But even in this case the personal suffering students endure must be properly compared. While many educational programs are less personally enjoyable than time spent in leisure, comparing discomfort during school with comfort during leisure is not the relevant comparison. In a universal public education system with living stipends the relevant comparison is between the discomfort students experience and the discomfort of *others*, who are working instead of going to school. If our criterion is greater personal sacrifice *than others*, then logic requires comparing the student's discomfort to the discomfort level of others, who work while the student is in school. Only if schooling is more disagreeable than working does it constitute a greater sacrifice than others make, and thereby deserve reward. So to the extent that the cost of education is born at public rather than private expense, including the opportunity cost of forgone wages, and to the extent that the personal discomfort of schooling is no greater than the discomfort others incur while working, extra schooling merits no compensation on moral grounds.

In sum, I call the problem with maxim 2 the *doctor-garbage collector problem*. How can it be fair to pay a brain surgeon who is on the first tee at his country club's golf course by 1 P.M. even on the four days a week he works, ten times more than a garbage collector who works under miserable conditions forty plus hours a week, if education is free and students are paid living stipends all the way through medical school? Despite the fact that many progressives continue to search for reasons that returns to human capital are more justified than returns to physical capital, I have yet to see a reason that holds up under scrutiny. Where does this difference in attitude many have toward rewards to physical and human capital come from?

No doubt the fact that the value of our labor contribution is the joint product of our human capital *and* our effort is responsible for part of the confusion. People *do* have some control over how valuable their labor contribution will be because we *do* have control over our effort, whereas most people have little, if any, control over how much physical capital we own, or how valuable its contribution will prove to be. Moreover, because our human capital only contributes when *we* work, and work entails sacrifice, human capital cannot make any contribution unless its owner makes sacrifices. On the other hand, when physical capital makes its contribution it is generally *not* its owner who makes any sacrifice, it is the owner's employees who work with the machinery and equipment and make the sacrifices associated with the contribution of the physical capital. But none of this is a reason to reward people according to the value of the contribution of their labor. If we reward effort we reward the only thing people have control over, and if we reward people according to their sacrifices then we precisely compensate people for the sacrifices they make when their human capital makes a contribution. In other words, if we reward people according to their efforts and sacrifices, we have already taken care of the two reasons people rightly feel that reward according to the value of one's labor contribution is more just than reward for the value of the contribution of the physical capital one happens to own. However, once rewards have compensated people for differences in effort and sacrifice, to pay some more than others because their efforts were more productive *because* they were expended alongside greater amounts of human capital is no more fair than paying some more than others because the physical capital they own makes a more valuable contribution.

Maxim 3: To Each According to Her Effort, or Personal Sacrifice

Whereas differences in contribution will be due to differences in talent, training, job assignment, luck, and effort, the only factor that deserves extra compensation according to maxim 3 is extra effort. By "effort," what is meant is personal sacrifice for the sake of the social endeavor. Of course effort can take many forms. It may be longer work hours, less pleasant work, or more intense, dangerous, unhealthy work. Or, it may consist of undergoing training that is less gratifying than the training experiences of others, or less pleasant than time others spend working who train less. The underlying rationale for maxim 3, which can be thought of as the *radical* conception of economic justice, is that people should eat from the stew pot according to the sacrifices they made to cook it. Compensation for sacrifices above average "evens things out" overall. According to maxim 3 no other consideration, besides differential sacrifice, can justify one person eating more stew than another.

One argument for why sacrifice deserves reward is that people have control over how much they sacrifice. I can decide to work longer hours, or work harder, whereas I cannot decide to be 6 foot 11 or have a high IQ. It is commonly considered unjust to punish someone for something she could do nothing about. On those grounds paying someone less just because she is not large or smart violates a fundamental precept of fair play. On the other hand, if someone doesn't work as long or hard as the rest of us, we don't feel it is inappropriate to punish her by paying her less because she *could* have worked longer or harder if she had chosen to. In the case of reward according to effort, avoiding punishment is possible, whereas in the case of reward according to contribution it is largely not.

But are all people equally able to sacrifice? Or is it easier for some to make sacrifices than it is for others, just as it is easier for some to perform difficult and valuable physical or mental tasks than it is for others? Questions such as these make me happy that I am not a philosopher. What can one say except, "perhaps." But even if it is only a matter of degree, are we delusional to think it is usually easier for people to affect how much effort they put into a task, or how much they sacrifice for the common good, than it is for them to affect how valuable a contribution they make? I happily leave philosophers to debate "free will," but I cannot persuade myself that we have no more control over our efforts and sacrifices than we do over how valuable our contribution will be.

In any case, the "punishment" meted out by maxim 3 to those who make fewer sacrifices than others is not even social disapproval. There is no reason for society to frown on those who prefer to make fewer sacrifices as long as they are willing to accept less economic benefits to go along with their lesser sacrifice. There is no reason that just because people enter into a system of equitable cooperation with others this precludes leaving the sacrifice/benefit trade-off to personal choice. Maxim 3 simply balances any differences in the burdens people choose to bear with commensurate differences in the benefits they receive. I think this is the strongest argument for reward according to sacrifice. Even if all were not equally able to make sacrifices, extra benefits to compensate for extra burdens seems only fair. When people enter into economic cooperation with one another, for the arrangement to be just should not all participants benefit equally? Since each participant bears burdens as well as enjoys benefits, it is equalization of *net* benefits, that is, benefits enjoyed minus burdens borne, that makes the economic cooperation fair. So if some bear more of the burdens justice requires that they be compensated with benefits commensurate with their greater sacrifice. Only then will all enjoy equal *net* benefits. Only then will the system of economic cooperation be treating all participants equally, that is, giving equal weight or priority to the interests of all participants. Notice that even if some are more able to sacrifice than others, the outcome for both the more and less able to sacrifice is the same when extra sacrifices are rewarded. In this way all receive the same net benefits from economic cooperation irrespective of any differences in their abilities to contribute *or* to sacrifice.

Many who object to maxim 3 as a distributive principle for real economies raise questions about measuring sacrifice, or about conflicts between reward according to sacrifice and economic efficiency. Since reward according to sacrifice is the distributive principle of the participatory economy described and defended in chapters 8 and 9, we will consider these criticisms of maxim 3 carefully in those chapters. But notice that measurement problems, or conflicts between equity and efficiency are *not* objections to maxim 3 as a definition of what is *fair*; in short, they are *not* objections to maxim 3 *on equity grounds*. To reject maxim 3 because effort or sacrifice may be difficult to measure, or because rewarding sacrifice may reduce efficiency is not to reject maxim 3 because it is unfair. No matter how weighty these arguments may prove to be, they are not arguments against maxim 3 on grounds that it somehow fails to accurately express what it means for the distribution of burdens and benefits in a system of economic cooperation to be just, or fair. Moreover, even should it prove that economic justice is difficult to achieve because it is difficult to measure something accurately, or costly to achieve because to do so generates a great deal of inefficiency, one presumably would still wish to know exactly what this elusive and costly economic justice *is*.

In any economy, some are unable to make contributions or sacrifices, and some should be exempted from doing so even if they are able. Disabilities prevent some people from being able to work, and we choose to exempt children and retirees from work as well. Whether we decide to base reward on contribution or sacrifice we must decide if some are exempt from whatever our general rule may be. Obviously issues of fairness must be considered in any system of exemptions: (1) Are the rules for exempting people fair? (2) Are the rewards for those exempted fair? While I will offer a few suggestions about rules of exemption and appropriate compensations for those exempted in a participatory economy in chapter 8, these matters are separable from the issue of just rewards for those not exempted. The different maxims refer to the general rules of compensation and different rules for exemptions could be appended to any of the maxims.

Of course proponents of maxims 1 and 2 reject maxim 3 because it fails to reward people according to the value of their contribution. Some whose contributions are of greater value may well receive no more than others whose contributions are less valuable in an economy where distribution is according to maxim 3. But we have found compelling reasons why contribution-based theories of economic justice fail to hold up under scrutiny: (1) contribution-based notions of equity will necessarily punish some people for something they are powerless to do anything about. And (2) reward according to contribution—whether of one's productive property *and* person, or *only* of one's person—inevitably awards greater benefits to some who sacrificed less than others, and distributes less benefits to some who sacrificed more than others. In sum, there *is* a good answer to the question: "Why should those who sacrifice more benefit more?" The answer is: "Because otherwise people do not receive equal *net* benefits from the system of economic cooperation. Because otherwise the economic system does not give equal priority to everyone's interests. Because otherwise the economy does not treat people equally." But I know of no good answer to the question: "Why should those who contribute more benefit more?" The only answer to this question is the proverbial child's response: "Because."

John O'Neill voiced a serious criticism of maxim 3 on equity grounds that is appropriate to consider here. "Distribution according to effort fails as a general principle because it is potentially humiliating, in particular for a low-output worker who is given a 'high-effort' score. It reflects badly on the evaluation of the worth of her capacities. The problem here is that the effort scores necessarily involve judging not just the performance of workers but their person."[14]

Being judged can prove unpleasant, and people understandably hesitate to volunteer to be judged by others no matter what the standards of judgment. But until we are willing to accept one another's self-evaluations without question, judgment at the hands of external parties may be regrettable, but it is unavoidable. O'Neill correctly points out that maxim 3 requires judging not only people's performance but their capabilities as well. But I think we only avoid making "double judgments" at the cost of justice. To spare people the embarrassment of judging their capabilities, and to judge only the value of their contributions, amounts to accepting maxim 2 as our notion of fairness. Of course maxim 2 has many supporters, but for those of us who cannot rationalize away the doctor-garbage collector problem, it fails the test of fairness. Is O'Neill willing to systematically punish the less able with lower economic rewards to avoid what he sees as their humiliation? Because that is what shying away from judging potentials as well as performance amounts to. I think a far better solution, which does not sacrifice economic justice, is to replace the misguided social norm that lower ability is humiliating with the valid norm that only failing to live up to one's abilities, or failing to accept responsibility for one's decision not to, is shameful. Moreover, until the unwarranted stigma that concerns O'Neill disappears, I suggest we let the less able decide for themselves whether they would like to have their performance compared to their abilities. Many of them may be quicker than their more able workmates to overcome the unwarranted assumption that to be less able is humiliating, and thereby free themselves to receive their just deserts—according to their sacrifices.

Even for those who reject contribution-based theories of economic justice like maxims 1 and 2 as inherently flawed, there is still a problem with maxim 3 from a moral point of view that I call the *AIDS victim problem*. Suppose someone has made average sacrifices for fifteen years, and consumed an average amount. Suddenly they contract AIDS through no fault of their own. In the early 1990s, a medical treatment program for an AIDS victim could cost as much as a half million dollars. That is, the cost to society of providing humane care for an AIDS victim sometimes ran as high as a half million dollars. If we limit people's consumption to the level warranted by their efforts, or the sacrifices they make in work, we would have to deny AIDS victims humane treatment, which many of us would find hard to defend on moral grounds.

Maxim 4: To Each According to Her Need

In chapter 8, I will argue that a participatory economy should distribute according to sacrifice *and* need. But whether taking differences in need into consideration is required by economic justice, or is required, instead, for an economy to be *humane* is debatable. For me this reduces to a question of semantics since I believe that ignoring differences in need in certain situations is morally unacceptable, just as I believe ignoring differences in sacrifice to be immoral. But in my personal view maxim 4, payment according to need, is in a different logical category than the other three, and expresses a commendable social value, but a value beyond economic justice. It seems to me that it is one thing for an economy to be an equitable economy, one that is fair and just. It is another thing for an economy also to be humane.

While I believe justice requires compensating people according to the sacrifices they make, it seems to me that it is our humanity that compels us to provide for those in need. But as we economists like to say, the policy implication is the same in either case. Just as greater sacrifice should receive greater reward, greater need should receive greater reward sometimes as well. Whether the ethical reasoning behind the conclusion is the same in the two cases may be of importance to philosophers who think it is important to understand that it is our sense of justice that requires rewarding greater sacrifice, whereas it is our humanity that requires rewarding greater need. In these terms an economy might be just but still morally lacking. A just economy that allowed AIDs victims to suffer for lack of proper medical care would, indeed, be unethical because it would be inhumane. In these terms, besides striving for economic justice, we must work to make our economies more humane as well, which will require distribution according to effort or sacrifice, tempered by need.

Social Contract Theories of Economic Justice

Modern philosophers do not always address social justice in terms of maxims. Robert Nozick explicitly rejects the "maxim approach" arguing against all "pattern models" of social justice as violations of individual liberty. Instead he proposes a theory of "historical entitlements." According to John Rawls's theory of "justice as fairness," what is fair is what rational people would agree to in a fair negotiating situation, and what they would agree to would be the "difference," or "maximin" principle, unequal outcomes are just if and only if they act to increase the economic well-being of the worst-off group absolutely. I pretend to no comprehensive evaluation or critique of the theories of Rawls and Nozick. I merely address a few points they raise either explicitly or implicitly that are relevant to a defense of maxim 3.

Robert Nozick

Nozick objects to the maxim approach altogether: "To think that the task of a theory of distributive justice is to fill in the blank in 'to each according to his ____ , is to be predisposed to search for a pattern, and no end-state principle or distributional pattern principle can be continuously realized without continuous interference in people's lives."[15] He goes on to provide a number of convincing examples to demonstrate that if people are completely free to do as they wish with what is their "just allotment" by hypothesis, they may well upset the pattern deemed to be just in the first place. A rebuttal to Nozick's claim that all pattern models—which includes maxim 3—infringe on people's individual liberty in ways that cannot be justified is in order.

The dilemma Nozick refers to was well illustrated in the previous discussion of inheritance. I argued that it is justifiable to limit bequests so as not to disrupt everyone's right to equal economic opportunities. The essential idea was that a reasonable conception of individual liberty should not mean that all conceivable uses of one's person and property must necessarily be permitted. Just because I recognize that you are the owner of a gun does not mean I agree that the principle of individual liberty allows you to use it to shoot at me, or at my dog, or even at a deer wandering through our neighborhood out of hunting season. Similarly, freedom to dispose of one's wealth, even if it was fairly acquired, need not include the right to dispose of it in a way that disrupts economic justice.

Of course people should be free to consume *x* rather than *y*, or consume more later and less now. But that does not mean people should be free to destroy economic justice by leaving large inheritances to some while others receive no inheritance at all, even if those leaving bequests acquired their wealth fairly. Just as it is reasonable for a community to establish zoning restrictions on people's use of their real estate through a fair and democratic process, it is reasonable for a society of moral beings to democratically decide to restrict disposition of personal property in ways that would be destructive of economic justice. Otherwise, it becomes impossible for communities to achieve economic justice. In other words, when Nozick rejects pattern models of economic justice on the grounds that they may require some restrictions on how people can dispose of what they acquired fairly, he effectively rejects economic justice itself because he disarms communities of the means necessary to secure economic justice.

It seems to me that Nozick operates with a very limited conception of property. Just because I recognize that something is your property, and I agree that you acquired it fairly, and I agree this means *in general* you can do what you want with it, this need not imply that I agree that your right to dispose of that property as you wish takes precedence over any and all other considerations, no matter what you decide you want to do with it, and no matter what the consequences of that choice might be. Nozick's conception of property is too black or white to be useful in a social world where individual rights conflict, or in a world with legitimate objectives besides individual liberty.

Finally, Nozick implies that only someone with an authoritarian bent would consider restricting liberty to preserve justice. But notice that regarding inheritance, it is not individual rights in general that are served by Nozick's solution since the right of a few to make particular kinds of bequests is only protected at the expense of the right of many to an equal economic opportunity. Nozick's answer, of course, is that no historical entitlements *earned* people the right to an equal economic opportunity, whereas, in his opinion, there are historical entitlements that *earn* people the right to dispose of their justly acquired property as they choose. But whether Nozick's theory of historic entitlements holds up or not on its own terms—and I do not believe it does—notice that it is not a defense based on the priority of individual rights over social justice. It is a defense based on the supposed moral legitimacy of the right of some—the older generation—to do some things—make any kind of bequest—and the presumed absence of any legitimate right of others—the younger generation—to do other things—start life with equal opportunities. Regarding inheritance, my disagreement with Nozick is *not* a disagreement over whether rights of individuals or economic justice should receive priority, as Nozick would have us believe. The difference is a difference of opinion over what individual rights and whose individual rights should take precedence when there are conflicts.

John Rawls

While Nozick appeals to conservative libertarians, John Rawls is an icon of modern liberalism. In the first part of his theory of "justice as fairness," Rawls argues that we should accept as just whatever outcome we believe would be agreed to by rational parties in a fair negotiating situation. Rawls carefully constructs such an "original position" using the ingenious device of a "veil of ignorance" that prevents negotiating parties from knowing whether they will be weak or strong, smart or dumb, lucky or unlucky, blessed or not blessed with wealthy and generous parents, and so on. In this way Rawls eliminates much unproductive debate about economic justice that is little more than rationalization for self-serving conceptions. In the second part of his theory he argues that what people in his original position would agree to is what he calls the difference, or maximin principle, namely, that unequal outcomes are just if and only if they act to increase the economic well-being of the worst-off group absolutely.

However, Rawls's difference principle has been interpreted in two different ways. One interpretation is that any Pareto improvement—any change that makes someone better off and nobody worse off and also improves the outcome for the worst off —passes the test of justice. In this interpretation it does not matter if the change improves the outcome for the better off by a great deal and the outcome for the worst off by only a little, and thereby increases inequality. So in this interpretation Rawls is read as providing a rationale for any form of trickle-down economics: no matter how small, if the merest trickle reaches the bottom, any cascade at the top is innocent of the charge of injustice. The second interpretation—which I am quite sure is the one Rawls himself intended—is that justice demands that society scan *all* Pareto optimal outcomes, outcomes where no change would make anyone better off without making someone else worse off, and enact the one that makes the worst off, best off. As all economists know, these are *not* the same thing at all.

Suppose you are originally better off than I am, and there are two possible changes we could make. The first change would make you much better off than you are initially, but only make me slightly better off than I was before. Since we are both better off than we were initially, the first change is a Pareto improvement on the status quo. The second change would make us both moderately better off than we were initially. Since we are both better off than we were initially, the second change is also a Pareto improvement on the status quo. Clearly the second change satisfies the difference principle: of all three possible outcomes—the status quo, the first change, and the second change—the second change makes me, the worst-off person, the best off I can be. But does the first change also satisfy Rawls's difference principle, in which case the large unequal outcome between you and me it creates would be deemed perfectly fair?

If we compare the first change with the status quo, it makes me, the worst-off person, slightly better off, and therefore seems to satisfy the difference principle as well, despite the fact that it mostly helps you, the better-off person. *And if the second change were not also possible,* the first change would pass the difference principle test because it would make me, the worst-off person, the best off I can be. But since the second change is also possible, by hypothesis, and the second change makes me, the worst off, both better off than I was originally, and better off than I would be under the first change, I do not believe the first change satisfies the difference principle as Rawls intended it to be interpreted. I believe that Rawls only intended the second change to pass his difference principle test, and only intended to argue that the inequality between us that remains after we make the second change is fair and unobjectionable.[16]

Rawls argued that people in his original position would rationally fear that they might prove to be the worst off after the veil of ignorance was lifted. Moreover, he argued people would have to weigh matters very cautiously in his original position because they would never be allowed to cry "foul" to any outcome they had agreed to while in the original position, no matter how bad the result proved to be for them. Rawls concluded that in these circumstances people would only agree to accept unequal outcomes if they worked to the advantage of the worst off. As I interpret Rawls, that means he concluded that while the second change would be agreed to by people in the original position, the first change would not.

But while I do not believe Rawls intended to sanction all trickle-down economics, even in the second interpretation Rawls can give the moral thumbs up to economic inequality. In fact, that was one of the purposes of his theory. Rawls asked if unequal outcomes were necessarily unjust. He reasoned that if the unequal outcomes would have been unanimously agreed to in a fair negotiation they could not be deemed unfair. And he reasoned that what all would agree to in a fair situation, in which nobody knew in advance where they were likely to end up in the income distribution, would be to maximize the outcome for the worst off. If the arrangement that accomplished this—maximizing the minimum outcome—happened also to be an unequal outcome, Rawls concluded that those inequalities would not be unfair, but perfectly just.

Philosophers have debated whether people would choose Rawls's difference principle in his original position for over thirty years. Some have argued that the difference principle is too conservative. Amartya Sen, among others, asked why people would not choose to maximize expected utility and argued that only an implicit assumption of extreme risk aversion would warrant choosing the difference principle instead.[17] Others have asked why people in the original position would forgo large benefits for all groups at the bottom of the income bracket *except* for the group at the very bottom in order to win a marginal gain for the bottommost group. Economists who debate the comparative merits of different measures of inequality are invariably surprised to hear Rawls argue for what amounts to a principle of poverty reduction that references only the well-being of the bottommost group. Robert Nozick and other conservatives have criticized the veil of ignorance for not permitting people to know how productive they are compared to others. Nozick argued that this information was morally relevant and hiding it from negotiators rendered the original position unfair, and consequently, agreements negotiated under these unfair conditions are unfair as well. While I am inclined to side with Rawls in debates with Nozick, I am more agnostic regarding debates between Rawls and others over rational choice by people blind to their own identities. But my main concern lies elsewhere.

While Rawls is most anxious to refute utilitarian notions of justice, theories that justify inequalities if they increase the total benefits of all people added together, notice that Rawls's theory provides good reasons to reject both maxims 1 and 2 as well. People behind the veil of ignorance would never agree to maxim 1 because they might discover after the veil was lifted that they would be revealed to be descendants of paupers, but would have forsworn all rights to call foul over the Rockefeller grandson problem. Similarly people behind the veil of ignorance would not agree to maxim 2 because when it was lifted they might discover they were garbage collectors rather than brain surgeons, with no right to complain.[18]

What about maxim 3? Could maxim 3 be chosen in Rawls's original position? Rawls makes no reference to sacrifice in his discussion of the difference principle. Maxim 3 sanctions inequalities only if they compensate for differences in sacrifice, whereas the difference principle sanctions inequalities only if they serve to improve outcomes for the worst off. But it is not clear that when Rawls speaks of "outcomes," and who is better or worse off, that he does not mean to include what I have called both benefits and burdens, or sacrifices, in the calculus. As a matter of fact, as I read his intent, he either does, or should do so. There is nothing in his theory that should lead him to distinguish between a dangerous job and a smaller portion of food rations as negative aspects of someone's "outcome." In which case, in Rawlsian terms maxim 3 is equivalent to the principle of *equal* outcomes, outcomes in which different sacrifices people make in work are precisely compensated for by different consumption benefits, yielding equal "outcomes" for all. But of course Rawls's difference principle is *not* the equality principle. Rawls began with the equality principle, explicitly asked if deviations from equal economic outcomes might be just, and came to the conclusion that unequal outcomes *were* fair if they made the worst off better off than any other possible outcome did, including equal outcomes for all.

As I interpret him, Rawls's defense of inequality hinges on two factual assumptions. *Only if* the economic system that maximizes the outcome of the worst off does so *only by* generating unequal outcomes, can Rawls judge those inequalities to be equitable. There are many who rush to cast capitalism and unequal property income in precisely this light, arguing that the poorest in a capitalist economy with unequal property incomes are absolutely better off than they would be in any other system. And others dispute the case for capitalism on factual grounds, but claim that market socialism with unequal marginal revenue product wages maximizes the economic well-being of the poorest, compared to all other feasible alternatives. I do not believe the *facts* justify inequalities according to Rawls's difference principle in *either* capitalism *or* market socialism. I do not believe the poorest in capitalist economies are as well off as the poorest would be in more than one kind of noncapitalist economy I can think of, and I do not believe most of the unequal property income in capitalist economies serves to raise the worst off. Nor do I believe that those at the bottom of the wage spectrum in market socialist economies would be as well off as the poorest in the kind of participatory economy I advocate in chapter 8, and I believe most of the inequality in marginal revenue product wages in market socialist economies would lower, not raise, the lowest wages in absolute terms. So, I could accept Rawls's theory and criticize inequalities in capitalism and in market socialism as unjust based on his theory. But I believe Rawls's theory of economic justice tends to focus attention other than where it should be. In my view those concerned with economic justice need not worry about the degree to which inequality helps the worst off, since it mostly hurts them. But I am inclined not only to dispute those who rationalize capitalist and market socialist inequalities in Rawlsian terms on empirical or factual grounds, I am inclined to protest on ethical grounds as well, which means I differ with Rawls's conception of economic justice.

Suppose we found an economic system that distributed the burdens and benefits of economic activity fairly. What the system is, and what we deem to be fair is irrelevant for the present purposes. Then suppose it turned out that by permitting some deviation from these fair outcomes, the outcome for the worst off improved without making the outcomes for others any worse. People in such an economy might well vote to permit the deviation. They might even vote to do so unanimously, as Rawls argues rational people in his original position would do. I, personally, might even join the consensus. But I would not call the outcomes with the deviation fair or just. By hypothesis, those outcomes deviate to some extent from what is just! Nor would I call the original economy that was just by hypothesis, unjust in light of the effect of the deviation. Yet this is what Rawls's theory would require me to do. According to Rawls's theory, the original economy was not actually just; I only mistakenly thought it to be so. According to Rawls, only the adjusted economy is truly fair.

Perhaps this reduces to semantics, but I find Rawls's conception unnecessarily confusing. Maybe I have been a practicing economist too long, but I find it far easier to distinguish between efficiency and equity rather than conflate them, as I believe Rawls has done, even if unintentionally. When Rawls has people in his original position consider distributive principles they must take *any* considerations they care about into account when doing so. So if distributive principles had implications not only for economic justice, but for economic efficiency as well, they would have to consider both effects when deciding what principle to agree to unless they did not care about one goal at all. As a philosopher Rawls is naturally prone to think of distributive principles as a matter of economic justice. But economists are long used to thinking of the effects of distributive principles on both efficiency and equity. Rawls implicitly recognizes what we economists call the efficiency effect when he recognizes the possibility that unequal outcomes may permit the worst off to do better than insisting on equal outcomes. But he treats distributive outcomes as if the *only* difference between them is that some are fair and others are not. Another difference between them is that some may be more efficient and others less so. Regarding my example above, why not simply say that the original economy was just, but we have assumed a conflict between efficiency and equity by hypothesizing that some particular deviation from equity yields an efficiency gain, part of which is distributed to the worst off. If nobody ends up any worse off from the deviation (i.e., it is a Pareto improvement) it might well be that all would join the worst off in voting unanimous approval for implementing the deviation. But that simply means people deem a particular efficiency gain of greater importance than a particular deviation from equity. Why call the second outcome more equitable and the first unjust? Does that add insight, or only obfuscate what is going on? Why not simply call the first outcome more equitable, and the second less equitable but more efficient?

Rawls's difference principle, in effect, conflates two different social goals, economic justice and efficiency. In my view it is better to recognize equity and efficiency as different goals, search for an economy that achieves both to the greatest degree, and search for policies within this economy that promote both to the greatest extent. *If it turns out there are conflicts, or trade-offs, between equity and efficiency* either in choosing between different kinds of economies, or in choosing policies within a particular economy, we can deal with that in a straightforward manner through a fair and democratic decision-making process.

When confronted with trade-offs between goals, most people are inclined to attach weights to different priorities, and the argument that precedes a democratic vote is over what those weights should be. Implicit in this approach—multiple priorities that requires us to choose weights when there are conflicts—is that the weights will not be one for one of the priorities and zero for all others![19] Rawls's difference principle compels us to proceed in a very different way. When faced with a possible conflict between equity and efficiency Rawls's difference principle directs us to scan all possible unequal outcomes and find the particular Pareto optimum that maximizes the outcome for the worst off. Then we are directed to compare this outcome with the best egalitarian outcome, that is, the outcome in which everyone achieves the highest level of well-being. If the worst off fares better in the best egalitarian outcome there is no conflict between equity and efficiency and we choose the egalitarian outcome. But if the worst off fares better in an unequal outcome there is a conflict between equity and efficiency, and Rawls's difference principle directs us to attach a weight of one to efficiency and zero to equity and choose the unequal outcome no matter how little the efficiency gain and how great the loss in equity. While I am no longer surprised when my fellow economists make this choice, I find it ironic that Rawls, a social philosopher who devoted his life to the investigation of social justice, implicitly gives absolute priority to efficiency over equity whenever there is a conflict between the two.[20]

In any case, I do not believe that either Nozick or Rawls provide good reasons to abandon maxim 3. Admittedly maxim 3 reduces economic justice to very simple terms, the kind of terms we nonphilosophers are used

to. But more convoluted approaches to difficult problems are only helpful if they prove more compelling. I find Nozick's argument against any
kind of pattern model, or maxim, unacceptable because I think it amounts
to giving up on economic justice altogether. In effect it grants equity no
weight whatsoever compared to a flawed notion of individual economic
freedom, which may well explain why it is held in such high esteem in
conservative circles. While I am more sympathetic to Rawls's difference
principle—actually, I would be delighted to live in a world that applied
it as he intended it to be interpreted—I am not surprised that philosophers continue to question his conclusion that the difference principle
would be chosen by rational people blind to their own identities over
maximizing expected utility or some other formula that considers the
well-being of groups below average as well as the well-being of the worst-
off group. But more importantly I believe Rawls has conflated equity and
efficiency in his difference principle in a way that obfuscates rather than
clarifies issues. Nor do I find any compelling argument in Rawls against
equal outcomes as fair outcomes, that is, against maxim 3, which achieves
overall equality by compensating unequal sacrifices with commensurate
benefits. Instead I find in Rawls a strong case for why we should seriously
consider prioritizing efficiency at the expense of equity if the efficiency
gain makes the worse off significantly better off than they would be if we
insisted on strict equality. I have little problem with this conclusion,
although unlike Rawls, who I believed was too easily swayed by mainstream economists in this regard, I do not expect to find many practical
situations where we will find it necessary to heed this advice.

Conclusion

There are understandable reasons why progressives find it difficult to
stand fast for economic justice. It is commonly assumed that the "price"
of economic justice is great because it necessarily entails significant losses
of economic efficiency. This "truth" is commonly assumed to be self-evi-
dent.[21] But the fact that it is so convenient for haves to insist that this is
"obviously" the case is reason enough to demand proof rather than mere
assertion. I have seen no compelling proof that greater inequality causes
greater economic efficiency, and a great deal of evidence to suggest the
contrary. Economic growth rates were highest during the "golden age of
capitalism" when the gap between haves and have-nots shrank and the
middle class expanded dramatically. The most egalitarian of the advanced

capitalist economies, the Scandinavian economies, have growth records over the past eighty years that should be the envy of their less egalitarian rivals. The ratio of CEO to average worker salaries in Japanese companies during the Japanese economic miracle from 1950 to 1980 was many times lower than in U.S. companies where managerial performance was far less impressive. Moreover, at a theoretical level nothing indicates that the "high road" to growth— wage-led growth—is less effective or plausible than the "low road" to growth, that is, suppressing wages to increase profits.[22]

There are also understandable reasons why it is easier for progressives to denounce unfair income from physical capital than unfair income from human capital. The magnitude of the injustice resulting from differential ownership of physical capital is commonly assumed to be greater than the magnitude of the injustice resulting from differences in human capital.

While this may be true, we should bear in mind that the conclusion may depend on how we measure the magnitude of injustice. The difference in income between those with the largest amounts of physical capital and those with none is no doubt far greater than the difference in income between those with the largest amounts of human capital and those with the least. But if we compare the sum total amount of undeserved income from unequal ownership of physical capital to the sum total amount of undeserved income from unequal ownership of human capital we may very well get a different result, in which case redistributing undeserved income from human capital might raise the incomes of the have-nots more than redistributing undeserved income from physical capital.[23]

When we preach economic justice from our bully pulpits the number in our audiences who receive undeserved income from productive property are no doubt fewer than the number who receive undeserved income from human capital. God knows it is never pleasant to displease the congregation!

For these reasons and others, no doubt it is more congenial to consider possible reasons it might be fair for those who sacrifice less to receive more than those who sacrifice more, rather than simply admit it is unfair. I can't help but suspect this may explain in part the great interest shown in Rawlsian approaches to economic justice over the past thirty years among those who profess a kindly disposition toward those less fortunate than themselves.

But the hammer of justice is only a fearsome weapon when permitted to strike wherever it must fall. If I refuse to abide by the logic of justice when others charge that the income I receive from my human capital is unfair to them, my appeal to justice when I complain that income someone else receives from productive property they own is unfair to me loses all force. The hammer of justice carries no force other than its moral power, which rests entirely on the principle that what is good for the goose is good for the gander.

2

Economic Democracy

The centerpiece of the ideological defense of capitalism is the concept of "economic freedom." While many victims have been lulled to sleep when the cheerleaders for capitalism equate economic justice with "to each according to the value of the contribution of her labor and productive property," even more have been hoodwinked when capitalist ideologues equate economic democracy with economic freedom, and pretend that all economic freedoms are treated equally in capitalism. Substituting the concept of economic freedom for a more meaningful definition of economic democracy plays on the obvious truth that it is good when we are free to do what we want. But what are we to do when the freedom of one person to do what she wants infringes on the freedom of others to do as they wish? Uncovering the slight of hand at play when economic freedom is cleverly substituted for the principle that people should control their own economic destinies is crucial to dispelling capitalist enabling myths. However, there is another reason to dig more deeply into the meaning of economic democracy. Not only did confusion about economic justice undermine efforts to promote equitable cooperation during the last century, confusion about economic democracy led many progressives astray as well. Substituting majority rule for economic freedom, which supporters of centrally planned "socialist" economies were prone to do, is not an adequate solution to the problem of economic democracy. The difficult subject of how to advance the cause of economic democracy is taken up in later chapters. In this chapter we tackle the much easier task of how economic democracy should be defined.

Economic Freedom

Conservative Abuses

Milton Friedman argues in *Capitalism and Freedom* (1964) that the greatest virtue of capitalism is that it provides people with "economic freedom." Friedman even stipulates that should capitalism, to his surprise, prove less fair or efficient than some other economy, he would still favor capitalism because in his view it is uniquely capable of delivering economic freedom. While Friedman never defines economic freedom, his discussion and examples in *Capitalism and Freedom* make clear that by economic freedom he means the freedom to do whatever one wishes with one's person and property, including the right to contract with others over their use of one's person or property.

The first problem with Friedman's concept of economic freedom is that in all economies, including capitalism, there are important situations where the economic freedom of one person conflicts with the economic freedom of another person. If polluters are free to pollute, then victims of pollution are not free to live in pollution-free environments. If employers are free to use their productive property as they see fit, then their employees are not free to use their laboring capacities as they see fit. If the wealthy are free to leave their children large bequests, then new generations will not be free to enjoy equal economic opportunities. If those who own banks are free from a government-imposed minimum reserve requirement, ordinary depositors are not free to save safely. So it is not enough simply to shout "let economic freedom ring," as appealing as that may sound.

The appeal of the concept of economic freedom largely rests on a presumption that when one person exercises her economic freedom she does not infringe on the economic freedom of others. It has often been remarked that John Locke envisioned a society of independent farmers and artisans, where each possessed his necessary means of production. Ignoring the presence of indigenous inhabitants, Locke reasoned that with an open frontier farmers could each have all the land they wanted without limiting the ability of other farmers to do likewise. Artisans were presumed to possess the necessary tools of their trade enabling them to produce anything in their individual "production possibility set" without relying on anyone else. In other words, in Locke's world everyone had sufficient wherewithal to produce whatever she wanted, and nobody's choices limited the choices open to anyone else. In this context the goal of increasing everyone's decision making discretion over more elements in her individual choice set was both noncontradictory and attractive. But it was only John Locke's imagination and the assumptions of classical liberalism that armed everyone with sufficient wherewithal to pursue their goals, and assured us that none could make choices that limited the choices open to others. Whether people were ever so armed and immune to the choices made by others is highly questionable. Certainly in today's world, where the natural environment is no longer bounteous relative to the human population and where large corporations not only own the preponderance of the means of production but have patented the most productive technologies as well, it is painfully obvious that the options for most of us are largely determined by choices made by others.

In any case, when there are conflicts between people's economic freedoms in capitalism, whose economic freedom takes priority over whose is settled by the property rights system. Once we realize economic freedom is meaningless without a specification of property rights—that it is the property rights system in capitalism that dictates who gets to decide when conflicts inevitably arise—the focus of attention shifts to where it should have been in the first place: How does a property rights system distribute decision-making authority? Does a property rights system distribute control over economic decisions in a way we would consider democratic? Or, by distributing property unequally, and by giving priority to some categories of property rights over others, does a particular property rights system leave most people little control over their economic destinies and award a few control over the economic fates of the many? So, the first problem with Milton Freidman's way of conceptualizing the notion that people should control their own economic lives is that it merely begs the question and defers all problems to an unspecified property rights system.

The second problem is that while Friedman and other champions of capitalism wax poetic on the subject of economic freedom, they have remarkably little to say about what is a better or worse property rights system. Most of what little they do say reduces to two observations: (1) whatever the distribution of property rights, it is crucial that property rights be clear cut and complete, since otherwise there will be inefficiency due to "property right ambiguity." And (2), since—in their opinion—it is difficult to argue that any distribution of property rights is preferable to any other on moral or theoretical grounds, there is no reason—again, in their opinion—to change the distribution of property rights history bequeathed us. If one can prove that property was acquired in clear violation of the law, Friedman and his followers are willing to consider redress. But they refuse to even consider the possibility of "legal theft," a distribution of property rights that effectively disenfranchises whole categories of economic actors. Friedman makes no objection when his fellow conservatives defend the property rights status quo and considers only clarification of ambiguities a legitimate area for public policy. What is entirely lacking is any attempt to develop criteria for better and worse distributions of property rights. The silence from conservative theoreticians is deafening on this point and those favored by existing property rights regimes can hardly be expected to object to the oversight.

Liberal Misuses

Over the past three decades, Amartya Sen has arguably done more to challenge the dogma that there is no remedy for poverty than any other living economist.[1] However, his latest work illustrates the dangers liberals court when they embrace the economic freedom metaphor. In *Development as Freedom* (1999), Sen goes beyond his earlier interpretation of economic development as the expansion of people's "capabilities" and argues that development can be defined as the expansion of freedom. According to Sen all the capabilities people may acquire are to be understood as exemplifying freedom. In his desire to describe all the good things that come with development as expansions of freedom Sen, for example, talks about mortality as a denial of "the freedom to survive." Paul Seabright took exception to reducing development to the expansion of freedoms in the March 29, 2001 issue of *The New York Review of Books*:

> Well yes, one can call death denial of the freedom to survive. But is it really illuminating to suggest that what matters about being dead is the lack of freedom that goes with it? Being dead is also bad for the health and has a significant statistical association with dropping out of college, but personally I think it's the deadness that would bother me. . . . We can always *say* that the society we like best is the one that most advances freedom, but a claim of that kind sounds remarkably like the claim in Molière that opium sends people to sleep because if its dormitive faculty.

I agree with Seabright that redefining everything that is good for someone to have as an increase in their freedom to have it, may be good salesmanship in the era of the free-market jubilee, but it is not good methodology. First, by conflating all "goods" into one—freedom—we not only reduce the power of language, we risk deceiving ourselves that something is more simple than it really is, a mistake Sen has correctly warned others against time and time again in other contexts. Economic development is *not* simply the expansion of freedoms. More generally, we have multiple economic goals—economic democracy, economic justice, environmental sustainability, and economic efficiency, to name four—that we should not attempt to reduce to a single goal, economic freedom. Second, as argued above, all too often when one person's freedom expands it does so at the expense of someone else's freedom that contracts. It is no less ambiguous and problematic when Amartya Sen says the goal of economic development is to maximize people's freedom than when Milton Friedman says the most important economic goal is to maximize economic freedom. What are we to do when people's freedoms conflict? Friedman's conservative disciples are happy to leave the answer to problems of conflicting personal freedoms to the reigning property rights system. Anyone who is familiar with Sen's work knows he is not willing to let the reigning system of property rights be the arbiter of some freedoms over others, and the freedoms of some people over the freedoms of other people. Sen has devoted his entire career to searching for answers to the paramount question of our time: What is the cause of so much poverty in the midst of so much wealth and prosperity? But if existing property rights regimes disenfranchise the have-nots, then what property rights deliver economic democracy? How does one argue for the superiority of one property rights regime over another? Just as conservatives sidestep this question by favoring existing property rights regimes, Sen sidesteps the basic philosophical question by simply favoring an expansion of property rights for the poor. In a world where property rights govern decision making power and life prospects, favoring an expansion of property rights for those with little or none is good politics. But it is not an attempt to justify a particular pattern of property rights as a means to achieve economic democracy. Neither conservatives nor Sen make a compelling philosophical case for the property rights they favor. In effect they assume their conclusion. These are among the difficulties that motivate the alternative conception of economic democracy defined below as "economic self-management."

Finally, by embracing the metaphor of economic freedom Sen unintentionally encourages the dominant rationalization for exploitation of our times. It is often asked: If people freely choose to enter into an arrangement, and are fully aware of the consequences, how can the outcome be considered unjust? This is a common rebuttal to legitimate complaints that wages are exploitative, that giant corporations price gouge, that the international credit system is usurious, and that free trade is a system of unequal exchange.[2] I am not suggesting that Sen falls victim to this sophistry, far from it. Sen has contributed greatly to the critique of neoliberal arguments for capital and trade liberalization, "flexible" labor markets, and the expansion of corporate rule in general. My point is simply that the freedom-encompasses-all metaphor Sen has recently championed unfortunately lends itself to this kind of abuse.

Majority Rule

If economic freedom is an inadequate and misleading conception of economic democracy, what are the alternatives? The other dominant conception of economic democracy is majority rule. This concept was borrowed from political science where the notion that no citizen should have more say over political matters than any other was enshrined in the doctrine of one person, one vote. The problem with majority rule is simple: when a decision has a greater effect on some people than others, by giving each person an equal vote, those more affected by a decision can find themselves overruled by those who are less affected. Even in the political sphere of social life, where many decisions affect all citizens more or less equally, some political decisions clearly affect the lives of some citizens more than the lives of others, and therefore these are individuals should be allowed to make, some choices regardless of how much others may disagree and claim to be affected. In these circumstances political scientists sensibly amend the principle of majority rule with other concepts like a bill of rights, civil liberties, and supermajority voting rules. But in the case of economic decisions the probability of unequal effects is much greater than in the case of political decisions. While some economic decisions affect only a single person, and some economic decisions affect us all to roughly the same extent, *most* economic decisions affect more than one person, but affect some people a great deal more than others. And therein lies the rub. While the concept of economic freedom works well for economic decisions that only affect one person, and the concept of majority rule works well for economic decisions that affect us all equally, neither conception of economic democracy works well for the overwhelming majority of economic decisions that affect some of us more than others.

Little Help from the Economics Profession

One would think the economics profession would have a great deal to say about economic democracy. But like economic justice, economic democracy is not a favorite subject of mainstream economists. What little they have to say on the subject comes under esoteric labels like "consumer and producer sovereignty," and intellectually difficult issues are buried under the unlikely heading of "externalities."

When mainstream economists think about economic democracy they do not begin from scratch. Instead they begin their thinking in the framework of a private enterprise market economy where there are already employers, employees, and consumers. In such an economy the employers—not the consumers of goods and services—are the ones who get to decide what goods will be available to consume. And the employers—not the employees who do the work—are the ones who get to decide how the work will be done. While this seems to obviously disen-franchise both consumers and workers from decisions that affect them greatly, mainstream economists caution us not to rush to verdict. They argue that while it is true that the employers do get to decide what to produce, consumers' preferences will guide owners of productive facili-ties to produce what consumers want, as long as many producers compete against one another to sell their goods in competitive goods markets. Mainstream economists also argue that while it is true that employers do get to tell their employees how to go about their work, employers will seek to please workers' preferences about how they work, as long as there are many employers competing against one another to hire employees in competitive labor markets.

There is no doubt that the more competitive goods markets are, the more consumer preferences will influence what they get to consume, and the more competitive labor markets are, the more workers' preferences about how they go about their work will be taken into account by their employers. But even when goods and labor markets are competitive, the degree of influence consumers and employees exert over the decisions that affect them in capitalist economies falls far short of anything deserving the title "consumer and producer (i.e., worker) sovereignty" for reasons explored at length in chapter 4. We will discover that a heterodox economic theory called "the conflict theory of the firm" demonstrates that even when labor markets are competitive, employers have incentives to organize work in ways that disempower employees, hardly something employees would choose if they were truly sovereign. And we will discover that even competitive goods markets bias the choices consumers face for different kinds of goods, and distribute votes in a way that can hardly be considered democratic. But for now, suffice it to say there are good reasons for rejecting the suggestion that consumers and workers are sovereign over the decisions that affect them in capitalist economies, and good reasons to conclude instead that the greater the power of corporations the more disenfranchised workers and consumers become. In other words, we will discover in chapter 4 that substituting discussion of producer and consumer sovereignty for a discussion of economic democracy, and engaging in a misleading evaluation of the extent of producer and consumer sovereignty in capitalism, is little more than a subtle sleight-of-hand maneuver to disguise the lack of economic democracy in capitalist economies.

However, mainstream economic theory creates another obstacle to clear thinking about economic democracy. Economists are taught to think about how economic choices affect people using individual utility functions. Moreover, in standard treatments a person's utility is defined as a function of the "consumption bundle" she consumes and the work tasks she performs. In this framework what affects an individual, that is, causes her to experience either more or less satisfaction or "utility," are only choices she makes herself. What should I consume? What tasks should I contract to perform?[3] What if instead, a person's utility were defined as a function of all human activity, in recognition of the fact that we are a social species and our individual well-being hinges on the activities of others as well as our own.[4] In this context individuals are seen to be affected by many more choices than mainstream economic theory recognizes, and it is apparent that the problem of economic democracy is much more complicated than mainstream theory leads us to expect. In fairness to mainstream theory, choices *others* make in market economies are sometimes recognized as affecting individuals. But these occurrences are seen as exceptions to the rule and special cases. They are given a nasty name—"externalities"—and consigned to a backwater of economic theory that is routinely underemphasized in economic curricula. In chapter 4, we will examine the basis for the presumption of external effect exceptionality in market economies, and discover why a growing number of heterodox economists are challenging this presumption, which dominates mainstream thinking. But for now it suffices to point out that by labeling the effects on an individual of choices made by others in market economies externalities, and by treating externalities as exceptions to the rule, mainstream economic theory (1) effectively relegates the difficult issues of economic democracy in market economies to an underdeveloped backwater of mainstream economic theory, and (2) neatly classifies all situations where people are disenfranchised in market economies as exceptions to the norm.

Unfortunately, those outside the mainstream of the profession have not been much more helpful than mainstream economists in clarifying how we should think about economic democracy. Progressive economists outside the mainstream invariably call for economic democracy, but just as invariably fail to specify what they mean in precise terms. To a great extent, "economic democracy" has been reduced to a feel-good phrase that, like "sustainable development," often obscures more than it clarifies. Heterodox economists who are openly critical of capitalism do make clear they do not believe employees in capitalist firms enjoy economic democracy or that producer and consumer sovereignty add up to economic democracy. And Marxists criticize capitalism because it "alienates" workers from their labor and its products and from their "species being." But besides sweeping generalizations to the effect that economic democracy will be achieved when economic decisions are made by "the associated producers," there is little concrete help from outside the mainstream toward defining our elusive goal.

Economic Self-Management

An alternative conception of economic democracy that takes into account the fact that most economic decisions affect more than one person, but not everyone equally, is quite straightforward: consider economic democracy as having decision-making input, or power, in proportion to the extent that you are affected by a choice or decision. If you are affected more than someone else by a particular decision, then you would have more say than they do. If you are affected less, you would have less input than they do. Then we can say that if everyone has decision-making input in proportion to the degree they are affected, for every economic decision, the economy is characterized by, or has achieved economic democracy. However, the phrase "economic democracy" is already used to mean different things by different people, and practically never used in the way suggested here. So it seems helpful to give this new way of thinking about economic democracy a name of its own. I define *economic self-management* as *decision-making input in proportion to the degree one is affected by different economic choices*, and suggest that thinking about achieving economic self-management for everyone is the best way to think about achieving economic democracy.

Of course it will never be possible to arrange for decisions to be made in ways that every person enjoys perfect economic self-management, any more than it is possible to ever achieve perfect economic justice no matter how well an economy is designed to promote justice. However, at least the goal of maximizing economic self-management, as defined above, is always meaningful, whereas the goal of maximizing people's economic freedom over the choice sets that affect them is only meaningful in a context where those choice sets do not intersect. As we saw, if choice sets intersect, increasing the economic freedom of one person over her choice set necessarily diminishes the economic freedom of someone else over the choice set that affects them. In other words, when choice sets intersect it is impossible to simultaneously maximize the economic freedom of both, in which case you must choose some set of rules that prioritize the economic freedom of some over the economic freedom of others, you cannot maximize economic freedom in general. But regardless of how intertwined the choice sets that affect people may be, no matter how often an economic decision affects more than one person, no matter how uneven the pattern of effects of economic decisions on multiple parties, it is still always possible to move from a decision-making procedure that less perfectly apportions decision making input in accord with the extent to which people are affected to a decision-making procedure that more perfectly apportions decision-making power according to how much people are affected. In other words, when we think of economic democracy as economic self-management we have a well-defined goal that offers a clear objective that is achievable in theory, if only imperfectly in practice even under the most democratic decision-making procedures conceivable. On the other hand, while individual economic freedom is well defined, it fails to offer a clear objective that could be achieved even in theory whenever economic choices affect multiple parties.[5]

Of course agreeing on a definition and a goal is not the same as achieving the goal. Just because we have a rigorous definition of economic self-management, and just because this gives us a coherent goal to shoot for and measure different decision-making procedures against, does not mean we know what procedures will best achieve economic self-management. Nor does it help us decide how we can best determine the degree to which different people are affected by different economic decisions. Nor does it help us identify and deal with situations where it is pointless to deny that people do feel affected by the behavior of others, but we may not think it is right to give them input in any case. In other words, having a clear idea of what we mean by economic democracy does not solve any of the hard problems of achieving it.

But getting clear about the goal is a first step in the right direction. As long as the phrase "economic democracy" remains vague, and is used to mean different things by different people, it is difficult to make progress toward achieving economic democracy. And as long as people labor under a misconception about what economic democracy means, we will continue to search in the wrong directions. As we discover in chapter 4, thinking of economic democracy as individual economic freedom can lead us to embrace antidemocratic economic institutions like private enterprise and markets. While thinking of economic democracy as majority rule can blind us to the fact that even the most democratic version of central planning conceivable would still deny people economic democracy by failing to let those who are more affected by a decision have more say over that choice.

3

Debilitating Myths

Besides being unclear about what economic justice and democracy mean, "we" on the left were wrong about many other things, some of them quite important. Of course who "we" were needs to be clarified. For every myth that plagued the left during the twentieth century, for every mistaken strategy based on some erroneous belief, invariably someone, or some group of people, recognized the mistake at the time. Sometimes their criticisms even became widely known and fostered great debates, but often objections received too little publicity and were soon forgotten. This is not to say that progressives never learned from their mistakes as the twentieth century progressed. There are many leftists today who have long since disabused themselves of many of the debilitating myths discussed below. So it is neither the case that none objected to these mistakes at the time, nor that many did not learn from mistakes afterward and modify programs, policies, strategies, and tactics in appropriate ways. Still, it is important to own up to major misconceptions that adversely affected left political practice during the last century and clarify the lessons to be learned. Confusion about the meaning and implications of economic justice and economic democracy were addressed in the previous two chapters and are the principle concerns of this book. In this chapter, I briefly touch on a few other confusions that are important to address before evaluating capitalism, communism, social democracy, and libertarian socialism in Part 2.

Capitalism in Crisis—But Not as Expected

Many twentieth-century progressives sustained themselves emotionally and psychologically with false beliefs that capitalism's dynamism and technological creativity would prove to be its undoing as well as its strength. In particular, two Marxist crisis theories influenced many on the left during much of the twentieth century. Marx hypothesized that capitalist development would be characterized more by capital-using, labor-saving technical changes than by capital-saving, labor-using changes. According to Marx this was problematic because his *labor theory of value* led him to believe that profits came only from exploiting *living labor*, not *dead labor*, that is, capital. In other words, Marx reasoned that when individual capitalists substituted machinery for labor to lower production costs they collectively produced a *long-run tendency for the rate of profit to fall*, in effect killing the goose that was laying their golden eggs. For over a hundred years Marxist economists predicted that such a crisis would eventually appear once all the *counteracting tendencies* played themselves out, and many anticapitalist activists wondered if every crisis that came along was "the big one." But in 1961, a Japanese political economist, Nobuo Okishio, published a theorem proving that if the wage rate did not fall, cost-reducing technical changes, including labor-saving, capital-using changes, would raise, not lower, the rate of profit in the long run, contrary to the expectations of generations of Marxist theorists. In other words, labor-saving, capital-using technical change does nothing, in and of itself, to depress the rate of profit in capitalism. Despite a number of attempts by die-hard Marxists during the 1970s and 1980s to rescue the falling rate of profit crisis theory from being relegated to the dust bin of history by the Okishio theorem, by the end of the century virtually all open-minded political economists recognized that this supposed *internal contradiction* within capitalism had been nothing more than a lengthy intellectual red herring.

Marx also predicted *crises of underconsumption* (or *overproduction*) as competition drives individual capitalists to reduce the wages of their employees and increase their accumulation out of profits, thereby increasing production at a pace that eventually outstrips consumption demand, causing a *realization crisis* when capitalists as a whole can no longer realize the profits they individually extracted in production. Paul Baran (*Political Economy of Growth*, 1957) and Paul Sweezy (*Monopoly Capital*, 1966) revived this theory in the 1960s when they interpreted postcolonial imperialism, Cold War military spending, modern advertising, and the expansion of public and private debt all as stop-gap solutions to what they presented as a chronic problem of insufficient demand for all the goods and services modern capitalist economies were capable of producing. In their interpretation these responses to the problem of insufficient aggregate demand were unlikely to provide a permanent solution. Baran argued that for a time advanced capitalist economies could dispose of unwanted consumption goods through trade surpluses with countries in the *periphery* of the global capitalist system, and unwanted investment goods through direct foreign investment in the periphery. But Baran argued that the solution to capitalist overproduction through imperial expansion would prove impermanent as capitalism developed in the periphery and the lesser-developed economies began to generate underconsumption problems of their own.[1] Sweezy argued that even highly seductive Madison Avenue advertising could only increase a household's propensity to consume so much. He also prophesied limits to how much consumption could be increased through expansion of private debt since this meant that banks would be, in Sweezy's words, "skating on ever thinner ice," thereby increasing the likelihood of financial crises. Sweezy argued that *military Keynesianism* financed by rising public indebtedness might fill the underconsumption gap for longer, but he also pointed out that this requires financial markets to tolerate indefinitely rising government debt and citizens to tolerate working more hours every day to produce ever-more useless military hardware.

Variants of this theory are still popular among some Marxist economists who insist that problems of insufficient aggregate demand in capitalism are endemic and increasing. The question is if there is an inherent tendency within capitalism to generate an ever-widening gap between all that can be produced and the demand necessary to purchase it so that the pressure to find new ways to buoy demand to ward off stagnation escalates as capitalism develops. To put it simply and bluntly, the answer is *no*. Modern political economy macroeconomic models of growth and distribution developed over the last quarter century have moved us considerably beyond Marxist underconsumptionist crisis literature that was less rigorous and therefore more conjectural. Don Harris (*Capital Accumulation and Income Distribution*, 1978), Stephen Marglin (*Growth, Distribution and Prices*, 1984), and Lance Taylor (*Income Distribution, Inflation and Growth*, 1991) were prominent pioneers of what is now a substantial theoretical literature that rigorously explores the relationship between distribution and growth in capitalist economies. In its totality this literature demonstrates conclusively that *the relationship between aggregate demand and supply is no more, nor less problematic in the long run than it is in the short run.* Keynes demonstrated long ago that demand in a given year can be insufficient to induce capitalists to produce all the economy is capable of that year. Similarly, modern political economy macroeconomic growth models demonstrate that permanently redistributing income from wages to profits can lower the long-run growth rate by permanently lowering capacity utilization and thereby permanently depressing investment.[2] But there is no tendency for the "demand gap," which must be filled to avoid stagnation, to increase over time. It turns out that at least at the theoretical level, managing aggregate demand to keep the economy producing at full capacity in the long run is no different than managing demand so the economy will produce at full capacity in the short run. In neither case will aggregate demand automatically yield full-capacity outcomes without helpful interventions orchestrated by government. In neither case should anyone expect fine-tuning by the government in practice to be easy or perfect, among other reasons because it is not easy to predict human behavior when speculative and strategic motives are at play. Moreover, both employers and the wealthy often bring pressure on governments *not* to stimulate aggregate demand even when it would increase GDP because it would decrease their share of GDP as well. So practical, technical difficulties of aggregate demand management in capitalism are invariably compounded by class interests that often cloak themselves in ideological garb. But there is no tendency for the problem of generating sufficient aggregate demand to get worse as capitalist economies grow, and no reason to believe that successful intervention will prove more difficult to achieve as capitalism develops, except if capitalist political power increases, enabling them to more successfully obstruct efficient demand management for selfish reasons.

The idea that capitalism contains *internal contradictions* that act as seeds for its own destruction is simply wrong and needs to be discarded once and for all. The belief that capitalism inevitably digs its own grave often buoyed the hopes of the faithful during the twentieth century in the face of setbacks for anticapitalist organizations and causes. Ironically, early in the century it was social democratic leaders of the second "socialist" international like Edouard Bernstein who argued most forcefully that internal contradictions could be relied on to soon bring capitalism to its knees, and therefore there was no need to prioritize insurrectionary over reform organizing. At that time it was those like V. I. Lenin and Rosa Luxemburg who broke away from the second international to form the third "communist" international who were more skeptical about the proximity of capitalist crisis without a strong push from a proletariat who needed to be prepared and organized for insurrection. After World War II roles were reversed. Social democratic parties officially abandoned their belief in fatal internal contradictions and argued that capitalism was not doomed, but that fortunately it was highly amenable to reform, while members of communist parties became more inclined to take refuge from their political defeats in the advanced economies in theories of internal capitalist contradictions. But no matter who believed them, and no matter what policy implications leftists drew from doctrines of fatal contradictions within capitalism, they were never true, and the sooner progressives realize that capitalism is no more plagued by endemic underconsumption than it is doomed by a tendency for the rate of profit to fall, the sooner we can focus on what is really wrong with capitalism, and what can be done to improve its performance until we can replace it.

What is true is that despite impressive technological advances that should dramatically improve our lives, laissez-faire capitalism will not satisfy the need for basic economic security for most of the third world, and a growing underclass in the advanced economies. What is true is that despite the fact that scientists are capable of devising technologies that would allow us to protect the natural environment, unrestrained global capitalism will unleash unthinkable environmental catastrophes within the next hundred years. What is true is that the new era of global robber baron capitalism in which financial capital reigns virtually unconstrained will continue to cause financial crises that destroy the livelihoods of billions who live in developing economies and increase the economic insecurity of the majority who live in developed economies. What is true about the present course of global capitalism is that it will doom most to struggle harder than their parents to meet their economic needs, while a tiny privileged minority accumulate fabulous wealth at an accelerating rate.

What is also true is that not even when capitalism is tamed by a full panoply of social democratic reforms can it satisfy the desires for self-managed, meaningful work that an increasingly educated populace will demand, or our longings for community, dignity, and economic justice. And while reforms within capitalism can slow the pace of environmental destruction, they will never make capitalism environmentally sustainable.

Nor, unfortunately, does capitalism nurture the seeds of its own replacement in ways most twentieth-century progressives believed it would. It does not generate a growing, homogeneous, working class whose economic activities lead them to see the advantages of seizing and managing the means of production themselves. Instead capitalism teaches those it disenfranchises that they are incapable of making good decisions and should be thankful that their fortunes rest on the decisions of their betters. Capitalism rationalizes exploitation, fosters commercial values and behaviors, and teaches myths about its desirability and inevitability. The transition to the economics of equitable cooperation, however, requires dispelling myths about the virtues of capitalism, challenging the legitimacy of all forms of exploitation, rejecting commercial values to embrace human values, and developing efficient democratic and cooperative patterns of behavior. Since all these behaviors are penalized rather than rewarded by market competition, capitalism provides less help and creates more obstacles for those seeking to tame it, and eventually replace it, than our twentieth-century predecessors expected, and leaves more hard swimming against the current than they dared to believe.

If the "doomed to destruction by internal contradictions" theories were wrong, if the "seek to heighten the contradictions" interpretation of the role of anticapitalist activists in history was misconceived, then what is an accurate interpretation of capitalist history, and how should progressive activists understand our role? During the second half of the second millennium A.D. the political sphere of social life witnessed an epic struggle between tyranny and freedom, followed by a continuing struggle between elite political rule versus democratic rule. Has there been a similar struggle going on in the economic sphere of social life? If so, I think it has been a struggle between the economics of competition and greed and the economics of equitable cooperation. Beside the rapid technological changes that distinguish our era—many of which were, indeed, wonderful advances, even if some will prove less so with hindsight—people have struggled over *how* to organize divisions of labor that improve the efficacy of our economic sacrifices. On the one side we have seen institutions grow that seek to organize our increasingly specialized economic endeavors based on a system of competition and greed, along with ideologies that preach the necessity and advantages of doing so. On the other side we have seen resistance to this epic trend. We have seen struggles of different kinds and sizes against the ravages of competition and greed and the miseries, inequities, wastefulness, and inefficiencies they create. We have seen intellectual critiques of its destructive dynamics. We have seen theories developed that insist there *is* another possibility, that the human species is not so socially feeble that we cannot organize a productive division of labor in a system of equitable cooperation. And we have seen not just macro projects attempting to replace the economics of competition and greed with the economics of equitable cooperation, we have witnessed hundreds of millions of micro attempts to do so as well.

I suggest progressive economic activists see ourselves as engaged in a struggle that is centuries old, a tug of war between those who would further refine and consolidate the system of competition and greed that has been spreading its sway for almost five centuries, and those who oppose its spread and struggle to achieve a more equitable system of economic cooperation. Naturally those who pull for the economics of competition and greed are usually those who enjoy more of the benefits and less of the burdens it distributes, while those pulling for equitable cooperation are often victims of the system of competition and greed. Not surprisingly over the past five hundred years the rope has sometimes moved slowly in one direction and sometimes in the other, sometimes lurched quickly, and sometimes remained stuck for a time. Not surprisingly some strategies and tactics for pulling the rope have proven more critical and decisive than others at particular junctures. And we should really not be surprised to discover that every once in a while when we thought we had achieved a significant lurch in the direction of equitable cooperation, we later discovered that we had grossly deceived ourselves.[3]

It remains to be seen whether this tug of war over how to manage our economic affairs will be never ending, or will some day be resolved in favor of equitable cooperation, and we will move on to a new era, where humans struggle over different issues altogether. At the beginning of the second millennium A.D. this hardly seems relevant as the forces of competition and greed have become much more powerful over the past thirty years, and those struggling for equitable cooperation have become much weaker. However, seeing ourselves in a centuries-old tug of war between two different ways of organizing our joint economic endeavors does affect expectations. It suggests that the transition from the economics of competition and greed to the economics of equitable cooperation will prove less abrupt and decisive than many twentieth-century anticapitalists hoped for. This does not diminish the importance of replacing key institutional knots in the rope that favor those pulling for competition and greed with different institutional knots that give those pulling for equitable cooperation stronger grips. The struggle is not only about pulling hard. Success also hinges on untying old knots that aid our opponents, and whenever opportunities arise, tying new knots that make our tugs more effective.

In chapter 4, we analyze why the large knots of private enterprise and markets all but guarantee victory for the economics of competition and greed if they are not loosened and eventually untied altogether. In chapters 5 and 11, we study small knots that make capitalism less destructive like financial regulation, full employment macroeconomic policies, industrial policy, universal old age and health insurance, tax reform, environmental regulation, and welfare programs, many of which have been recently untied to our detriment. In chapters 6, 7, 8,and 9 we discuss replacing the large knots of capitalism with different large knots that greatly improve the likelihood of advancing the cause of equitable cooperation. We discuss replacing the employer-employee knot with the knot of democratic worker councils, replacing the knot of markets with the knot of participatory planning, and replacing the habit of rewarding people according to contribution with the habit of rewarding people according to sacrifice.

The Invisible Coordinator Class

Marx predicted that as capitalism developed the class between what he called the proletariat and the bourgeoisie, the "petite bourgeoisie," would shrink and join the ranks of an increasingly homogeneous working class. Instead a class between ordinary workers and capitalists grew in size and importance, and the working class itself grew increasingly heterogeneous. While most Marxists ridiculed the term "middle class" for lack of analytical rigor in the mid-1970s John and Barbara Ehrenreich challenged Marxist orthodoxy insisting that a "professional managerial class" (PMC) with interests antagonistic to the interests of both capitalists and workers had grown in size and importance in advanced capitalist economies.[4] In the early 1980s, Michael Albert and I argued that not only had advanced capitalism spawned an important new "coordinator class" in its midst, this class had succeeded in becoming the new "ruling class" in various twentieth-century communist economies by preventing the working class from exercising collective self-management after capitalist domination was eliminated.[5]

The Ehrenreichs argued that as long as the left refused to recognize the existence of a professional managerial class in capitalism we would continue to fail to understand why the working class was repelled by left movements dominated by PMC culture and outlook. Albert and I argued that as long as the left refused to recognize that a class of coordinators could rise to ruling-class status in public enterprise economies we would continue to fail to understand the nonsocialist nature of the so-called socialist economies. We argued that neither the class struggles in twentieth-century capitalist economies, nor class dynamics in communist economies could be understood without recognizing the importance of a new class whose power was based on monopolizing knowledge and administrative authority, a new class that Marxist theory was completely blind to.

Unfortunately, for all its emphasis on class analysis, Marxism blinded many fighting against the economics of competition and greed to important antagonisms between the working class and the new, professional managerial, or coordinator class. In chapter 4, I argue that this blind spot contributed to profound misunderstandings about communist economies. In chapter 5, I suggest that as the twentieth century progressed, social democracy increasingly represented the perspectives and interests of this new class at the expense of the working class. In chapters 8 and 9, I argue for the importance of institutional safeguards to prevent this new class from usurping economic power in postcapitalist economies. And in chapters 11, 12, and 13, I explore ways the working class can protect its interests against the PMC while working along with progressive elements within the PMC to overthrow capitalist rule.

Economism

By *economism* I mean attributing unwarranted importance to economics in some way or another. It can take the form of assuming that the economic sphere of social life in a particular society is more important than it really is, compared to the political, kinship, or community spheres of social life. It can take the form of assuming in a particular situation that economic classes are more important agents of history than they really are, compared to racial, religious, or gender groups. It can take the form of assuming that a social problem derives from some economic cause when it actually is rooted in dynamics in some other sphere of social life. Or it can take the form of referring to a society as "capitalist" when it is also patriarchal and racist. The truth is most of us got two things completely wrong about classes in twentieth-century societies. Not only were we blind to the emergence and importance of a new professional managerial, or coordinator class, most of us also overestimated the importance of class struggle and underestimated the importance of struggles between privileged and oppressed historical communities and gender groups. We underestimated the importance of struggles over national sovereignty. We underestimated the power of struggles between dominant and subordinate racial and religious communities. We underestimated the extent to which patriarchal gender relations privilege men over women, and we underestimated the pressures unleashed by struggles to transform them.

By century's end, the peace and antiimperialist movements, the civil rights and antiracist movements, and the women's and gay rights movements had gone a long way toward correcting this economistic bias among those fighting for progressive social change. But for much of the century the economistic bias in Marxism permeated the programs and strategies of those fighting for progressive economic change. Until late in the century, the grand alliance of progressive forces was invariably conceived as a united front of all workers against the capitalist class, as oppressed minorities and women were expected to subordinate their struggles for equality and liberation to the strategic necessity of class unity. For much of the century, antiracists and feminists were told they could best achieve their goals by prioritizing the overthrow of capitalism.

This is not to say that the economic sphere of social life is not of great importance, or that classes are not important agents of history, or that economic dynamics do not affect gender, community, and political relations. This is not even to say that there are not situations where economic dynamics and class struggle are the most important forces molding events. Class struggle is far from over. Quite the contrary. In an implicit economic social contract after World War II, labor conceded control of the workplace to their employers in exchange for wage increases commensurate with productivity increases. In the early 1980s, the capitalist class in the United States and Europe tore up this social contract, which underwrote the postwar golden age of capitalism and launched all out class war to suppress wages in the advanced economies that continues today. But to assume that economic forces and class struggle are *always* most important is unwarranted, to reduce explanations of war, gender oppression, and racial discrimination to economic motives is untenable, and to demand that oppressed racial and gender groups always subordinate their struggles to the class struggle is unconscionable.[6]

It's the Environment, Stupid!

By the end of the twentieth century, many of us fighting against the economics of competition and greed had added to our litany of complaints about capitalism that it leads us to abuse the natural environment in ever more frightening ways. But prior to the first Earth Day in 1970, with few exceptions, anticapitalists were missing in action in the battle to protect the environment. In other words, until barely thirty years ago those who specialized in criticizing capitalism were largely oblivious to one of its most serious, and potentially fatal shortcomings. Moreover, there is still an unfortunate dichotomy between most who criticize capitalism because it disenfranchises the majority from economic decision making, distributes economic burdens and rewards unfairly, and wastes human productive potentials, and those who criticize capitalism because it is destroying the biosphere. It is crucial for those who have long criticized capitalism for other reasons to get up to speed about the threat capitalism poses to the environment. What follows is a brief explanation of four different reasons that another hundred years of capitalism may well destroy the environment beyond repair.

Overexploitation of Common Property Resources

Fisheries are the examples of common property resources most often discussed by environmental economists. The problem for fisheries is that individual fishers have no reason to take into account: (1) the more fish they catch from a fishery the fewer fish others will catch for a given amount of effort this year, and (2) the more fish they catch this year the fewer fish will be available for all to catch next year. In other words, individual fishers have no incentive to consider the external costs their increased fishing imposes on other fishers this year and next. When every potential fisher ignores these external costs we predictably get overfishing, or *overexploitation* of the fishery. It is important to notice that we get overexploitation even if the fish are not overfished to the point of extinction. Even if the fishery survives we still have overexploitation in the sense that the net benefits from this year's fishing will be less than they could have been had fewer fishers spent less time fishing. And even if the fishery survives, we would have overexploitation in the sense that the net benefits in the two years together could have been higher had fewer fish been caught this year so more could be caught next year. Unfortunately, not just fisheries, but a great deal of the natural environment is a "common property resource" and is therefore currently subjected to the logic of overexploitation when individual users are free to pursue profit maximization. To name a few important examples, the air we breathe, the upper atmosphere where greenhouse gases accumulate, much of the world's tropical forests, and most aquifers are common property resources, too, so when users motivated by individual concerns have free access, they predictably overexploit these and other crucial common property resources as well. While capitalism has always stimulated humans to overexploit nature's commons, the consequences have now reached critical levels. Current population levels, current technological capabilities, and the extent to which capitalism has now penetrated every society threaten to turn overexploitation into global ecocide in the twenty-first century.

Overpollution

Pollution is a "negative externality" of production or consumption activity. It is well known that market economies predictably over-produce goods and services whose production or consumption entails negative external effects because those who make decisions in market economies—buyers and sellers—have no incentive to take negative effects on others into account. This means that while it may be efficient to pollute to some extent—when the benefits from the goods or services produced along with the pollution exceed the costs of producing them *including* the damage, or cost of the pollution—markets will predictably lead us to pollute beyond this point. When car producers and buyers ignore the negative effects of car emissions on local air quality and greenhouse gas accumulations they not only lead us to produce and consume too many cars, they also lead us to engage in too much air pollution. But many industries are like the automobile industry, to a greater or lesser extent. Cement factories emit particulates that cause urban air pollution as well as produce cement. Utility companies emit sulfur dioxide that causes acid rain while they produce electricity. And modern agriculture produces pesticide runoff contaminating ground water and rivers, as well as fruits and vegetables. In a market economy it is predictable that we will emit too much particulates and sulfur dioxide and use too much pesticide.

The biosphere provides resources, assimilates wastes, provides amenities, and performs life-support services. Whenever production or consumption diminishes the usefulness of the environment in any of these regards, it is likely to go unaccounted for in a market system since most of those affected will be third parties whose interests will not be considered by the buyer or seller in a market transaction. In other words, expecting a free-market system not to pollute too much is like waiting for a lead balloon to rise.

But surely environmentally conscious people take the environmental effects of their actions into account. Isn't the answer more environmental education so we all become "green consumers?" We *should* consume so as not to pollute, and the environment certainly is better off because many who have become aware of the environmental consequences of their choices take those effects into account. But it is important to realize that a market system provides no incentives for people to engage in green consumerism. Quite the opposite, markets provide powerful incentives for consumers to behave in environmentally irresponsible ways even when they are aware of the consequences. To understand this, we need to consider a third major reason market economies destroy the environment.

Too Little Pollution Cleanup

Not only will markets lead us to pollute too much in the first place, they will lead us to clean up too little of the pollution we do emit. Since everyone benefits from pollution cleanup, and none can be excluded from the benefits, cleaning up pollution is a public good. However, market economies tend to underproduce public goods in general due to something called the "free-rider problem." In a market system there is an incentive for everyone who benefits from a public good to try to avoid paying the cost of providing the good, and instead to ride for free on the purchases of others. When someone else buys a private good I do not benefit. But when others buy a public good I can often benefit as much as they do. Hence the temptation to try to free-ride on the purchases of others when it comes to public goods. But of course when each individual pursues her rational strategy and rides for free, there is little or no demand in the market for public goods. In other words, markets provide incentives for individuals to express their desires for private goods in the marketplace by offering to buy them, since otherwise they cannot benefit. But markets provide no incentives for individuals to express their desires for public goods in the marketplace by offering to purchase them. Quite the contrary, in a market economy it is almost always foolish for individuals to buy public goods no matter how much they may want them. In the words of Robert Heilbroner, "Markets have a keen ear for private wants but a deaf ear for public needs." And therein lies the problem for green consumerism in market economies. The problem is not that when people choose to engage in green consumerism the world is not better off because of it. The problem is that markets penalize those who practice green con-

sumerism and reward those who do not, which means that socially beneficial campaigns encouraging green consumption must always swim
upstream in market economies.

The problem of climate change nicely illustrates all of the above ways in
which capitalism contributes to environmental destruction. Human
economic activity over the past hundred years has led to dramatic
increases in atmospheric concentrations of carbon dioxide. Between 1860
and 1990, global carbon emissions rose from less than 200 million to
almost 6 billion metric tons per year. At the same time, deforestation has
considerably reduced the recycling of carbon dioxide into oxygen. The
result of increased carbon emissions and reduced sequestration is that the
stock of greenhouse gases in the atmosphere has increased to the point
that it is leading to climate change with serious adverse affects. At its old
equilibrium level the greenhouse effect was part of making the earth habit-
able, preventing the earth's mean temperature from falling well below
freezing and reducing temperature fluctuation between day and night. But
today's higher levels of greenhouse gases in the atmosphere mean global
temperatures will rise and extreme climate conditions will intensify.
Droughts will be longer, floods more severe, hurricanes and tornadoes
more frequent, and melting polar ice caps will raise sea levels and threaten
a large percentage of the world's population who live in coastal cities.

This is happening because in our market economy businesses and
households who burn fossil fuels are not charged for the adverse effects
their actions have on the atmosphere; carbon emissions are a negative
externality. This is happening because in a market economy those who
control tropical forests are not paid for the beneficial effect of carbon
storage and sequestration if they choose to preserve the forests. Carbon
storage and sequestration is a positive externality.[7] Markets lead us to
engage in too many activities with negative external effects and too little
activities with positive external effects. Hence, too much fossil-fuel
burning and too little forest preservation goes on under market incentives.
Moreover, reductions in carbon emissions are a public good, as is preservation of forests that sequester and store carbon. But since none can be
excluded from benefiting from these public goods, and they do entail
private sacrifices for those who provide them, all businesses, consumers,
and nations wait for someone else to shoulder the burden of providing
these public goods in hopes of riding for free on the sacrifices of others.
Every country wants to enjoy the benefits associated with carbon-emitting
activity and commercial forest use, and hopes other countries will reduce
their carbon emissions and preserve their forests.

It is not hard to see why international negotiations over greenhouse gas emissions get stuck. Per-capita emissions in 1990 were only 0.489 metric tons in poor countries, but 3.426 in rich countries. Rich countries point to the unthinkable effects on the environment of poor countries following the industrialization path of the rich countries, while poor countries point to the inequity inherent in freezing emissions at present levels or demanding equal percentage reductions from all countries. Meanwhile, every country continues to use its own forests to best commercial advantage while hoping other countries will refrain from deforestation and provide free carbon sequestration and storage services for all. Since owners of tropical forests get paid for timber they cut, or cattle they raise after burning forests off, but do not get paid for carbon their forests sequester and store, countries like Brazil, Zaire, and Indonesia, whose forests provide major global carbon storage and sequestration services, have no incentive to preserve them. The free market has given us global warming and continues to provide powerful *dis*incentives to any country who moves to do anything constructive about it.

Overconsumption

Thorstein Veblen explained how capitalism breeds "conspicuous consumption" in *The Theory of the Leisure Class: An Economic Study of Institutions* published in 1899. John Kenneth Galbraith explained why private goods are prioritized at the expense of public services in advanced capitalist societies in *The Affluent Society* published in 1958. In *Quiet Revolution in Welfare Economics* (1990), Michael Albert and I developed a model of endogenous preference formation to provide a rigorous explanation of why it is individually rational for people to adjust to biases in the economies they live in, and therefore why it is predictable that people living in capitalist economies will develop their preferences for consumption at the expense of leisure, and for private consumption at the expense of social consumption. In three books, *The Overworked American: The Unexpected Decline of Leisure* (1992), *The Overspent American: Upscaling, Downshifting, and the New Consumer* (1998), and *Do Americans Shop Too Much?* (2000), Juliet Schor dissected the irrationality of overwork and overconsumption during the past half century in the United States in all its gory details. Schor traced the reasons why we cash in our productivity increases on more private consumption rather than on more leisure and more social consumption—even when it is contrary to our best interests—once again, to incentives embedded in the economic system. Since consumption damages the environment more than leisure, and private consumption damages the environment more than social consumption, these well-documented dynamics are an important part of a full understanding of all the ways that capitalism adversely affects the environment.

Capitalism inevitably leads us to overexploit the global commons, to over tax the waste storage capacities of the natural environment, to underprotect and restore the natural environment, and to work and consume too much, all to the detriment of the environment. To say the left neglected these problems far too long in the twentieth century is a gross understatement. The fact that capitalism contains perverse incentives that make environmentally responsible behavior individually irrational must be front and center when we make our case against the economics of competition and greed in the century ahead.

Conclusion

Having clarified important issues about economic justice and economic democracy in the previous two chapters, and having dispelled some myths that plagued much of the left during the twentieth century in this chapter, we are now ready in Part 2 to evaluate the two economic systems that dominated the twentieth century—capitalism and communism—and the two movements that offered themselves as alternatives to both, social democracy and libertarian socialism.

Part II

Rethinking Our Past

4

Neither Capitalism Nor Communism

Now that the twentieth century has drawn to a close, what have we learned about how to manage our economic affairs? This chapter reviews our most recent failures to design a desirable economic system hoping to avoid repeating history as farce. First I summarize what is wrong with laissez-faire capitalism, the economic system that stands triumphant at the beginning of the new millennium poised to sentence billions to abject poverty and destroy the biosphere if unchecked over the century to come. Then I examine what was wrong with communism and command planning, the first misguided attempt to transcend the economics of competition and greed, which is now in the dustbin of history itself.

Capitalism

The Nobel laureate and dean of conservative economists, Milton Friedman, argued in *Capitalism and Freedom* (1964) that only capitalism can provide economic freedom, allocate resources efficiently, and motivate people successfully. He also argued that capitalism tends to eradicate discriminatory prejudices, rewards people as fairly as can be hoped for, and is a necessary condition for political freedom. The truth is capitalism aggravates prejudice, is the most inequitable economy ever devised, is grossly inefficient—even if highly energetic—and is incompatible with both economic and political democracy. In the present era of free-market triumphalism it is useful to organize a sober evaluation of capitalism by responding to Friedman's claims one by one.

Capitalism and Freedom

Friedman says the most important virtue of capitalism is that it provides economic freedom, by which he means the freedom to do whatever one wishes with one's person and property, including the right to contract with others over their use of your person or property. He says economic freedom is important in and of itself, but also important because it unleashes people's economic creativity and because economic freedom promotes political freedom.

Friedman's concept of individual economic freedom is an inadequate and misleading conceptualization of economic democracy for reasons discussed in chapter 2. But disagreements over how best to define economic democracy aside, Friedman's argument that free enterprise and markets allow people to control their economic lives is misleading, and his conclusion that capitalism promotes political democracy is totally unpersuasive.

According to Friedman there is no conflict between the economic freedoms of employees and employers as long as employment contracts are agreed to by both parties under competitive conditions. As long as the employment relation is voluntary, and as long as labor markets are competitive so that no one is compelled to work for a particular employer, or compelled to hire a particular employee, the economic freedoms of all are preserved according to Friedman and his conservative followers. In their eyes, when an employee agrees to work for an employer she is merely exercising her economic freedom to do with her laboring capacities as she sees fit. She could employ her human capital herself if she wished. But if she is offered what she decides is a better deal—relinquish her right to use her laboring capacities to another for a wage payment she finds suitable—she should be free to do so. What's more, if she is prohibited from making this choice her economic freedom would be violated, just as the economic freedom of the employer to use his productive property as he sees fit would be violated if he is barred from hiring employees to work with it under his direction. Accordingly, Friedman concludes that "union shops" are violations of employee as well as employer economic freedom under capitalism, and the socialist ban on private enterprise altogether is the ultimate violation of people's economic freedom to hire and be hired by one another should they so choose.

The first problem with this defense of private enterprise as the cornerstone of economic freedom is that not all people have, or could ever have, an equal opportunity to become employers rather than employees. In real capitalist economies a few will become employers, the vast majority will work for someone else, and some will be self-employed. Moreover, *who* will be employers, employees, or self-employed is determined for the most part *neither* randomly *nor* by peoples' relative preferences for self-managed versus other-directed work. Simple models reveal that *only* under egalitarian distributions of capital would relative preferences for self-managed work determine who become employers and who become employees. Under inegalitarian distributions, those with more capital inevitably become the employers while those with less capital become the employees, *irrespective* of peoples' relative preferences for self-management or aversions to being bossed around.[1] One of the most profound insights provided by these simple models is that while it is true, in a sense, that employees "choose" alienated labor, they do not necessarily do so because they have a weaker desire for self-management than those for whom they work. The distribution of wealth tilts the playing field so that some will benefit more by becoming employers and others will benefit more by becoming employees *independent* of work preferences. Put differently, the poor have to pay a steep price if they "choose" to manage their own laboring capacities while the rich are amply rewarded for "choosing" to boss others.[2]

Defenders of capitalism answer this criticism by arguing that anyone who wants to work badly enough for herself can borrow whatever is necessary to become self-employed or to become an employer in the credit market. They go on to point out that *assuming perfect credit markets*, anyone who can run an efficient business can borrow enough to do so, and thereby avoid having to play the role of employee herself. But this line of reasoning assumes more than any real capitalism can offer—credit on equal terms for all—and ignores the fact that even competitive credit markets can impose a steep price on the poor for self-management that the wealthy are not required to pay. In a world with uncertainty and imperfect information—not to speak of patents and technological and financial economies of scale—those with more collateral and credentials will receive credit on preferential terms, while the rest of us will be subject to credit rationing in one form or another. To expect anything different is to expect lenders to be fools. So being referred to the credit market is not going to even the playing field for the poor. But even if all did receive credit on equal terms, the simple models I referred to above, which assume that anyone can borrow as much as they want at the market rate of interest and nobody has access to credit for less, demonstrate that those who avoid the status of employer by borrowing in credit markets in effect pay their wealthy creditors for a right that should be as inalienable as the right to vote on political issues. There is a bottom line and the buck must stop somewhere: those without wealth to begin with would face an uphill road to avoid employee status even if credit markets were perfect, and they face a much steeper uphill road when credit markets are less than perfect, which they always are.

The second problem with the argument that capitalism promotes economic freedom is that even if the capitalist playing field were even, and the probability of becoming an employer rather than an employee was the same for everyone regardless of wealth, this would not mean that the employer-employee relationship was a desirable one. Of course random assignment would be a far sight better than having relative wealth determine who will boss and who will be bossed. But is it better than having neither bosses nor bossed? That is, is it better than an economy where all enjoy self-management? Consider this useful analogy: a slave system where blacks apply to be slaves for white slave masters of their choice is better than one where white slave owners trade black slaves among themselves. A slave system where people are assigned randomly to be slaves or slave masters is better than one where only blacks can be slaves and only whites can be slave owners. But abolition of slavery is better than even the least objectionable kind of slavery. The same holds for wage slavery. A labor market where the poor are free to apply to work for employers of their choice is better than one where wealthy employers trade poor employees among themselves, as major league baseball players discovered. A system that assigns people to be employers or employees randomly is better than one where the wealthy predictably become the employers and the poor predictably become their employees. But abolition of wage slavery—replacing the roles of employer and employee with self-management for all—is better than even the least objectionable system of private enterprise.

If the claim that private enterprise is a bulwark of economic freedom holds little water, what of the argument that markets promote economic freedom? In one of his most quoted passages, Milton Friedman argues that the principle virtue of competitive markets is that they are uniquely compatible with economic freedom:

> The basic problem of social organization is how to coordinate the economic activities of large numbers of people. The challenge to the believer in liberty is to reconcile this widespread interdependence with individual freedom. Fundamentally there are only two ways of

coordinating the economic activities of millions. One is central direction involving the use of coercion—the technique of the army and of the modern totalitarian state. The other is voluntary cooperation of individuals—the technique of the market place. The possibility of coordination through voluntary cooperation rests on the elementary, yet frequently denied, proposition that both parties to an economic transaction benefit from it, *provided the transaction is bilaterally voluntary and informed*. So long as effective freedom of exchange is maintained, the central feature of the market organization of economic activity is that it prevents one person from interfering with another in respect of most of his activities. The consumer is protected from coercion by the seller because of the presence of other sellers with whom he can deal. The seller is protected from coercion by the consumer because of other consumers to whom he can sell. The employee is protected from coercion by the employer because of other employers for whom he can work, and so on. And the market does this impersonally and without centralized authority.[3]

The first problem with this argument is it is not one person, one vote, but one dollar, one vote in the marketplace. Some claim this as a virtue: if I have a particularly strong preference for a good I can cast more dollar ballots to reflect the intensity of my desire. But this argument conflates two issues. There is nothing wrong with a system of social choice that permits people to express the intensity of their desires. In fact, this is necessary if we are to achieve self-managed decision making. But, *there is something wrong when people have vastly different numbers of dollar ballots to cast in market elections*. Few would describe a political election in which some were permitted to vote thousands of times and others were permitted to vote only once as a system to be admired and emulated. But this is exactly the kind of democracy the market provides. Those with more income have a greater impact on what suppliers in markets will be signaled to provide than those with less income, which explains why market freedom often leads to outcomes we know do not reflect what most people need or want. Why are there so many plastic surgeons in Hollywood when many poor, rural communities suffer for lack of family practitioners? How can the demand for cosmetic plastic surgery in Hollywood be so high, and the demand for basic healthcare in poor, rural communities be so low? There are many more rural poor who vote in the healthcare market for basic healthcare than there are wealthy Hollywood residents who vote for plastic surgery. And the intensity of poor people's desires for basic healthcare is higher than the intensity of Hollywood residents' desires for plastic surgery as well. But those voting for plastic surgery in Hollywood have many more votes to cast for even their less pressing desires than poor, rural residents have to cast for basic healthcare even regarding life and death needs. Hence the provision of medical services of marginal benefit, like plastic surgery in Hollywood, and the failure to provide essential medical services for the rural poor, when healthcare decisions are left to the marketplace.

Second, simple models like those mentioned above demonstrate that exchanges in labor and credit markets that are bilaterally voluntary and informed can still lead to growing inequalities that cannot be morally justified, even when employees and borrowers are supposedly protected from coercion by a multiplicity of employers and lenders to choose from. The lie behind Friedman's portrayal of market exchanges as noncoercive is that he ignores the critical importance of what those who confront each other in the marketplace arrive with. When some arrive at the labor market with more capital than others, it is entirely predictable that those with more capital will end up being the employers and those with less their employees. Moreover, as long as capital is scarce it is predictable that employers will capture the lion's share of the efficiency gain from the labor exchange that puts employees to work with more capital than they would otherwise have been able to work with. Similarly, those who arrive at the credit market with more capital will lend to those with less, and as long as capital is scarce the lenders will capture the lion's share of the resulting increase in the borrower's productivity. Friedman can call these outcomes noncoercive on the grounds that those without capital volunteered to exchange their laboring capacities for a wage, and borrowers agreed to pay interest knowing full well what the consequences would be. But this merely displaces the source of coercion. It is their lack of capital in the first place that coerces employees and borrowers to "volunteer" to be fleeced in labor and credit markets. Are we to believe they would have volunteered to be the ones who showed up at the labor or credit market with less capital in the first place?

Friedman opens the door when he acknowledges that exchanges under noncompetitive conditions are coercive. Note that when people buy from the only firm selling a product, or sell to the only buyer available, these exchanges are still bilaterally voluntary, informed, and mutually beneficial. In a one-company town since I am free to remain unemployed, I am presumably better off working than not working if you find me employed. In a one-bank town since I am free not to borrow at all, I am presumably better off if I borrow than I would have been had I not. But not even Milton Friedman has the *chutzpah* to call these noncompetitive market outcomes noncoercive, even though the agreement is voluntary and mutually beneficial. Once we recognize that voluntary exchanges under noncompetitive conditions are coercive—only one party to the exchange has the opportunity to choose among *different* partners—it is easy to see how exchanges even under competitive conditions can be coercive as well. *When initial conditions are unequal,* voluntary, informed, and mutually beneficial exchanges will still be coercive and lead to inequitable outcomes, even if exchanges take place under competitive conditions.

The third problem with Friedman's assertion that market decisions are free from coercion is that buyers and sellers often come to agreements with adverse consequences for third parties who have no say in the matter whatsoever. Friedman acknowledges that victims of what he labels "neighborhood effects" are coerced, but presumes these are minor inconveniences that seldom occur. As I discuss below, a growing percentage of nonmainstream economists are convinced that what most economists call "external effects" may prove to be the rule rather than the exception in market exchanges, thereby leaving many disenfranchised and coerced external parties when buyers and sellers make decisions that affect them.

The fourth problem is that Friedman assumes away the best solution for coordinating economic activities. He simply asserts "there are only two ways of coordinating the economic activities of millions—central direction involving the use of coercion—and voluntary cooperation, the technique of the market place." In chapter 8, we will see how a participatory economy can permit all to partake in economic decision making in proportion to the degree they are affected by outcomes. Since a participatory economy uses a system of participatory planning instead of markets to coordinate economic activities, Friedman would have us believe that participatory planning must fall into the category of "central direction involving the use of coercion." Readers will be able to judge for themselves. If after reading chapters 8 and 9 you decide that participatory planning is clearly not central direction through coercion, no matter what else you may like or dislike about the procedure, you will have discovered that Friedman's assertion that there are only two ways of coordinating economic activities—for which he offers no argument whatsoever—is erroneous.

Finally, Friedman claims that beside providing economic freedom, capitalism promotes political freedom as well. His first argument is that in a free-enterprise economy people have a choice of nongovernment employers. Friedman points out this means people are not reliant on the government for their economic livelihood and therefore will be free to speak their minds, and in particular, free to oppose government policies. Friedman's second argument is that if wealth were distributed equally none would have sufficient discretionary wealth to fund political causes. Since wealth is distributed very unequally in capitalist economies, Friedman concludes there are always multiple funding sources available for any and all political causes.

Economic democracy *is* political democracy's best friend, and authoritarian economies *are* political democracy's worst enemy. But that does not mean capitalism promotes political freedom and democracy. One problem with Friedman's first argument is that private employers can intimidate employees who are afraid of losing their jobs, just as a government employer can. In other words, Friedman is blind to the dictatorship of the employer and sees government as the only conceivable source of coercion. A more important fallacy with his first argument is that a monolithic state employer is not the only alternative to a wealthy capitalist employer. State monopoly on employment opportunities in Soviet-style economies *was* a serious obstacle to freedom of political expression in those societies. But in chapters 7 and 8 we will see that nobody has reason to fear for their job because of their political views in a participatory economy, or in an employee-managed, market socialist economy for that matter. The state exerts no influence over who gets hired or fired in enterprises in either of these economies.

The obvious problem with Friedman's second argument—that unequal wealth provides alternative sources of funding for political causes—is that by his own admission, those with vastly greater wealth will control access to the means of political expression. This effectively disenfranchises the poor who have no recourse but to appeal to the wealthy to finance their political causes. Jerry Brown was right when he argued in the 1992 Democratic party presidential primaries that politicians in both major parties are essentially bought and paid for by wealthy financial interests whose contributions are critical for TV ads that determine success in a daunting gauntlet of state primaries. Ralph Nader was right when he argued during the 2000 general election that both the Republican *and* Democratic parties had been effectively bought by corporations, and should be seen for what they are, two wings of a single party of business, the "Republicrats." Every viable politician in America has to ask how his stand on an issue will affect both his voter appeal *and* his funding appeal, with the effect on donations from wealthy contributors becoming increasingly more vital to electability. The fact that Ross Perot and Steve Forbes Jr. could gain serious public consideration for their rather harebrained political ideas by financing presidential bids out of their own deep pockets, whereas 99 percent of the population can't afford a moderate-sized ad in *The New York Times*, much less fund a serious presidential campaign, is hardly evidence that capitalism makes it possible for all political opinions to get a hearing. The fact that pundits considered Senator John Kerry the frontrunner for the Democratic Party presidential nomination in 2004 long before the first primary in no small part because he is married to an heiress who announced that her entire family fortune was available to her husband for his campaign demonstrates that money obstructs equal political opportunities for all, not that it promotes political democracy. And the rare cases where grass-roots activism and true voter appeal win out in a phase of the political process—such as the McGovern primary campaign in 1972 and the early stage of the Dean campaign in 2003—demonstrate how *much* money *usually* distorts political democracy, not that the system is free from bias.

Finally, why does Milton Friedman think the economically powerful and wealthy will finance political causes aimed at reducing their wealth and power? At best, the wealthy in private enterprise economies who Friedman paints as "patrons of the political arts" would predictably provide more adequate funding for some schools of "political art" than others. Simply put, Friedman's attempt to make a political virtue out of the unequal economic power that characterizes capitalist economies is absurd. Unequal economic power breeds unequal political power, not political democracy, as any schoolchild knows.

Capitalism and Efficiency

Friedman and mainstream economists argue that markets allocate scarce productive resources efficiently, while free enterprise guarantees that profit-maximizing capitalists will search diligently for ever more efficient technologies and implement them quickly whenever they are discovered. Of course this vision has been with us since the time of Adam Smith who popularized the idea of a beneficent "invisible hand" at work in capitalist economies over two hundred years ago. In his *Wealth of Nations*, Smith actually postulated two invisible hands at work in capitalism. How do they work, and when do beneficent invisible hands turn into malevolent invisible feet?

Smith reasoned that sellers would keep supplying more goods as long as the price they received covered the additional costs of producing them. In other words, Smith assumed that market supply curves would be the same as marginal cost curves. He also reasoned buyers would keep demanding more of a good as long as the satisfaction they got from an additional unit was greater than the price they had to pay for it, in which case market-demand curves would be the same as marginal benefit curves. But if market price keeps adjusting until the quantity suppliers want to sell is the same as the quantity buyers want to buy this means that every unit that benefits buyers more than it costs producers to make will get produced, and no units that would cost more to produce than the benefits buyers would enjoy from them will be produced. Smith pointed out this means every unit we should want to be produced will be, while none we should not want produced will be produced; the market will lead us—as if guided by a beneficent invisible hand—to produce exactly the socially optimal, or efficient amount of the good. What can go wrong?

Externalities

In his defense, nobody in Smith's day distinguished between private costs to sellers and costs to society as a whole, or between private benefits to buyers and benefits to society as a whole. If there are what economists now call external costs—costs not borne by the seller but costs borne by someone nonetheless, then the marginal social cost of producing something will be greater than the marginal private cost. And if parties other than the buyer of a good are affected when it is consumed, either positively or negatively, if there are external effects when a buyer consumes a good, then the marginal social benefit that comes from consuming the good is different from the marginal private benefit to the buyer. Problems arise because neither sellers nor buyers have any incentive to take consequences for third parties into account, which means the market decision-making process, in which only buyers and sellers participate, will fail to take external effects into account. If the external effects are negative consequences for third parties, the market will end up leading us to make more of the good than is socially efficient by effectively disenfranchising parties other than the buyer and seller who are negatively affected. If the effects on external parties are positive, the market will lead us to make less of the good than is socially efficient by excluding third parties who are positively affected from the decision making process.

Today everyone agrees that Adam Smith's vision of the market as a mechanism that successfully harnesses individual desires to the social purpose of using scarce productive resources efficiently hinges on the assumption that external effects are insignificant. The assumption of no external effects is explicit in theorems about market efficiency in graduate texts, although usually only implicit when most mainstream economists conclude that markets are remarkable efficiency machines that require little social effort on our part. However, more and more economists outside the mainstream are challenging this assumption, and a growing number of skeptics now dare to suggest that externalities are prevalent, and often substantial. Or, as E. K. Hunt put it, externalities are the rule rather than the exception, and therefore markets often work as if they were guided by a "malevolent invisible foot" that keeps kicking us to produce more of some things, and less of others than is socially efficient.[4]

First, critics point to the absence of empirical evidence supporting the claim of external-effect exceptionality. It is truly remarkable that this crucial assumption has never been subjected to serious scrutiny. We economists are well known for engaging in exhaustive empirical debates over assumptions that are far less important. But in this case, perhaps the most critical assumption about market economies—the assumption that externalities are small and few and far between—has not given rise to serious empirical debate, and remains unsubstantiated by any empirical studies. It remains untested, an assumption of ideological convenience.

Lacking empirical evidence, are there theoretical reasons to believe that externalities *should* be exceptional rather than prevalent? Obviously, increasing the value of goods and services produced, and decreasing the unpleasantness of what we have to do to get them, are two ways producers can increase their profits in a market economy. And competitive pressures will drive producers to do both, although, as we will see below not as perfectly as Adam Smith presumed. But maneuvering to appropriate a greater share of the goods and services produced by externalizing costs and internalizing benefits without compensation is also a way to increase profits. And presumably competitive pressures will drive producers to pursue this route to greater profitability just as assiduously. Of course the problem is, while the first kind of behavior serves social interests as well as the private interests of producers, the second kind of behavior does not. Instead, when buyers or sellers promote their private interests by externalizing

costs onto those not party to the market exchange, or internalizing benefits from third parties without compensation, their behavior introduces
inefficiencies that lead to a misallocation of productive resources.

Market admirers seldom ask: Where are firms most likely to find the
easiest opportunities to expand their profits? How easy is it usually to
increase the size or quality of the economic pie we bake? How easy is it
to reduce the time or discomfort it takes to bake it? Alternatively, how
easy is it to enlarge one's slice of the pie by externalizing a cost, or by
appropriating a benefit without payment? Why should we assume that it
is always easier to expand profits by productive behavior than by redistributive behavior? Yet the implicit assumption that it is always easier to
increase profits through productive behavior than redistributive manuev-
ering is what lies behind the view of markets as efficiency machines.

Market enthusiasts fail to notice that the same feature of market
exchanges primarily responsible for small transaction costs—excluding
all affected parties but two from the transaction—is also a major source
of potential gain for the buyer and seller. When the buyer and seller of
an automobile strike their convenient deal, the size of the benefit they
have to divide between them is greatly enlarged by externalizing the costs
onto others of the acid rain produced by car production, and the costs
of urban smog, noise pollution, traffic congestion, and greenhouse gas
emissions caused by car consumption. Those who pay these costs, and
thereby enlarge car-maker profits and car-consumer benefits, are easy
marks for car sellers and buyers because they are geographically and
chronologically dispersed, and because the magnitude of the effect on
each of them is small yet not equal. Individually they have little incentive to insist on being party to the transaction. Collectively they face
transaction cost and free-rider obstacles to forming a voluntary coalition
to represent a large number of people, each with little, but different
amounts at stake.[5]

Moreover, the opportunity for this kind of cost-shifting behavior is
not eliminated by making markets more competitive or entry costless,
as is commonly assumed. Even if there were countless perfectly informed
sellers and buyers in every market, even if the appearance of the slightest
differences in average profit rates in different industries induced instan-
taneous self-correcting entries and exits of firms, even if every economic
participant were equally powerful and therefore equally powerless—in
other words, even if we embrace the full fantasy of market enthusiasts—
as long as there are numerous external parties with small but unequal
interests in market transactions, those external parties will face greater

transaction costs and free-rider obstacles to a full and effective representation of their collective interest than that faced by the buyer and seller in the exchange. And it is this unavoidable disadvantage that makes external parties easy prey to cost-shifting behavior on the part of buyers and sellers.

Even if we could organize a market economy so that buyers and sellers never faced a more or less powerful opponent in a market exchange, this would not change the fact that each of us has smaller interests at stake in many transactions where we are neither the buyer nor the seller. Yet there is every reason to believe that the *sum total* interest of *all* external parties can be considerable compared to the interests of the buyer and the seller. It is the transaction cost and free-rider problems that put those with lesser individual interests at a disadvantage compared to buyers and sellers in market exchanges, which, in turn, gives rise to the opportunity for individually profitable but socially counterproductive cost shifting behavior on the part of buyers and sellers. So not only is there no empirical evidence that external effects are truly small and exceptional, there are strong theoretical reasons for expecting just the opposite to be the case. There is every reason to expect that individual rationality and competition for profit will drive buyers and sellers in even the most competitive markets to seek out ways to externalize costs onto large numbers of disempowered third parties who are relatively easy marks, and create significant allocative inefficiencies in the process.

Smith not only believed markets were guided by a beneficent invisible hand guiding us to allocate scarce resources precisely to the productive tasks where they created the greatest well-being, he also believed a second invisible hand was at work in competitive markets leading capitalists to search for and implement only new technologies that were more socially efficient. He pointed out that any capitalist who discovers a way to reduce the amount of an input necessary to make an output will be able to lower her production costs below those of her competitors, and thereby earn higher-than-average profits. Moreover, Smith pointed out that other producers will be driven to adopt the new, more productive technique for fear of being driven out of business by more innovative competitors. In this way Smith, Friedman, and all mainstream economists argue competition for profit promotes the search for, and adoption of, more socially efficient technologies. However, there are a number of reasons competition for profits can drive capitalist firms to make technological choices that are *contrary* to the social interest that supporters of capitalism are usually reluctant to discuss.

NONCOMPETITIVE MARKET STRUCTURES

There is one reason mainstream economists have been willing to discuss why profit-maximizing firms may not adopt more socially efficient technologies. It is conceded that noncompetitive market structures lead to allocative inefficiencies since monopolistic and oligopolistic market structures contain incentives for profit-maximizing producers to hold output below socially efficient levels. But noncompetitive market structures promote dynamic inefficiencies as well. A substantial literature exists in which mainstream economists document cases where large companies have conspired to suppress technological innovations because they would have depreciated their fixed capital or reduced opportunities for repeated sales.

BIASED PRICE SIGNALS

Externalities not only lead to a misallocation of productive resources as explained above, they also lead to market prices that do not accurately reflect the true social costs of producing things. Since capitalists use market prices when deciding if a new technology will reduce their costs, discrepancies between market prices and true opportunity costs due to external effects can lead to socially counterproductive decisions by profit-maximizing capitalists regarding technologies. Significant negative externalities associated with producing energy by burning oil are unreflected in the market price of energy produced by burning oil compared to energy produced using solar or wind sources. Therefore, research into new oil-drilling technologies would have been prioritized over research into renewable energy sources more than it should have been *even if* the oil industry had not long been the beneficiary of massive government tax subsidies, and *even if* the oil industry had not recently captured the executive branch of the U.S. government outright.

A further problem arises when there is a bias in the price of labor relative to capital. Many labor economists acknowledge that factors other than relative scarcities of labor and capital play an important role in determining wage and profit rates. If this were not the case, there would be no reason for workers to try to unionize, and no reason for employers to try to prevent them from doing so! In any case, when employers use their power to suppress wage rates and increase profit rates, this will predictably bias their choice between labor- and capital-saving technical changes. Simple models reveal that when the rate of profit in the economy rises and the wage rate falls it becomes increasingly likely capitalists will implement new capital-saving, labor-using technologies that are profitable but socially inefficient, and reject new capital-using, labor-saving technologies that are socially efficient but unprofitable.[6] In other words, when bargaining power affects the "prices" of labor and capital—as it inevitably does—it introduces a bias in the prices for different "factors of production," and profit-maximizing capitalists responding to these biased signals will sometimes make socially counterproductive, or inefficient choices when choosing between alternative technologies.

CONFLICT THEORY OF THE FIRM

A number of political economists over the past thirty years have contributed to what is now called the "conflict theory of the firm." This nonmainstream theory spells out why profit-maximization requires capitalists to choose less efficient technologies if more efficient technologies lower their bargaining power over their employees sufficiently. The argument is as follows: an inherent conflict of interest exists between employers and employees over how high or low the wage rate will be, and how much effort employees will exert for their wages. If we define the real wage in this context in terms of dollars of compensation per unit of effort expended, this reduces to a struggle over the real wage. For the most part, employers are free to choose among alternative technologies available. Or at least, employers have considerable discretion over choice of technologies. It would be irrational for employers to consider the impact of technological choices on productivity *only* when these choices *also* affect employers' bargaining power *vis á vis* their employees. Since profits depend not only on the size of net output—productivity—but on how the net output is divided between wages and profits, rational employers will consider how their choice of technology affect *both*. For example, consider an automobile maker's choice between assembly-line versus work-team technologies. Suppose when quality and reliability are taken into account, making automobiles in work teams is slightly more productive than making cars on an assembly line, but team production is more skill enhancing and builds employee solidarity while assembly-line production reduces the knowledge component of work for most employees and reduces employee solidarity by isolating employees from one another. If the "bargaining-power effect" outweighs the "productivity effect," competition for profits will drive auto makers to opt for assembly-line production even though it is less efficient.

Adam Smith's second invisible hand, whereby profit-maximizing capitalists can supposedly be relied on to search for and select socially efficient new technologies is flawed, just like his first invisible hand, whereby competitive markets can supposedly be relied on to allocate scarce productive resources efficiently. Upon careful examination it turns out that proponents of capitalism confuse "energetic"—which capitalism certainly *is*—with "efficient"—which capitalism definitely is *not*.

Capitalism and Economic Discrimination

Friedman and most mainstream economists insist that competition for profits among employers will reduce discrimination. They point out that if an employer has a taste for discrimination and insists on paying white, or male employees, more than equivalent black, or female employees, the employer who discriminates will have a higher wage bill than the employer who pays equivalent employees equally. So mainstream theorists insist that eventually employers who do not engage in wage discrimination should compete those who do out of business. Similarly, Friedman points out that the business of any employer who fails to hire or promote the most qualified people due to overt or unconscious discrimination will be less productive than businesses that hire and promote purely on merit. So according to mainstream economists a firm that engages in discriminatory personnel practices should also be competed out of business by firms that do not. While mainstream theory is quick to see the profit-reducing effects of economic discrimination on the part of employers, it is blind to the profit-increasing effects of discrimination. The conflict theory of the firm helps explain why profit-maximization does not preclude, but in fact requires a degree of discriminatory behavior even when employers operate in competitive labor and goods markets.

Discrimination in hiring, assignment, promotion, and payment have all been used to aggravate suspicions and antagonisms that already exist between people of different races and ethnic backgrounds and between men and women. Historical settings where ample reasons for suspicion and mistrust abound provide ready-made pressure points that employers can manipulate to divide and conquer their employees. When employees are mutually suspicious they can be more easily induced to inform on one another regarding lackadaisical efforts, making it easier for the employer to extract more effort. When employees are unsupportive of one another they will be easier for their employer to bargain with over wages when their contract comes up. What the conflict theory reveals is that since discriminatory practices by an individual employer have these positive effects on profits, profit-maximization requires engaging in discriminatory practices up to the point where the negative effects of discrimination on profits—which are the exclusive focus of mainstream theory—outweigh the profit-enhancing effects—which only nonmainstream economists identify. In other words, competition for profits will drive employers to engage in discriminatory practices up to the point where the redistributive effect of discrimination—increasing the employer's share of value added by decreasing employees' bargaining power—equals the negative impact of discrimination on productivity or the wage bill.[7]

The implications of discovering that economic discrimination is part and parcel of profit-maximization under capitalism are important. First, since mainstream theorists are correct that discrimination often reduces economic efficiency, it provides yet another reason to believe that capitalism will not be efficient. But more importantly it means that it is not the employers who discriminate who will eventually be driven out of business by those who do not, but just the reverse. Employers who steadfastly refuse to discriminate will be driven out of business by those who pay attention only to the bottom line, and therefore engage in profit-enhancing discriminatory behavior. The implication for public policy is huge. If mainstream economists were correct, competitive labor and capital markets would tend to eliminate discriminatory employment practices, at least in the long run, in which case, if minorities and women were willing to continue to pay the price for society's patience, we could expect discrimination to diminish without government involvement. But the conflict theory demonstrates that even assuming no collusion among employers, it is profitable for individual employers to aggravate racial antagonisms among their employees up to the point where the costs of doing so outweigh the additional profits that come from negotiating with a less powerful group of employees. Therefore, it is foolish to wait for capitalism to eliminate discrimination if unaided. Instead, laws outlawing discrimination and affirmative action programs are necessary if discrimination is to be reduced. But unfortunately, not only is active intervention necessary, the struggle against discrimination must constantly swim upstream in capitalist economies because employers who do discriminate are rewarded with higher profits, and employers who refuse to discriminate will be punished by shareholders who care only about their bottom line.

The increasingly popular view in the United States that government protection and affirmative action have done their job and are no longer necessary could not be farther from the truth.[8] When the government scaled back programs to prevent economic discrimination the discrepancy between the wages of equivalent black and white workers increased by 50 percent from 10.9 percent in 1979 to 16.4 percent in 1989.[9]

Capitalism and Economic Justice

Under the best of circumstances private-enterprise market economies distribute the burdens and benefits of economic activity according to the conservative maxim 1: to each according to the market value of the contribution of his or her labor and productive property. But we have already seen why capitalist distribution is inequitable. Distribution according to this maxim means that the grandson of a Rockefeller who never works a day in his life will consume a thousand times more than a hardworking doctor simply because the former inherited ownership of large amounts of productive property. In chapter 9 of *Capitalism and Freedom* Friedman points to examples of inequities in precapitalist feudal economies and in communist economies, and points out there would be inequities even in market socialist economies that eliminate property income altogether. But injustices in other economies do not make inequities in capitalist economies any smaller. In a world where recent estimates indicate the combined wealth of the world's 447 billionaires is greater than the income of the poorest half of the world's people, capitalist inequity can hardly be dismissed as a minor liability as Friedman would have us do. As long as there are feasible economies that distribute the burdens and benefits of economic activity more equitably than free-market capitalism, those who offer rationalizations for capitalist inequities are nothing more than accomplices in the crime of economic injustice.

But capitalism is not unfair only because people get unjustifiable income from ownership of productive property. Labor markets reward people unfairly as well. Even if wages and salaries were determined in competitive labor markets free from discrimination, a surgeon who is on the golf course by 1 P.M. would consume ten times more than a garbage collector working forty hours a week because the surgeon was genetically gifted and benefited from vast quantities of socially costly education. Free labor and capital markets mean that most who are wealthy are so *not* because they worked harder or sacrificed more than others, but because they inherited wealth, talent, or simply got lucky. In chapter 1 we concluded that distribution of labor income according to the value of work contibution—which is the *best* one could hope for if labor markets were free from discrimination and worked perfectly—is inequitable because differences in the values of people's contributions for reasons *other than* differences in effort or sacrifice are beyond people's abilities to control, and carry no moral weight in any case.

Conclusion

Private enterprise and markets *both* cause systematic inequities that cannot be morally justified. As energetic as capitalism may be, private enterprise and markets *both* cause significant inefficiencies. Despite the facile equation of capitalism with freedom and democracy that is ubiquitous not only among mainstream politicians and in the mainstream media but in academia as well, private enterprise and markets *both* disenfranchise the vast majority from participating in economic decision making in proportion to the degree they are affected, and stand as a growing danger to, rather than a bulwark of, political freedom. Capitalism can also be expected to aggravate rather than ameliorate social prejudice and discrimination. Finally, as explained in the last chapter, capitalism creates powerful incentives to abuse the natural environment and disincentives for individual parties to undertake environmental protection and restoration. The difference between twenty-first century and twentieth-century capitalism will be that "born-again" capitalism may well kill us all since it begins with initial conditions—6 billion people, modern technology, and an already damaged ecosystem—that can do in mother earth in fairly short order. God has given capitalism the rainbow sign. No more water, the fire next time.

Unfortunately, the first alternative to capitalism to appear, communist central planning, was fatally flawed as well. While most of the centrally planned economies that expanded their global influence from 1917 to 1989 no longer remain to be undone, their intellectual legacy must be undone if we are to understand what a desirable economy looks like.

Communism

The first postcapitalist economies were popularly referred to as communist. While communism stood for something quite different at the beginning of the century, by the end of the twentieth century, in common usage communism referred to a particular kind of political system, as well as a particular kind of economic system. The communist political system was a single-party state, where the single party was governed by undemocratic rules ironically called "democratic centralism." The communist economy was a system of public enterprises governed by a procedure known as central planning. This communist economic system did not suffer from the same deficiencies as capitalism, but the centrally planned economies of the Soviet Bloc were terribly flawed in other ways. At the risk of oversimplifying, while the fatal flaw in capitalism is its antisocial bias, the fatal flaw in central planning is its antidemocratic bias. But besides their totalitarian dynamics, there was every reason to expect centrally planned economies to prove inequitable and inefficient as well.

Central Planning

Central planning cannot be efficient unless central planners: (1) know the quantities of available resources and equipment; (2) know all the ways production units can combine inputs to yield outputs; (3) are informed of the relative social worth of different final goods and services; (4) have sufficient computing facilities to carry out large-scale quantitative manipulations; and (5) can induce mangers and workers to carry out the tasks central planners assign them.

If we generously grant all these assumptions, central planners could, *in theory*, calculate an efficient production plan, and then choose from a variety of options for how to assign workers to jobs and distribute goods to consumers efficiently. Essentially central planners solve a giant, economywide maximization problem. First they formulate what mathematicians call an objective function, which represents the social value of all the final goods and services produced in the economy. Then they formulate a number of inequalities that represent constraints on the economy's production possibilities. For every primary resource there is a resource constraint that says the amount of that resource the plan would use cannot exceed the amount available in the economy, since otherwise the plan would be unfeasible. And for every produced good there is a "Leontiev constraint,"[10] which says the amount of every good produced must be at least as large as the final consumption plus intermediate consumption of that good called for by the plan, since otherwise the plan would also be unfeasible. The central planners then solve the economy planning problem by choosing how much of each good to produce, via each technique that can be used to make the good, to maximize the objective function, that is, to maximize the social value of final output, subject to the condition that none of the resource or Leontiev constraints are violated. In other words, the planners choose from among all the feasible production plans—the plans that satisfy the resource and Leontiev constraints—the one that yields the greatest social value of final output. The first four assumptions above guarantee the plan they find will be optimal. The fifth assumption guarantees that the planners can get the optimal plan they calculated produced.

Theoretical Problems

In all versions of central planning: (1) the famous "down/up, up/down" process between the central planners and the production units that admirers present as participatory, consensual decision making is actually down-go-questions from the planners, up-come-answers from the production units and down-go-orders from the planners, up-comes-obedience from the production units; (2) qualitative information about the human and social effects of production and consumption essential to an accurate evaluation of outcomes is never generated; (3) elite "conceptual workers"—central planners and plant managers I call coordinators—monopolize the technical information required for decision making; and (4) not even plant managers, much less workers, make suggestions, much less decisions about what they want to produce and how they want to produce it. Instead, plant managers and central planners play a cat-and-mouse game trying to mislead and manipulate each other, and the only management left to individual production units is to "manage" to fulfill the targets and quotas the central planners assign them with the inputs the central planners allot them.

In other words, central planners gather information, calculate a plan, and issue marching orders for production units to obey. The relationship between the central planning agency and the production units is authoritarian and hierarchical rather than democratic and participatory. Moreover, since each unit is subordinate to the planning board, and a superior agent must have effective means for holding subordinates accountable, methods of surveillance and verification are needed to minimize what economists call "malfeasance," more popularly known as lying and shirking. Central planners predictably prefer to appoint managers whom they can reward and punish according to the performance of their units, rather than establish more complicated procedures to try to control rambunctious worker councils. And, having appointed managers of production units, central planners will logically wish to grant them dictatorial powers over the workers in their employ since it makes no sense to punish managers for the behavior of workers whom managers don't control. So what begins as a totalitarian relationship between the central planning agency and production units, ends up with dictatorial relations between plant managers and workers as well. Not only do workers have no say over what they produce—central planners decide this—they have little say over how they meet their output quotas—plant managers decide that.

Suppose we give central planning every benefit of the doubt. We assume the planners have all information listed above. We assume the social values of final goods are determined by a completely democratic voting procedure among consumers. We assume central planners accurately calculate the optimal plan. We assume workers carry out the plan to the letter. Even if all these assumptions were fulfilled, best-case central planning would still fail to deliver economic self-management for two reasons.

Since central planners monopolize all quantitative information generated in the planning process, workers and consumers would still be denied access to information about the opportunity costs of final goods and the productivities of different primary inputs. And since very little, if any, qualitative information is generated in central planning about the human aspects of different work and consumption experiences, workers and consumers would lack information about the situations of other workers and consumers as well. This means workers and consumers in centrally planned economies cannot receive the information they must have if they are to engage in intelligent, responsible self-management. How could they sensibly decide what to produce and consume without knowing how their choices affect others, even if they were allowed to make their own choices?

Second, in theory central planners could let every consumer vote, say, a thousand points, indicating her relative preferences for different final goods and services. But this fair and democratic voting procedure among consumers fails to provide self-management for workers. Once votes are tallied and used to formulate the planning objective function, central planners translate those preferences into specific work plans for each production unit. This means every consumer-worker has had the exact same decision-making input as every other consumer-worker over what to produce and how to produce it in every single workplace. This is democratic, and allows consumers to express the intensity of their preferences for different goods and services, but it does *not* provide self-management for workers because it does not give workers input into production decisions according to how much they are affected. My opinion about what to produce and how to produce it in *my* workplace should count more than the opinion of someone who works somewhere else, just as their opinion should count more than mine about *their* workplace. But the best central planning can do is give everyone equal input in all economic decisions via a democratic determination of the planning objective function. The problem is central planning is inherently ill-suited for accommodating the differential impacts different economic decisions have on different groups of workers.

Moreover, it is rational for individuals to orient their preferences toward opportunities that will be relatively plentiful and away from those that will be relatively scarce in any economy. If a bias arises in the expected future supply of particular work roles, people will orient their development accordingly. In the case of central planning, the bias against providing self-managed work opportunities militates against people developing greater desires and capacities for self-management, and instead promotes apathy among the work force. The apathy of workers often noted by those who studied the Soviet and Eastern European centrally planned economies was a logical result of the bias against self-managed work opportunities in their centrally planned economies. What makes less sense than for a worker in a centrally planned economy to develop a keen interest in what she will produce or how she will produce it? Better not to care.

Practical Problems

I deliberately ignored the problems most critics of central planning focus on because I wanted to explain why even best-case central planning is fundamentally flawed, and because I wanted to focus on what I believe is the true Achilles' heel of central planning, its authoritarian structure and bias against self-management. But real-world settings were not as kind to central planning as the generous assumptions we made above. Most critics concentrate on how difficult it is for central planners to gather accurate information and induce managers and workers to carry out planners' directives, and therefore how inefficient central planning becomes.

While it is relatively easy for a central agency to catalog the availability of all the primary resources in the economy, including the availability of different categories of labor, it is a formidable task for central planners to learn the productive capabilities of local enterprises. Exactly what mixes of inputs a particular enterprise can combine to achieve its outputs is information best known to workers, engineers, and managers at individual plants. But in order to calculate an efficient plan the central planners need accurate information about the technical capabilities of all the enterprises. Unfortunately for central planning, there are strong incentives for enterprises to lie to central planners about their true capabilities. Since enterprises know central planners will use the information they provide to order them to produce as much output as possible using as little inputs as possible, an enterprise can make its life easier by deceiving central planners into thinking the enterprise is not capable of as much as it truly is. By underreporting their true capabilities local enterprises can trick central planners into asking them to produce less than they could if they tried their hardest, and/or allocating them more inputs than they would need if they were as efficient as possible. Especially since central planning punishes managers of enterprises that fail to meet output quotas, and rewards managers for overfulfillment, there is everything to gain and nothing to lose by underreporting capabilities.

Procapitalist critics of central planning pretended there was nothing that could be done about this problem, which is not actually true. For decades central planning agencies employed their own team of experts to advise them whether plant managers were reporting truthfully. But having a B team of engineers and technicians working for the central planners to second-guess the A team in the enterprises was a wasteful and imperfect solution to an intractable practical problem. And central planning disappeared before recent theoretical solutions to this principal-agent problem could be tested in centrally planned economies.[11]

Most critics also pointed out that prices in centrally planned economies do not reflect true opportunity costs. It was common in centrally planned economies to price goods considered staples like bread, cooking oil, and work clothes well below their true opportunity costs while pricing goods considered to be luxuries above their opportunity costs. How could what seemed like such a good idea to progressives be the object of so much scorn by mainstream economists? Who was right? The answer is nothing was wrong with the instincts of progressive activists. It is true that prices in centrally planned economies differed from opportunity costs.[12] But unlike market economies where prices play the pivotal role in determining how much of our scarce resources to devote to producing different goods, and how to produce them, in centrally planned economies what and how to produce is determined by the central plan *without reference to the prices in the economy*. This is so counterintuitive to those who live in and study market economies, that otherwise competent professional economists committed simple logical errors when analyzing this unfamiliar context. Choosing the relative social values of final goods in the planners' objective function is ultimately a political decision in centrally planned economies. Once this is done, central planners calculate what to produce and how to produce it without resort to prices, by specifying the resource and Leontiev constraints and solving the planning problem. If the planners calculate any prices they do so *after* having already calculated the economy plan. And if any prices are used to distribute final goods among consumers and evaluate enterprise performance they do so without having any effect on what was produced and how it was produced in the first place. Consequently, any divergence between prices in centrally planned economies and true social opportunity costs *cannot possibly be the cause of inefficient decisions about what and how to produce.*

In fact, the divergence from true opportunity costs was even greater than most critics of central planning bothered to point out. Not only were the prices of consumption goods set with political goals in mind, the entire accounting cost structure of centrally planned economies failed to reflect true opportunity costs. While it is theoretically possible to accurately determine opportunity costs for primary resources in a centrally planned system this was seldom done. So inputs like land, water, and minerals— much less clean air—were seldom valued "rationally." Moreover, wage rates and salaries were set according to political criteria rather than according to their marginal revenue products. As a result the labor and resource costs of different goods, as calculated in centrally planned economies bore little resemblance to their true opportunity costs. Moreover, this would have been true even had authorities priced consumer goods to clear their markets. But critics who understand why prices that diverge from opportunity costs generate inefficiencies in market systems jumped to the erroneous conclusion that the same must be true in centrally planned economies. In their leap they forgot another of their criticisms of central planning—namely that decisions were not based on prices in the first place! If you don't use the prices to decide what and how to produce things, then whatever deficiencies the prices have hardly matter regarding production decisions.

Another common criticism was that central planning did not satisfy consumers, and in particular did not respond to the diversity of needs and desires modern consumers develop. This was absolutely true in fact, but not because central planning is inherently incapable of satisfying consumer desires. In communist central planning the decision to emphasize investment rather than consumption priorities, and decisions about what consumer goods to prioritize were made by political authorities who were in turn not subject to democratic control. While it was never done—and I am not recommending we revive central planning to do it right—there is no theoretical reason the priorities given different final goods in the planners' objective function could not be determined by equitable, democratic voting procedures rather than by undemocratic political dictate.

Finally, we come to the infamous problem of rationing and queues in centrally planned economies. Nothing is more obviously idiotic than having people waste time and grow cynical standing in lines for major parts of their lives. Yet every centrally planned economy was plagued by this counterproductive stupidity, which became the most visible symbol to the outside world that something was terribly wrong about communist economies. The first best solution would have been to distribute income fairly—make wage rates reflect only effort and sacrifice and give those who are disabled a fair income as well—and then set retail prices so markets clear. Result: no lines for anything, no inequities. The second best solution would have been to compensate for inequities in income distribution—that were for some reason thought to be unavoidable—by rationing staples, giving every family an equitable amount, and distributing nonessentials by setting prices as high as necessary to keep demand from exceeding supply. When everyone is guaranteed their rationed allotment, there is no reason to stand in line for staples for fear the supplies will run out. The distribution centers for rationed goods simply need to notify families when their rations have arrived and are ready to be picked up. Result: no lines for either staples or nonessentials, and less inequity than present in the wage and salary structure. The worst solution is to keep prices of nonessentials below the level needed to eliminate excess demand since that guarantees lines for nonstaples; and to fail to deliver the quantity of rationed goods one has authorized for people since that guarantees lines for necessities! Don't ask me why communist planners never grasped this simple truth. In three personal visits to Cuba over twenty-five years I never got a satisfactory answer from anyone.[13]

Obviously, best case central planning was never tried. And it is clear centrally planned economies run by totalitarian political parties largely immune from popular pressure and increasingly free to feather the nests of their leaders and members, was not likely to produce the best outcomes. Some progressives are still reluctant to abandon central planning on grounds that many of the problems that occurred can be blamed on poor practice and the impact of an undemocratic political system on the economy. But this conclusion fails to recognize central planning's fatal bias against meaningful popular participation in economic decision making. It was precisely this fatal flaw that made central planning such a convenient accomplice for totalitarian political elites. The marriage of the single-vanguard party state and central planning was truly a marriage made in hell between two totalitarian dynamics, where political and economic democracy were the first victims. Combined with a more democratic political system and redone to closer approximate a best-case version, centrally planned economies would have done better than they did. But they could never have delivered economic self-management, and would have always been susceptible to growing inequities and inefficiencies as the inevitable effects of differential economic power appeared.

Perestroika

How are we to interpret the last-ditch attempt to reform the Soviet economic system that Mikhail Gorbachev called *perestroika*? Socialism was originally supposed to be a system of democratic planning, a system in which democratically organized groups of workers and consumers planned their economic endeavors. While the old system of bureaucratic, central planning was neither participatory nor efficient, *perestroika* explicitly abandoned the goal of democratic planning. In *Perestroika: New Thinking for Our Country and the World* (1987), Gorbachev wrote: "The reform is based on dramatically increased independence of enterprises and associations, their transition to full self-accounting and self-financing. They will now be fully responsible for efficient management and the end results. In this connection, a radical reorganization of centralized economic management is envisaged in the interests of enterprises. We will free the central management of operational functions in the running of enterprises." In other words, *perestroika* was a program to replace bureaucratic planning with markets, rather than with democratic planning.

Socialism was also supposed to be based on the principle: From each according to ability, to each according to work effort. In the beginning, socialists did not consider differences in contributions due to differences in luck, talent, education, and training provided at social rather than personal expense to be legitimate reasons for differential reward. The original vision was that under socialism personal sacrifice for the social interest, or effort, for short, was to be rewarded until mutual trust and solidarity proved sufficient to permit distribution according to need. But while popular support for this principle was strong in the early years after the Russian Revolution: (1) socialist distributive principles were never practiced by any Bolshevik government, and (2) Stalin moved exactly in the opposite direction during forced industrialization when skilled labor was in short supply and wage and salary differentials increased dramatically. As a matter of fact, it was Stalin who first coined the phrase "levelers" as an epithet aimed at his opponents who dared support the original socialist distributive principle Stalin was intent on violating. So rather than correcting what he called the "leveling mistakes of Stalin," Gorbachev was actually following in Stalin's antisocialist tradition of rationalizing unjust inequalities when Gorbachev wrote: "Equalizing attitudes crop up from time to time even today. Some citizens understood the call for social justice as 'equalizing everyone.' . . . But what we value most is a citizen's contribution to the affairs of the country—the talent of a writer, scientist, or any other upright citizen. . . . On this point we want to be perfectly clear: socialism has nothing to do with equalizing. . . . Much is said about benefits and privileges for individuals and groups of individuals. We have benefits and privileges that have been established by the state, and they are granted on the basis of the quantity and quality of work." In other words, *perestroika* was a program to embrace distribution according to the liberal maxim 2—to each according to the value of her labor's contribution—and officially abandon the original socialist maxim 3—to each according to work effort or sacrifice.

Finally, socialists traditionally claimed that every citizen had a *right* to a socially useful job, and unlike capitalism, socialism should guarantee everyone socially useful work. But Gorbachev warned that "the high degree of social protection in our society makes some people spongers," and complained that "the state has assumed concern for ensuring employment [so] even a person dismissed for laziness or a breach of labor discipline must be given another job." Gorbachev promised that *perestroika* would put an end to this. In other words, *perestroika* abandoned the one traditional socialist goal central planning had actually delivered on, the right to a job.

My point is not that Gorbachev was yet another Soviet leader who betrayed socialist principles, since that would not distinguish him from most Soviet leaders before him.[14] My point is that Gorbachev wrote and said all these things because *perestroika* required it. *Perestroika* was an attempt to move the Soviet economy from the old centrally planned system to a new and different public-enterprise market system. I do not believe either system is consistent with traditional socialist principles, so I see *perestroika* as a desperate attempt by Soviet rulers to move from one nonsocialist system to a different nonsocialist system. Since the new system was to be based on markets rather than planning, and could not function coherently if wages were not based on marginal revenue products, *perestroika* meant renouncing the remnants of socialist ideology that had been part of the social contract that held the old system together, but were incompatible with the new system and obstacles to its birth.

The Soviet economy has long been what I call a coordinator economy—one in which a class of central planners, plant managers, and technocrats—or coordinators—make all important economic decisions. The original coordinator economy combined hierarchical relations of production with bureaucratic central planning. The social contract that held the system together for over sixty years consisted of job security and a wage/price system that did not altogether reject effort and need as legitimate distributive criteria, in exchange for worker and consumer toleration of inefficiency, corruption, and acquiescence in their economic disenfranchisement. In a nutshell, this was the traditional coordinator economy, an economy without capitalists, but with a ruling class of planners and administrators who controlled economic decision making with their own interests in mind, first and foremost.

Perestroika was a strategy for moving to a slicker kind of coordinator economy, a strategy that failed in the Soviet Union but succeeded for more than a decade in China. The new version of a coordinator economy maintains public ownership and hierarchical relations of production, but features markets rather than planning, and consequently allows a much greater role for local managers. But a market-based coordinator economy requires a new social contract as well. And in particular, parts of the ideological underpinnings of the old social contract are dysfunctional in a market-based coordinator economy. As we saw, central planning can operate coherently with a system of wages and prices that are political compromises designed to reward elites and pacify "the masses," since decisions about what and how to produce under central planning are not determined by wages and prices in any case. Since resource allocation and production decisions in central planning do not depend on wages and prices, they are free to play a purely distributive role, deciding who gets what after it has already been decided what will be produced and how it will be produced. But in market-based coordinator economies wages and prices must play an allocative as well as a distributive role. And if wages, resource prices, and costs based on them are not reflective of relative scarcities and productivities, the economic decisions based on them will be inefficient to the point of incoherence. Hence the need to forge a new social contract that abrogated employment security and eschewed economic rewards based on effort and need in order to create a free labor market that would reward performance according to how much a worker contributes to enterprise profits and prices reflective of opportunity costs rather than political compromises.

If wage and price reform was a prerequisite for a workable, market-based coordinator economy, why did Gorbachev hesitate so long to impose one? The answer is simple. The clean, technical phrase "wage and price reform" actually means breaking the old social contract and hammering out a new one. These are difficult political matters, requiring troublesome negotiations, fraught with danger, especially when important parts of society's old elite stand to lose in the bargain, along with a majority of the working class. The difficulty and danger were so great that Gorbachev postponed the crucial wage and price reform for five years, at the cost of economic coherency. What existed in the Soviet Union from 1986 to 1991 was a noneconomic system. People didn't expect the old system to stay in place, but were unsure if the new system would ever materialize. Parts of the old system remained, but only parts of the new system were implemented. The economy was in chaos because there was no predictable system of incentives. When nobody knows what to expect, or what they will be rewarded or punished for, people do the only rational thing; they sit and wait. And when people wait in any economy there is always crisis.

Contrary to popular and professional opinion in the West, the centrally planned coordinator economies were not in an economic crisis that threatened the system prior to the advent of *perestroika*.[15] There was a political crisis of universally acknowledged corruption and hypocrisy in the Soviet Union. And there was a long overdue crisis of Soviet imperialism in Eastern Europe, where politically bankrupt, puppet regimes tried to pacify their subjects in the 1970s and 1980s with consumption financed by massive loans from the West, thereby generating a debt crisis by the end of the 1980s and providing global capitalism with a Trojan horse to undermine the Eastern European regimes. But the traditional, centrally planned coordinator economies did not generate a tailspin of their own making. The Polish economy was in full crisis by 1989 because the Poles had been on a slow-down strike against their quisling military government since 1981. And the Soviet economy was in crisis from 1986 to 1991 because nobody knew what to expect. But otherwise, the traditional coordinator economies were plugging along in the late 1980s more or less like they always had, and in some Eastern European countries like Hungary and

Czechoslovakia the transition from centrally planned coordinator economies to market-based coordinator economies was well underway.

What was alarming was that after decades of *outperforming* their Western capitalist competitors, growth rates in the centrally planned economies had dipped below Western growth rates by the beginning of the 1980s, and the most significant technological revolution since the industrial revolution appeared to be taking off in the West but passing the Eastern economies by. This is what filled Gorbachev and his far-sighted allies with desperation and urgency. Their answer, *perestroika*, was a risky preemptive strike to change from a centrally planned to a market-based coordinator economy before the relative economic decline worsened. But to talk about lower positive rates of growth as if they were negative, or to point out a "luxury gap" as evidence of economic crisis is deceitful. The Soviet economy was a hundred years behind the U.S. economy in 1920, and it was still thirty years behind in 1980. That explains the luxury gap and unflattering comparisons of any number of economic indices. After 1985, the Soviet economy was in crisis because it was in a never-never land between an old system and a new one that was never successfully put into place.

Whereas Gorbachev's *perestroika* failed, the Chinese communist party did succeed in replacing central planning with a market-based coordinator economy in the late 1980s. In part this was because the Chinese communist party defended its totalitarian political power with a vengeance—Tiannamen Square—whereas Gorbachev embraced *glasnost*—political openness. Even now when the Chinese communist party has moved down the road replacing market-based coordinatorism with full-blown capitalism, it maintains its monopoly on political power at all costs. I am a staunch critic of market-based coordinator economies. I believe Chinese growth rates are overestimated. And I think those who interpret high Chinese growth rates as evidence of a healthy economy performing admirably are in great error. Nonetheless, Chinese growth rates in the late 1980s and early 1990s do suggest that market-based coordinator economies are capable of considerable economic dynamism, just as Gorbachev had hoped for.

Conclusion

Centrally planned coordinator economies superficially resembled the kind of economy nineteenth century socialists envisioned in some respects: there was no private ownership of productive property and therefore there were no capitalists. Wages were determined politically, not dictated by the law of supply and demand in labor markets. And bureaucratic, central planning *is* planning—just not democratic, much less participatory planning. Market-based coordinator economies, on the other hand, are hard to confuse with the visions of early socialists. While capitalists remain absent, state-appointed enterprise managers take their place, and market-based coordinator economies replace planning with markets and pay marginal revenue product wages. It is clearly not an economy where workers and consumers plan their joint endeavors, nor an economy where rewards are based on effort, or sacrifice for the common good.

In the end communist parties sacrificed economic democracy along with political democracy in the name of economic justice and efficiency they never delivered. Central planning combined with hierarchical management[16] disenfranchised ordinary workers and consumers who predictably lapsed into apathy once revolutionary fever subsided and corruption in the *nomenclatura* escalated. Appending markets for final goods to the central planning system failed to enfranchise consumers in meaningful ways, and clumsy attempts to compensate for inequitable salaries with flawed ration systems that forced people to stand in lines for necessities and luxuries alike only added insult to injury. Under central planning planners, managers, and workers operated under a system of counterproductive incentives where it was in the interest of each group to deceive the others, curbed only by fear of retribution. But central planning would have been incompatible with economic democracy even if it had overcome its information and incentive liabilities, even if wages had been equitable, even if planning objectives were voted on democratically, and even if consumption goods had been distributed efficiently. The truth is central planning survived as long as it did only because it was propped up by unprecedented totalitarian political power, and there is no reason to mourn its demise.

5

Social Democracy:
Losing the Faith

If both communism and free-market capitalism are highly undesirable, this raises a difficult question for the democratic left to answer: Why was every alternative to communism and laissez-faire capitalism in decline as the twentieth century closed? If social democracy was a desirable alternative to both free-market capitalism and communism, why has its message weakened and its influence declined since the 1970s? If a libertarian socialist economy is superior to both capitalism and communism, why did no libertarian socialist economy materialize in the twentieth century, and why did libertarian socialists become all but invisible by midcentury? If the new left was an advance over the old left, why did the new left never achieve as much political success as the old left in its heyday, and why were the new social movements spawned by the new left weaker at century's end than during the 1970s and 1980s?

Of course, for proponents of free-market capitalism, these are not difficult questions to answer. In their view every feasible alternative is inferior to free-market capitalism. For them capitalism stood triumphant at century's end because it proved to be superior to all its challengers. For the few who cling to nostalgic memories of communist bygone glories, the answer lies in betrayal of the communist cause from within or relentless military, political, and economic pressure applied by the international capitalist ruling class from without. For these diehards, more democratic forms of central planning *would* have triumphed if only the playing field had been even. But for all of us who believe there is a desirable alternative to capitalism that is *not* command planning, the above questions do not have easy answers.

The most convenient place for the democratic left to search for answers is in the uneven playing field. Compared not only to capitalism, but to communism as well, democratic left movements and governments in the twentieth century invariably struggled against more powerful opponents. Scandinavian social democratic parties governed in small countries supported by neither superpower during the Cold War. When François Mitterrand tried to pursue social democratic reforms in the early 1980s he had to contend with hostile free-market governments in Washington, London, and Bonn, and with a well-orchestrated boycott by international financial capital. And Spanish anarchists not only had to contend with Spanish fascism supported by Mussolini and Hitler, they found themselves at a disadvantage compared to their communist "allies" who enjoyed Stalin's full backing, and their social democratic "allies" who enjoyed support from the capitalist "democracies."

The second easiest way to explain why one part of the democratic left was unsuccessful is to complain that other parts denied it the support it deserved. Social democrats and libertarian socialists have not only criticized free-market capitalism and communism, they both spent a great deal of time and energy criticizing one another's views and practices. This is only natural since social democrats and libertarian socialists inevitably compete with one another for the allegiance of those who are dissatisfied with free-market capitalism and totalitarian communism alike. However this natural competition can be healthy or destructive. Since I believe different tendencies within the democratic left are destined to continue competing with one another for a good part of the century ahead, in Part 4 we will be on the lookout for ways to make their competion more healthy and less destructive. But it remains true that sometimes failures of one tendency on the democratic left to achieve greater success in the twentieth century was due to lack of support it should have received from allies. Social democrats failed to acknowledge the legitimacy of libertarian socialist criticism that social democratic reforms did not go far enough, while libertarian socialists were prone to accuse social democrats of "selling out" rather than acknowledge what their reforms did achieve. To cite one poignant example, it is clear, with hindsight, that Spanish social democrats and anarchists failed to support each other against the machinations of their communist allies during the Spanish Civil War to their mutual detriment.

The hardest place to search for reasons why the movement one favors was unsuccessful is within, and that is what I will attempt to do in this chapter and the next. For all that social democrats and libertarian social-ists have gotten right about economic justice and democracy, and about capitalism and communism as well, I believe they have each also gotten important things wrong. Not only is this an important part of the reason why no part of the old or new democratic left proved more successful in the twentieth century, it is why even the best ideas and organiza-tions from the twentieth century are inadequate to guide and lead the struggle to replace the economics of competition and greed with the economics of equitable cooperation in the century ahead. This chapter draws on misconceptions about economic justice and democracy and debilitating myths discussed in Part 1 to help explain the failures of social democracy. The next chapter examines the failures of libertarian socialism.

The Accomplishments of Social Democracy

I mean it as a great compliment when I say that capitalism functions poorly indeed without social democrats.[1] The "golden age of capitalism" was due more to the influence social democrats exerted over capitalism than any other single cause. Only when social democratic policies have been ascendant has capitalism proved able to avoid major crises and distribute the benefits of rising productivity widely enough to sustain rapid rates of economic growth and create a middle class. Political democracy in the twentieth century also received more nurturing from social democratic parties than from any other single source. However, despite their important accomplishments, crucial compromises social democrats made with capitalism bear a major responsibility for the failure of the economics of equitable cooperation to make greater headway against the economics of competition and greed in the twen-tieth century.

Of all the political tendencies critical of capitalism, social democrats have participated in reform campaigns and electoral democracy most effectively. Sometimes social democratic parties won elections and formed governments that carried out major economic reforms. Other times reforms that began as planks in platforms of social democratic parties out of power were implemented by rival parties decades later. Some of the major reforms for which social democrats deserve a great deal of credit include old-age insurance, universal healthcare coverage, welfare for those unable to work or find work, financial regulation, stabilization of the business cycle through fiscal and monetary policies, incomes policies to combat cost-push inflation while reducing income inequalities, and long-run, comprehensive planning policies to promote growth and development. Wherever and whenever social democrats were politically stronger, reforms were more numerous and went deeper. Social democrats were strongest in Sweden from the mid-1950s to the mid-1970s where social democratic reforms achieved their apogee. Social democracy in Germany was strongest under Helmut Schmidt and Willy Brandt in the 1970s. The high point for social democratic reforms in the United States occurred prior to World War II during the New Deal of President Franklin Delano Roosevelt. The high point in France and Great Britain occurred immediately after World War II when a united front government in France and Labor Party government in Great Britain each ruled briefly. Lyndon Johnson's "war on poverty" in the mid-1960s and François Mitterrand's first year in power in 1981 proved to be short-lived resurgencies of social democratic agendas in their respective countries.

A comprehensive critique of twentieth-century social democracy would require at least one whole book written by a writer who had devoted decades to studying the history of social democracy. I am not such a specialist, nor is this a book primarily about social democracy. I will concentrate on what I believe to be the crucial strengths and weaknesses of twentieth-century social democracy, and review the work of two authors whom I consider particularly insightful. Michael Harrington and Magnus Ryner are peerless students of social democratic history whose support for their cause did not prevent either of them from writing critically.

As the leading social democrat in the United States from the 1960s until his untimely death in 1989, Michael Harrington combined insider knowledge with a critical detachment derived from viewing powerful European social democratic parties from the perspective of a small party in the United States that could not have been farther from the halls of power itself. In *The Next Left: The History of the Future* (1986) and in *Socialism: Past and Future* (1989) Harrington provides a sympathetic, but critical evaluation of social democracy. In "Neoliberal Globalization and The Crisis of Swedish Social Democracy" published in *Economic and Industrial Democracy* (1999), and in *Capitalist Restructuring, Globalization and the Third Way: Lessons from the Swedish Model* (2002), Magnus Ryner provides an insightful, up-to-date analysis of the "Swedish model." Harrington and Ryner both try to explain why social democratic reforms were not more successful in their heyday, lost momentum in the 1970s, and were rolled back over the last two decades.[2] I will emphasize where I think we must go beyond their criticisms.

The Decline of Social Democracy through the Eyes of Michael Harrington

Michael Harrington opened his thoughtful evaluation of social democracy in the twentieth century with the following observation:

> Once upon a time, to be precise, on July 14, 1889, when the nascent socialist parties of the world came together in Paris on the centenary of the Bastille, it was reasonable to take socialism seriously. It confidently announced itself as the inheritor of the great bourgeois revolutions, the movement that would redeem a promise of *liberté, egalité, et fraternité* that could not possibly be fulfilled within capitalist limits. A century later the social democratic parties of Europe, Latin America, Canada, and the Pacific are a major political force, either in government or in the opposition. Yet none of them has a precise sense of what socialism means, even if they have often proved to be more humane and efficient trustees of capitalism than the capitalists themselves (*Socialism*, 1, 2)

In other words, over the course of a century Harrington tells us that parties initially dedicated to replacing the economics of competition and greed with the economics of equitable cooperation became parties who ameliorated the pernicious effects of a system based on competition and greed that they accepted. How does Harrington explain this transformation? How can we avoid the same outcome in the century ahead? Harrington begins his answer by pointing out that social democrats never figured out what kind of economy they wanted instead of capitalism.

What Is *The Alternative to Capitalism?*

As the twentieth century progressed, social democrats' answer to this crucial question became increasingly more vague, ambiguous, and self-contradictory. In the early part of the century they dealt in rhetorical flourishes counterpoising democratic direction of the economy to rule by profit-seeking capitalists, but in Harrington's words, social democrats "were woefully imprecise about what it meant, much less as to how to put it into practice" (*Socialism*, 20, 21). Harrington concludes that for the first half of the twentieth-century social democrats "attempted, with notable lack of success, to figure out what they meant by socialism, and remained inexcusably confused about its content. Was there a socialist substitute for capitalist markets, either a plan or a new kind of market? Even if one could solve the political difficulties and achieve a sudden and decisive socialist take over, that would simply postpone all the other problems to the next morning, as happened, catastrophically, with the Bolsheviks after the Revolution" (*Socialism*, 20, 21, 24). I could not agree more with Harrington on this point. It is a central contention of this book that until progressives clarify how the economics of equitable cooperation can work convincingly and concretely, we are unlikely to avoid the fate that befell twentieth-century social democrats.

Harrington went on to point out that after World War II social democrats gave up on their search for an answer to the question that eluded them, and instead embraced a concrete answer to a *different* question: "John Maynard Keynes miraculously provided the answer that Marx had neglected: socialization was the socialist administration of an expanding capitalist economy whose surplus was then partly directed to the work of justice and freedom" (*Socialism*, 21). While Keynesian policies humanized capitalism significantly, unfortunately that was all they did, or ever can do. Harrington tells us that when the "Keynesian era came to an end sometime in the seventies, the socialists were once more thrown into confusion" (*Socialism*, 21). By then, however, social democrats had long forgotten the original question whose answer had always eluded them: Exactly how does the economics of equitable cooperation work?

Unfortunately, even social democrats like Harrington who recognized the above problem contributed nothing to its solution. In an entire chapter on "Market and Plan," Harrington fails to remove any of the vagueness from social democratic rhetoric about how equitable cooperation could actually function. He tells us "only under socialism and democratic planning will it be possible for markets to serve the common good as Adam Smith thought they did under capitalism" (*Socialism*, 219). But he provides no compelling reasons for why this would be the case. He sits squarely on the fence, contributing nothing to the debate over the existence of an alternative to markets and command planning. "Alec Nove argues either there is a centralized and authoritarian plan for the allocation of resources or there must be markets. Nove, I think, overstates this counter position. Ernest Mandel projects a vision of democratic planning, but I am not sure it is feasible" (*Socialism*, 242). Harrington concludes his chapter in a paroxysm of ambiguity and double talk surrounding reiteration of the obvious:

> Markets are obviously not acceptable to socialists if they are seen as automatic and infallible mechanisms for making decisions behind the backs of those who are affected by them. But within the context of a plan, markets could, *for the first time*, be an instrument for truly maximizing the freedom of choice of individuals and communities. I would not, however, use the phrase "market socialism" to designate this process. What is critical is the *use* of markets to implement democratically planned goals in the most effective way. That, it must be said, involves a danger: that the means will turn into ends. There is no guarantee that this will not happen short of a people genuinely committed to solidaristic values and mobilized against the threat inherent even in the planned employment of the market mechanism. The aim, then, is a socialism that makes markets a tool of its nonmarket purposes (*Socialism*, 247).

What Harrington completely fails to address in his confusion is whether or not when people interact through markets this subverts their commitment to Harrington's vaunted "nonmarket purposes." If participation in markets systematically undermines the "solidaristic values" of even those most "mobilized against the threat inherent in the market mechanism," then why would Harrington believe that "means" will not "turn into ends?" What is particularly galling about this abject failure of intellectual leadership regarding plan versus market is that it effectively endorses the unofficial policy of social democracy in favor of market socialism while avoiding responsibility for renouncing the idea of a *system* of democratic planning. Harrington tells us that "putting market mechanisms at the service of social priorities rather than in command of the economy is an area in which democratic socialists have contributions to make" (*Socialism*, 233), and reminds us that social democrats in the Swedish Labor Federation (LO) were taming the labor market through a labor market board and incomes policy as early as 1950. This is all well and good. But the question remains: Is the phrase "democratic planning" to mean something more than political intervention in particular markets in particular ways? After reading an entire chapter on the subject, readers of Harrington's book remain as clueless about his answer to this fundamental question as they were before beginning.[3]

Coping with a Fractured Working Class

Harrington's second explanation for the failure of social democracy is that the homogeneous, majoritarian working class prophesied by Marx never materialized. Instead the working class "divided on the basis of skill, gender, religion, and the like, and in the post-World War II period, when the shift toward the professionals and the service sector became blatantly evident, the socialists were forced to confront the fact that their historic ideal had been shorn of its supposed agency" (*Socialism*, 21, 22). While social democrats may have been slow to give up on the myth of a homogeneous working class, they were quicker to adapt than most communists and libertarian socialists who continued to labor far longer under the illusion of a growing working-class majority who would eventually identify primarily in class terms. So I am less inclined than Harrington to chastise social democrats for coming to grips slowly with the fact that a majoritarian movement for the economics of equitable cooperation would have to be built not only from segments of the working class who saw themselves as different and with interests at odds with one another, but from nonclass "agents of history" as well. However, I am more critical than Harrington of *how* social democrats chose to adapt to something that came as a surprise to all leftists. As explained below, I believe social democratic union leaders and politicians too often found it convenient to prioritize more privileged sectors of an increasingly diverse working class at the expense of less privileged ones, and embraced theories that rationalized their behavior by obfuscating the meaning of economic justice.

The Pitfalls of Gradualism

I think Harrington's third reason for social democratic failures is critical. He points out that even when social democrats realized they were "stuck with gradualism and all its attendant problems," and responded in the only sensible way—"have socialists permeate the society from top to bottom"—unfortunately they "overlooked one of capitalism's most surprising characteristics: its ability to co-opt reforms, and even radical changes, of the opponents of the system" (*Socialism*, 24). Harrington clearly understands the problem well. He points out: "Capitalists themselves were, in the main, not shrewd enough to maneuver in this way. The American corporate rich fought Roosevelt's functional equivalent of social democracy with a passionate scorn for the 'traitor to his class' who was the president. Yet these same reactionaries benefited from the changes that the New Deal introduced far more than did the workers and the poor who actively struggled for them. The structures of capitalist society successfully assimilated the socialist reforms even if the capitalists did not want that to happen" (*Socialism*, 25). But while Harrington goes to great lengths to search for what new leftists called "nonreformist reforms," he has little to say about the only real way to confront the problem that capitalism will co-opt reforms and co-opt reformers as well: create institutions of equitable cooperation for people to live in even while they are engaged in the lengthy process of fighting for reforms and convincing the victims of capitalism to jettison the economics of competition and greed entirely.

It is not enough to complain, as Harrington tells us Karl Kautsky did in a letter after World War I, "that it had become impossible to get anyone in the movement to do anything as a volunteer," or to agree with Robert Michels who demonstrated in his famous study of German social democracy how "outcast revolutionaries had turned into staffers" (*Socialism*, 21). There is only so long activists will volunteer while others secure positions in the movement that allow them to wield more power and secure economic livelihoods for themselves that are more commodious than most of those whom they lead. Social democracy insufficiently inoculated its members against the virus of capitalist values, and failed to ensure that leaders lived up to the values they preached. More importantly social democratic practice provided too little institutional support for members who wanted to live in ways that "keep the dream alive," even while most around them competed individualistically in the capitalist marketplace. I will offer suggestions about how this problem can be better addressed in chapters 12 and 13. But I do not think the answer lies in searching for reforms that are somehow less "reformist" than most reforms social democrats pursued in the twentieth century. Because new leftists were particularly prone to futile searches for the holy grail of nonreformist reforms, I treat this issue at greater length next chapter. But let me put the matter squarely here: reforms *are* reformist. They *do* make capitalism less harmful while leaving capitalism intact. It does no good to think we can resolve this dilemma by finding some kind of nonreformist reform. Instead, the answer lies in how we fight for the only kind of reforms there are, and in providing people who reject capitalist values practical ways to personally live according to human values, and insisting that those who would lead the movement for equitable cooperation do so as well.

Harrington's last two reasons why social democracy did not fare better are important historically, but there was no way social democrats could have avoided them in the twentieth century, just as there will be no way for us to avoid them in the century ahead. Therefore, lessons must take the form of how to mitigate predictable damage from circumstances we cannot prevent.

The Pitfalls of "Lemon" Socialism

Harrington complains: "In ordinary times, when the system was working on its own terms, the socialists never had the political power to make decisive changes and were thus fated to make marginal adjustments of a basically unfair structure. In the extraordinary times when the socialists did come to power, after wars or in the midst of economic crises, they had a broader mandate, but never a support for revolution, and they inherited almost insoluble problems from their capitalist predecessors" (*Socialism*, 25). A popular joke in Peru in the mid-1980s captured this dilemma perfectly. For more than sixty years the Peruvian military assassinated and arrested leaders of the Peruvian social democratic party, APRA, and prevented APRA from taking power after it won elections on numerous occasions. According to the joke, the cruelest punishment the Peruvian military ever meted out to APRA was to finally allow the party to take power after winning elections in 1985. The oligarchy had so badly mismanaged the economy that neither they nor the military wanted to take responsibility for the economic crisis that was unavoidable. The jokesters proved to be remarkably prescient. In twelve months, the approval ratings for Alan Garcia dropped from 60 to 15 percent, and it took more than a decade for APRA to recover its position as a significant political force after his disastrous term in office ended.

    This problem is also referred to as "lemon socialism": when social democrats were able to nationalize companies, or industries, it was usually because they were in terrible shape. Consequently they often performed badly as public enterprises simply because they were going to perform badly in any case. After World War II this was a problem for the Labor government in Great Britain and for the popular-front government in France. Harrington comments that François Mitterrand's Socialist Party failed to realize in 1981 "how run down the industrial plant had been allowed to become," and quotes from a 1984 retrospective on the Mitterrand victory in *The Economist* that concluded: "The Socialists thought they would nationalize a phalanx of rich industrial concerns that could be used to boost output, jobs, and national wealth. Instead, with one or two exceptions, the state had acquired, at high cost, a collection of debt-ridden, wheezing remnants of the go-go years of Gaullist giantism" (*Next Left*, 123–124). On a smaller scale this problem plagued steel companies in Pittsburgh, Pennsylvania, and Youngstown, Ohio in the 1980s that were taken over in employee buyouts with support from local governments anxious to preserve their tax base. Of course it is always more advantageous to take over winners than losers for public and employee management. But we will no doubt find ourselves faced with less attractive options in the future, just as social democrats were in the past. What lessons are to be learned?

There may be circumstances so unfavorable that they are literally programmed for failure, in which case we must be patient enough to refrain from taking over only to preside over a disaster. However, rather than turn away from opportunities because they are risky, I think wisdom will more often take the form of negotiating for a larger mandate. After all, with a large enough mandate we believe there is no social problem we cannot tackle successfully! Problems arise when one takes over a lemon with insufficient financial resources, or takes over a government with an insufficient voting majority in the legislature, or with debilitating constraints imposed by the military or by hostile financial interests. My own reading of twentieth-century social democratic history leads me to the conclusion that tougher negotiations over how much leeway our opponents permit us when we take over a situation our opponents do not want to take responsibility for themselves, and a greater willingness to turn down the job if we are not given the tools necessary to do it, will often serve us well. But these are always tough calls, and there will no doubt be disagreements among those fighting to replace the economics of competition and greed with equitable cooperation over this kind of tough call in the century ahead, just as there were in the past.

Global Capital Markets: The Nine-Hundred-Pound Gorilla

Finally, Harrington tells us social democrats were "utterly unprepared for the internationalization of politics and economics that has been one of the decisive trends of the twentieth century." (*Socialism*, 25) In particular Harrington blames the failure of the socialist government of François Mitterrand in France in the early 1980s primarily on hostile global capital markets. "The failure of the bold plans of the Mitterrand government in 1981–1982 were caused, above all, by an open economy that had to bow to the discipline of capitalist world markets rather than follow a program that had been democratically voted by the French people." (*Socialism*,

27) And as we will see below, globalization features prominently in Magnus Ryner's explanation of the decline of social democracy in Sweden. The extent to which social democratic reforms in a single country can be vetoed by global financial markets in the neoliberal era is of great importance to consider carefully.

A mushrooming pool of liquid global wealth—created by record profits due to stagnant wages, downsizing, megamergers, and rapid technical innovation in computers and telecommunications—is now more free to move in and out of national economies at will than at any time in history. A trend away from prudent restraints on international capital flows built into the Bretton Woods system, toward full-blown "capital liberalization" began with the unregulated Eurodollar market in the 1960s and culminated in a successful neoliberal crusade to remove any and all restrictions on capital mobility in the context of a global credit system with minimal monitoring and regulation, no lender of last resort, and serious regional rivalries that obstruct timely interventions. Neoliberal global managers have literally created the financial equivalent of the proverbial nine-hundred-pound gorilla: *Where does the nine-hundred-pound gorilla—global liquid wealth—sit? Wherever it wants!* And when a derivative tickles, and savvy investors—who realize they are functioning in a highly leveraged, largely unregulated credit system— rush to pull out before others do, currencies, stock markets, banking systems, and formerly productive economies can all collapse in their wake. What this does, of course, is give international investors a powerful veto over any government policies they deem unfriendly to their interests. If neoliberal global capitalism could trump Mitterrand's program in an advanced economy like France that was not facing international bankruptcy in the early 1980s, and forced the most powerful of all social democrats in Sweden to abandon their reforms in the late 1980s and early 1990s, what hope is there for social democratic programs that attempt to spur equitable growth in bankrupt Third World economies facing even more powerful global financial markets and an even more implacable International Monetary Fund early in the twenty-first century? Chapter 11 considers the crucial question of what progressive movements in Third World countries can do when they are voted into national office in a global economy where international financial capital rules supreme. Both Harrington and Ryner provide useful insights based on twentieth-century social democratic experiences that I will add to more than disagree with.

In chapter 6 of *The Next Left*, Harrington provides a detailed analysis of the failure of the Mitterrand Socialist government in France in the early 1980s that is extremely instructive. He begins: "President Mitterrand and the French Socialists received an absolute majority in 1981 and proceeded faithfully to carry out a program that had been carefully worked out over a decade. Within a year they were forced to sound retreat, and by the spring of 1983 they had effectively reversed almost every priority of their original plan. . . . Had a movement that had boldly promised a 'rupture with capitalism' on the road to power become more capitalist than the capitalists once in power?" (*Next Left*, 116, 117). Harrington admits that "rupture with capitalism" rhetoric was partly hype, but points out that practically every campaign promise was redeemed during the first year, in which the Mitterrand government "honored the clenched fist of working class history and the poetic rose of May 1968" (*Next Left*, 119). The program was, indeed, every bit as "audacious" as one could have hoped for. It consisted not only of left Keynesian policies to stimulate equitable growth, but aggressive nationalizations and a "new model of consumption," that is, "a qualitative rather than merely a quantitative change" (*Next Left*, 119). It is worth taking a close look at what happened precisely because unlike many other twentieth-century social democratic governments, on taking office the Mitterrand government did *not* immediately back off from bold campaign promises.

The French Socialists immediately increased the buying power for the least-paid workers through dramatic increases in the minimum wage and a "solidaristic wage policy" giving the greatest wage increases "to those at the bottom of the occupational structure" (*Next Left*, 127). To increase the demand for labor the government increased hiring in the public sector and increased government spending on social programs. To decrease the supply of labor and shift use of society's social surplus from more consumption to more leisure the government sponsored programs for early retirement at age sixty, increased annual paid vacation from four to five weeks, and tried to reduce the work week from forty to thirty-five hours. All this is hard to fault. Unfortunately the last program fell victim to political machinations within the left over whether it would be reduced hours for the same pay—a real wage increase— or reduced hours for less pay, "work sharing." The Communist-led federation of unions and the more traditional business unions opposed any reduction in pay. The Catholic Democratic Confederation of Labor supported work sharing, as did the government's Minister of Labor arguing that real wages had already been increased in other ways and that work sharing benefited the least advantaged—the unemployed—and encouraged leisure over consumerism. The end result was thirty-nine hours for thirty-nine hours of pay, an insignificant work sharing that left nobody satisfied and everyone bitter.

Proclaiming themselves different from social democrats elsewhere in Europe who had long since abandoned nationalization, the French socialists went through with an impressive list of nationalizations they had promised during the election campaign. Again the courage displayed by the nationalizations is hard to fault. However, besides the fact that many of the companies they took over were much weaker than they realized, two other problems limited benefits from the nationalizations. Harrington tells us: "At the cabinet meeting at which the decision was made to go ahead with the nationalizations, there was a fateful debate that pitted Michel Rocard, Jacques Delors, and Robert Badinter against most of the rest of the ministers and, the decisive factor, against the president. There is no need, Rocard and Delors argued, for Paris to pay for one-hundred percent of an enterprise that is targeted for government ownership. Fifty percent is quite enough, and much less expensive. But Mitterrand went ahead with one-hundred percent buy outs" (*Next Left*, 136, 137). Harrington points out that the consequences were not dissimilar to corporate takeovers with borrowed money in the United States— "the acquired company had to be starved for cash in order to finance its own acquisition" (*Next Left*, 137). The second problem, how the newly nationalized companies were managed, was caused, in part, by the first. Harrington quotes from a letter sent to the new administrators that said: "You will seek, first of all, economic efficiency through a constant bettering of productivity. The normal criteria of the management of industrial enterprises will apply to your group. The different activities should realize results that will assure the development of the enterprise and guarantee that the profitability of the invested capital will be normal" (*Next Left*, 135, 136). In other words, the new managers were given marching orders no different than those stockholders would send to a CEO they had just hired! Harrington goes on to tell us: "Alain Gomez, a founder of the Marxist left wing of the Socialist party, CERES, and a new official in the public sector, was even blunter: 'My job is to get surplus value'" (*Next Left*, 136).

The problem is, of course, that if capitalists are paid the full present discounted value for their assets, and if nationalized enterprises are managed no differently than private enterprises, the only thing that will change is who employees and taxpayers will resent. Instead of resenting greedy capitalists they will resent the socialist government, the socialist ministers, and their new socialist bosses. Like Harrington, I can understand this is easier to see from the outside free from budgetary and managerial pressures, but it is true nonetheless. Moreover, the government's efforts to promote decentralization and worker participation were no more successful in state enterprises than in the private sector. Harrington tells us: "Although the Auroux laws were unquestionably progressive, they fell far, far short of the ideal of self-managed socialism. In essence, the workers were given the right to speak up on issues affecting their industry—which was a gain—but they got no power to make decisions. One of the consequences of genuine worker control is that productivity goes up. But given the extremely limited nature of the workers' new rights—and the mood of moroseness that settled over the society not too long after the euphoria of May 1981—that pragmatic bonus from living up to an ideal was not forthcoming" (*Next Left*, 137). Unfortunately the administrators of newly nationalized enterprises who received the letter quoted above were no more inclined than their counterparts in the private sector to accede power to make decisions to their employees from whom they were busy extracting "surplus value."

Finally, the government launched strong expansionary fiscal and monetary policies to provide plenty of demand for goods and services so the private sector would produce up to the economy's full potential and employ the entire labor force. Again, there is nothing to find fault with here. Everyone deserves an opportunity to perform socially useful work and be fairly compensated for doing so. However, there is only so much any progressive government can do about this as long as most employment opportunities are still with private employers. Mitterrand deserves praise for doing the most effective thing any government in an economy that is still capitalist can do in this regard: ignore the inevitable warnings and threats from business and financial circles and their mainstream economist lackeys preaching fiscal "responsibility" and monetary restraint, and unleash strong expansionary fiscal and monetary policy.[4]

Unfortunately this is where the Mitterrand government had its worst luck and discovered just how powerful global financial markets can be. They were unlucky when OECD projections in June 1981 of a strong global recovery proved completely wrong. They were unlucky that French trade had shifted toward the Third World over the previous decade where the global slump was most severe. They were unlucky that "the Socialist stimulus created new jobs in West Germany, Japan, and the United States, as much as, or more than, in France" (*Next Left*, 133). More to the point, they were unlucky that conservative governments in Washington, London, and Bonn led by Reagan, Thatcher, and Kohl all helped each other juggle expansions at crucial political junctures, but could not have been more pleased when capital flight and growing trade and budget deficits brought the French socialist program to a grinding halt. Mostly, Harrington tells us they were unlucky "because France could not afford to run a relatively large internal (government) deficit and an external (balance of trade) deficit at the same time" (*Next Left*, 117). The only government fortunate enough to be able to do that, Harrington pointed out, is the U.S. government, as the Reagan administration proved with their military Keynesianism accompanied by tax cuts for the rich during exactly the same years when international financial markets prevented France from running much smaller budget and trade deficits as a percentage of its GDP.[5] However, with the benefit of hindsight it is apparent the Mitterrand government did not handle an admittedly difficult situation as well as it might have.

Harrington points out that trying to avoid devaluing the franc was a mistake. Whether it was because the advice to devalue came from Mitterrand's "arch interparty rival, Michel Rocard," or due to false pride— "one does not devalue the money of a country that has just given you a vote of confidence"—matters little (*Next Left*, 132). Of course hindsight is twenty-twenty, particularly regarding currency devaluations. Nonetheless, devaluation would have reduced the balance of payments deficit, thereby buying the government more time for its program. But the most important lesson is one Harrington shied away from, just as the African National Congress government in South Africa and the Lula Worker Party government in Brazil have shied away from it more recently. There are only three options: (1) don't stimulate the domestic economy in the first place because you are not willing to stand the inevitable heat in your kitchen; (2) stimulate, but back off as soon as new international investment boycotts your economy, domestic wealth takes flight, financial markets drive interest rates on government debt through the ceiling, and the value of your currency drops like a hot potato; or (3) stimulate, but be prepared to face the heat international capital markets will bring with strong measures restricting imports and capital flight, by substituting government investment for declines in international and private investment, and by telling creditors you will default unless they agree to rollovers and concessions. Option three *is* the economic equivalent in the neoliberal era of not only playing hardball with international creditors, but going to financial war if need be. As daunting as option three is, it is important to remember that the Mitterrand government in France proved that option two does not work. As Harrington admitted, "within less than two years the Socialists were engaged in administering a regime of 'rigor,' otherwise known as capitalist austerity" (*Socialism*, 20). Moreover, option two almost always leads to even worse austerity measures than option one because regaining credibility with global financial markets is usually more difficult than not losing it in the first place. Option two also creates more political damage because voters understandably hold the reformers responsible for the pain caused by the austerity program reformers preside over. On the other hand, the ANC government in South Africa has proved that option one inevitably undermines support from the social sectors that bring progressive governments to power in the first place. If you make no serious attempt to fulfill campaign promises, you inevitably alienate those who voted you into office. Unfortunately it appears the Worker Party in Brazil intends to repeat this mistake. If they continue to renege on campaign promises I fear "comrade" Lula's political base may prove even less forgiving than the ANC base in South Africa who did have the ANC to thank for delivering them from apartheid, if not from economic subjugation and poverty.

Drawing Lessons

So what are the lessons to be learned? Unlike some left critics, I do not believe that social democracy's success in taming capitalism was responsible for the failure to replace capitalism in the twentieth century. Had social democratic parties been less successful at reducing capitalist irrationality and injustice, I believe twentieth-century capitalism would simply have been more crisis ridden and inhumane than it was. Had Herbert Hoover presided over the Great Depression instead of Franklin Delano Roosevelt, I believe the depression would only have been deeper and caused more unnecessary suffering. Without New Deal reforms to build on, I believe socialists' chances of replacing capitalism in the United States in the years before World War II would have been even slimmer than they were. Without social security, unemployment insurance, and a minimum wage, and without the example of more robust social democratic reforms in Sweden during the 1960s and 1970s, I believe even fewer people today would believe that equitable cooperation is possible. Broadly speaking, I believe the road to equitable cooperation lies through more and more successful equitable cooperation, not through less. Crises that sometimes trigger the overthrow of structures of privilege are crises of legitimacy, crises of public confidence in ruling elites, or ideological crises that free people from the myths that make them unwitting accomplices in their own oppression. Cracks in the ideological hegemony that undergirds the status quo are the catalysts of social change precisely because they allow people to see that a better world *is* possible. More suffering in and of itself does not lead people to revolt. Becoming convinced that suffering can be prevented is what motivates people to take risks and stand up for change. Since winning reforms rather than standing by and pointing accusatory fingers at deteriorating conditions is what convinces people that suffering is unnecessary, in my opinion the problem with social democratic reforms was not that they were too successful, but that they were not successful enough.

Nor do I believe that more competition and greed teaches people how to cooperate more equitably. Quite the opposite, the more people practice competition and greed the more difficult it is for them to develop the trust and social skills necessary for equitable cooperation. And the more competition and greed is tolerated the stronger becomes the capitalist enabling myth that people are capable of no better. Unfortunately social democrats eventually accepted the necessity of a system based on competition and greed. Michael Harrington formulates the "great social democratic compromise" accurately enough: social democrats "settled for a situation in which they would regulate and tax capitalism but not challenge it in any fundamental way" (*Socialism*, 105). But I don't think even Harrington fully appreciated the full consequences of the compromise. It is one thing to say: We are committed to democracy above all else. Therefore we promise that as long as a majority of the population does not want to replace capitalism we have no intentions of trying to do so. It is quite another thing to say: Despite our best efforts we have failed to convince a majority of the population that capitalism is fundamentally incompatible with economic justice and democracy. Therefore we will cease to challenge the legitimacy of the capitalist system and confine our efforts to reforming it. The first position is one I believe must guide the movement for equitable cooperation in the century ahead. Unfortunately, the second proposition was the compromise accepted by the leadership of social democratic parties, and eventually by all who remained members.

The first proposition does not promise to refrain from voting capitalism out when the majority is ready to do so. Nor does it promise to refrain from taking effective action against capitalists and their supporters should they try to thwart the will of a majority if and when the majority decide they wish to dispense with capitalism in favor of a new system of equitable cooperation. It does not promise to refrain from explaining how private enterprise and markets subvert economic justice and democracy no matter how many believe otherwise. It does not promise to refrain from campaigning in favor of replacing capitalism with something different even when polls indicate that a majority still favors capitalism. It is a simple, unwavering promise to always respect and abide by the will of the majority. The second proposition, on the other hand, bars social democrats from continuing to argue that private enterprise and markets are incompatible with economic justice and democracy. It bars social democrats from campaigning for the replacement of capitalism with a system more compatible with economic justice and democracy. The second proposition implies that if capitalism precludes certain outcomes, then social democrats must cease to lobby on behalf of such outcomes. Therefore the second proposition implies either: (1) social democrats were historically wrong, and economic justice and democracy are fully compatible with capitalism, or (2) while social democrats can continue to fight for some aspects of economic justice and democracy they can no longer support full economic justice and democracy. In effect the second proposition buys political legitimacy within capitalism for social democratic parties in exchange for accepting the legitimacy of a system based on competition and greed. So in my view the problem was not that social democrats fought, often successfully, for reforms to mitigate the effects of competition and greed. The problem was that they ceased to keep fighting for further reforms when their initial reforms fell short of achieving economic justice and democracy because they agreed to accept a system of competition and greed even though the system obstructed the economic justice and democracy they had pledged to fight for.

But eventually the damage went deeper. To his credit Harrington admits that by midcentury social democrats he describes as "bewildered and half-exhausted" no longer had any "precise sense of what socialism means" and no longer "challenged capitalism in any fundamental way." By accepting the economics of competition and greed the "social democratic compromise" led social democrats to lose sight of what economic democracy and economic justice are as well.

By the end of the twentieth century, social democrats no longer agreed among themselves about what economic democracy meant. Moreover, they no longer debated these disagreements vigorously, preferring not to engage in divisive debates they convinced themselves were irrelevant to the immediate tasks that confronted them. Consequently, many social democrats no longer understood why leaving economic decisions in the hands of private employers who survived the rigors of market competition was not an acceptable way to capture expertise. Many no longer understood why "consumer and producer sovereignty" provided by markets was not, by and large, sufficient means of securing economic democracy. Many social democrats no longer understood why joint labor-management advisory committees in capitalist firms were usually fig leafs rather than meaningful vehicles for self-management. By century's end, the debate among social democrats over plan versus market was merely a debate about situations where markets were relatively more efficient and circumstances when efficiency required more "planning" in the form of policy interventions of one kind or another in the market system. Why markets violate economic democracy, and how planning by bureaucrats and corporations can obstruct economic self-management for workers and consumers were no longer issues addressed by social democratic parties by the 1980s.

Similarly, by century's end social democrats no longer knew what economic justice was. Were workers exploited only when they were paid less than their marginal revenue products? If who deserves what is to be decided according to the value of contributions, why do owners of machines and land that increase the amount it is possible to produce not deserve compensation commensurate with those contributions? Unable to answer these questions, social democrats increasingly avoided them. Social democratic union leaders fell into the trap of justifying wage demands on the basis of labor productivity. By doing so they lost track of the fundamental Marxist truth that profits are nothing more than tribute extracted by those who own the means of production, but do no work themselves, from those who do all the work. Moreover, having accepted the morality of reward according to the value of contribution, it was a short step to concentrating on winning wage increases for employees with more human capital and abandoning workers with less human capital. According to a contribution-based theory of economic justice, who is more exploited is determined by whose wage is farthest below their marginal revenue product. No matter how much lower the wages of some workers are than the wages of other workers, if the *difference* between the marginal revenue product and wage of high wage workers is greater than the *difference* between the marginal revenue product and wage of low-wage workers, it would be the workers with higher wages, not those with lower wages, who are more exploited. So social democratic leaders could justify abandoning the worst-off sectors of the working class and prioritizing the interests of high-wage sectors on (false) grounds that workers with higher wages were often "more exploited." Had they remained clear about what economic justice really means—reward according to effort or sacrifice—it would also have remained clear that workers with lower wages are not only worse off, they are also more exploited. But losing their moral compass provided a convenient excuse for social democratic union leaders and politicians since those with less human capital are often harder to organize, harder to win wage increases for, harder to collect dues from, harder to solicit campaign contributions from, and harder to motivate to get out and vote. In short, accepting reward according to contribution provided a ready-made excuse for a shift in priorities toward a constituency that could increase social democratic political power within capitalism more easily.

Accepting capitalism in a strategic compromise turned into accepting the ideology that justifies capitalism as well. While the effect of strategic concessions on electoral results was always hotly debated, the effects of theoretical and moral concessions were less debated in social democratic circles. In my opinion, however, it was the theoretical and moral concessions that were primarily responsible for slowing social democratic reform momentum, and finally rendering social democracy powerless to fight back against right-wing campaigns that rolled back reforms with remarkable speed and ease at century's end.

Imperialism and Eurocentrism

However, the greatest failing of twentieth-century social democracy was its failure to effectively oppose Western imperialism and resolutely support Third World movements for national liberation. An associated weakness was social democratic cultural eurocentrism and a propensity to credit capitalism for much more than it deserves. In this regard social democrats were just as prone to lapse into unwarranted "economism" as Marx's more orthodox disciples, underestimating the importance of noneconomic spheres of social life and crediting capitalism for achievements Western civilization has every right to be proud of, but for which capitalism deserved little, if any, of the credit. Harrington is as guilty of the misleading conflation of Western civilization with capitalism as any of his social democratic counterparts. "Capitalism was a radical new innovation, the greatest achievement of humankind in history, a culture and a civilization as well as an economy" (Socialism, 4). He proceeds to credit capitalism for creating modern science, marrying for love, the novel, painting of the Flemish Renaissance, and Reason itself (*Socialism*, 4, 5). The presumption that any praiseworthy innovation of European society was due to the rise of capitalism in Europe is a particular favorite of social democrats. But it was one practical consequence in particular of this misguided economism and eurocentrism that most sapped twentieth-century social democracy of its transformative powers: social democracy failed to respond to the challenge of Western imperialism.

In some cases social democratic leaders, parties, and governments shamelessly supported colonialism. The last line in the French movie *Black and White in Color* speaks to a century of such betrayals. Set in West Africa, when French and German settlers in adjacent colonies get belated news of the outbreak of World War I, each side kidnaps natives they force to fight each other under white command, copying trench warfare tactics they read about in newspapers arriving belatedly from Europe. Two sensitive, educated, young men rise to become the leaders of the French and German sides. When news of peace in Europe finally arrives months after the armistice, and the two meet for the first time to arrange an end to their imitation war fought with native troops, the Frenchman confesses to his German counterpart: "I'm going to make you laugh. I was a socialist." The young German answers: "So was I." *The Battle of Algiers*, directed by Gillo Pontecorvo assisted by Franco Solinas, opened the eyes of many like myself from the Vietnam War generation in the United States to the horrors that inevitably accompany attempts to preserve imperial rule when it is challenged by popular rebellion. French social democrats not only supported colonial rule in Algeria, from 1954 when the Algerians began their uprising until 1958, the high commissioner of the French Republic in Algiers who prosecuted the war with increasing brutality was the Socialist, Max Lejeune.

In other cases social democrats were anti-imperialist in name, but less often in deed. Even the best among them, including Michael Harrington, displayed serious shortcomings in their opposition to Western imperialism. Harrington is far too quick to make excuses. He complains that social democratic parties sometimes suffered at the polls when they opposed imperial policies: "When the German socialists refused to vote in support of a military campaign against the people of Southwest Africa in 1906, they went on to suffer, in the campaign of 1907, their first electoral setback since 1884" (*Socialism*, 26). Does this justify subsequent failures of German social democrats to oppose German imperial ventures? Harrington points out that social democratic parties sometimes only had "partial power in capitalist parliaments of imperial countries engaged in the exploitation of subject peoples" (*Socialism*, 26). Does that excuse them from going along with imperial policies of governments they participated in? Harrington excuses the Belgian socialists on grounds that they were forced to choose "between a Congo that was the personal property of the king or a Congo that was under the imperial rule of the nation" (*Socialism*, 26). Since when is it impossible to vote "none of the above?" The only thing Harrington has to say about the Labor Party and British Imperial rule in India was that "the British Labor Party government of 1945 played an important role in making India independent, a policy Winston Churchill opposed" (*Socialism*, 26). No doubt Mahatma Gandhi would have found other things worthy of mention about the Labor Party and British Imperial rule! Moreover, the fact that the Labor Party adopted a relatively benign position regarding Indian independence did not deter it from supporting subsequent British imperial ventures in Egypt, Kenya, Malaysia, and Iran where the Labor Party gave its support to British military intervention to stop Mossadegh's nationalization of oil before the CIA organized a coup to topple him and reinstall the Shah. Harrington neglects to mention these abject moral failures of the British Labor Party, nor its open hostility to the Campaign for Nuclear Disarmament, which led a mass movement in Britain challenging British government support for Washington Cold War policies. Unfortunately, there is much in Labor Party history since World War II that is perfectly consistent with Tony Blair as foremost cheerleader for Clinton's war on Yugoslavia and Bush's war on Iraq.

Harrington heaps praise on Willy Brandt and Olof Palme for leading the Socialist International in the late 1970s to support policies to "create employment and growth in both the advanced and underdeveloped economies" (*Socialism*, 26). But what Harrington fails to mention is the hostile relationship between the Socialist International and most national liberation struggles during the same time period. In a few cases where Third World governments pressured by U.S. imperialism were headed by social democrats, like Michael Manley in Jamaica, the Socialist International could be relied on to provide diplomatic support and economic aid for their fellow social democrats. In all other cases social democrats considered it more important to find fault with the leadership and policies of successful national liberation movements than to denounce the imperial ambitions and interventions of the United States, much less lend effective diplomatic or military support to national liberation movements under attack. Since resistance to U.S. imperialism throughout the Third World during the second half of the twentieth century was overwhelmingly led by parties that were not social democratic, social democracy found itself sitting on the fence, or worse, with respect to *the* defining issue of the era. It would take a whole book to do justice to the sad history of social democracy and Western imperialism. Suffice it to say I do not believe we would find many positive lessons about how to relate to imperialism in the century ahead by studying how social democracy responded to the challenges of imperialism in the century just past. When a social demo-crat as introspective and self-critical as Michael Harrington has only this to say about "Third World socialism" in a book written from his deathbed: "The problem was that Third World 'Socialism' turned out to be either naively utopian or, worse, a cover for new authoritarian, exploitative, and inefficient regimes" (*Socialism*, 26), we need to look elsewhere for guidance about how First World citizens fighting for equi-table cooperation should relate to Third World national liberation move-ments. Honest criticism of those fighting for their national political and economic liberation is one thing. Criticism as an excuse for being "missing in action" in the movement to end Western imperialism is another thing entirely.

The Decline of the "Swedish Model"

Magnus Ryner introduces his insightful discussion of the crisis of Swedish social democracy as follows:

> The overall theme of my argument is that it is important to neither reduce the crisis of social democracy to a set of external constraints totally outside the control of social democratic actors, nor to argue that nothing fundamental in the structural environment has changed, and that the crisis is simply an effect of a betrayal of ideas by social democratic elites. The former approach ignores actual tactical and strategic failures of actors, fails to appreciate alternative options and strategies that might have been pursued and that might provide lessons also for the future. The latter approach ignores the profound structural change that has taken place, and that has redefined the terms of social democratic politicss (*Crisis of Swedish Social Democracy*, 40).[6]

Not only is this a realistic and useful way to look at the issue, Ryner provides insightful particulars to flesh out the picture. He remarks that "the transformation of international monetary institutions and global financial markets, the emergence of the Eurodollar and other offshore markets, the flexible exchange rate system, mounting government debt, and the growing asymmetries between creditor and debtor nations has made high finance the pivotal agent in the allocation of economic resources" (*Crisis*, 42). And he fingers the crucial difference between "the 'double screen' of Bretton Woods that ensured the capacity of states to manage aggregate demand and to mitigate market-generated social disruptions" and the neoliberal transformation that "deliberately reshapes state-market boundaries so as to maximize the exposure of states to international capital markets and discipline social actors to conform to market constraints and criteria" (*Crisis*, 43, 44).

As far as I'm concerned Ryner could have dispensed with questionable theories like "Taylorist production norms reaching their sociotechnological frontiers," "the end of Fordism," and "flexible specialization replacing economies of scale" others have written much about in explaining why Sweden's social democrats faced more difficult circumstances at the end of the twentieth century than they had in midcentury. The success of multinational corporations in getting the rules of the international economy rewritten in their favor, and in favor of financial capital in particular, is sufficient to explain why it became more difficult for Swedish unions and the Swedish government to wrestle part of the social surplus away from Swedish and multinational corporations for those who actually produced it. But not only do all social democrats bear some of the blame for permitting the rules of the international economy to be rewritten in ways that were detrimental to the interests of their traditional constituencies, Swedish social democrats played into the hands of Swedish capitalists allowing them to regain their dominant position in the Swedish economy.

Failure to Wage Class War

Ryner tells us "one should not underestimate the sense of weakness in business circles" in 1970 when Swedish capital faced "the profit squeeze, increased employers' contributions to finance social consumption, juridification of the labour process, and an outright challenge to private ownership of the means of production." (58) But instead of pushing for a new social compromise that won employees greater participation as the Meidner plan called for, and instead of increasing the role of the state in accumulation and investment, Swedish social democrats concentrated on preserving the status quo and their distributive gains in face of a worsening international economic situation. In other words, when they had the chance, Swedish social democrats balked at taking that next reformist step no social democrats ever dared take in the twentieth century, which would also have permanently weakened the power of Swedish capitalists.

What went little noticed at the time was that by frightening Swedish capitalists but leaving them breathing room, the social democrats allowed the Skandinaviska Enskilda Ganken/Wallenberg group, which had only reluctantly accepted the social democratic compromise in the first place, to take over the Swedish employers association (SAF) from the Handelsbank group, which had supported the "Swedish model." The shift in power became clear to all when "Asea's Curt Nicolin was appointed executive director of the SAF in 1978, an event described as a 'culture shock' by senior officials of the organization" (*Crisis*, 59) Under new "hyperliberal leadership" Ryner tells us the SAF "assumed a position of total non-accommodation in the public commission responsible to iron out a compromise on wage earner funds, attempts to overcome difference with the Swedish Labor Confederation (LO) on wage levels and collective savings were abandoned, and by January of 1992 the SAF had unilaterally exited from all corporatist forms of bargaining." In short, frightened Swedish capitalists embraced new internal leadership willing to battle not only against social democratic programs but social democratic ideology as well. Taking advantage of neoliberal international conditions that strengthened their cause, and a retreat offered by moderate proponents of "the third way" within the Swedish social democratic party, the SAF went on to roll back the "Swedish model" in the late 1990s.

The Third Way: A Trojan Horse

Ryner argues convincingly that despite external shocks to an overly specialized and vulnerable Swedish export sector, and despite the increasingly hostile neoliberal international environment, Swedish social democrats still had options they failed to pursue that could have changed the outcome. Moderate "third way" social democrats called for a retreat in face of more difficult economic and political conditions, while the more progressive wing of the Swedish social democratic party (SAP) called for an expansion of economic democracy. Ryner provides an invaluable description of how third-way policies paved the road to economic failure and political defeat that all who are attracted to such policies would do well to heed. This lesson is so important I quote Ryner at length:

The economic policy of the SAP 1982–90, coined "the third way" (between Thatcherism and Keynesianism), presupposed that "supply-side" selective labour market policy measures and a coordinated restraint in collective bargaining would be sufficient measures to contain unemployment and inflation. The policy ultimately faltered because long-term GDP and productivity growth were not realized, and the implicit incomes policy failed. A basic fallacy of the policy was the premise that increased private profits and investments would regenerate GDP and productivity growth. Apart from the success of pharmaceuticals, there was little growth in new dynamic sectors and enterprises. Instead the strategy benefited existing firms, which had a "golden decade" despite the lack-luster performance of Sweden's economy (*Crisis*, 60).

The government deregulated capital and money markets in 1985, and this was followed by a formal deregulation of foreign exchange markets in 1989. Moreover, the strategy in managing the public debt changed. Together with a vow not to devalue again, the government declared it would no longer borrow abroad directly to finance the debt or cover balance of payments deficits, but would rather only borrow on the domestic market. This meant that in order to maintain balance of payments, the Swedish interest rate would have to increase to a level where private agents would hold bonds or other debts in Swedish krona, despite the devaluation risk. In other words, the Ministry of Finance and the Central Bank deliberately sought to use global financial markets for disciplinary purposes on unions (LO and TCO) and social service agencies in wage and budget bargaining. The LO and TCO did not consent to their marginalization, and continued to demand support for solidaristic wage policy and did not heed the "moral suasion" of incomes policy since there no longer was a coherent common moral framework. It led to what became known as the "War of the Roses" between the Ministry of Finance on the one hand and the unions and social service cadres on the other (*Crisis*, 62).

It should be noted that these policy changes were not subjected to debate and approval in any party congresses or in the electoral arena. Only the Central Bank and the Ministry of Finance were effectively involved. Concurrently, just as these policies were implemented, the "third way" was still presented to party ranks and in the electoral arena as a reformist socialist response to the crisis in opposition to neoliberalism (*Crisis*, 63).

These third-way economic failures Ryner describes so well also led to electoral defeat. "It was in the context of the 'extraordinary measures' of a wage freeze and a temporary ban on strikes that the electoral support of the SAP plummeted to a historical low, ultimately leading to a humiliating electoral defeat in 1991" (*Crisis*, 63). But more importantly Ryner explains how third-way politics led to a rightward shift in the entire Swedish political spectrum.

> The SAF began to assume the role of an aspiring hegemonic party, attempting to shape intellectual and popular discourse and the terrain of contestability in civil society in a market friendly direction. Although this strategy has fallen short of realizing a Thatcherite national-popular hegemony in Sweden, it has nevertheless been quite a success. It ensured the defeat of wage earner funds in the electoral arena. More broadly, it has made neoliberal ideas popular in the middle-class strata, which is reflected in the successes of the Moderaterna (the neoconservative party) and the rightward shift of the liberal Folkpariet on economic issues. The subsequent shift in the substance of academic discourse in economics also took place in the context of strategic business funding of economic research (*Crisis*, 59).

Is "Economic Democracy" Still Possible?

Rearguard measures clearly failed to save the Swedish model, and it should now be apparent to all that third way politics functioned as a Trojan horse for the economics of competition and greed inside the walls of the Swedish Social Democratic Party. But was there a viable alternative that could have produced better results? Ryner admits conditions were unfavorable, and there is no way to know for sure. But he goes to great lengths to point out ways that moving the reform agenda forward—increasing what Swedish social democrats call "economic democracy" rather than unleashing market forces—might have had more success.

Ryner argues that continued expansion of social-welfare programs that were the hallmark of the Swedish model in its heyday eventually required increases in productivity. But he points out that the left within the SAP consistently offered proposals aimed at these objectives. Contrary to complaints from neoliberals abroad, Swedish conservatives, and third wayers inside the SAP that the Swedish left was only about redistribution, the LO, social service agency cadre, and their progressive intellectual allies inside the SAP had a coherent program to stimulate productivity, investment, and growth. In other words, they were *neither* short sighted *nor* exclusively about redistribution.

The LO launched an offensive for "industrial democracy" in the early 1970s that led to the Codetermination Act, the Work Environment Act, and Legislation of Employment Protection. But all attempts to build on these beginnings came to naught. In 1976, the LO endorsed the "Meidner Plan" to expand worker participation and gradually give them partial ownership of the firms where they worked. On numerous subsequent occasions the LO proposed ways to increase "collective savings and investment" through excess profit taxes and wage-earner funds (The fourth AP fund, the Waldenstrom Report, and the LO wage-earner fund proposal of 1981). Unfortunately, "the LO never managed to convince the rest of the social democratic movement that it was worth the electoral risks to mobilize around the issue" (57). In their excellent chapter on what they call the Swedish "Middle Way," Charles Sackrey and Geoffrey Schneider describe what reformers hoped would be the effect of wage earner funds: "The funds were intended to be used to buy up shares of companies, so workers could gradually gain a voice in all business decisions. Once labor leaders became owners, they would sit on corporate boards and directly influence corporate decision making. Laborers could then keep firms from moving overseas, or downsizing workers unnecessarily. The funds would also inject Swedish firms with new capital for investment."[7] But of course, this is not the kind of program for investment and growth that Swedish capitalists were interested in. More to the point, advocates of "the third way" in SAP did not buy it. As we saw, they preferred instead to put their faith in private savings and investment, and in market discipline and financial liberalization to promote investment and growth. It is widely acknowledged that increasing participation increases worker productivity. Unfortunately there is no telling to what extent this might have happened in Sweden because it was never tried.

The second plank in an alternative response to the crisis of Swedish social democracy would have been to strengthen government control over credit, rather than loosen it. Gregg Olsen provides a mind-numbing description of the disaster unleashed by third-way social democrats who succumbed to the croonings of neoliberal financial reformers instead of heeding the warnings of Keynes and the old guard leadership of SAP.

The Swedish credit market was rapidly deregulated throughout the 1980s. By the end of the decade, Sweden's long standing system of controls over foreign investment and exchange and the financial sector were effectively eliminated. Finance houses proliferated during this period, and money flooded into office buildings and real estate. However, the speculative boom ended in short order. The Swedish credit system foundered by the end of 1991, forcing the government to divert tax revenues to bail out several of its major banks *at a cost of 3% of GDP.*[8]

Along with retaining strong controls over domestic credit, Swedish social democrats would also have had to adopt strong measures to prevent capital flight and prevent international finance from exercising de facto veto power over Swedish social democratic policies. But unlike underdeveloped economies where it is more important to achieve a net inflow of investment, as a highly developed economy Sweden faced the less daunting task of merely preventing a net capital outflow. With sufficient controls on Swedish capital flight, Swedish social democrats could have withstood a virtual boycott by international investors. It is not unreasonable to believe that once having done so, international investors would have eventually reentered profitable Swedish markets on terms acceptable to social democratic governments.

There is no telling if Swedish social democrats could have mobilized enough popular support to sustain an alternative program along these lines. Ryner provides compelling evidence that there was strong support for such policies among workers and beneficiaries of Sweden's social programs. Quoting surveys, Ryner tells us "there is a profound divide between the increasingly neoliberal paradigm of Swedish elites and the continued welfarist 'common sense' of the Swedish people" (39). So according to Ryner support for a program to deepen "economic democracy" was lacking in the SAP leadership and its economic advisors rather than in the SAP base. Nor is there any way to know if the SAP had mobilized support behind such a program whether international conditions would have permitted Sweden to move from a left Keynesian welfare state toward deeper and more productive "economic democracy." What is now known is that the third way was a huge step back toward the economics of competition and greed, and the vast majority of the Swedish people are worse off for it.

6

Libertarian Socialism:
What Went Wrong?

Libertarian socialists[1] were by far the worst underachievers among twentieth-century anticapitalists. Even so, I count myself a libertarian socialist, and believe "we" have the most to offer those fighting to replace the economics of competition and greed with the economics of equitable cooperation in the century ahead. I realize this means I have a lot of explaining to do about why libertarian socialists did so poorly during the last century if we truly were more insightful than others. I should begin by admitting that not even I find the explanations that follow completely satisfying. No doubt many readers will find them even less so.[2] Nonetheless, I try to explain why I believe libertarian socialists have much to offer in the years ahead, if we can overcome reasons for past failures.

As we saw in the last chapter, social democrats renounced the necessity of replacing private enterprise and markets with fundamentally different economic institutions, and concentrated instead on reforms to humanize a system based on competition and greed. As a result social democrats were doomed to grapple with two dilemmas: (1) what to do when leaving the system intact makes it impossible to further promote economic justice and democracy, much less environmental sustainability; and (2) what to do when further reforms destabilize a system one has agreed to accept while the system constantly threatens to undermine hard-won gains. Social democrats struggled unsuccessfully with these dilemmas, all too often abandoning important components of economic justice and democracy and denouncing political tendencies to their left whose programs they considered politically or economically destabilizing. Libertarian socialists avoided these dilemmas only to fall into a different trap. I believe the principle failure of libertarian socialists during the twentieth century was their inability to understand the necessity and importance of reform organizing. When anticapitalist uprisings were few and far between, and libertarian socialists proved incapable of sustaining the few that did occur early in the twentieth century, their ineptness in reform campaigns doomed libertarian socialists to more than a half century of decline after their devastating defeat during the Spanish Civil War (1936–1939).

After 1939, libertarian socialism became almost invisible as a political force on the left for twenty-five years. The eclipse was so complete that most progressives today are unaware that libertarian socialism was even more than an intellectual footnote on the left, an early warning against the totalitarian dangers of communism. But this was not always the case. Early in the twentieth century, libertarian socialism was as powerful a force as social democracy and communism. The Libertarian International—founded at the Congress of Saint-Imier a few days after the split between Marxists and libertarians at the Congress of the Socialist International held in The Hague in 1872—competed successfully against social democrats and communists alike for the loyalty of anticapitalist activists, revolutionaries, workers, unions, and political parties for over fifty years. Libertarian socialists played a major role in the Russian revolutions of 1905 and 1917. Libertarian socialists played a dominant role in the Mexican Revolution of 1911. Libertarian socialists competed with some success against social democrats for influence inside the British Fabian Society, later to become the British Labor Party. Before and after World War I, libertarian socialists competed against social democrats and communists in Germany, and were more influential than both in the Low Countries, France, and Italy. In uprisings that failed to overthrow capitalism in Europe in the aftermath of World War I, revolutionaries allied with the Bolsheviks in the new Communist International were more active in Germany, but anarchists allied with the Libertarian International were more influential in rebellions that lasted longer in Italy. And twenty years after World War I was over, libertarian socialists were still strong enough to spearhead the largest and most successful revolution against capitalism to ever take place in any industrial economy, the social revolution that swept across Republican Spain in 1936 and 1937.

After their defeat in Spain, libertarian socialists vanished to all intents and purposes for a quarter century. When libertarian socialist themes reappeared in the 1960s in the new left it took on different forms and never again resembled the movement that played such an important role in the first third of the century. More recently the vacuum left by the demise of communism and decline of social democracy in the 1990s has given rise to a resurgence of interest in libertarian socialist thought on the left. But if all that comes of this "rethinking" is that tiny anarchist groups replace tiny communist sects on the far left of the political spectrum, little will be accomplished.[3] On the other hand, if large segments of the anticapitalist left can learn what libertarian socialism has to teach about why neither capitalism nor communism is the answer to our economic problems; if new libertarian socialists can remember that we are only *one* of the social movements that will be required to transform today's oppressive societies; if new libertarian socialists can hold onto our anticapitalist convictions while learning the art of reform organizing; if new libertarian socialists can relearn from our own past the importance of building imperfect experiments in equitable cooperation that reach out to those who want and need them; if new libertarian socialists can face up to the intellectual challenge of developing procedures that implement grassroots economic self-rule efficiently, we libertarian socialists just may discover we can live up to our potential, and make important contributions to building the better world that eluded us last century.

Michael Harrington was a rare social democrat capable of admiring libertarian socialism on occasion. Referring to the nineteenth century utopian socialists Henri de Saint-Simon, Charles Fourier, and Robert Owen, Harrington wrote: "Utopian socialism was not the preserve of scholars in their studies. It was a movement that gave the first serious definition of socialism as communitarian, moral, feminist, committed to the transformation of work, and profoundly democratic. *If there is to be a twenty-first century socialism worthy of the name, it will, among other things, have to go two hundred years into the past to recover the practical and theoretical ideals of the utopians.*"[4] I think Harrington is correct. I think when people struggling to achieve equitable cooperation in the future take the time to seriously review the history of the utopian socialists and the libertarian socialist movements who followed them, they will find a great deal to build from. In any case my goal here is to make a small contribution to that kind of "rethinking" about libertarian socialism. First I briefly summarize what I believe libertarian socialists "got right" about capitalism, communism, and the alternative kind of economy we need and can have. Then I consider reasons why libertarian socialists were more successful early in the twentieth century than during the past fifty years, focusing on the Russian and Spanish Revolutions. Finally, I address what I believe were the principle failures that plagued libertarian socialists, particularly in the latter half of the century.

Libertarian Socialist Successes

Twentieth-century libertarian socialists were right about capitalism. They saw it as a system based on competition and greed, disenfranchising and exploiting producers while manipulating consumers. They objected to capitalism first and foremost on moral grounds and believed in organizing people to overthrow capitalism irrespective of whether capitalism contained the seeds of its own destruction. Libertarian socialists were also right about communism, or more properly, Marxism-Leninism, and central planning. They believed that communism merely substituted rule by commissars for rule by capitalists, no matter what differences there were between centrally planned, public enterprise economies and private enterprise, market economies. Chapter 4 explained why I think the history of twentieth-century capitalism and communism has vindicated libertarian socialists in these regards. However, the linchpin of all libertarian socialist thinking is the conviction that workers and consumers are quite capable of managing themselves and their own division of labor efficiently and equitably. That, of course, is why libertarian socialists believe people can do very well, not only without capitalist employers to boss them and market competition to drive them, but also without communist overseers and bureaucrats from the central planning ministry to tell them what to produce. I believe libertarian socialists are correct in this belief. But I do not think the intellectual case for how this can be done is as obvious as twentieth-century libertarian socialists claimed, or how to do it is as simple and nonproblematic as libertarian socialists pretended. On the contrary, I think much more careful thinking needs to be done about exactly how to organize equitable cooperation so that injustice and elite rule do not reappear, and so people do not despair that their time and energies are being wasted.[5] In any case, if history is going to vindicate libertarian socialism regarding the feasibility of economic self-rule by ordinary workers and consumers it will have to be twenty-first century history because the history of the twentieth century certainly did not.

What was responsible for the organizational successes of libertarian socialists early in the twentieth century and their singular lack of success in the second half of the century? I think careful investigation by future historians will reveal that behind every success lay decades of agitation and organization building in which the message of libertarian socialism resonated strongly with large segments of the population, who, for one reason or another, were largely unaffected by rival messages about what people could and should do. I believe the notion that popular uprisings with real possibilities of consolidating self-rule occur spontaneously will be dispelled by careful historical examination. I also suspect investigation will confirm that the lack of success of libertarian socialists in the second half of the century was largely due to their inability to participate effectively in reform organizing during an era when this was the only way to reach significant numbers of people. The brief analyses below of libertarian socialist successes in building mass movements in Russia and Spain early in the century, compared to later failures, is intended only to outline a prima facie case for this hypothesis. If I say enough to stimulate others to investigate more thoroughly I will consider my meager efforts successful.

Libertarian Socialism in the Russian Revolution

The Narodniki, the Left Social Revolutionary Party, and various anarchist groups had been agitating for land reform and leading the opposition to Czarist tyranny in Russia for more than half a century before these Russian libertarian socialists were politically powerful enough to play a prominent role in the Russian Revolutions of 1905 and 1917.[6] The ideological hegemony of the Czar and the Russian landed aristocracy was in eclipse, and the best efforts of powerful officials like Prime Minister Stolypyn to promote capitalism in the Russian countryside were mostly unsuccessful, as bourgeois ideology made little headway with Russian landlords and peasants alike. Instead, Narodniki and anarchist intellectuals became the teachers of Russian peasants creating countless clandestine and legal organizations over fifty years. The rural "soviets" that later formed the spearhead for revolution and land reform in Russia were not the creations of Mensheviks or Bolsheviks—who were virtually unknown in the Russian countryside prior to 1917—but the fruit of decades of organizing by different groups of rural Russian libertarian socialists. Nor did the rural soviets spontaneously appear from the untutored consciousness of the exploited peasant "masses" without organizational precedent. Rural soviets only appeared suddenly and acted decisively because the idea of radical land reform had been nurtured for decades in most Russian villages by Narodniki, anarchists, and cadre from the Left Social Revolutionary Party, and because village committees with battle-tested leadership already existed to form the backbone of the rural soviets. The message of rural libertarian socialists resonated strongly with land-starved Russian peasants: eliminate the landed aristocracy—who do nothing but collect exorbitant rents from peasant tenants already responsible for organizing as well as carrying out production—so village assemblies can distribute land to the tillers and reclaim the traditional *mir* as common land to be managed, once again, collectively by the village. In other words, libertarian socialists sank roots for generations in the Russian countryside, organizing peasants to do what they wanted to do and came to believe they were capable of doing once they eliminated the parasites who prevented them from becoming masters of their fate.[7]

In Russian cities, anarchists enjoyed great success even though they had stiffer competition for the loyalty of workers from other anticapitalist groups. First, the fact that much of Russian industry was foreign owned reduced the appeal of foreign employers to their Russian employees in general. Second, the fact that much of the Russian proletariat was newly arrived from the countryside and maintained ties with their native villages gave anarchists an advantage over Mensheviks and Bolsheviks, since many workers were more familiar and trusting of anarchists to begin with. Finally, anarchists' preference for clandestine, revolutionary factory committees over reformist unions turned out not to work to their disadvantage in recruiting supporters in Czarist Russia. For the most part the Czarist government banned unions and factory committees alike, meting out the same punishment to activists in both kinds of organization if caught, assassination, imprisonment, or exile to Siberia. So if anything, the willingness of Mensheviks and Bolsheviks to organize through more reformist organizations like unions, where they had to reveal themselves to negotiate with employers, worked to their competitive disadvantage and to the advantage of the more secretive anarchists. Anarchist influence among Russian workers was so dominant that when Bolshevik cadre showed up in factories in order not to be ignored they had to preach the same message as the anarchist cadre who were already there: Owners be gone! The factory committee is ready to take over.[8] How it was that Russian anarchists and Left Social Revolutionaries found themselves banned, assassinated, arrested, deported to Siberia, and thoroughly politically defeated after building a significant popular following and playing crucially roles in both the February and October Revolutions, is an important question to address. But it is a different story and irrelevant to my purpose here, which is only to explore the basis for the considerable organizational successes of libertarian socialists in Russia prior to 1919.[9]

Libertarian Socialism in the Spanish Revolution

For the same reason we need not explore why Spanish anarchists found themselves on the losing end of revolutionary history after building an even larger following and playing an even greater role in the Spanish Revolution of 1936 and 1937. Our question is how and why Spanish anarchists were able to build a mass following and establish themselves as a powerful political force in the first place. Just as traditions of grass-roots economic self-management like the *mir* long preceded the arrival of anarchist agitators in Russian villages, strong traditions of economic self-management in various parts of Spain dated back to the fifteenth century or earlier. Drawing on primary research by T. F. Glick (*Irrigation and Society in Medieval Valencia*, 1970) and A. Maass and R. L. Anderson (*And the Desert Shall Rejoice: Conflict, Growth and Justice in Arid Environments*, 1986), Elnor Ostrom brought the centuries-old practice of collective self-management of irrigation systems in Valencia (Turia River), Alicante (Monnegre River), and Murcia and Orihuela (Segura River) to the attention of modern scholars studying democratic self-management of common property resources in *Governing the Commons* (1990). Reading from historical accounts of the Spanish Civil War we discover that this region of Spain, the Levant, was one of the hotbeds of rural anarchist collectives. In *The Anarchist Collectives: Workers Self-management in the Spanish Revolution 1936–1939* (1974), Sam Dolgoff quotes Gaston Leval who provided a firsthand study of the collectives:

> The regional federation of Levant, organized by our comrades of the CNT, was an agrarian federation embracing 5 provinces with a total population of 1,650,000 at the outbreak of the Civil War, with 78% of the most fertile land in Spain. It is in the Levant where, thanks to the creative spirit of our comrades, the most and best developed collectives were organized. (The number of collectives grew from 340 in 1937 to 900 at the end of 1938, and 40% of the total population of these provinces lived in collectives.) These achievements will not surprise those acquainted with the social history of the region. Since 1870 the libertarian peasants were among the most determined and persistent militants. While at certain times the movement in the cities (particularly Valencia) was altogether suppressed, the movement remained alive in the countryside. The peasants carried on. For them the Revolution was not confined only to fighting on the barricades. For them the Revolution

meant taking possession of the land and building libertarian communism. In the Levant, the collectives were almost always organized by the peasant syndicates on the grass roots level. But they remained as autonomous organizations. The syndicates constituted the necessary intermediary connection between the "individualists" and the collectives. Mixed commissions did the purchasing for the collectives as well as for the individual farmers (machines, fertilizers, insecticides, seeds, etc.). They used the same trucks and wagons. This practical demonstration of solidarity brought many formerly recalcitrant "individualists" into the collectives. This method of organization served a double function: it encompassed everything that could be usefully coordinated, and, thanks to the syndicates, succeeded in spreading the spirit of the collectives among new layers of the population rendered receptive to our influence.[10]

What Leval describes above is remarkable. The movement was popular and massive, but hardly spontaneous since it had been thoroughly prepared by anarchist agitation and organization building for sixty years. Moreover, thanks to Ostrom we know this libertarian socialist movement that was more than fifty years in the making was itself built on the social achievements of hundreds of years of democratic management of river irrigation systems in the region. The anarchist collectives were voluntary, yet comprised 40% of the population. Relations of solidarity with autonomy between collectives and more reformist, all-inclusive syndicates permitted both efficient economic coordination and friendly political relations between "individualist" and "collectivist" peasants. In other parts of his account Leval tells us that the federation of collectives sponsored large-scale improvements to irrigation systems and programs on animal husbandry and plant cross breeding. The collectives established schools in every village, reducing the rate of illiteracy from 70 percent to below 10 percent in a little over two years, and the federation of collectives ran a school for accounting and bookkeeping in Valencia, as well as the University of Moncada, which the regional federation of the Levant placed at the disposal of the Spanish National Federation of Peasants. In sum, we have quite a remarkable example of energetic and efficient economic and cultural self-management occurring despite disruptions from the Civil War and suppression from a hostile government of social democrats and communists centered in Valencia. But "remarkable" should not be confused with "spontaneous."

When we look at other regions even more famous for their revolutionary accomplishments like Aragon, Catalonia, and the city of Barcelona, we find a similar pattern: sixty years of libertarian socialist agitation and institution building on top of democratic, collectivist experiences and practices, in some cases dating back centuries.[11] In *The Spanish Labyrinth*, Gerald Brenan—by no means an anarchist sympathizer—provides the following description of Port de la Selva in Catalonia *before* the Civil War based on investigations by J. Langdon Davies and Joaquin Costa:

> The village was run by a fishermen's cooperative. They owned the nets, the boats, the curing factory, the store house, the refrigerating plant, all the shops, the transport lorries, the olive groves and the oil refinery, the café, the theater, and the assembly rooms. They had developed the *posito*, or municipal credit fund possessed by every village in Spain, into an insurance against death, accident, and loss of boats. They coined their own money. What is interesting is to see how naturally these cooperatives have fitted into the Spanish scene. For Port de la Selva is one of the old fishermen's communes of Catalonia which have existed from time immemorial. Here then we have a modern productive cooperative grafted on to an ancient communal organization and functioning perfectly.[12]

Far from presuming the masses would spontaneously organize their own self-rule, Spanish libertarian socialists devoted a great deal of time and energy to discussing exactly how the new society should be reorganized and how and by whom different kinds of decisions should be made. Dolgoff tells us "the intense preoccupation of the Spanish anarchists with libertarian reconstruction of society as been called an 'obsession' and not altogether without reason. At their Saragossa Congress in May 1936, there were lengthy resolutions on 'The Establishment of Communes, Their Function and Structure,' 'Plan of Economic Organization,' 'Coordination and Exchange,' 'Economic Conception of the Revolution,' 'Federation of Industrial and Agricultural Associations,' 'Art, Culture and Education,' and sessions on relations with nonlibertarian individuals and groupings, crime, delinquency, equality of sexes, and individual rights."[13] But what is even more telling about the topics taken up at the Saragossa Congress is that the resolutions debated, refined, and approved there had been worked on by every congress of the Spanish section of the Libertarian International beginning in 1870. In other words, policies put into effect by the agrarian collectives and socialized industries during the Spanish Revolution had been debated by tens of thousands of delegates in dozens of major congresses dating back over thirty years.

Moreover, Dolgoff tells us "the resolutions mentioned above were more than just show pieces; they were widely discussed. In a largely illiterate country, tremendous quantities of literature on social revolution were disseminated and read many times over. There were tens of thousands of books, pamphlets and tracts, vast and daring cultural and popular educational experiments (the Ferrer schools) that reached into almost every village and hamlet throughout Spain."[14] According to Brenan, "by 1918 more than fifty towns in Andalusia alone had libertarian newspapers of their own."[15] And based on statistics derived from Gaston Leval's *Espagne Libertaire*, Dolgoff reports that in Barcelona the CNT published a daily, *Solidaridad Obrera*, with a circulation of thirty thousand. *Tierra y Libertad* (a magazine) of Barcelona reached a circulation of twenty thousand; *Vida Obrera* of Giron, *El Productor* of Seville, and *Acción y Cultura* of Saragossa had large circulations. The magazines *La Revista Blanca*, *Tiempos Nuevos*, and *Estudios* reached circulations of five thousand, fifteen thousand, and seventy-five thousand, respectively. In Dolgoff's words, "by 1934 the anarchist press blanketed Spain."[16]

The revolutionary Barcelona George Orwell made famous in his eyewitness account in the first chapter of *Homage to Catalonia* (1955) clearly did not appear spontaneously. But not only was the intellectual and organizational groundwork for the Spanish Revolution painstakingly laid over six decades; not only was the anarchist-led confederation of labor, the CNT, the oldest and largest organization of workers in Spain with a million and a half members by 1934; the popular impression that revolutionary Spain was inefficient and undisciplined, and that anarchists were sectarian, divisive, and bear much of the responsibility for the defeat of the Spanish Republic by Franco's fascist-backed military, is almost entirely unsubstantiated. Noam Chomsky, citing sources friendly and unfriendly to anarchists alike in "Objectivity and Liberal Scholarship," demonstrates that industrial and agricultural production and deliveries were strongest in anarchist areas, and that military courage and discipline of anarchist troops was unparalleled. In case after case Chomsky refutes accusations made at the time by their communist and social democratic rivals that it was anarchists who engaged in sectarian politics, showing that available evidence indicates that exactly the opposite occurred. Chomsky also demonstrates in case after case that the presumption of liberal scholars writing after the fact that the libertarian revolution that swept over much of Spain was dysfunctional was almost entirely lacking in credible evidence.

The Demise of Libertarian Socialism

Libertarian socialism never recovered from its defeat in Spain. After World War II, social democrats and communists dominated left politics in Western and Third World societies alike for over forty years. Lacking a comprehensive history of libertarian socialism we are at a disadvantage in trying to learn what contributed to its demise in the middle third of the century. No doubt many factors contributed, not the least of which was that both social democrats and communists achieved state power in various countries allowing them to provide ideological, material, political, diplomatic, and even military aid for allied parties elsewhere, while no libertarian socialist group enjoyed help from any outside source. But what strikes me is that ingredients crucial to libertarian socialist successes early in the century were absent later in the century: (1) Nowhere did they exercise significant influence or enjoy a substantial following in the labor movement, as unions and their federations became dominated by social democrats, communists, or business unionists. (2) Their message that reforms were doomed and worker takeovers were the only answer fell on deaf ears. In the "golden age of capitalism" reformist unions were winning significant wage increases, and takeovers by individual groups of workers from employers fully backed by the power of the state seemed particularly unrealistic and suicidal. (3) As Taylorism deskilled ordinary workers and concentrated productive knowledge in the hands of supervisory staff, worker self-management became less appealing to industrial workers than to their predecessors with living memories of craft and guild-controlled production, and instead had only esoteric appeal to small groups of intellectuals and students. (4) Only where Third World national liberation movements came to power did realistic possibilities of organizing noncapitalist economies present themselves, but this invariably occurred where communist influence and the Soviet model held sway. Always unwilling to engage in electoral politics, fixated on organizing workers "at the point of production" but unable to make any headway in convincing them to reject capitalism in toto, libertarian socialists were left with no connections to any significant segment of the body politic. It was not until the rise of the new left in the late 1960s that libertarian socialists were able to do more than provide a left critique of totalitarian socialism—that was completely drowned out by the conservative critique of communism backed by the full force of the Western intellectual establishment—and a radical critique of capitalism—that was at odds with more elaborate Marxist treatments that enjoyed hegemony in anticapitalist circles.

The New Left

The rise of the new left in the 1960s led to a revival of libertarian socialist themes but not libertarian socialism itself. New left activists were largely unaware of their own parentage, which had become all but invisible over the previous thirty years. Many new left leaders reinvented libertarian socialist wheels without being aware of their intellectual antecedents. Grassroots democracy, control over one's community and work life, solidarity combined with autonomy, and rejection of materialism became powerful new left themes whose allure may even have been increased by the vagueness and lack of intellectual rigor with which they were expressed.

　　The popularity of the new left—of which I am a proud product—derived from the power of themes that had long been libertarian socialist staples in modern capitalist societies where the gap between the hollow rhetoric of justice and democracy for all and the hard reality of discrimination and oligarchic rule was becoming ever more apparent. The popularity of the new left also derived from the intellectual and moral bankruptcy of both social democratic and communist parties in Western democracies. Blinded by fear of communism, and unwilling to risk their fragile status in the political mainstream of Western societies, social democrats were unreliable allies against imperialism and more likely to exaggerate the accomplishments of Western capitalism than to criticize its systematic failings. Communists in Western societies, on the other hand, were doomed to political oblivion by their betrayal of democracy, which manifested itself in the excuses they offered for totalitarian regimes abroad and in their own undemocratic practices. But nowhere did the new left succeed in establishing a coherent intellectual analysis and program. Nowhere did the new left create organizational vehicles to participate successfully in electoral politics. Nowhere did the new left succeed in maintaining the libertarian, antimaterialist cultural revolution that accompanied its emergence in the 1960s. And nowhere did the new left establish a solid and lasting base in any significant segment of the body politic. Instead, most of the relatively privileged participants in the new left drifted back into their original life trajectories in mainstream society, while a minority went on to pursue their radicalism in the mainstream labor movement or in one of the new social movements that grew in the 1970s and 1980s, the feminist and gay liberation movements, the environmental movement, and solidarity movements associated with particular Third World liberation struggles.

New Social Movements

While new social movements have each made invaluable contributions, they accelerated the trend begun in the new left away from developing a comprehensive libertarian socialist theory and practice. Progressive activism became more compartmentalized, more practical, and more reform oriented. Theoretical discussion receded further into discussions of "core values" that were often not clearly spelled out, allowing people to conveniently assume they agreed even when phrases like economic justice, economic democracy, and sustainable development meant quite different things to different interpreters. Activists in the 1970s and 1980s with libertarian socialist values did *not* further develop their theoretical critique of capitalism. Instead, confusion about why capitalism was unacceptable and what was wrong with both mainstream and Marxist analyses of capitalism increased. They did *not* deepen their understanding of how the economics of equitable cooperation guided by democratic planning rather than markets or central planning could operate. Instead their answers to the question: "What do you want instead of capitalism?" became even more self-contradictory and confused. Finally, most of them did *not* learn how to throw themselves into reform campaigns without abandoning their anticapitalism and commitment to economic self-rule. Instead many new leftists leapfrogged right over social democrats they once regarded as stodgy and overly cautious, to flaunt the flag of pragmatism they had scorned in their "idealistic youth." Very few retained any commitment to the libertarian socialist "big picture." Most who moved on to work in the labor movement, the women's movement, the gay rights movement, the environmental movement, or in Third World solidarity movements renounced "big picture politics" altogether, and focused instead on writing grants and press releases, fundraising from foundations and through bulk mail solicitations, lobbying local, state, and national officials, running shelters and petition campaigns, contract negotiation, and learning to use the Internet to publicize campaigns and create alternative media outlets. Whatever knowledge was required by a particular campaign, whatever skills were needed by the particular organization and social movement one worked in, became the almost exclusive focus of intellectual inquiry. Only a very few former new leftists, usually hidden away along with old left die-hards in left caucuses of organizations in the social movements, continued to adhere to libertarian socialist politics. For the most part the revival of interest in anarchism and libertarian socialism in general that has taken place in the past half dozen years has come from a new generation of young activists, as unfamiliar with the new left as they are with the old left, looking for democratic, fair, and sustainable alternatives to neolib-eral, global capitalism.

New social movement activism has more to its credit than reform victo-ries and successful efforts to minimize rollbacks, which are important enough. For one, by brute force, that is, by building large, lasting move-ments on a par with the labor movement, as much as through intellec-tual discourse, they have shattered the hold of economistic theories and bankrupt political strategies based on them that handicapped progressive activists for most of the twentieth century. The women's and gay rights movements have revolutionized thinking about gender relations and created a mind set that makes explanations that insist on tracing the roots of gender oppression to economic dynamics unacceptable to a majority of women and gay activists. Failure to treat gender oppression and patri-archy as central to the project of human liberation will never again be tolerated by a large constituency necessary for its achievement. Similarly, the antiracist movement will no longer accept treating racism as nothing more than a ruling-class trick to divide the working class, and will never again limit its goals to demanding *only* minimal civil rights. The various ways that whole communities who were once conquered or enslaved continue to be oppressed by other communities will have to be dealt with as a central part of social reconstruction rather than as secondary or deriv-ative issues. Nor will the anti-imperialist movement any longer put up with explanations in purely economic terms that ignore the important roles that national chauvinism, jingoism, racism, sexism, authoritari-anism, and militarism all play in imperial politics. The environmental movement has wisely conditioned its supporters to always question whether any theoretical framework fully incorporates all the implications of human dependence on the biosphere, and made sure they will never take claims on face value that any economic system can be trusted to preserve and restore the natural environment. The women's, gay, civil rights, peace, and environmental movements are forces to be reckoned with and are here to stay. While the labor movement rightly insists that class exploitation is very much still with us and on the rise, never again will labor or leftist leaders be able to successfully insist that the class struggle must *always* take precedence over other struggles, or that classes are the only important agents of progressive social change.

The new social movements have created a promising new starting point for social change activism in the twenty-first century. Oppressed communities and genders as well as classes are now recognized as important agents of historical change. Transformations of oppressive community and gender relations as well as economic relations are now accepted as high-priority goals. And the need for dramatic rethinking about the very meaning of human progress in light of environmental constraints is now taken for granted by the majority of progressive-minded people. Since much of traditional libertarian socialist theory was plagued by economism and lacking in environmental awareness, the theoretical analyses by those active in new social movements provide a welcome theoretical corrective. Since libertarian socialist practice focused almost exclusively on class issues, the existence of multiple social movements provides a corrective social environment as well.

I have suggested that in large part because of their hostility to reformist organizations libertarian socialists in the middle of the twentieth century became isolated from large movements fighting against their oppressors. Moreover, their insistence that little could be accomplished until capitalism was overthrown despite the fact that sensible people came to realize that capitalism was going to be with us for quite some time, only served to keep them isolated. New social movements have spread awareness that there is always much to be accomplished in different spheres of social life, and that no single revolutionary break is going to be the be-all and end-all for those working for social reconstruction. Hopefully the power of the new social movements will help libertarian socialists to see this as well, and having learned that the forces shaping history are different in important ways from what they long believed, libertarian socialists will adjust their strategy and practice accordingly. If not, I think libertarian socialists will ignore the lessons new social movements teach at their own peril.

Libertarian Socialists and Capitalist Reform

I suspect that twentieth-century libertarian socialists were always too "purist" and reluctant to enter into reform campaigns. I suspect they were always too quick to assume that reformist unions and cooperatives were largely ineffectual. They were too quick to conclude electoral politics was pointless because they believed capitalists would never tolerate interference in their control over government policy. They tended to believe that lobbying the government for policy reforms favorable to workers was useless since the state was the executive committee of the capitalist class. And they feared that failing to overthrow capitalism, you only mislead workers into thinking things can get better. But one of the great lessons of the twentieth century is that considerable room for maneuver exists within capitalism, and that reforms can make a great deal of difference in how the majority fares. So it turns out that twentieth-century libertarian socialists greatly underestimated the possibility of improvement through reform. Moreover, I suspect that libertarian socialists who did participate in reform campaigns often did so less than wholeheartedly because they were convinced that little could be accomplished. Armed with a ready-made theoretical explanation for the failure of reforms, libertarian socialists were programmed to give up too easily and I suspect they often abandoned campaigns prematurely. I suspect their negative attitude about reform work also put them at a competitive disadvantage in leadership battles within reform organizations *vis á vis* their social democratic rivals who arrived with unshakable faith that meaningful reforms were possible and a sneaking suspicion that anything beyond reform was a pipe dream.

While always a handicap, I believe early in the century libertarian socialists got away with their misguided policy on reforms within capitalism for peculiar historical reasons. I suspect they were able to build large mass organizations of their own because sometimes there were no alternative reform organizations for people to choose from. When this happened, libertarian socialists could become the dominant ideological force within large organizations, as we saw in both prerevolutionary Russia and Spain. Libertarian socialists did not consider these to be reformist organizations because they were led by dedicated revolutionaries, namely themselves, and because they were staunchly anticapitalist, since their memberships routinely approved anticapitalist resolutions introduced by the libertarian socialist leadership. But I believe these organizations attracted large numbers of members because they met crucial needs within capitalism no other organizations addressed. In this respect the organizations *were* reform organizations, they were just hard to recognize as such because they routinely rubber-stamped revolutionary proclamations. In other words, my hypothesis is this: libertarian socialists early in the century owed their successes in large part to their wholehearted participation in reform campaigns and organizations. They were able to trick themselves into doing effective reform work because these campaigns and organizations took on revolutionary trappings that were largely irrelevant to the majority of participants they attracted, but which allowed libertarian socialists to participate without violating their ideological pledge to eschew the politics of reform. As a result, early in the century libertarian socialists were often able to reach large numbers of people and participate in enduring, mass organizations despite their official policy of boycotting organizations dedicated solely to achieving reforms within capitalism. But by midcentury a plethora of reform organizations and campaigns had filled this vacuum, at least in most advanced democratic capitalist economies, and that is where large numbers of people struggling to improve their lives through collective action have been found ever since. Consequently, since World War II libertarian socialists' long-time policy of turning up their noses at reform work has doomed them to isolation.

Beside the mistaken belief that meaningful reforms within capitalism were impossible, other factors influenced libertarian socialists to shy away from reform organizing. Many fell victim to false theories of capitalist crisis. If capitalist development was inevitably killing the goose that laid the golden eggs by substituting capital—dead labor—for living labor, when profits in the long run come only from exploiting living labor, then capitalism could be relied on to dig its own grave. If by keeping wages depressed capitalists witlessly created crises of over production leading to ever more severe depressions, what was the point in fighting for higher wages or lobbying governments to stimulate demand through expansionary fiscal and monetary policies? Believing in misguided theories of capitalist crisis such as these led some libertarian socialists to conclude it was better to concentrate on criticizing the immorality of profit income altogether and agitate for an uprising to replace capitalism with a libertarian socialist economy when the next crisis arrived. But faith in false theories of capitalist crisis proved debilitating for two reasons. Most obviously, strategy premised on crises that do not occur is like waiting for Godot, and unlikely to prove effective. Second, people don't appreciate those who give them up for dead and fail to extend a helping hand. If my misery can be even slightly alleviated, I will judge those around me according to how hard and effectively they work to do so. The idea that bystanders are waiting for me to be further abused, even hoping I might be if this stimulates me to revolt, is hardly ingratiating.

I think libertarian socialists were also loath to dirty their hands in reform campaigns and participate in institutions like unions and legislatures because they considered them to be breeding grounds where anticapitalists eventually betray the cause. In this regard they were not wrong. The anticapitalist movement has long suffered from a steady hemorrhage of former members who are worn down and corrupted by the roles they play in various reform institutions and who eventually sell out. But the question is how libertarian socialists should respond to this very real danger. Unfortunately they usually decided to avoid becoming corrupted by not participating in reform campaigns and organizations. Why risk being corrupted like the social democrats by becoming union officials or elected politicians? Better to stay intellectually pure and committed to the libertarian socialist vision of a wholly new economy while waiting for capitalism to crumble. Libertarian socialists' main task would then become to prevent authoritarian socialist groups from seizing and fortifying the state to fill the vacuum created by the collapse of capitalism and capitalist class rule. Many libertarian socialists convinced themselves that if the danger of usurpation by a self-appointed vanguard could be avoided, with minimal encouragement workers and citizens would quickly learn how to manage their own economic and political affairs free, at last, from authoritarian power of all kinds. But of course, none of this proved to be true.

The Myth of Nonreformist Reforms

What many libertarian socialists failed to realize was that any transition to a democratic and equitable economy has no choice but to pass through reform campaigns, organizations, and institutions however tainted and corrupting they may be. The new left tried to exorcise the dilemma that reform work is necessary but corrupting with the concept of *nonreformist reforms*. According to this theory social democrats erred in embracing reformist reforms while early libertarian socialists erred in rejecting reforms altogether. According to new left theorists the solution was for activists to work on nonreformist reforms, that is, reforms that improved people's lives while undermining the material, social, or ideological underpinnings of the capitalist system. There is nothing wrong with the notion of winning reforms while undermining capitalism. As a matter of fact, that is a concise description of pecisely what we should be about! What was misleading was the notion that there are particular reforms that are like silver bullets and accomplish this because of something special about the nature of those reforms themselves.

There is no such thing as a nonreformist reform. Social democrats and libertarian socialists did not err because they somehow failed to find and campaign for this miraculous kind of reform. Nor would new leftists prove successful where others had failed because new leftists found a special kind of reform different from those social democrats pursued and libertarian socialists rejected. Some reforms improve peoples lives more, and some less. Some reforms are easier to win, and some are harder to win. Some reforms are easier to defend, and some are less so. And of course, different reforms benefit different groups of people. Those are ways reforms, themselves, differ. On the other hand, there are also crucial differences in how reforms are fought for. Reformers preaching the virtues of capitalism can fight for reforms. Or reforms can be fought for by anti-capitalists pointing out that only by replacing capitalism will it be possible to fully achieve what reformers want. Reforms can be fought for while leaving institutions of repression intact. Or a reform struggle can at least weaken repressive institutions, if not destroy them. Reforms can be fought for by hierarchical organizations that reinforce authoritarian, racist, and sexist dynamics and thereby weaken the overall movement for progressive change. Or reforms can be fought for by democratic organizations that uproot counterproductive patterns of behavior and empower people to become masters and mistresses of their fates. Reforms can be fought for in ways that leave no new organizations or institutions in their aftermath. Or reforms can be fought for in ways that create new organizations and institutions that fortify progressive forces in the next battle. Reforms can be fought for through alliances that obstruct possibilities for further gains. Or the alliances forged to win a reform can establish the basis for winning more reforms. Reforms can be fought for in ways that provide tempting possibilities for participants, and particularly leaders, to take unfair personal advantage of *group* success. Or they can be fought for in ways that minimize the likelihood of corrupting influences. Finally, reform organizing can be the entire program of organizations and movements. Or, recognizing that reform organizing within capitalism is prone to weaken the personal and political resolve of participants to pursue a full system of equitable cooperation, reform work can be combined with other kinds of activities, programs, and institutions that rejuvenate the battle weary and prevent burnout and sellout.

Any reform can be fought for in ways that diminish the chances of further gains and limit progressive change in other areas, or fought for in ways that make further progress more likely and facilitate other progressive changes as well. But if reforms are successful they will make capitalism less harmful to some extent. There is no way around this, and even if there were such a thing as a nonreformist reform, it would not change this fact. However, the fact that every reform success makes capitalism less harmful does not mean successful reforms necessarily prolong the life of capitalism, although it might, and this is something anticapitalists must simply learn to accept. But if winning a reform further empowers the reformers, and whets their appetite for more democracy, more economic justice, and more environmental protection than capitalism can provide, it can hasten the fall of capitalism.

In any case, it turns out we are a more cautious and social species than twentieth-century libertarian socialists realized. And it turns out that capitalism is far more resilient than libertarian socialists expected. More than a half century of libertarian socialist failures belie the myth that it is possible for social revolutionaries committed to democracy to eschew reform work without becoming socially isolated. Avoidance of participation in reform work is simply not a viable option and only guarantees defeat for any who opt out. Moreover, no miraculous nonreformist reform is going to come riding to our rescue. Though most twentieth-century libertarian socialists failed to realize it, their only hope was to throw themselves wholeheartedly into reform struggles while searching for ways to minimize the corrupting pressures that inevitably are brought to bear on their members as a result. While admittedly a caricature, the image of libertarian socialists in the latter part of the last century shunning "tainted" reform organizations and campaigns to knock only on working-class strangers' doors seeking to enlist them directly into the anticapitalist revolution gives an idea of how I think they went wrong on this crucial issue.

The Myth of Spontaneous Revolt

After World War II, some libertarian socialists lapsed into a naïve belief in spontaneous anticapitalist revolts, and an unwarranted faith that once having risen, workers would quickly leapfrog to smoothly functioning systems of equitable cooperation. If I am correct, this was very much at odds with their own historical experience earlier in the century where decades of successful agitating and organizing on a mass scale invariably proved necessary. Nonetheless, isolated libertarian socialists in midcentury sometimes convinced themselves that exemplary actions on their part could lead the masses to reject the cautionary advice of corrupt officials in reformist organizations, and spark a spontaneous worker uprising to replace capitalism with libertarian socialism. However, there is a world of difference between believing that capitalism is dysfunctional and that ordinary people can figure this out, and believing people will spontaneously decide they want to replace capitalism stimulated by agitation and exemplary action alone. There is also a world of difference between believing a majoritarian movement can overthrow capitalism, and believing such a movement will suddenly arise like a phoenix without the aid of a myriad of imperfect social institutions through which millions of people have struggled for decade after decade to better their lives. And there is a world of difference between believing that workers and consumers can coordinate their economic endeavors equitably and efficiently, and believing participation in the economics of competition and greed under capitalism will prepare them to do so. Finally, it is one thing to think workers and consumers can engage in participatory planning and self-management, and quite another to believe they can do so without prior deliberation over appropriate procedures, and without a great deal of practical experience in economic self-governance. Libertarian socialists in the latter part of the twentieth century all too often confused these differences.

Finally, libertarian socialists were misled by the myth that the grinding of the gears of capitalism would generate revolutionary consciousness in the working class. They underestimated the extent to which capitalism instead teaches people to accept the desirability and inevitability of the economics of competition and greed. Unfortunately capitalism does not nurture the seeds of its own replacement in the way twentieth-century libertarian socialists hoped it would. Instead capitalism fosters commercial values, teaches people they are incapable of behaving except out of greed or fear, and teaches that only market competition can harness human egotism to socially useful purposes. Capitalism teaches people to accommodate and make their peace with capitalism because it is inevitable. In the later part of the twentieth century, libertarian socialists ignored this feature of capitalism to their detriment. Unlike their predecessors early in the century, they underestimated the importance of creating practical examples of equitable cooperation no matter how imperfect and impermanent. They forgot it was necessary to create institutions for workers that served as "schools" to teach the habits of equitable cooperation, and failed to realize the longer capitalism endures the more important this task becomes. They did not understand that besides dispelling myths about capitalism's supposed virtues and criticizing its commercial values, they had to create opportunities for people to learn and practice efficient, democratic, and cooperative behavior patterns in accord with human values, precisely because this kind of behavior and these values are not rewarded by market competition. As precapitalist cultures of cooperation like the Russian *mir* and Spanish common property irrigation systems receded in the collective memory, new cultures of cooperation swimming against the capitalist tide became more, not less important, to create and nurture. Ways to address this component of a successful strategy to advance the cause of equitable cooperation in the twenty-first century are addressed in chapter 13.

Postscript:
In Defense of Libertarian Socialism

Noam Chomsky

I had a few comments on your interesting observations on libertarian socialism.

In the main, I agree, but I think there is one questionable part. You stress the fact that in midcentury, libertarian socialists basically disappeared from the scene, with some revival (but without much historical memory) in the new left. You attribute this failure to unwillingness to recognize the need for reformist measures as a step toward the more radical changes they looked forward to, to the "naïve beliefs," and so forth, of libertarian socialists—who you don't name, but I think for a good reason.

It seems to me that there are a number of problems with this. First, as you point out, the earlier successes were not based particularly on "reform organizing," but were more a matter of "creating the facts of the future within the present society," in accord with the Bakuninist (etc.) program. And as you point out, it was quite successful, until destroyed by violence: by the Bolsheviks from 1917 when they immediately began wiping out factory councils, Soviets, the Constituent Assembly (because of social revolutionary influence), Ukrainian peasant organizations, and in fact every popular and socialist element in the pre-Bolshevik society. And in Spain it was remarkably successful—though for a brief period—before it was destroyed by violence, by a coalition of Stalinists, liberal democracies, and fascists. From that point on there was no option of undertaking reformist programs within the dictatorships, so the criticism you raise doesn't apply there. In Germany, most libertarian elements were destroyed by 1918 or 1919, by violence again, led by Social Democrats this time.

What about the West? By the end of World War II, there was a powerful spirit of radical democracy throughout much of the world, including the United States, and a desire to overturn the traditional order and to institute the basic elements of a much more free and just society. Sometimes these efforts were Communist-led, sometimes not—and the notion "Communist" is pretty complex as well. Sometimes there were concrete achievements, as in northern Italy, where the partisans basically drove out the Nazis and established the beginnings of what could have become a populist/cooperative socioeconomic structure, with strong worker influence that was even leading to worker ownership and self-management (the ideas were in the air, and some early steps were taken). This terrified U.S. liberals and the British (including the Labor Party), which pretty much conquered northern Italy from its own people, dismantled the hated popular organizations rather in Leninist style, and reinstituted something like the traditional order (as they had already done in the south from 1943). The reasons were explicit: the new structures were threatening the prerogatives of ownership and management (and potentially foreign investment). This continued: the first memo of the newly founded NSC called for national mobilization and support for paramilitary activities to overthrow the Italian government if the 1948 election was won by the left (Communist, but actually rather complex—the Cold War was hardly an issue). The United States' subversion of Italian democracy to prevent left/worker influence went on at least into the 1970s, when the internal record runs dry. It was one of the most important CIA enterprises in those years. There were similar developments elsewhere in Europe, varying with circumstances, but always with the goal of subverting democracy if it threatened to allow anything very different from the traditional order. Same in Japan, where the 1947 "reverse course" instituted by Washington liberals eliminated worker self-management, independent unions, and other intolerable forms of democracy, and pretty much reinstituted the traditional society, which largely remains intact now. All very similar to Latin America and other domains. For more libertarian elements, there were few options, because they were mostly destroyed.

Even where radical democratic forces were suppressed, there were consequences. The impact found expression in the Western industrial democracies in the social democratic policies of "welfare states," and was also a core factor in the establishment of the Bretton Woods system in the international economy. But libertarian socialist elements barely survived the postwar repression. Maybe they would have been naïve if they'd existed, but they hardly did.

I think that is why you cannot mention specifics (names, organizations) when you talk about the libertarian socialist failures in midcentury. Little remained. Options were very limited.

I think your criticism is correct about certain elements of what remained, but by no means all. And that continues to the present. You can find examples in forums on Znet, for example. Thus a couple of years ago I had an interview with David Barsamian called something like "expanding the floor of the cage," a metaphor borrowed from very successful efforts of Brazilian rural workers to form unions in the face of really brutal repression. I argued in the interview that they were right: they had long-term radical objectives, which they didn't hide, and knew they were in a cage, but wanted to expand its floor. And they also wanted to preserve "the cage" (that is, the state) because they knew that awful as it was, they could potentially have some influence over it (as was correct), and the cage was protecting them from far more dangerous predators right outside: concentrated Brazilian capital, foreign investors, the IMF, and so on.

These comments were partially in response to young anarchists who condemn everything if it does not overthrow the state. They elicited a torrent of protest, and arguments over whether anarchists believe they will be able to appeal to and organize working people by calling for dismantling such protections for workers as exist in the workplace (OSHA, etc.) and whatever structure there is of workers' rights, health care, pensions, and so forth. So yes, the issue you point to is very much alive, and splits sectors that call themselves "anarchist" (a very broad brush, as always).

Furthermore, this extends well beyond libertarian socialism. There is often, I think, lack of sufficient willingness to assess the consequences of actions that are undertaken, including the effect they will have on the population one is hoping to reach with them. I won't go on with other examples, but we wouldn't have much difficulty in identifying them, across a considerable spectrum. And there is of course often lively debate about these matters among people who basically agree on goals, and often work closely together with mutual support and cooperation, but disagree on the assessment of likely consequences, or even—a bit surprisingly to me—on the importance of taking careful account of likely consequences as long as one is following one's conscience.

Another observation that I think is relevant is that anarchism does not leave an "intellectual tradition" in the manner that Marxism-Leninism does. For a good reason. Serious libertarian socialism leaves no place for bosses, including the radical intelligentsia, who are, naturally, far more attracted by Marxism-Leninism, which provides them with a rationale to "beat the people with the people's stick" (borrowing from Bakunin again). Therefore, if they join, it is as participants, not rulers. And the result is that the intellectual legacy is thin and where it exists virtually suppressed. It gives the wrong message, from the point of view of the custodians of history and doctrine.

On the history, it might not be a bad idea to bring up the developments in the workers movements, including the United States from the mid-

1850s, which were very interesting. Some are reviewed in Norman Ware's book on the Lowell-Lawrence labor press, other examples can be found in the Knights of Labor, which had some kind of intellectual resonance, even among such central figures of U.S. intellectual life as John Dewey, who sometimes called for replacing "industrial feudalism" by "industrial democracy" (basically, worker self-management) if democracy is to exist in any substantive form.

Basically, I agree with your critique, but I think it leaves out a number of factors.

Noam
(Personal Communication, 2004)

Part III

What Do We Want?

7

Postcapitalist Visions

As the twenty-first century begins some progressive economists have given up on the search for a desirable alternative to capitalism. They say those who react to the failures of capitalism by becoming anticapitalist only delude themselves into thinking there is a better kind of economy. For these chastened progressives the only kind of "visionary" economic thinking that is worthwhile is thinking of ways to make capitalism more equitable and humane. They accuse anticapitalists of exaggeration, and preach the politics of damage control. Others continue to believe a better alternative to capitalism exists, but argue it is not important to spend time now thinking about what that alternative is and how it could work. According to these anticapitalists we should organize against the excesses of capitalism and forthrightly denounce capitalism as the root source of most of the problems. But when asked what kind of economy anticapitalists want, they suggest we answer in deliberately vague and general terms: "We want a just and democratic economy," or, "we want an economy that is not wasteful and destructive of the environment." There are understandable reasons to be concerned about the pitfalls of visionary thinking. But to reject discussion and debate over how we can better organize our economic activities to achieve economic justice, economic democracy, and sustainability has never been more self-defeating than it is today.

The Importance of Economic Vision

Some hesitate to spell out how we think the economy should be run for fear of putting people off. But saying we are anticapitalist risks alienating people we work with in reform campaigns and movements since most of them assume the capitalist system is sound, only its application is flawed. To run the risk of putting these people off by saying we reject the capitalist system itself without trying to explain in concrete terms what we are for instead makes little sense. Others eschew debates about economic vision for fear it will lead to sectarianism that divides us unnecessarily and distracts us from focusing on more urgent tasks. Given the history of sectarianism on the left there is every reason to fear this dynamic. But we must guard against sectarianism on many issues, and the advice to table economic vision would only be sensible if it were true that deliberations on this issue are unnecessary. Others claim that describing how to make better economic decisions is totalitarian because it robs those who will live in postcapitalist economies of their democratic right to manage their economy as they see fit when the time comes. This argument is nonsense. Since when did discussing difficult and momentous issues in advance impede deliberative democracy rather than advance it? Only if those debating such matters attempt to impose their formulas on future generations would this be a problem. And I know of none who discuss *democratic* postcapitalist possibilities who have any such pretensions.

Of course there is a time and place for everything. There are venues where pontificating on the inherent evils of the capitalist system is out of place and counterproductive. Similarly there are venues where discussing arrangements for how those in worker councils could manage themselves, or how different groups of workers and consumers might coordinate their interrelated activities fairly and efficiently is out of place. The question is not whether every commentary, every speech, every conference document, every article, or every book must explain how a problem today is linked to capitalism, or how it could be solved in an alternative economy. The question is whether theorizing about economic vision, and testing our convictions in the flesh where possible, play an important role in the movement to replace the economics of competition and greed with the economics of equitable cooperation.

The simplest argument for the value of visionary thinking lies in the question: How can we know what steps to take unless we know where we want to go? For those of us who believe we are attempting to build a bridge from the economics of competition and greed to the economics of equitable cooperation we must have some idea where we want the bridge to end as well as where it must begin. But the strongest reason for not avoiding the issue of what we would do when capitalism falters is our track record of failure. This is not the first time people have been entreated to jettison capitalism for a better alternative. In chapter 4, I argued that communist economies were not failures for the reasons widely believed, but they were colossal failures nonetheless. And they were certainly *not* the desirable alternative to capitalism that was promised. So people have every reason to be skeptical of those who claim there is a desirable alternative to capitalism. People have every right to demand more than platitudes and generalities. Reasonable people, not only doubting Thomases, want to know how our alternative to capitalism would differ from the last one, and how it would work in concrete terms. Our anticapitalist predecessors misled literally billions of people, with terrible consequences. We should not deceive ourselves that many today are willing to accept our assurances on faith that we have it right this time. We avoid contentious issues about the alternative to capitalism only at our own peril. It may be that God has given twenty-first century capitalism the rainbow sign, but salvation from doomsday will be no faith-based initiative. If we cannot show an overwhelming majority of the victims of capitalism how a better system can work, if we cannot provide convincing answers to hard questions about why our procedures will not break down, or get hijacked by new elites, the economics of equitable cooperation will remain little more than a prayer on the lips of the victims of competition and greed.

So while we fight for reforms within capitalism we must also explain what is wrong with capitalism. And when we win concessions we must also explain why victories are in constant danger of being rolled back as long as the basic institutions of capitalism are left in place. Finally, if we believe that environmental preservation, economic justice, and economic democracy can be achieved without sacrificing efficiency we must explain concretely how a different way of organizing our economic activities can achieve these lofty goals. Rosy rhetoric and vague generalities no longer suffice, if they ever did.

Alternatives to Capitalism

What have we learned about how to manage our economic affairs from our disappointing experiences in the twentieth century? What should we do if we had the opportunity to start again? We could hold a lottery, or perhaps have a brawl, to decide who owns what productive resources. The unfortunate losers would have to hire themselves out to work for the more fortunate winners, and the goods the losers produced could then be "freely" exchanged by their owners, the people who didn't produce them. Of course, this is the *capitalist* "solution" to the economic problem criticized in chapter 4, which has been spreading its sway for over three centuries.

Alternatively, we could make the best educated, or perhaps most ruthless among us, responsible for planning how to use society's scarce productive resources and for telling the rest of us what to do. But that was tried with unsatisfactory results. After a troubled half century, *command planning* is in the dustbins of history where it belongs. So whether public enterprise, centrally planned economies yielded more or less alienation, apathy, inefficiency, and environmental destruction than their capitalist rivals during their half century of nonpeaceful coexistence is, practically speaking, a moot point. In any case, we know authoritarian planning does not yield economic democracy, equity, and efficiency. So, what options remain for those of us who are convinced, for all the reasons explained in chapter 4, that neither capitalism nor communism is the answer to our economic problems?

One alternative is to declare all physical means of production and natural resources part of the public domain, and have everyone work for public enterprises that would then exchange the goods they produced with each other and with consumers in more or less free markets. The state could select, train, appoint, monitor, reward, and punish managers of these publicly owned enterprises. Or, alternatively, employees could hire and reward their own managers. New investment in the enterprises could be self-financed out of their own revenues. Or new investment could be financed out of a state budget. Many anticapitalist economists now support one or another variant of public enterprise, market economies, more commonly known as *market socialism.*

Others propose to avoid the problems of markets and authoritarian planning by breaking large economies down into autonomous communities. Largely economically self-sufficient communities, consistent with the boundaries of natural ecosystems, would manage their own economies democratically. Small is beautiful. Communication and democracy works face-to-face, even though it breaks down in larger groups where people cannot know one another. A variety of new proposals for *community-based economics* have appeared since the demise of communism, and some communitarian anarchist visions from the past have been revived as well.

Finally, some of us who reject capitalism, authoritarian planning, and market socialism, but who believe community-based economics fails to address crucial economic issues and arbitrarily forswears the benefits of a division of labor, ask ourselves: Why can't workers in different enterprises and industries, and consumers in different neighborhoods and regions of the country, coordinate their joint endeavors *themselves*? Why can't councils of consumers and workers propose what they would like to do, and revise their own proposals as they discover more about the impact of their decisions on others in a national planning process? What is impossible about the "associated producers"—and consumers—planning their related activities themselves? Those who believe there is no reason we cannot organize our economic affairs in this way champion a vision of *democratic*, or *participatory planning*.

In the aftermath of the collapse of communism, debate about alternatives to capitalism has divided into three camps: proponents of market socialism, supporters of community-based economics, and proponents of national democratic planning. Since few in any of these camps believe there is even a substantial minority in any of the advanced economies ready to replace capitalism at this time, and since everyone in all three groups is thoroughly committed to democracy, all understand that the struggle to eventually replace capitalism must necessarily take the form of fighting for reforms within capitalism for the foreseeable future. Partisans in all camps should also understand that their differences about the future do not mean they cannot agree for the most part on economic policies and reforms we should pursue right now. Advocates of market socialism, community-based economics, and democratic planning should all be able to agree on reforms to advance the cause of equitable cooperation discussed in chapter 11.[1] So while I urge people to actively pursue the debate over the best alternative to capitalism openly, forthrightly, and without pulling punches, this does not mean I believe we cannot agree on most parts of an economic program for the present.

In this chapter, I describe market socialism, explain what it could accomplish, and explain what problems I believe it would inevitably fail to address. Then I explain why, however appealing they may be, proposals for community-based economics leave crucial questions unanswered. In the next chapter, I present the model of democratic planning I favor called "participatory economics," and explain why I believe a participatory economy can achieve economic justice and democracy without sacrificing efficiency, while promoting solidarity and variety. Important questions about participatory economics and the environment, and participatory economics and the global economy are also addressed for the first time in chapter 8. Major concerns critics have raised about the feasibility and desirability of participatory economics are carefully considered in chapter 9.

Market Socialism

Public enterprise market economies, or what are usually called market socialist models, come in both managerial and worker-managed forms. In the earliest model of market socialism developed by Oscar Lange, Abba Lerner, and Frederick Taylor in the 1930s, enterprises were financed by the state and managers were appointed by the state. Below I discuss a more recent version of managerial market socialism by John Roemer where enterprises are self-financed. Finally I discuss what advocates call worker self-managed market socialism, which I believe is far superior to state-managed models, but intrinsically flawed nonetheless.

In *A Future for Socialism* (1994), John Roemer recommends changing capitalism in two respects:

(1) Void present ownership of corporations and issue everyone identical portfolios of stocks, or "coupons," giving each person, initially, an equal share of ownership in every corporation in the economy. People would then be free to trade their shares of stock in one company for shares in another, but not permitted to trade shares of stock for money or goods.

(2) Organize corporations into Japanese-style conglomerates, or *Keiretsu*, headed by a major investment bank that would (a) own significant blocks of stock in the corporations under its tutelage, (b) loan its corporate clients funds for investment, and (c) monitor the performance of corporate management.

The rationale for the first change is to diminish nonlabor income differentials. The rationale for the second is to create a mechanism for financing investment and weeding out managers who fail to maximize profits from those who do. Roemer claimed this economy would be more egalitarian than capitalism and no less efficient, and urged progressives to define their goal as replacing capitalism with a "coupon economy." While any reform that reduces wealth and income inequality would be a welcome improvement over capitalism, I believe adopting Roemer's coupon economy as our economic goal would be a tragic step backward.

The first problem with Roemer's downsizing of progressive economic vision is that the human costs of transition would remain high while the benefits of changing from capitalism to a coupon economy would be meager. According to his own calculations the coupon system would only have increased median African-American income in the United States by 2 percent in 1989. Yet a more egalitarian income distribution is the major benefit Roemer claims for his coupon economy! Roemer admits people would have no more control over their work lives in a coupon economy than in capitalism since firm managers monitored by investment banks and mutual funds would decide what and how their employees would produce. Nor does he offer any compelling reason to believe the market failures discussed in chapter 4 would be significantly less in a coupon economy than in capitalism. So a coupon economy would be no less alienating, and only marginally more fair and efficient than capitalism. Moreover, it would certainly be an economy where a class of corporate, bank, and mutual fund managers dominated economic decision making and eventually appropriated significant material rewards.

Yet moving from capitalism to a coupon economy would require dispossessing the present owners of the means of production, just as surely as changing from capitalism to a kind of market socialism where workers had the right to manage themselves, or to the participatory economy described in the next chapter with democratic worker and consumer councils, jobs balanced for empowerment and desirability, consumption based on effort, and participatory planning. So, presumably, the human price the capitalist ruling class would exact before succumbing to any of the three changes would be roughly comparable. To put it bluntly, given the strength and viciousness of the opposition that can reasonably be anticipated from today's capitalist ruling class, a coupon economy is hardly worth risking one's life for.

What would the coupon system accomplish? Roemer wants to outlaw trading shares of stock for money or goods so those who are poor in goods, poor in human capital, or both will not sell off their shares of stock and end up with as little income as they have now in a few years. But he wants to permit trading stocks in one company for stocks in another to generate coupon market prices that signal which companies are performing efficiently and which are not. The problem is dividend rich and poor would reappear as coupons are traded, and the coupon price signals would be largely useless window dressing in any case. Those who are luckier, more skillful, or privy to "insider information" would make more successful trades on the coupon stock exchange. So when the lions are done fleecing the lambs, not only will labor income be just as unequal as in capitalism, dividend or profit income in Roemer's coupon economy will eventually become highly unequal as well when those who are coupon-trading challenged end up owning shares in corporate lemons.[2] Moreover, it is unclear why Roemer considers the opinions of coupon stockholders to be valuable indicators of firm performance since actual profit records of companies would be a matter of public record and could therefore serve as the basis for managerial reward and punishment and investment allocations. Besides, Roemer recommends staffing the investment departments of his large banks with personnel he expects to be as knowledgeable about the performance and prospects of the companies under their financial tutelage as the corporate management they are monitoring. Why would such bankers, the apex of Roemer's new power elite, pay heed to the uninformed speculations of small time stockholders rather than their own more knowledgeable evaluations?

Roemer suggests that mutual funds could become the owners of the majority of stocks—thereby creating a few, large watchdogs over corporate performance—and citizens could trade shares in companies for shares in mutual funds—thereby preserving a more egalitarian income distribution. But the option of investing in mutual funds has not eliminated large inequalities in dividend income in today's economies, so why would it prevent inequality in a coupon economy? It turns out not all mutual funds are created equal, so the problem of what happens to the losers in any mutual fund coupon sweepstakes that replaces the firm coupon sweepstakes does not go away. And just as Roemer has no answer to the question who would judge and control the big bankers, he has no answer to the question who would judge and control the managers of the mutual funds. He does not trust the government to use economic rather than political criteria in managing public enterprises—including mutual funds—and small-fry coupon holders in mutual funds can hardly be expected to monitor and control big enchilada fund managers.

If Roemer's managerial version of a public-enterprise market economy is alienating and authoritarian, what about employee-managed models of market socialism? Permitting workers to manage themselves, or hire and fire those who do, is a far sight better than having managers appointed and monitored by the state, large public investment banks, or mutual funds. Advocates of worker self-managed market socialism in Yugoslavia in the early 1950s sought to give workers control over their own labor by freeing them from the dictatorship of the central plan *and* from managers appointed by the central planners. Having dissolved central planning and abandoned state appointed management, these reformers embraced markets as the only known way to coordinate the activities of different workers managed enterprises without central direction.[3]

Just as managerial market socialism is an improvement over capitalism because it reduces nonlabor income inequality somewhat, employee-managed market socialism is a significant improvement over its more technocratic cousin because it gives groups of workers the power to manage themselves. But there are three problems with employee-managed market economies that I believe are unavoidable: (1) even when property income differentials are eliminated, labor markets distribute labor income unfairly; (2) if workers must coordinate their activities through markets, significant inefficiencies and antisocial dynamics are inevitable; and finally, (3) while no central planners would dictate to workers in employee-managed market economies, there is every reason to expect class divisions to grow between workers and their managers and worker self-management to atrophy.

LABOR MARKETS ARE UNFAIR

If we eliminate inequities that stem from private ownership of productive property, would public-enterprise market economies be fair?[4] Unfortunately, the answer is *no*. While public enterprise market economies are more just than their private enterprise counterparts, they are still unfair because free-labor markets do not lead to equitable wage rates. If wages are determined by the laws of supply and demand in labor markets the best that can be hoped for is distribution according to maxim 2: to each according to the value of the contribution of his or her labor. Chapter 1 explained why this is unfair. Productivity is not only the result of how much effort or sacrifice one expends. It is also the result of talent (the genetic lottery), education and training (provided in large part, if not entirely, at public expense), the quantity and quality of other productive inputs one works with, and luck. Therefore payment according to productivity is unfair to those who are human capital-poor or unlucky through no fault of their own. Significant differences in people's productivity *will* result from differences in factors *other than* effort or sacrifice. Moreover, no economy could ever hope to make people equally productive. Therefore, while they may not suffer from the Rockefeller grandson problem, employee-managed market economies, like state-managed market economies, do suffer from the doctor/garbage collector problem.

But market socialist economies cannot even reward people according to the true social benefits of their contributions. They will reward people instead according to the market value of their contributions, which differ from the true social benefits of their contributions for two reasons. First, the market weighs people's desires by the income behind them, the value of contributions in the marketplace is determined not only by consumers' needs and desires but by the distribution of income. As we saw in chapter 4, according to the market, the value of the contribution of a plastic surgeon with a practice in Hollywood is greater than the market value of the contribution of a family practitioner saving lives in a poor, rural area. Maybe we can see that the social benefit of the contribution of the doctor in a poor, rural area is greater than that of the plastic surgeon in Hollywood, but the market cannot. And second, the market has "a keen ear for private wants but a deaf ear for public needs," the market over values private goods and undervalues public goods. This implies that those who produce goods or services whose benefits are limited to a few will have the value of their contributions overvalued by the market, while those who produce goods or services whose benefits extend to many will have the value of their contributions undervalued by the market.

Finally, the inequity of people receiving higher wages and salaries than others who make greater personal sacrifices cannot be corrected in public enterprise market economies without causing a great deal of inefficiency. Efficiency requires charging a firm that uses a particular kind of labor as much as that labor could have contributed to social benefits if it were employed elsewhere. Otherwise firms will hire workers who contribute less to social benefits than had they been employed elsewhere. On the other hand, equity requires paying workers according to their effort or sacrifices. As we have seen these are not the same thing at all, giving rise to the following dilemma: if we allow the labor market to determine wage rates, we will get something approximating marginal revenue product wages. Even though market-determined marginal-revenue products deviate from the true marginal social benefits from different kinds of labor for the reasons explained above, nonetheless, they do reflect significant portions of the opportunity costs of different kinds of labor, therefore if those who use different categories of labor pay their marginal-revenue products we will allocate different kinds of labor to their most productive uses in many cases. However, if people are paid according to their marginal-revenue products the compensation workers receive will be very unfair. On the other hand, if we try to overcome this inequity by substituting effort, or sacrifice wages for market determined wages, firms in market socialism no longer have any incentive to employ workers where their contribution to social benefits is greatest. If a market socialist community health clinic only has to pay a highly trained brain surgeon her "effort wage," the clinic may find it cost effective to hire a brain surgeon even though she would be far more productive working in a major hospital surgical center.

There is no way around the dilemma that any modification of market-determined wage rates in the direction of equitable wage rates will generate efficiency losses in market socialist economies as labor is misallocated. Moreover, labor costs form a substantial portion of total production costs of most goods and services in modern economies. So if wages are made equitable, not only wage rates, but the entire cost structure of the economy will deviate systematically and substantially from true social opportunity costs. Goods made directly or indirectly by labor whose effort wages are higher than their marginal-revenue product wages will sell at prices higher than their true social opportunity costs. While goods made directly or indirectly by labor whose effort wages are lower than their marginal-revenue product wages will sell at prices lower than their true social opportunity costs. This means that any attempt to make wages more equitable will create gross allocative inefficiencies in a market economy.

All variants of public enterprise market economies distribute the burdens and benefits of social labor unfairly because workers will be rewarded according to the market value of their contributions rather than their effort or personal sacrifice. However, making wages more fair necessarily generates systematic inefficiencies in market economies, including all market socialist economies. Some advocates of market socialism, such as Thomas Weisskopf, recognize that people would not be fairly rewarded and admit the inequity is not necessary to generate motivational efficiency.

A more just system of economic remuneration would arguably link payment solely to differential personal effort and personal sacrifice, not to the luck of the genetic draw. . . . In market socialist economies people are rewarded primarily for productive contributions due to their own labor . . . even though such rewards may *not* really be necessary to elicit the deployment of those abilities in production.[5]

Others, such as David Schweickart, claim remuneration in market socialist firms could be decided by one's coworkers through some sort of democratic procedure: "Beyond minimum wage specifications and the requirement that the value of the capital stock be kept intact, income distribution within the firm should be left to the enterprise itself."[6] But to suggest that workers in an enterprise would be able to set their wages relative to one another in any way they please when there is a market for labor in the economy is either naïve or disingenuous. While formally true that workers in one of Schweickart's self-managed enterprises could set their wages however they wish, one could also claim that capitalist employers are free to set the wages of their employees however they wish. The problem with this reasoning in an economy with labor markets—whether capitalist or market socialist—is that it ignores the necessity of attracting employees who are free to work elsewhere. If a group of workers in Schweickart's model of self-managed market socialism decided democratically that they did not wish to pay a skilled engineer any more than they paid a coworker who swept the factory floor—provided their effort and sacrifices were equal—they would soon find themselves without any skilled engineers! The fact is there *are* labor markets in employee self-managed market economies, which means wage rates *will* be highly influenced by differences in marginal revenue products.

Michael Howard, like Weisskopf, recognizes that market-based wages are unfair. To his credit he proposes doing something about it by giving everyone a guaranteed income sufficient to live on, financed out of general tax revenues, independent of whether a person works or chooses not to.[7] While Howard's proposal prevents people with very low productivities from suffering severe economic hardship, it does not eliminate inequities due to differences in people's marginal-revenue products that are not the result of differences in sacrifice. Moreover, it creates motivational inefficiencies that Schweickart takes Howard to task for with good reason. I argue below that whether need-based consumption leads to resentment and motivational inefficiency depends very much on circumstances. While I find good reason to believe that a long track record of sacrifice-based remuneration can build a tradition of solidarity sufficient for people to eventually be willing to allow one another to consume increasingly according to need—without resentment and inefficiency—I agree with Schweickart that hard-working people who are underpaid for their sacrifices by market-based wages would have every reason to resent others who receive a generous living allowance for doing nothing, as Howard proposes. My reading of the history of the politics surrounding welfare programs is that as long as a great many who work receive less compensation than they deserve, paying able-bodied people who do not work breeds resentment. Since capitalism does not guarantee everyone socially useful work and fair remuneration one is forced to choose between inhumanity—inadequate or no welfare programs—and injustice—work for some of the able-bodied but welfare for others under capitalism. But this dilemma should not and need not arise in a desirable economy. The fact that Howard finds it necessary to append a welfare program to market socialism to avoid inhumanity I believe is further evidence that there is something fundamentally wrong with market socialism in the first place.

Of course all advocates of market socialism point out that capitalism is even *more* inequitable, and argue that progressive income taxes can be used to reduce wage inequities. While true, proponents conveniently ignore political and psychological obstacles that would predictably work against the kind of tax correctives they recommend. Why would the economically advantaged in market socialist economies not translate their advantages in resources and leisure into disproportionate political power? And why would they not use their disproportionate political power to obstruct attempts to correct wage and salary inequities? Moreover, people inevitably tend to rationalize their behavior. The logic of the labor market is: "She who contributes more gets more." So when people participate in the labor market they must defend their right to a wage on the basis of their contribution. The logic of redistribution through progressive taxation runs counter to this logic. Therefore, participation in market socialist labor markets not only does not lead people to see the moral logic of progressive taxation, it inclines them to be receptive to the argument of opponents, which is: "Everyone already got what they contributed, so it is *re*distribution that is unfair."

Finally, there is one further ethical dilemma inherent in market socialism. To their credit, almost all advocates treat education as a fundamental human right, and champion universal public education to advance the causes of equal opportunity and political democracy. But where is the justice in permitting individuals to appropriate the benefits of the greater productivity that comes from education and training if the cost of that education and training is born at public expense? Logic would seem to dictate *either* that individuals bear the expense of education from which they reap the benefits in the form of higher wages and salaries in market socialism, *or* that education at public expense not give rise to private benefits. Since the latter is impossible in market socialism, I do not see how advocates can embrace universal public education without serious inconsistency.[8]

MARKETS ALLOCATE RESOURCES INEFFICIENCY

Chapter 3 explained how the free-rider problem leads markets to underproduce public goods. Chapter 4 explained how external effects mean markets are guided by an invisible foot as well as an invisible hand leading to inefficient uses of resources, and why market inefficiencies increase over time as people adjust to the antisocial bias inherent in the market system. Moreover, mainstream microeconomic theory concedes that noncompetitive market structures create allocative inefficiencies, and Keynesian macroeconomic theory identifies multiple sources of disequilibrium dynamics in markets that also generate significant inefficiencies. Unfortunately for advocates of market socialism, every reason markets are inefficient applies to private *and* public-enterprise market systems alike. Moreover, if taxes and subsidies do not adequately internalize externalities, if stabilization policies do not sufficiently counter disequilibrium dynamics, and if antitrust policies fail to make markets perfectly competitive in private-enterprise market economies, they will fail to do so in public-enterprise market economies as well. In other words, there is little reason to believe markets will be any more efficient in market socialist economies than they are in capitalist economies.

MARKETS DESTROY THE SOCIAL TIES THAT BIND US

By making individual choice easy compared to social choice, markets not only allocate productive resources inefficiently they promote a warped, antisocial pattern of human development. Sam Bowles—an advocate of market socialism himself—provides an eloquent explanation of the antisocial bias in market systems:

> Even if market allocations *did* yield Pareto-optimal [i.e. efficient] results, and even if the resulting income distribution *was* thought to be fair (two very big "ifs"), the market would still fail if it supported an undemocratic structure of power or if it rewarded greed, opportunism, political passivity, and indifference toward others. The central idea here is that our evaluation of markets—and with it the concept of market failure—must be expanded to include the effects of markets on both the structure of power and the process of human development. As anthropologists have long stressed, how we regulate our exchanges and coordinate our disparate economic activities influences what kind of people we become. Markets may be considered to be social settings that foster specific types of personal development and penalize others. . . . The beauty of the market, some would say, is precisely this: It works well even if people *are* indifferent toward one another. And it does not require complex communication or even trust among its participants. But that is also the problem. The economy—its markets, work places and other sites—is a gigantic school. Its rewards encourage the development of particular skills and attitudes while

other potentials lie fallow or atrophy. We learn to function in these environments, and in so doing become someone we might not have become in a different setting. . . . By economizing on valuable traits— feelings of solidarity with others, the ability to empathize, the capacity for complex communication and collective decision making, for example—markets are said to cope with the scarcity of these worthy traits. But in the long run markets contribute to their erosion and even disappearance. What looks like a hardheaded adaptation to the infirmity of human nature may in fact be part of the problem.[9]

Market economies cast people into the antagonistic roles of buyers and sellers every day where empathizing with one's opponent is counterproductive to one's own well-being. Market prices are systematically biased against social activities in favor of individual activities. Markets make it easier to pursue well-being through individual rather than social activity by minimizing the transaction costs associated with the former and maximizing the transaction costs associated with the latter. Private consumption faces no obstacles in market economies whereas joint, or social consumption, runs smack into free-rider and transaction-cost problems. In a word, the hallmark of markets is their antisocial bias.

Markets and hierarchical decision making economize on the use of valuable but scarce human traits like "feelings of solidarity with others, the ability to empathize, the capacity for complex communication and collective decision making." But more importantly, markets and hierarchical relations contribute to the erosion and disappearance of these worthy traits by rewarding those who ignore democratic and social considerations and penalizing those who try to take them into account. It is no accident that despite a monumental increase in education levels, the work force was less capable of exercising its self-management potential at the end of the twentieth century than it was at the beginning, or that people feel more alone, alienated, suspicious of one another, and rootless than ever before. Robert Bellah, Jean Bethke Elshtain, and Robert Putnam, among others, have documented the general decay of civic life and weakening of trust and participation across all income and educational levels. There is no longer any doubt that "the social fabric is becoming visibly thinner, we don't trust one another as much, and we don't know one another as much" in Putnam's words.[10] While it is easier to blame the spread of television than a major economic institution, the atomizing effect of markets as they penetrate more areas of our lives bears a major responsibility for this trend.

MARKETS CREATE CLASS DIVISIONS

Markets create a social environment in which a class of managers, professionals, intellectuals, and technicians—whom I call "coordinators"—can increasingly dominate and ultimately exploit ordinary workers. Tom Weisskopf admits as much when he says:

> It is certainly true that under market socialism there must be some people occupying positions of key decision-making responsibility, and in all likelihood such people will have higher incomes as well as greater power than most of the rest of the population. . . . There would be ample scope for inequalities associated with differential skills, talents and responsibilities.[11]

Sam Bowles explains why markets undermine rather than nurture economic democracy.

> If democratic governance is a value, it seems reasonable to favor institutions that foster the development of people likely to support democratic institutions and able to function effectively in a democratic environment. As we have seen, markets may provide a hostile environment for the cultivation of the necessary traits. The complex decision-making and information processing skills required of the modern democratic citizen are not likely to be fostered in markets.[12]

What Bowles fails to point out is that the erosion of "complex decision-making and information processing skills" in market economies is not even and across the board for all participants. Instead the effects are highly unequal, as a few are singled out to play decision-making and communicative roles while most are relegated to the tasks of carrying out orders, all of which makes markets breeding grounds for coordinator class dynamics and distinctions. While workers in employee-managed market economies have the formal right to make any and all decisions, the organization of work and assignment of tasks in market socialist enterprises empowers only a few and disempowers most workers. Managers and professional employees will increasingly dominate enterprise decision making because most employees will have neither the information nor self-confidence to express their views effectively. Moreover, since the need to survive in the competitive marketplace rules out many options for improving the quality of work life, disempowered workers will increasingly be willing to leave bottom-line calculations to professional hired guns. If the Yugoslav experience has anything to teach us it is that the impulse to participate in economic self-management of ordinary workers wanes in the context of competitive market dynamics and job structures that empower their managers while disempowering them.

The question for advocates of market socialism is whether their vision turns out to be an oxymoron. How can one free people from the negative effects of socially irresponsible greed as well as fear of economic insecurity, while continuing to rely on greed and fear as the principal means of motivation? Doesn't every step taken within a market socialist system to limit inequities and insecurities also undermine its motivational system?

Community-Based Economics

Some who reject capitalism, authoritarian planning, and market socialism, offer a vision of largely self-reliant, local economies governed by the kind of direct democracy once used in New England town meetings. A growing number of radical environmentalists and young anarchists argue that only reducing the scale of economic institutions, and increasing the self-sufficiency of local communities can satisfy libertarian goals, reduce alienation, and promote ecological balance.[13] They seek to avoid the negative repercussions of both markets and planning by eliminating the "problem" these allocative mechanisms address, coordinating a division of labor among geographically dispersed groups. By decentralizing large, national economies into small, autonomous economic communities they also hope to promote face-to-face democratic decision making and create incentives for local communities to take the environmental effects of their activities into account. They argue that while participatory democracy doesn't work in large groups where people do not know one another and cannot discuss things in person, it can work in small communities. They also reason that once the consequences of choices all fall "in my back yard" (IMBY), the IMBY principle will force local communities to protect their environment. Of course, just as there are different models of market socialism and democratic planning, community-based economics comes in different flavors. Social ecology and libertarian municipalism,[14] an ecological society through democratic pluralism,[15] Buddhist economics,[16] bioregionalism,[17] ecological economics,[18] and ecosocialism[19] are some of the versions, and they all differ from one another in significant ways. While I sympathize with the participatory and ecological goals of radicals who propose small scale, democratic autarky, all versions of community-based economics suffer from major problems.

ILL-DEFINED MODELS

Unlike many versions of market socialism and democratic planning, no "model" of community-based economics is a real model in the sense that it specifies rules and procedures for how to make all the decisions that must be made in any economy. For this reason all versions of community-based economics are really visions, not coherent models. Sometimes proponents are blissfully unaware that they have failed to address important issues that will inevitably arise. Sometimes proponents refer to the lack of specific, concrete answers regarding *how* something would be decided, as a virtue compared to what they criticize as deterministic models of market socialism and democratic planning. But this response misses the point. It is impossible to evaluate a proposal for how to run the economy until it is a full and complete proposal. This failure should not be confused with the problem of explaining how to move from today's capitalist system to a community-based economy. Advocates of community-based economics often address this issue more extensively than they answer exactly how they propose particular issues be decided once we get to a community-based economy. Nor should the failure be confused with lack of speculation about what kinds of decisions they imagine people will make in a community-based economy. Since proponents of community-based economics are motivated by strong convictions that people need to choose radically different technologies and products, need to change their priorities regarding leisure versus work, and need to accept the necessity of zero growth of "material throughput," authors usually write at length about the differences between the decisions *they believe* will be made in their community-based economy and the decisions made in today's capitalist economies. The problem is that any professional economist knows there are certain categories of decisions that must be made in any economy, and until a proposal is comprehensive enough to specify how a proponent suggests these necessary decisions be made—until we have what economists call a formal model—it is literally impossible to evaluate whether the economy would do what its proponents claim it would.

HOW TO INTEGRATE SEMI-AUTONOMOUS COMMUNITIES?

One manifestation of this first problem is that when push comes to shove, no version of community-based economics proposes that communities be entirely self-sufficient—for understandable reasons. In other words, it turns out that autonomous communities are only semi-autonomous. And when it comes down to explaining precisely how the "semi" part be handled, we invariably find no answer beyond hand waving, and declarations of faith that democratic communities can work this out between themselves satisfactorily.[20] Of course if communities were completely self-sufficient there would be inefficient duplication of efforts and inequities. But in the likely event that communities rediscovered the advantages of the division of labor, no proposal in this literature— precisely because they are not truly models—provides an answer to the question how communities that are no longer completely autonomous should arrange their division of labor.

How would communities decide how much of a division of labor they want to engage in? What if one community wants a greater division of labor than another community wants? A careful reading of Bookchin's vision of libertarian municipalism reveals that no community must acquiesce to a greater division of labor than it wants to. While this is a specific rule, it is a problematic one. This rule means the community that wants the least division of labor among communities can impose its preference over the preferences of all other communities. Why a community that is better endowed with natural, human, and/or physical capital would not be tempted—even if unconsciously—to take unfair advantage of this veto right is unclear. Even if communities could agree on a division of labor with other communities, how would they go about deciding how to distribute the burdens and benefits of this division of labor? How would they jointly manage the division of labor? Should goods and services not produced by every community be traded between them in free markets? If so, why would this not lead to the usual litany of inequities, instabilities, and inefficiencies that advocates of community-based economics (correctly) criticize in capitalism and market socialism? Should communities attempt to plan mutually beneficial economic relations? If so, how would they go about it, and how would the authoritarian dynamics of central planning be avoided? Simply asserting that the communities will decide all this "democratically" is not a good enough answer.

Joel Kovel's model of ecosocialism, defined as an expanding network of "ecological ensembles," is in many ways even more opaque than others in this literature. In truth it is more an interesting and insightful proposal about movement strategy than a coherent postcapitalist economic model. But Kovel provides an excellent critique of the disadvantages of extreme localism:

A pure community, or even 'bioregional' economy is a fantasy. Strict localism belongs to the aboriginal stages of society: it cannot be reproduced today, and even if it could, it would be an ecological nightmare

at present population levels. Imagine the heat losses from a multitude
of dispersed sites, the squandering of scarce resources, the needless
reproduction of effort. . . . This is by no means to be interpreted as a
denial of the great value of small-scale and local endeavors. . . . It is
rather an insistence that the local and particular exists in and through
the global whole; that there needs to be, in any economy, an interde-
pendence whose walls are not confinable to any township or bioregion;
and that, fundamentally, the issue is the relationship of parts to the
whole.[21]

Proposals for community-based economics simply fail to address this
fundamental issue. In the end, the problem of devising desirable allocative mechanisms to coordinate the division of labor between communities won't go away, and advocates of autonomous economic communities
provide no coherent or satisfactory answer to how they would coordinate cooperation between communities that always turn out to be only
"semi-autonomous" under careful cross-examination.

ONE BIG MEETING DOESN'T WORK

Advocates of community-based economics also fail to provide concrete
answers to crucial questions about how communities would make
different kinds of internal decisions. Even in a community of several
thousand people there will be different groups of workers and consumers. There will be different kinds of economic decisions to make. It
is impractical for the whole community to vote on each and every
economic question that comes up. What would the agenda for such a
meeting look like? Who would be responsible for setting this agenda?
Moreover, a democratic vote of a community does not provide its citizens with decision making power *in proportion to the degree they are
affected* in cases where not all members of the community are equally
affected by a particular economic choice. Nor can all decisions be left to
the work groups who form within these communities. Many of the decisions groups of workers make affect other groups of workers and must
be coordinated with consumers in the community as well. Proponents
of community-based economics unfortunately have precious little to say
about how these internal decision-making problems should be solved.
Saying that the ultimate power over all economic decisions resides in the
community assembly where all have voice and one vote is not a good
enough answer.

Not all proponents of community-based economics reject private enterprise and markets altogether. Some whose vision includes space for private firms alongside producer cooperatives, and for markets when "properly socialized," seem to do so because they confuse what we must tolerate during the transition from competition and greed with economic relations that are truly consistent with equitable cooperation itself. Others mistakenly believe that some private enterprise and some markets are compatible with equitable cooperation. They fail to realize, in the words of Joel Kovel, that combining private enterprise and market forces with people seeking to practice equitable cooperation is like trying to raise weasels and chickens in the same pen. More radical visions of community-based economics do reject private enterprise and markets entirely. Like those of us who support participatory economics, advocates of libertarian municipalism, ecosocialism, and communitarian anarchism all argue that there is no place for either private enterprise or markets in a truly desirable economy.

However, all who espouse community-based economics—whether inclined to abolish or to retain markets and private enterprise to some degree—are staunchly democratic, egalitarian, and proenvironment. Because advocates of community-based economics and supporters of participatory economics share these same values, I believe as discussion continues we will become even closer allies than many of us already are. I see nothing in a participatory economy that I believe should displease proponents of community-based economics. In fact, I think those attracted to community-based economics will find that some features of a participatory economy resolve many problems for which they lack solutions. This is not to say that critiques of participatory economics have not appeared in anarchist journals.[22] But in my view there is little if any disagreement over values, and much of the disagreement over institutions and procedures voiced by our anarchist critics is based on a misreading and misinterpretation of what supporters of participatory economics have actually proposed. In other words, I regard most modern, libertarian communalist visionaries as allies—like our council communist, syndicalist, anarchist, and guild socialist forebears—and ask them to consider the procedures of participatory planning when they think further about how they would coordinate economic relations among semi-autonomous communities, and about how they would propose communities comprised of different groups of workers and consumers apportion decision-making authority internally as well.

Democratic Planning

As in the case of market socialism and community-based economics, different versions of democratic planning have been proposed over the past dozen years, and there are important differences between them. The Spring 2002 issue of *Science & Society* was devoted entirely to different models of democratic planning. Nine economists presented their ideas about how democratic planning can best be organized, and commented on one another's proposals. In his introduction the special editor for the issue, Pat Devine, who calls his own model of democratic planning "negotiated coordination,"[23] explained:

> Michael Albert, Al Campbell, Paul Cockshott, Alin Cottrell, Robin Hahnel, David Kotz, David Laibman, John O'Neill and I all share a commitment to democratic, participatory planning as the eventual replacement for market forces. But while there are many other points of agreement among all or some of us, there are also disagreements over fundamental principles and values as well as details.

The next three chapters present and defend one version of democratic planning popularly known as participatory economics. It is an economic vision those committed to fighting for the economics of equitable cooperation can explain to people when they want to know concretely how we propose to achieve economic justice, democracy, and efficiency while protecting the environment and promoting solidarity and variety, without either capitalist corporations and markets, or commissars and authoritarian plans. It is also a comprehensive proposal, a formal model, that answers exactly how all the different kinds of decisions that must be made in any economy would be made, and explains concretely how the economic activities of different democratic worker and consumer councils can be coordinated efficiently and fairly through a participatory, democratic planning procedure. In other words, besides being a vision of equitable cooperation, it is a rigorous model that can be subjected to formal analysis and criticism.

8

Participatory Economics

In the 1970s, Michael Albert and I came to the conclusion that the vision
of a self-managed economy shared by many council communists, syndi-
calists, anarchists, and guild socialists was essentially sound, but, unfortunately, these economic visionaries had failed to provide a coherent
model explaining precisely how their alternative to capitalism could work.
Our libertarian socialist predecessors provided moving comparisons of
the advantages of worker and community self-management over capitalism and authoritarian planning. But all too often they did not respond
to difficult questions about precisely how necessary decisions would be
made, how the democratic procedures they championed would yield a
coherent plan, why there was any reason to believe the plan that emerged
would be efficient, or how people would be motivated to work and inno-
vate. But we did not believe this meant their vision was an impossible
dream. It simply meant more theoretical work was required to flesh out
the vision and demonstrate its feasibility.

In the 1980s, a number of progressive economists joined conservative
critics who had long claimed it was impossible to coordinate the activities of separate groups of producers and consumers except via markets
or authoritarian planning. As George Scialabba explained: "Most economists believe that a modern economy can function only through one of
two mechanisms: market exchange, with perhaps some degree of regulation; or central planning by a state bureaucracy. Since the collapse of the
Soviet empire, and long before, the inferiority of central planning has
been obvious. The desirability of markets, within whatever limits, is now

an article of faith among political and economic writers, the premise even of democratic socialists including recent writers in *Dissent*.[1] Skepticism regarding the feasibility of democratic planning was part of the reason many democratic socialists supported various versions of market socialism or mixed economies. They proclaimed there was no third way, and accused those, such as ourselves, who called for planning by producers and consumers themselves of deluding ourselves and others. Alec Nove was one who threw down the gauntlet in no uncertain terms: "In a complex industrial economy the interrelation between its parts can be based in principle either on freely chosen negotiated contracts [i.e., markets], or on a system of binding instructions from planning offices [i.e., central planning.] *There is no third way*."[2]

In two books published in 1991, Michael Albert and I set out to rectify intellectual weaknesses in the case for participatory planning by spelling out precisely how worker and consumer councils *could* coordinate their joint endeavors themselves consciously, democratically, equitably, and efficiently. In *The Political Economy of Participatory Economics*, (Princeton University Press) we presented a theoretical model of participatory planning and carried out a rigorous analysis of its properties. In *Looking Forward: Participatory Economics for the Twenty-First Century*, (South End Press) we examined the intricacies of participatory decision making in a variety of realistic settings, and addressed practical issues conveniently ignored by theoretical models. After publication, critics suddenly dropped the objection that participatory planning is technically impossible, and raised new objections. Some argued that a participatory economy was undesirable in any case. Others argued that it was incompatible with human nature. And still others argued that no matter how feasible and desirable it might be, there was no way to move from the economics of competition and greed we are ensnared into a participatory economy.

This chapter describes the main features of a participatory economy, and examines two important issues that were not addressed in earlier presentations: how a participatory economy would protect the environment, and how a participatory economy could benefit from international trade and investment without undermining its core principles. Legitimate concerns about the desirability and feasibility of participatory economics that critics have raised over the past dozen years are carefully examined in the following chapter. How to move from competition and greed to the kind of equitable cooperation embodied in a participatory economy is the subject of the four chapters comprising Part 4 of the book.

A Participatory Economy

The model of a participatory economy was designed to promote: (a) economic justice, or *equity*, defined as economic reward commensurate with effort, or sacrifice; (b) economic democracy, or *self-management*, defined as decision-making power in proportion to the degree one is affected by a decision; and (c) *solidarity*, defined as concern for the well-being of others, all to be achieved without sacrificing economic *efficiency* while promoting a *diversity* of economic life styles. The major institutions used to achieve these goals are: (1) *democratic councils* of workers and consumers, (2) *jobs balanced* for empowerment and desirability, (3) *remuneration according to effort* as judged by one's work mates, and (4) a *participatory planning* procedure in which councils and federations of workers and consumers propose and revise their own activities under rules designed to yield outcomes that are both efficient and equitable.

Worker Councils

In a participatory economy production is carried out by worker councils, where each member has one vote. Everyone is free to apply for membership in the council of her choice, or form a new worker council with whomever she wishes. There is an ample literature documenting the advantages of employee management. Evidence is overwhelming that people with a say and stake in how they work not only find work more enjoyable, they are more productive and efficient as well.[3] So rather than dwell on the advantages of self-management—which should be beyond question—I focus here on the proposal to expand self-management through balancing work assignments for desirability and empowerment, which is more unusual and controversial.

Every economy organizes work into "jobs" that define what tasks a single individual will perform. In hierarchical economies most jobs contain a number of similar, relatively undesirable, and relatively unempowering tasks, while a few jobs contain a number of relatively desirable and empowering tasks. But why should some people's work lives be less desirable than others? Doesn't taking equity seriously require balancing work for desirability? And why should work empower a few while disempowering most? If we want everyone to have an equal opportunity to participate in economic decision making—if we want to ensure that a *formal* right to participate translates into an *effective* right to participate—doesn't this require balancing work for empowerment? If some sweep floors all week, year in and year out, while others evaluate new technological options and attend planning meetings all week, year in and year out, is it realistic to believe they have an equal opportunity to participate simply because they each have one vote in the worker council? Doesn't taking participation seriously require balancing work for empowerment?

The proposal is not that everyone perform every task, which is impossible in any case. Each person would still perform a small number of tasks in her "balanced job complex" (BJC) just as she does now. Therefore BJCs do *not* mean an end to specialization. But some tasks in every BJC will be more enjoyable and some less so, and some will be more empowering and some less so. Moreover, the balancing can be achieved over a reasonable period of time. The tasks I perform do not have to be balanced for desirability and empowerment every hour, day, week, or even every month. While the reaction from economists against BCJs has been particularly fierce, advocates of participatory economics believe ample leeway exists in organizing work to accommodate practical considerations while eliminating *persistent* differences in desirability and empowerment. In any case, criticisms that BJCs waste scarce talent and expertise are carefully considered in chapter 9.

Finally, every worker council must provide each member with an "effort rating." The purpose is to recognize that not everyone always makes equal sacrifices in work, and those who make greater sacrifices are entitled to compensation in the form of extra consumption rights. Effort-rating committees in worker councils will collect information and testimony about people's work and establish some kind of grievance procedure. And presumably all workers will serve on the effort-rating committee according to some system of rotation. But different worker councils need not go about rating themselves in the same way, any more than they have to organize their work in the same way. Again, many have expressed concerns about rewarding effort and problems that may arise when efforts are judged by one's work mates. These concerns will be carefully considered in chapter 9. However, I should point out here that to prevent the possibility of "effort-rating inflation" the average effort rating a council awards its members cannot exceed the worker council's ratio of the social benefits of its outputs divided by the social costs of its inputs, to be calculated as explained below.

Consumer Councils

Every individual, family, or living unit belongs to a neighborhood consumption council. Each neighborhood council belongs to a federation of neighborhood councils the size of a precinct. Each precinct federation belongs to a city ward, or rural county federation. Each ward belongs to a city consumption council, each city and county council belong to a state council, and each state council belongs to the national consumption council. The major purpose for "nesting" consumer councils into ever larger federations is to allow for the fact that different kinds of consumption affect different numbers of people. Some decisions affect only local residents, while others affect all who live in a city, county, state, or the entire country. Failure to arrange for all those affected by consumption activities to participate in choosing them not only implies a loss of self-management, but, if the preferences of some who are affected by a choice are disregarded or misrepresented, it also implies a loss of efficiency as well. As we saw, one of the serious liabilities of market systems is their systematic failure to allow for expression of desires for social consumption on an equal footing with desires for private consumption. Having different levels of consumer federations participate on an equal footing with individual worker and neighborhood councils in the planning procedure described below prevents this bias from occurring in a participatory economy.

Individual members of neighborhood councils present their consumption requests accompanied by the effort ratings they receive from peers in their workplace. Using indicative prices generated by the participatory planning process described below, the social cost of each proposal is calculated. While no consumption request justified by an effort rating can be denied by a neighborhood consumption council, neighbors can express their opinion that a request is unwise, and neighborhood councils can also approve requests on the basis of need in addition to merit. Someone can borrow or save by consuming more or less than warranted by her effort level for the year, and anyone wishing to submit an anonymous request to protect her privacy can do so. A major question is whether distribution according to effort is consistent with efficiency. Why reward according to effort—interpreted as personal sacrifice in training and work—is more equitable than reward according to the market value of the contribution of one's labor has already been argued. What remains is to explain why payment according to effort, rather than productivity, does not interfere with allocative efficiency and is consistent with motivational efficiency.

In a participatory economy, while individuals consume according to their work effort, users of scarce labor resources—worker councils—are *charged* according to the opportunity costs of employing different kinds of workers, as described below. This avoids the contradiction that plagues market economies between equity—wages based on sacrifice—and allocative efficiency—labor costs for users that reflect social opportunity costs. But what about the common view that reward according to the value of one's personal contribution provides efficient motivational incentives while reward according to effort does not?

Differences in the value of people's contributions are due to differences in talent, training, job placement, luck, and effort. Once we clarify that "effort" includes personal sacrifices incurred in training, the only factor influencing performance over which an individual has any discretion is effort. By definition, neither talent nor luck can be induced by reward. Rewarding the occupant of a job for the contribution inherent in the job itself does not enhance her performance. And provided that training is undertaken at public rather than private expense, substantial material rewards should not be necessary to induce people to seek training for tasks they would generally rather perform than other tasks in any case. If we include above-average sacrifices a person makes in training in our definition of the effort that is rewarded, the only discretionary factor influencing performance is effort, and therefore the only factor we should reward to enhance performance is effort. In other words, not only is rewarding effort consistent with efficiency, but rewarding the combined effects of talent, training incurred at public not private expense, job placement, luck, and effort, that is, productivity, is *not* consistent with motivational efficiency.

Suppose we want to induce maximum effort from runners in a ten-kilometer race. Should prize money be awarded according to place of finish, or according to improvements in personal-best times? Rewarding outcome provides no incentive for poor runners with no chance of finishing "in the money," and no incentive for a clearly superior runner to run faster than necessary to finish first. Paying in accord with improvements in personal-best times gives everyone an incentive to maximize her effort. Since the claim that rewarding effort is not only more equitable than rewarding contribution, but also is more consistent with motivational efficiency turns common wisdom on its head, it is hardly surprising that it is one aspect of participatory economics that has been most vigorously challenged. Objections that have been raised are considered at length in chapter 9.

Participatory Planning

The participants in the planning procedure are the worker councils and federations, the consumer councils and federations, and an Iteration Facilitation Board (IFB). Conceptually, the planning procedure is quite simple. (1) The IFB announces what we call "indicative prices" for all final goods and services, capital goods, natural resources, and categories of labor. (2) Consumer councils and federations respond with consumption proposals. Worker councils and federations respond with production proposals listing the outputs they propose to make and the inputs they need to make them. (3) The IFB then calculates the excess demand or supply for each final good and service, capital good, natural resource, and category of labor, and adjusts the indicative price for the good up, or down, in light of the excess demand or supply. (4) Using the new indicative prices consumer and worker councils and federations revise and resubmit their proposals. Individual worker and consumer councils must continue to revise their proposals until they submit one that is accepted by the other councils. The planning process continues until there are no longer excess demands for any goods, any categories of labor, any primary inputs, or any capital stocks; in other words, until a feasible plan is reached.

The IFB has no discretionary power to set prices, much less to dictate what workers or consumers can do. The IFB bears no resemblance to GOSPLAN in the former Soviet Union, which was a central planning bureaucracy that *did* have tremendous power over who would produce what, and how they would produce it. But in participatory planning workers and consumers propose and revise their *own* activities in a process that reveals the social costs and benefits of their proposals for them and others to take into account. Not only does each worker and consumer council make its own initial proposal, they are responsible for revising their own proposals as well. The planning procedure is designed to make it clear when proposals are inefficient or unfair. And other workers and consumer councils can disapprove of proposals when they are unfair or inefficient, but revisions are entirely up to individual worker and consumer councils themselves. This aspect of the participatory planning procedure distinguishes it from all other planning models I know, and is a critical means of providing workers and consumers with the opportunity for self-management. Participatory planning gives individual groups of workers and consumers a great deal of power over their own activities, who are only constrained by the legitimate interests of others whom they affect. As long as what a group proposes to do is fair to others and does not misuse scarce productive resources it will be approved by the other worker and consumer councils because it is either beneficial, or, at least not detrimental to their interests.

The planning procedure is discussed further in chapter 9 when addressing concerns, but essentially the planning process whittles overly optimistic, unfeasible proposals down to a feasible plan in two different ways: Consumers requesting more than their effort ratings warrant are forced to either reduce their requests, or shift their requests to less socially costly items if they expect to win the approval of other consumer councils who have no reason to approve consumption requests whose social costs are not justified by the sacrifices of those making them. Similarly, worker councils are forced to either increase their efforts, shift toward producing a more desirable mix of outputs, or shift to a less costly mix of inputs to win approval for their proposals. By multiplying outputs by their indicative prices and dividing by inputs multiplied by their indicative prices it is possible to calculate the *ratio of social benefits to social costs* of any worker council proposal. Worker councils whose proposals have lower than average social benefit-to-social cost ratios will be forced to increase either their efforts or their efficiency to win approval from other worker councils. Efficiency is promoted as consumers and workers attempt to shift their proposals and avoid reductions in consumption or increases in work effort. Equity is promoted when further shifting is no longer productive and approval of fellow consumers and workers can only be achieved through consumption reduction or greater work effort. Each new round of revised proposals moves the overall plan closer to feasibility, and moves the indicative prices closer to true social opportunity costs. No participant in the planning procedure enjoys any advantage over any other, and the procedure generates equity and efficiency simultaneously.

Since further discussion of the planning procedure in chapter 9 focuses on substantive issues, readers concerned with more technical issues should consult other readings. Chapter 4 in *The Political Economy of Participatory Economics* provides a rigorous examination of the conditions under which the planning procedure generates a feasible and efficient plan, and the conditions under which the indicative prices generated by participatory planning equal true social opportunity costs. A comparison of the efficiency *advantages* of participatory planning and its estimates of social opportunity costs over market allocations and market prices can also be found there.

Protecting the Environment in a Participatory Economy

As we saw in chapters 3 and 4, capitalism's defining features—private enterprise and markets—both lead to abuse of the natural environment. And since those who commanded in most communist economies ignored environmental sustainability as a goal, and were even more insulated from popular discontent over environmental destruction than political rulers in some capitalist economies, the environmental record of the command economies was largely indistinguishable from that of their capitalist competitors. Participatory economics attracted immediate interest among left greens because it rejected the profit motive, market competition, consumerism and hierarchical decision making, and promised to take into account external effects that go ignored in market economies. However, in neither *Looking Forward* nor *The Political Economy of Participatory Economics* did we adequately explain *how* a participatory economy would protect the environment. We mentioned that externalities, such as pollution, and public goods, such as environmental preservation, would be more efficiently accounted for by participatory planning than by markets, but we did not spell out how specific procedures and features of a participatory economy could lead to a more judicious use of the environment. Therefore, it is not surprising that serious environmentalists were skeptical of claims that remained vague. Carl Boggs wrote: "It is unclear precisely how Albert and Hahnel's participatory economy establishes mechanisms for determining overall ecological impacts, for setting limits to the production of harmful goods, or for ascertaining how much industrial growth is desirable."[4] And Howard Hawkins reported: "One Left Green who read *Looking Forward* scoffed at it as 'industrialism with a human face.' He wondered how in the world—given our contemporary situation of ozone depletion, greenhouse effect, radioactive and toxic poisoning, and general ecological breakdown—can one lay out an economic vision without going into some detail on ecological issues?"[5] Boggs and Hawkins were completely justified in demanding to know what "mechanisms" in a participatory economy would determine ecological impacts and set limits on harmful production and growth.

I do not believe environmentalists should ever be satisfied that any proposal for how to conduct human activities will adequately protect the environment. Unlike other species, we humans proved so adept at shifting from preying on one species to others, that even before we invented agriculture we were already a bull in the ecological china closet for whom the normal ecological constraints on over hunting and grazing were largely absent. First the agricultural and then the industrial revolution greatly compounded the damage we wreaked. As we enter the third millennium A.D. none should doubt that the 6 billion humans on earth stand poised to damage the biosphere irreparably in a number of different ways, and we have only very recently begun to understand the havoc we create and the dangers we court.

But environmentalists must be satisfied with something less than zero pollution and no depletion of nonrenewable resources. Zero pollution often means not producing and consuming goods and services whose benefits far outweigh their costs, including the damage the pollution associated with producing and consuming them does to the environment. Never tapping nonrenewable resources is a debilitating constraint when it proves possible to develop substitutes before a nonrenewable resource runs out. Unless we plan to vacate planet earth, zero pollution and no resource depletion are impossible. But fortunately, they are also unnecessary. A sustainable economy does not mean going back to scattered clans of hunter gatherers, who hunted most large mammal species to extinction in short order wherever they spread in any case. Humans *will* affect the environment, but we must learn to do so in ways that do not produce catastrophic climate change. Human activity *will* drive some species to extinction, but we must learn to do so in ways that minimize species extinctions and do not destroy vital ecosystems. Human activity *will* affect fauna and flora, but we need to learn how to affect the living environment in ways that preserve a rich and diverse biosphere capable of sustaining human and nonhuman life of the same quality that we presently enjoy. It would be foolish as well as impossible to strive to have no impact whatsoever on the biosphere.

But we should plan the transition to a sustainable interaction with the environment with both efficiency and intergenerational equity in mind. If the transition is too slow we risk environmental collapse and consign future generations to oblivion. Even if collapse is avoided, if the transition is too slow it will unfairly advantage the present generation over future generations and inefficiently reject opportunities to achieve future environmental benefits that exceed present social costs. Clearly, moving too slowly is the mistake we are making presently and the mistake capitalism virtually guarantees. But besides being impractical, attempting an immediate transition imposes unnecessarily high costs on the present generation. Therefore, once capitalism has been replaced we will need to calibrate nonzero levels of pollution and resource depletion over long periods of time. This means environmentalists should not cringe when they read below that in a participatory economy, while victims have the right not to be polluted, they are afforded the opportunity to permit some pollution to take place as long as it is "judicious." *Pollution and resource depletion is judicious if it is part of an environmentally sustainable trajectory that is equitable and efficient over time.*

I must also warn that I am not able to respond to some issues environmentalists hold dear. I cannot satisfy environmentalists who want to know what specific technologies will be chosen or banned in a participatory economy, what the rate of growth of production will be, or how great the division of labor between different communities and regions will be. In their great nineteenth-century utopian novels *Looking Backward* and *News from Nowhere*, Edward Bellamy and William Morris each attempted to motivate a desirable alternative to capitalism not only by describing new economic institutions and patterns of behavior, but also by describing new products and technologies they hoped their postcapitalist economies would feature. I think greens who research and write about new products and technologies that are more environmentally friendly in the energy, transportation, agricultural, and industrial sectors are doing crucial intellectual work. I think activists who experiment with environmentally friendly modes of production, consumption, and living in an economy hostile to their efforts are an important part of the hope for the future, as will become apparent in chapter 13. But I am neither an expert on green technologies, nor competent to judge which ideas about environmentally friendly technologies and products are more fruitful and which will prove to be less so. I must leave the job of pointing out the advantages of particular technologies and products to scientists and engineers, and the task of conveying what life might be like in ecotopia to more talented novelists and science fiction writers than I. The focus of my attention is on whether basic economic institutions afford creative ideas and proposals about how we relate to the natural environment a fair and friendly hearing.

The profit motive ignores many environmental effects unmeasured in the commercial nexus. Markets are biased in favor of economic activities that pollute and biased against activities that preserve and restore valuable ecological systems. And capitalism promotes private consumption over social consumption and leisure to the detriment of the environment as well. In other words, capitalism is incapable of granting ideas about how to better relate to the natural environment a fair hearing. The question in this chapter is whether the basic institutions of participatory economics—democratic worker and consumer councils and federations, remuneration according to effort, and participatory planning—create an institutional setting and incentives that promote judicious relations with our natural environment. In other words, when ideas environmentalists— and I—think are promising, ideas like organic farming, locally grown produce, smart growth, deautomobilization, solar and wind power, recycling, and more leisure, are proposed in a participatory economy, will we discover they must swim against the current, as they do in capitalist economies, or will they find the stream is flowing in their direction?

PROTECTING THE ENVIRONMENT IN ANNUAL PLANS

As long as producers and consumers are not forced to bear the costs of pollution that results from their decisions we will continue to pollute too much. How does participatory planning internalize the negative external effects of pollution? In each iteration in the annual planning procedure there is an indicative price for every pollutant in every relevant region representing the current estimate of the damage, or social cost of releasing a unit of that pollutant into the region. What is a pollutant and what is not are decided by federations representing those who live in a region, who are advised by scientists employed in research and development operations run by the resident federation. For example, if only the residents of ward 2 of Washington, D.C., feel they are adversely affected by a pollutant released in ward 2, then ward 2 is the relevant region. But if the federation representing residents of all wards of Washington, D.C., decides that a pollutant released in ward 2 affects residents of all wards, then the entire city of Washington is the relevant region. Whereas, if the federation representing all who live in the Chesapeake Bay watershed feels that all who live in the watershed are adversely impacted by a pollutant released in ward 2, then the relevant region includes the District of Columbia, Maryland, and parts of Virginia, Delaware, Pennsylvania, and New York State.

If a worker council located in an affected region proposes to emit x units of a particular pollutant they are "charged" the indicative price for that pollutant in that region times x, just like they are charged y times the indicative price of a ton of steel if they propose to use y tons of steel as inputs in their production process, and just like they are charged z times the indicative price of an hour of welding labor if they propose to use z hours of welding labor. In other words, any pollutants the worker council proposes to emit is counted as part of the social cost of their proposal, just as the cost of making the steel inputs and the opportunity cost of the welding labor they propose to use are counted as part of the social cost of their proposal: all to be weighed against the social benefits of the outputs they propose to make. The consumer federation for the relevant region looks at the indicative price for a unit of every pollutant that impacts the region and decides how many units it wishes to allow to be emitted. *The federation can decide they do not wish to permit any units of a pollutant to be emitted: in which case no worker council operating in the region will be allowed to emit any units of that pollutant. But, if the federation decides to allow x units of a pollutant to be emitted in the region, then the regional federation is "credited" with x times the indicative price for that pollutant.* What does it mean for a consumer federation to be "credited?" It means the federation will be permitted to buy more public goods for its members to consume than would otherwise be possible given the effort ratings of its members. Or, it means the members of the federation will be able to consume more individually than their effort ratings would otherwise warrant. In other words, residents of a region have a right not to be polluted if they so choose. On the other hand, if they choose to permit a certain amount of pollution to occur in their region they are compensated for the damage they choose to endure.

This procedure allows people in different regions to choose different trade-offs between less pollution and more consumption. Why? Citizens in different communities might have different opinions about how damaging pollution is, or how beneficial consumption is. Or, even if all effects could be estimated with certainty, not all people feel the same about how much they value environmental preservation versus consumption, and citizens in different regions may feel differently on average as well. Does this create the kind of "race to the bottom effect" environmentalists point out that local, as opposed to national standards, do today?[6] Note we are not talking about allowing localities to make decisions about pollution that affects nonresidents, spillover effects. That problem is handled by the rule that emissions are governed during the planning procedure by federations that include *all* those affected. The question here is whether there is reason to fear a race to be bottom effect if standards for truly local pollutants are left to localities rather than set by higher-level authorities. It is important to remember that in a participatory economy no significant differences exist in income and wealth between communities. It is for that reason I do not believe permitting communities to choose their own environmental standards risks creating a "race to the bottom effect" in a participatory economy, as it certainly does in a society where poor communities are unfairly tempted to permit greater environmental destruction to attract jobs and income while only wealthy communities can afford the luxury of strict pollution controls.

However, the above procedure in the annual planning process protects the environment sufficiently only if present residents in the region of impact are the only ones who suffer adverse consequences. While this is the case for some pollutants, it is often the case that future generations bear a great deal of the cost of pollution today. The interests of future generations must be protected in the long-run participatory planning process and by an active environmental movement, as I explain below. However, before moving on to the long-run planning process and other features of a participatory economy that help protect the environment, I hasten to point out how much of an improvement the annual participatory planning process provides over market systems. Under traditional assumptions the above procedure will: (1) reduce pollution to "efficient" levels, (2) satisfy the "polluter pays principle," (3) compensate the actual victims of pollution for the damage they suffer, and (4) induce worker councils and consumer federations to truthfully reveal the benefits and costs of pollution. In other words, the procedure is what economists call "incentive compatible."

The fact that a participatory economy can treat pollution and environmental preservation in an "incentive-compatible" way is crucial. When producers or consumers have incentives to ignore damaging effects on the environment of their choices about what and how to produce and consume, the economic system is not incentive compatible. And when polluters and pollution victims lack incentives to reveal the true costs of pollution to victims and the true benefits of pollution to consumers of the products produced jointly with the pollution, the system is not incentive compatible. But in a participatory economy since producers are charged for harmful emissions the damage from pollution is included in the cost of a worker council proposal, giving producers just as much incentive to reduce pollution as any other cost of production. And since the indicative prices consumers are charged for goods in participatory planning include the costs of pollution associated with their consumption, there is just as much incentive for consumers to reduce consumption of goods that cause pollution as there is for them to reduce consumption of goods that require scarce productive resources or unpleasant labor to produce.

But does the procedure yield an efficient indicative price for pollutants? In most cases it is reasonable to assume that as emission levels increase the costs to victims of *additional* pollution rise and the benefits to producers and consumers of permitting *additional* pollution fall, in which case the efficient level of pollution is the level at which the cost of the last unit emitted is equal to the benefit from the last unit emitted. What will happen if the IFB quotes a price for a pollutant less than the "efficient" price, that is, less than the price at which the last unit of emissions causes damage equal to its benefits? In this case the pollution victims, represented by their federation, will not find it in their interest to permit as much pollution as polluters would like, in which case there will be excess demand for permission to pollute, and the IFB will increase the indicative price for the pollutant in the next round of planning. If the IFB quotes a price higher than the efficient price the federation representing pollution victims will offer to permit more pollution than polluters will ask to emit and there will be an excess supply of permission to pollute, and the IFB will decrease the indicative price in the next round. There is no incentive for pollution victims to pretend they are damaged either more or less than they really are, or for polluters to pretend they benefit more or less than they really do from being allowed to pollute, because each would fare worse by responding untruthfully than by responding truthfully to the quotes from the IFB. Consequently, when the IFB adjusts the indicative prices for pollutants until requests to pollute equal permission to pollute, the efficient level of pollution is reached.

Uncorrected markets accomplish none of the four goals above. Markets corrected by pollution taxes can only reduce pollution to efficient levels if the taxes are set equal to the magnitude of the negative external effect. *But because markets are not incentive compatible for polluters and pollution victims, markets provide no reliable way to estimate the magnitudes of efficient taxes for pollutants.* Ambiguity over who has the property right, polluters or pollution victims, free-rider problems among multiple victims, and the transaction costs of forming and maintaining an effective coalition of pollution victims—each of whom is affected to a small but unequal degree—all combine to render market systems incapable of eliciting accurate information from pollution victims about the damages they suffer, or acting upon that information even if it were known. A participatory economy, on the other hand, awards victims an incontestable right *not* to be polluted, and arms them with a federation that includes every victim to express and represent their interests. Moreover, the context of participatory planning makes it in the best interests of a federation's members for their federation to truthfully express the magnitude of the damage pollution does to all its victims.

Since the market system contains no mechanism for generating accurate estimates of the damage from pollution, how can levels of pollution taxes be set in a market economy? Leaving the level of pollution taxes to be determined by the relative power of polluters and victims to influence politicians clearly has no claim to efficiency, and in an age of overweaning corporate power invariably leads to taxes that are too low and too much pollution. The problems with "contingent valuation surveys" that try to estimate the magnitude of damages from pollution by questioning a sample of the victims are well documented. Hypothetical bias, embedded bias, ignorance bias, and dramatic discrepancies between "willingness to pay" and "willingness to accept damage" surveys when they should yield similar results, combine to greatly undermine the credibility of estimates from contingent valuation surveys. Finally, "hedonic regression" studies are unreliable among other reasons because they systematically exclude whole categories of environmental benefits like existence and option value. In any case, in market economies when power politics, unreliable surveys, or flawed studies lead to emission taxes that are too low, of course there is too much pollution and polluters pay less than the damage they cause. On the rare occasion when a tax may be set too high, there would be too little pollution, with polluters paying too much.

The crucial difference between participatory planning and market economies in this regard is that *the participatory-planning procedure generates reliable quantitative estimates of the costs and benefits of pollution while markets generate no quantitative estimates whatsoever.* Consequently, even "good-faith" efforts to internalize the cost of pollution through taxes in market economies are "flying blind," and opportunities for "bad-faith" intervention are ever present. Estimates from surveys and studies are less accurate than the indicative prices for pollutants that would be automatically generated by the participatory planning procedure. Moreover, because everyone knows estimates based on surveys and studies are unreliable, it is possible for interested parties to challenge estimates they find inconvenient. Interested parties frequently finance alternative surveys and studies that arrive at predictably different conclusions regarding the damage from pollution and benefits from environmental preservation. Since, unlike participatory planning, market systems generate no "objective" estimates that could serve as arbiters, debates over the size of pollution taxes in market economies invariably devolve into a cacophony of *he said, she said.*

Trying to correct market bias with tradable pollution permit programs face similar problems. Permit programs can only reduce pollution to efficient levels if the efficient number of permits is issued and if the permit market equilibrates perfectly. But since markets provide no way to estimate the damages to victims, there is no way to estimate the efficient number of permits to issue. Obviously, when too many are issued we pollute more than the efficient amount, while if it ever happened that too few were issued, we would pollute too little. In other words, the fact that markets provide no information about the magnitude of damages from pollution leads to the same problems of flying blind, and the same opportunities for bad faith lobbying in permit programs as in tax programs. Moreover, no market has ever equilibrated perfectly, including markets for pollution permits. Which means tradable permit programs will be even less efficient than equivalent pollution taxes. Finally, only if all permits were auctioned off by the government would permit programs satisfy the polluter pays principle. Since all tradable permit programs to date have operated on the grandfather system whereby permits are issued largely free of charge to polluters who are then free to trade them among themselves, no tradable permit program has ever satisfied the "polluter pays" principle. In effect tradable permit programs with free distribution award the property right to pollute to polluters, whereas pollution taxes implicitly award the property right to pollution victims. Regulation in the form of equal percentage reductions for all polluters offers no improvement over taxes or permits as far as reaching the efficient level of pollution, compensating victims, or making sure polluters pay, while creating an additional inefficiency: failure to minimize the cost of achieving whatever level of pollution reduction is mandated when marginal reduction costs differ among polluters. While pollution taxes, tradable pollution permits, and regulations *can and do improve* outcomes in market economies, there is no reason to expect any of them to accomplish even one of the four achievements that come from empowering neighborhood councils and federations representing pollution victims within the participatory planning process: achieving efficient levels of pollution, making polluters pay, compensating victims, and inducing truthful reporting about pollution costs and benefits.

Protecting the Environment in Long-Run Plans

The fact that a participatory economy can treat pollution and environmental preservation in an "incentive-compatible" way is a major accomplishment and significant improvement over market economies. But while participatory planning may "settle accounts" efficiently and equitably concerning the environment for all those taking part in the various councils and federations, what protects the interests of future generations who cannot speak for themselves? How can we avoid intergenerational inequities and inefficiencies while preserving economic democracy when much of the adverse effects of environmental deterioration is borne by the unborn, who obviously cannot be part of democratic decision making processes today?

The interests of future generations—which includes the future state of the natural environment—must always be protected (or ignored) by the present generation. This is true whether it is a political or economic elite in the present generation that weighs the interests of the present generation against those of future generations, or a democratic decision-making process involving all members of the present generation that weighs the competing interests of different generations. In a participatory economy intergenerational efficiency and equity regarding the environment must be achieved in the same way intergenerational efficiency and equity is achieved in all other regards, by means of restraints the present generation places on itself in its democratic deliberations concerning the long-run plan. In a participatory economy the same rules and procedures are used to determine the long-run plan as are used for the annual plan. Federations rather than individual worker and consumer councils play a larger role in long-run planning, as do research and development facilities attached to federations. But federations of workers propose and revise investments they would like to make in their own industries, together with federations of consumers who propose and revise what they would like to be able to consume more and less of in the future, in a process that settles on particular investment priorities and time tables. Each annual plan is then hammered out within constraints imposed by choices already agreed to in the long-run planning process.[7]

If the long-run plan calls for more overall investment, this decreases the amount of consumption available in this year's annual plan. If the long-run plan calls for reducing the automobile fleet and expanding rail and bus service in the future, this reduces the amount of investment and productive resources this year's annual plan is permitted to allocate to worker councils making automobiles, and increases the amount of investment and resources to be allocated to worker councils making trains. And if the long-run plan calls for a 25 percent reduction in carbon emissions over five years, the national consumer federation must reduce the amount of carbon emissions it permits in each of the next five annual plans accordingly. Major changes in the energy, transportation, and housing sectors, as well as conversions from polluting to "green" technologies and products, are all determined by the long-run planning process where it is as easy for federations to express preferences for environmental protection and restoration as for investments that permit increases in private consumption. When consumer federations demand more green space and improvements in air and water quality for the future during this process, investment priorities in energy, transportation, and housing are affected, and timetables for phasing in "green" technologies and products are settled on.

Sometimes when the present generation draws up the long-run plan they are making choices that affect *only* the future generation. Will people in the future transport themselves in cars or trains? But often when the present generation agrees on the long-run plan they make choices that favor one generation over another. Will the present generation consume less, so more can be invested and future generations will be able to consume more? Will the present generation consume less, so carbon emissions can be reduced more and future generations will suffer less from climate change? Will the present generation consume less so green technologies and products can be phased in more quickly and future generations can enjoy increased environmental amenities sooner rather than later? I can think of no way to guarantee that members of the present generation will take the interests of future generations sufficiently to heart, or, for that matter, choose wisely for them even when there is no intergenerational conflict of interest. Whether the present generation decides on a long-run plan democratically or autocratically, there is no way to guarantee they will not make mistakes that damage future generations: maybe replacing cars with trains for our descendants is a mistake because solar-powered cars would be as environmentally friendly as trains and more convenient. Nor is there any way to make sure the present generation will not behave like Louis XV and simply decide, *"apre mois le deluge."* I can hope that people who practice economic justice diligently among themselves, as a participatory economy requires, will practice it on behalf of their children, grandchildren, and great grandchildren as well. I can hope that people used to permitting pollution only when the benefits outweigh the costs will apply the same principle in their long-run planning and include the costs to those they know will follow them. And I can hope that when people have choices posed in ways that make perfectly clear when they would be favoring themselves unfairly at the expense of their descendants, that they will be too ashamed to do so. Long-run participatory planning is designed to make issues of intergenerational equity and efficiency as clear as possible. It is also designed to estimate the detrimental and beneficial effects of economic choices on the environment accurately and incorporate them into the overall costs and benefits that must be weighed. But even so, there is no guarantee that future generations and the environment might not be slighted. Some will have to speak up in the long-run participatory planning process when they think others in their generation are unmindful of future generations. And some will have to speak up during long-run planning when they think others are neglectful of the future of the environment.

OTHER FEATURES THAT PROTECT THE ENVIRONMENT

Besides specific features of the annual and long-run planning processes discussed above, there are other features of a participatory economy that make it more likely people will treat the natural environment judiciously. (1) An egalitarian distribution of wealth and income means nobody will be so poor and desperate that they cannot afford to prioritize environmental preservation over material consumption. There will be no destitute colonists cutting down and burning valuable rain forests because they have no other way to stay alive. There will be no poverty-stricken local communities who acquiesce to host unsafe waste dumps because they are desparate for additional income. An egalitarian distribution of income and wealth also means nobody will be so rich they can buy private environmental amenities while leaving the public environment to deteriorate. (2) A system that minimizes the use of material incentives and emphasizes rewards for social serviceability greatly dimishes the environmentally destructive effects of conspicuous consumption. (3) An allocative system that provides productive resources to workers as long as the social benefits of their work exceed the social costs—including the environmental costs and the cost of lost leisure—eliminates the competitive rat race for producers to accumulate and grow despite the environmental consequences, and despite the fact that after a certain point our extra consumption is not worth the leisure we sacrifice. In other words, unlike capitalist economies, and communist economies ruled by leaders who chose to compete with them in an economic growth race, there is no bias toward injudicious growth in a participatory economy.

However, in the end there is nothing a democratic economy can do to prevent environmental abuse if people make unwise or selfish choices. This can happen because people are simply unaware of the detrimental environmental consequences of their choices, or underestimate their severity. This can occur because the present generation is selfish and cares more about itself than about future generations. Or, if one believes that other species have rights or interests that deserve to be taken into account, it can be because people refuse to do so. An active environmental movement educating and agitating for its causes will be necessary in a participatory economy, and the health of the biosphere will depend on this movement's wisdom, strength, and persuasive powers. The difference is that in a participatory economy the environmental movement will find favorable settings for presenting its case whereas in capitalism the deck is heavily stacked against them.

CONCLUSION

The relevant question to ask regarding how the environment will fare under any economic system is this: Does the system contain incentives for those who make decisions to abuse the environment, or incentives for decision makers to protect the environment and use it wisely? Unlike capitalism and communism, each of which contain powerful incentives for decision makers to ignore adverse affects on the environment—and unlike market socialism, which is little better suited to accounting for environmental externalities, avoiding conspicuous consumption, and avoiding injudicious growth—in a participatory economy it is in the individual interests of decision makers to treat the environment wisely. There is no bias favoring growth of output over growth of leisure. Status cannot be achieved through conspicuous consumption. There are no perverse incentives that make it in the interests of producers or consumers to over-pollute because of neglected externalities. Instead, those who benefit from environmental preservation have the power necessary to protect their interests. Long-term plans place constraints on annual plans in ways that balance the interests of present and future generations. And the interests of future generations—which depend on environmental preservation— are given every opportunity to receive their due in the long-run, participatory planning process. A participatory economy provides no guarantee that people will treat the environment wisely, which is to say it does not make the environmental movement obsolete. A participatory economy merely eliminates perverse incentives that create biases against environmental preservation and restoration on a playing field where people weigh their competing goals democratically and fairly.

Participating in the Global Economy

When Michael Albert and I published *Looking Forward* and *The Political Economy of Participatory Economics* in 1991 we wrote nothing about how a participatory economy might relate to the global economy. Since we did not address international economic issues it is not surprising that some asked if participatory economics hinged on a transition from capitalism to participatory economics on a global scale. Twentieth-century leftists debated whether a revolution in a single country—Russia—was doomed to failure unless soon accompanied by socialist revolutions in other countries: the advanced economies in Europe. So it is hardly surprising that skeptics wondered if participatory economics was perhaps a new, impractical version of Trotskyist all-or-nothingism. Others, who believe important benefits come from international trade and investment, feared that a participatory economy would have to forgo these benefits if it had to withdraw from the international economy because the global economy was still governed by commercial principles. Still others, who believe international trade and investment curtail local economic democracy and aggravate global inequalities, feared that a participatory economy would be corrupted by participating in the capitalist global economy. Is it possible for a country practicing participatory economics to function in a global economy that is still largely capitalist? Is it possible for a country seeking to practice participatory economics to benefit from international economic relationships without betraying its core principles?

The Answer in a Nutshell

As long as a participatory economy is interacting with a wealthier economy, its principles of justice do not prevent it from trying to strike the best bargain it can get. A moral problem only arises when a participatory economy interacts with a poorer economy. But a participatory economy can always agree to terms of trade that would give a poorer trading partner more than 50 percent of the efficiency gain from specialization and trade. Similarly, a participatory economy can always agree to interest rates that give a poorer country it lends to more than 50 percent of the efficiency gain from international financial investment. As long as efficiency gains from international economic relations are shared according to this "greater-than-50-percent rule," both the participatory economy and its poorer international partners will benefit, and the benefits will be shared in a way so the gap between the wealthier participatory economy and its poorer international partners is diminished by their interaction.

The Problem

A participatory economy recognizes that justice means reward commensurate with effort or sacrifice. The problem is that citizens of poorer national economies receive less economic reward for their efforts, on average, than citizens of wealthier national economies. The reasons for these differences may be important when considering some issues, such as reparations, international patent and copyright laws, technology sharing, and foreign aid. But regardless of how they arose, the principle of economic justice in participatory economies requires effective measures to eliminate differences in the amount of reward people receive for equal sacrifices. It does no good to point out that citizens of poorer capitalist economies may not have committed themselves to this principle of distributive justice, hoping this exempts citizens of a participatory economy from applying the principle to them. That would be like saying that because a prisoner I capture in war has not committed to refrain from torturing me if I am captured, I am free to torture him. The point is that *my* principles preclude *me* from torturing others. Similarly, the point is participatory economic principles preclude a participatory economy from interacting with other economies on terms members of the participatory economy believe to be unfair. But fortunately it *is* possible for citizens of a participatory economy to apply their own principles of justice in international economic relations with others, whether regard less of other nations subscribe to those principles. And it *is* possible for a participatory economy to benefit itself even while doing so. As long as a participatory economy applies the greater-than-50-percent rule it can benefit from international trade and investment without violating its own principles of economic justice.

COMPLICATIONS

One might argue that anything less than immediate and complete rectification of international economic injustice—elimination of all differences in the average reward received for sacrifice among countries—is unacceptable. On the other hand, if one is willing to settle for *effective* policies that eliminate international economic injustice *over time*, then the greater-than-50-percent rule for sharing benefits works. After all, present levels of international economic injustice were generated over thousands of years by differences in luck as well as by different forms of international exploitation between communities that only recently have begun to see themselves as part of a single, human community struggling to achieve a system of equitable cooperation. If one accepts that, like Rome, international economic justice cannot be built in a day, a greater-than-50-percent rule that can be expanded to 60 percent, 70 percent, and so on through democratic deliberation between international economic partners may not seem so unsatisfying.

Of course the key insight is to recognize that there is no reason to believe that the terms of trade, interest rates, and profit rates generated by the laws of supply and demand in international markets for goods, services, credit, and capital will implement the greater-than-50-percent rule! Quite the contrary, there are good reasons to believe that *even when international markets are competitive*, equilibrium terms of trade and interest rates will almost always distribute more than 50 percent of any efficiency gains from international trade and investment to the wealthier countries, not to the poorer ones, thereby aggravating, not ameliorating global inequality and injustice.[8] In other words, international market forces usually implement the reverse 50-percent rule, and thereby systematically aggravate international economic injustice. But no practical obstacles prevent a participatory economy from applying the greater-than-50 percent sharing rule of justice in its international economic dealings with poorer countries. And as long as a participatory economy gives something less than 100 percent of the efficiency gain to a poorer international partner, the participatory economy will still be better off. Things will always prove more complicated in practice. But before considering complications let me situate the question of international economics in a broader context in hopes of clarifying some general principles of equitable cooperation that should guide us when complications arise.

I failed my first oral examination for a Ph.D. in economics because I did not recognize that the "indicated response" to my examiner's question: "Why do I hire a housekeeper and work as a university department chair?" was: "The benefits of comparative advantage." Instead, I answered using concepts like social conditioning, discrimination, exploitation, and racism—rather incoherently—and concluded—rather awkwardly—that in a good society we would all work at things we were good at, but we would all clean up our own messes as well. Thirty years later, I can at least state the problem more clearly: "When should we avail ourselves of the benefits of social cooperation, and how should we distribute the burdens and benefits when we do so?"

In many areas of life, humans have discovered significant benefits from social cooperation. We can educate our children better when some of us teach elementary school, others teach high school, and most do no formal teaching at all. And we all can eat and dress better when some of us grow food and others weave clothes. In other words, while we could try to satisfy our economic needs self-sufficiently, we seldom do so because establishing social relations that mediate divisions of responsibilities and rewards has often proven more efficient. Yet while we have been adept at arranging divisions of labor that lessen overall burdens and increase overall benefits, we have proven considerably less clever at distributing the burdens and benefits equitably, not to speak of managing the cooperative process democratically.

International economic cooperation is a particularly poignant case in point. Frequently the advantages of international cooperation are overestimated, and sometimes commercial prices misidentify true comparative advantages and greater international specialization leads to efficiency losses, not gains. For example, international markets systematically ignore important environmental and human effects associated with increased international specialization and transportation. Market prices underestimate damage to the environment and human health from large-scale, chemical-based agriculture, and also underestimate many of the environmental and human benefits of small-scale, organic local farming. Since greater international specialization usually means growth of the former at the expense of the latter, net benefits are systematically overestimated, and in some cases comparative advantages are misidentified leading to counterproductive new patterns of specialization and efficiency losses not gains. The human and public costs associated with the dislocation of work patterns due to changes in the international division of labor are also typically ignored by the market-price system since those who reap the benefits from international specialization are often able to externalize the costs of adjustment onto others. This is an additional reason that benefits from greater international specialization are overestimated, and in some cases may not even exceed the adjustment costs that go unmeasured in the market nexus. Finally, those who sing the praises of "capital liberalization" fail to count the efficiency losses from the depressions unleashed on developing economies when the ever more leveraged and unsafe international financial system breaks down in crisis and contagion, as it has done repeatedly over the past decade. Even when there are efficiency gains from international trade and investment, market forces invariably distribute those gains between countries unfairly. As long as capital is scarce globally, countries with more capital will usually be able to command more than 50 percent of the efficiency gains from international trade and investment when the terms of trade and international interest rates are determined by market forces, thereby aggravating global inequalities. No wonder some in the antiglobalization movement argue it is best to dispense with international trade and investment altogether!

However, while withdrawal from the international economy may be a wise choice for countries who cannot avoid severe neoliberal conditionalities, withdrawal is not always the best course of action. When true comparative advantages can be correctly identified and efficiency gains shared equitably, international economic cooperation *can* be advantageous. In any case, there is nothing in the nature of a participatory economy that precludes it from taking advantage of the benefits of international cooperation when they present themselves. Get all you can when dealing with wealthier international economic partners. Make sure poorer partners get at least 50 percent of any efficiency gains.

CONCLUSION

When there are significant differences in the *true* opportunity costs of producing different goods and services between countries, there *are* potential efficiency gains from specialization and trade. Moreover, there *are* terms of trade that can distribute the efficiency gain between trading partners in any way we like. There are always terms of trade that would give the entire efficiency gain from specialization and trade to country A and none to country B, just as there are (different) terms of trade that would give the whole efficiency gain to country B and none to country A. Generally speaking, there are terms of trade that give x percent of the efficiency gain to country A and 100 minus x percent to country B for any x between zero and one hundred. Similarly, when there are differences between how much another dollar of credit can increase the productivity of someone working in one country compared to someone working in another country, there *are* potential efficiency gains from international lending, and there are interest rates that can distribute the efficiency gain between the lending and borrowing countries any way we like. In other words, there are situations in which international trade and investment *can* yield efficiency gains, and there *are* ways the efficiency gain can be divided so as to reduce inequality and injustice while still yielding mutual benefits— leaving both partners better off. All a participatory economy in a global capitalist economy has to do is identify which countries have a lower average level of reward for effort than it does, and which countries have a higher level of reward for effort. Readily available figures on GDP per capita for different countries will suffice until more accurate measures of average economic well-being are developed. When dealing with countries with a GDP per capita higher than its own, a participatory economy is free to negotiate "no holds barred." In this case, the better the terms the participatory economy secures, the more it serves the cause of international justice as well as its own interests. However, when dealing with countries with a lower GDP per capita than its own, a participatory economy must share more than 50 percent of the efficiency gain with its poorer international economic partner, or otherwise violate its own principles of economic justice and risk undermining the moral logic that underlies its own system of cooperation.

What Do We Want?

As the new millennium opens the question of economic vision boils down to this: Do we want to try to measure the value of each person's contribution to social production and allow individuals to withdraw from social production accordingly? Or do we want to base differences in consumption on differences in the sacrifices people make in the system of economic cooperation as judged by one's work mates? In other words, do we want an economy that obeys the maxim, "to each according to the value of contribution," or the maxim "to each according to effort and sacrifice?"

Do we want a few to plan and coordinate the work of the many? Or do we want everyone to have the opportunity to participate in economic decision making to the degree they are affected by the outcome? In other words, do we want to continue to organize work hierarchically with conceptual tasks monopolized by a few, or do we want workplace democracy and job complexes balanced for empowerment?

Do we want a structure for expressing preferences that is biased in favor of individual consumption over social consumption? Or do we want it to be as easy for people to register preferences for social as it is for individual consumption? In other words, do we want markets or nested federations of consumer councils?

Do we want economic decisions to be determined by competition between groups pitted against one another for their well-being and survival? Or do we want workers and consumers to be able to plan their joint endeavors democratically, efficiently, and equitably? In other words, do we want to abdicate economic decision making to the marketplace or do we want to embrace the possibility of participatory planning?

As long as the problem is viewed as how to get an economic elite to make decisions in the public interest rather than its own, we won't get very far in thinking about a truly desirable economy. Whether they be capitalists, central planners, or managers of public enterprises, economic elites will imperfectly serve the public interest at best, and more often than not end by subverting the public interest to serve their own. Moreover, *the social process of consciously, democratically, and equitably coordinating our interconnected economic activities is fundamentally different from the social process of competing against one another in the marketplace exchanging goods and services.* While both "solutions" to the economic problem are feasible, only the former is compatible with self-management (decision-making input in proportion to the degree one is affected by the outcome), equity (to each according to personal sacrifice), and efficiency (maximizing benefits from using scarce productive resources), not to speak of solidarity (concern for the well-being of others) and environmental sustainability.

The question is *not* whether it is possible to achieve the kind of desirable economy described in this chapter in the near future. The answer to that question is obviously *no*. Instead, the question is what it means for an economy to be just and democratic, and what economic institutions are capable of achieving economic democracy and justice without sacrificing economic efficiency. Only after we are clear about what we really mean when we speak of the economics of equitable cooperation does the question *then* become how to get there from where we find ourselves today. After addressing important concerns that have been raised about participatory economics in chapter 9, we proceed to explore ideas about how to answer the second question in Part 4 where we consider economic reform campaigns and movements, and "prefigurative" experiments that can start us on the long march toward equitable cooperation.

9

Legitimate Concerns

Twentieth-century critics of capitalism promised that eliminating private ownership of the means of production and replacing markets with rational economic planning would give people control over their economic lives, eliminate economic injustice, and improve economic efficiency. To say critics of capitalism failed to live up to our promises would be a gross understatement. People today have every right to be skeptical when those who criticize capitalism claim they know how to organize an economy of equitable cooperation. In this chapter, I answer as best I can criticisms that have been raised over the past dozen years to the kind of participatory economy described in the last chapter. In some cases I am convinced critics have little reason to worry and have been overly influenced by conservative dogma. In other cases I worry as well, even though I think there is a reasonable chance of success. In all cases I think a skeptical attitude is fully justified, provided this does not turn into pretending that capitalism, or market socialism for that matter, is better than it is or can be. In any case, if we finally succeed in organizing an economy that deserves to be called a system of "equitable cooperation," it will be partly because we thought through how to do so much more clearly and concretely than we have in the past, and this will not happen unless critics vigorously challenge proposals like participatory economics.

Too Many Meetings? Cybernetic Overload? Misinformation?

Wouldn't the allocation of resources in a complex economy by means of participatory decision-making institutions place impossible demands on information processing and inordinate demands on people's time? . . . The mere listing of the requirements for decision-making in a participatory economy is enough to generate skepticism about whether and how they can possibly be met. Even if, in principle, institutions and processes can be developed to accomplish the necessary tasks . . . one is bound to wonder whether the whole system would actually function in practice. Assuming that computer technology could be relied upon to process and disseminate the enormous amount of information needed to make the system work, how would people be persuaded to provide the needed information in an unbiased and disinterested manner? And even if all the needed information could be accurately compiled, wouldn't participatory planning require each individual to dedicate so much time, interest and energy to assessing the information and participating in decision-making meetings that most people would get sick and tired of doing it?[1]

—Thomas Weisskopf

How many damn meetings would we all have to go to?[2]

—George Scialabba

There is good reason to ask if making economic decisions democratically might not bog down in endless debate. Anyone who has not attended meetings where discussion took up more of people's time than it was worth needs to attend more meetings, or meetings of more idealistic and radical organizations! We also have little experience with democratic economic planning on a national scale where so many things must be coordinated before a plan is put into motion. Perhaps the only reason national planning was feasible under communism was *because* it was autocratic and undemocratic. Finally, our limited experience with political democracy at the national level, where decisions are arguably fewer than economic decisions, has invariably ended by delegating decision making to elected representatives. No wonder when Alec Nove, a life-long student of the Soviet economy and planning system, confronts people with an endless list of decisions that must be coordinated in a modern economy, many are inclined to agree with him that there is no choice but to embrace the market as the only feasible alternative to authoritarian planning. But is decision making in a participatory economy really as daunting as Nove, Weisskopf, and others assume it must be?

First of all, information processing and meeting time is far from zero in capitalist economies, which critics of the idea of democratic planning conveniently ignore. As Pat Devine pointed out:

> In modern societies a large and possibly increasing proportion of overall social time is already spent on administration, on negotiation, on organizing and running systems and people. In existing societies much of this activity is concerned with commercial rivalry and the management of the social conflict and consequences of alienation that stem from exploitation, oppression, inequality and subalternity. One recent estimate has suggested that as much as half the GDP of advanced western countries may now be accounted for by transaction costs arising from increasing division of labour and the growth of alienation associated with it.[3]

David Levy reminded those skeptical that participatory planning could "coordinate and integrate consumption and production plans among millions of people," that:

> Within capitalist manufacturing firms we find echelons of managers and staff whose job it is to try to forecast demand and supply. Indeed, only a small fraction of workers directly produce goods and services. Moreover, the existing system requires millions of government employees, many of whom are in jobs created precisely because the market system provides massive incentives to engage in fraud, theft, environmental destruction, and abuse of workers' health and safety. And even during our "leisure time," we must fill in tax forms and pay bills.[4]

But would a participatory economy waste even more of our time in decision making? We can break the issue down into meeting time inside worker councils, meeting time in consumer councils, meeting time in federations, and meeting time in the participatory planning process itself.

Conception and coordination is part of the organization of production in any economic system. Under hierarchical organizations of production relatively few employees spend most, if not all, of their time thinking, meeting, coordinating, and monitoring others while most employees simply do as they're told. So it is true, most people would spend more time in workplace meetings in a participatory economy than in a hierarchical one. But this is because most people are excluded from workplace decision making under capitalism and authoritarian planning, as they largely would be under market socialism as well. It does not necessarily mean the total amount of time spent on thinking and meeting, rather than producing, would be greater in a participatory workplace. Moreover, autocratic meetings and procedures can waste time and be inefficient just as democratic meetings and procedures can be. Whether the decision-making process regarding production is efficient and streamlined need not be related to whether it is democratic. Finally, while it might prove to be the case that democratic decision making about production requires more "meeting time" than autocratic decision making, it should also be the case that less time is required to monitor and enforce democratic decisions about work than autocratic ones. When workers participate in making a decision they are more likely to require less oversight to carry it out. In any case, meeting time in worker councils is part of people's balanced job complexes: it is part of the normal workday in a participatory economy, just as it is for managers and supervisors in existing economies. It is not an infringement on workers' leisure time.

We plead guilty to suggesting that more social interaction go into making consumption decisions than is the case in market economies. One of the great failures of market systems is that they do not provide a suitable vehicle through which people can express and coordinate their consumption desires. Social consumption is disadvantaged compared to individual consumption in market economies precisely because appropriate institutional vehicles to make social choice easy and efficient are lacking. It is through a layered network of consumer federations that we propose overcoming alienation in public choice and isolated expression of individual choice that is the hallmark of market economies. Whether this will take more time than the present organization of consumption depends on a number of trade-offs.

Presently political and economic elites dominate local, state, and national public choice. For the most part they operate relatively free from restraint by the affected majority, but periodically time-consuming campaigns are mounted by popular organizations in attempts to rectify matters when they get grossly out of hand. In a participatory economy people would vote directly on matters of public choice. But that doesn't require a great deal of time, nor require attending any meetings at all. Expert testimony and differing opinions would be aired through a public-service media. Individuals and interest groups with strong feelings on particular issues would participate in these forum, but others would be free to pay as much or little attention to these debates as they wished. The key is that expressing one's preferences regarding local and national public good consumption is just as easy for individuals in a participatory economy as expressing one's preferences for beef versus chicken versus fish versus tofu. At each level of public-good consumption the options are formulated by delegates chosen democratically, then voted on by all those affected in economic referenda within consumer federations rather than voted on by delegates. It is true consumers will vote more in a participatory economy than in market systems. But this does not mean consumers spend more time in meetings.

The big issue, however, is how much meeting time is required by participatory planning itself, which we do proudly advertise as a "social, iterative, procedure." Contrary to the presumptions of critics, we did *not* propose a model of democratic planning in which different groups of workers and consumers, or their elected representatives, meet face to face to discuss and negotiate how to coordinate their activities. Instead we proposed a procedure in which councils and federations submit proposals only for their own activities, receive new information including revised estimates of social costs, and resubmit proposals, again, only for their own activities.[5] There is no meeting. Councils and federations submit their own proposals and vote thumbs up or down on the proposals of others. Nor did we propose meetings of delegates to define different feasible, comprehensive plans to be voted on. Delegates to particular federations will formulate public-good consumption options for those in their federations to vote on, but there are no meetings of delegates from *different* councils and federations to negotiate changes in the proposals coming from different councils and federations until they are mutually feasible. The participatory planning procedure we proposed is precisely an alternative to the "big-meeting" notion of how to democratically plan a national economy. We *agree* with critics who think the big-meeting version of national, democratic, economic planning is impractical, and would prove more a nightmare than a dream, which is why we proposed the participatory planning procedure *instead*.

We did suggest one time-saving procedure that *could* be used if people in a participatory economy want to. After a number of iterations had already settled the major contours of the plan—without meetings between delegates from different councils—the professional staff of the Iteration Facilitation Board (IFB) *could* define a few feasible plans within those contours for all to vote on without ever meeting and debating at all. The purpose would be to save the time otherwise required to go through further iterations to whittle proposals down to a feasible plan when there is very little left to be decided in any case. For example, if 97 percent of the plan is already settled in the first seven iterations, people may decide it is not worth another seven iterations to resolve the remaining 3 percent. If they wish, they could ask the IFB staff to formulate, say, five different ways to settle the remaining 3 percent of the plan and submit them to a referendum. In any case, this option *reduces* planning time rather than increases it. It could be used, or not, depending on how participants felt about the diminishing productivity of further iterations and how much people were willing to trust the IFB to formulate different "end-game" options. Finally, it bears pointing out that we did not even propose face-to-face meetings where people from different councils or federations could plead their cases for unusual consumption or production proposals. Instead we proposed that councils submit qualitative information as part of their proposals so that higher level federations could grant exceptions in unusual cases should they choose to. Moreover, the procedure we proposed for approving or disapproving unusual proposals is a simple up, down vote rather than a rancorous meeting.

But even if meeting time proves not to be overwhelming, Weisskopf also asked *"How would people be persuaded to provide the needed information in an unbiased and disinterested manner?"* In light of the Soviet experience this is a reasonable concern. When left economists wrote about the advantages of comprehensive planning in the 1950s and 1960s they pointed out that advances in mathematical programming theory and computer technology finally made it possible for central planners to calculate an efficient plan. They pointed out that all planners had to do was gather information about the availabilities of different kinds of labor and primary inputs, as well as information about the technologies available to the state-owned enterprises, then, provided the planners were supplied with accurate information about the relative values to society of different final goods and services, there were no longer any theoretical or practical obstacles to calculating the "rational economic plan," advertised as an alternative to the anarchic inefficiency of market economies. However, the assumption that central planners could discover the productive capabilities of state-owned enterprises proved terribly naïve. As explained in chapter 4, a plant manager has every reason to lie to her superiors on the central planning board about the true capabilities of her plant because she knows the plan she is eventually ordered to carry out can be influenced by what the central planners believe her enterprise is capable of. If plant managers are rewarded for fulfilling their plan targets, and penalized for failing to do so—as they most certainly were in the Soviet system—they have every reason to pretend their plants are capable of less than they really are. Of course, central planners come to expect plant managers to do just this. So central planners are left no alternative but to employ industry experts themselves to provide alternative estimates of plant capabilities. Therefore, Weisskopf is correct to point out that this becomes a massive, inefficient system of disinformation. Plant managers lie. Central planners don't believe them. Scarce expertise is duplicated in ministries and plants in a futile effort to estimate the magnitude of disinformation occurring. In short, the dream of a rational plan to use the nation's scarce productive resources to maximize the fulfillment of human needs turns into a nightmare of bureaucratic inefficiency because the information system of central planning is not "incentive compatible."

But participatory planning is *not* central planning. The procedures are completely different and the incentives are completely different. And one of the important ways in which it is different from central planning is that it *is* incentive compatible, that is, actors have an incentive to report truthfully rather than an incentive to misrepresent their capabilities or preferences. We make no naïve assumption that everyone will behave truthfully in a participatory economy even if there is an incentive for them not to. Instead we assume individuals, worker councils, consumer councils, and federations will all behave in their own self-interests. In other words, we assume they will reveal information truthfully only if it is in their interests, and we designed a planning mechanism where it is in their interests to do so.

In market economies the most serious incentive incompatibility regards consumer's expression of preferences for public goods, known as the free-rider problem. Consumers have an incentive to underrepresent their true preferences for public goods. In central planning the most serious incentive incompatibility regards enterprise management deceiving central planners about the productive capabilities of the enterprise, as explained above. But neither of the major incentive incompatibilities that plagued twentieth-century economies exist in a participatory economy. In a participatory economy consumers would rationally expect to lose well-being by misrepresenting their preferences for public goods. Members of a council or federation who receive a public good are charged their proportionate share of its social cost in participatory planning, regardless of how they individually voted. Therefore, any consumer who pretends to benefit less from a public good than she truly does when voting her preferences only lowers the probability of getting the amount of the public good she truly wants without appreciably diminishing her own payment. Pretending to benefit more than one truly does is also personally counterproductive. And in a participatory economy workers would rationally expect to diminish the likelihood of being allocated the productive resources they want by under representing their true productive capabilities. If workers pretend they cannot produce as much as they truly can with a set of inputs they only run the risk of not being allocated the inputs they want because they are given to another worker council that reports it can make better use of them. If critics avoid prejudgement based on the experience of central planning and reexamine participatory planning regarding incentive compatibility, I believe they will discover that, at least in this regard, their concerns are not warranted.

While I also think many concerns about endless meetings do not apply to our proposal, I do not want to be misleading. Informed, democratic decision making *is* different than autocratic decision making. And conscious, equitable coordination of the social division of labor *is* different than leaving economic choice to the impersonal laws of supply and demand. Supporters of participatory planning obviously think the advantages of self-management and equitable cooperation are well worth any extra inconvenience. But this is not to say we do not understand this requires, almost by definition, more meaningful social intercourse, which is why every effort should be made to minimize the trouble people must go to when we engage in collective economic self-management. Many of the procedures we recommended were motivated precisely to avoid pitfalls in the naïve illusion that "the people" can make all economic decisions that affect them in what amounts to "one big meeting." No doubt other procedures will be discovered by people living in participatory economies with rich and busy lives to reduce the time and energy required to manage their economic affairs.

Dictatorship of the Sociable? Overtaxing Democracy?

Isn't the practice of participatory democracy sufficiently difficult, time-consuming and emotionally draining that it would in practice have to be limited to a relatively small range of decisions? In practice such a system might well enable some people to exercise much greater influence over decisions than others. Disproportionate influence would not arise from disproportionate wealth or income, but from disproportionate interest in and aptitude for the relevant decision-making processes.[6]

—Thomas Weisskopf

One perverse incentive could be labeled "The Dictatorship of the Sociable." Some people really like meetings. They like to talk, to negotiate, to debate. As a result, they often attend meetings enthusiastically, and they often prevail at them.[7]

—Nancy Folbre

We do not want our economic system to divert people's participatory energies from more to less important issues. But we do want people to be able to participate in making the economic decisions that most affect their lives. People are certainly affected by the tasks they perform at work. That is why we let workers in their councils decide on their own tasks and how to combine tasks into job complexes, and why people are free to apply for whatever job complex they prefer as long as they are qualified to perform all the tasks it contains. People are also affected by what they consume personally. That is why consumers are free to consume whatever they wish consistent with their effort rating. But all who work in a council are affected by the products made and the technologies used there. That is why we let worker councils decide on their own inputs and outputs as long as their proposal uses scarce social resources efficiently. All who live in an area served by public goods are affected by the mixture of public goods available and the quality of the natural environment in the area. That is why we let neighborhood consumer councils decide what local environmental amenities and local public goods they want, and let federations representing larger groups of consumers and residents make decisions about regional and national environmental issues and decide what regional and national public goods they want. Finally, since major investment decisions determine what goods and services will be prioritized, what work processes will be transformed first, and what new products will be developed, these choices affect all who work and consume. That is why we let worker and consumer federations control their own research and development operations and allow these federations to determine the long-run plan for the economy.

Regarding long-run national planning the options are: (1) relegate long-run planning to the vagaries of the marketplace, (2) entrust long-run planning to a political or technical elite, (3) pretend the long-run plan can be efficiently hashed out in "one big meeting" where all participate, or (4) permit federations of workers and consumers to propose, revise, and reconcile the different components of the long-run plan. Leaving long-run planning to the market is responsible for the inefficient and unsustainable course we are presently on. If the planning elite is not chosen democratically, the dangers and disadvantages should now be obvious in light of the history of communist planning. But even if those who are entrusted to conceive and coordinate the long-term plan were chosen democratically, there would be far less room for popular participation than under the procedures of participatory planning. Finally, the impossibility of inviting everyone to one big meeting to come up with a comprehensive, long-run plan would become apparent as soon as someone tried to make up an agenda for the meeting.

Not all desirable changes in the economy can be accomplished all at once. In the next five years we cannot simultaneously replace highway travel with a high-speed rail system, transform agriculture to conform to ecological norms, replace fossil fuels with renewable energy sources, and undo urban sprawl. So besides identifying the long-run changes we want to make, we must prioritize those changes. Since the choices made in these regards have very important impacts on people's lives it is important to maximize popular participation in long-run planning. I think the best way to do this is to use participatory-planning procedures in which federations and *their* research and development units play the dominant role for developing the long-run plan. Then annual plans—which must conform to the long-run plan previously agreed to—can be developed using participatory planning procedures where individual councils play a more important role.

The issue boils down to how can ordinary people best become involved in a particular kind of decision making? In our view the federations of automobile workers, rail workers, agricultural workers, coal miners, oil, chemical and atomic workers, as well as the transportation, food, energy, housing, and environment departments of the national federation of consumers, should all play a prominent role in formulating, evaluating, and prioritizing the alternatives listed above. Even regarding major, long-term choices, we think people participate best in areas closest to their personal concerns, and participatory planning is designed to take advantage of this. So even though everyone will eventually have a vote when we choose between major long-run alternatives, different federations will play key roles in developing those alternatives, as will experts working for federations. Besides the professional staff of the IFB that helps guide the participatory-planning process, professionals in research and development units working directly for different federations will play an active role in defining long-term options for their members to consider. With the aid of the most accurate estimates of social costs and benefits possible provided by the participatory-planning procedure, I remain confident that workers and consumers, through their councils and federations, can guide the long-term planning process, run the annual planning process, and manage their own work and consumption without wasting their valuable time.

Too Inefficient?

Workers might not be sufficiently motivated to train or work. Scarce productive resources might not be used where they are most productive. People might not search for innovations, or workplaces might fail to implement productive innovations even after they are discovered. In other words, economies can suffer from motivational inefficiencies, allocative inefficiencies, or dynamic inefficiencies.

Incentives to Work

Albert & Hahnel's proposal would surely lead to greater equity in the reward for labor than the market-based alternative, but their claim of greater efficiency is misguided. First, it is very difficult to observe and measure an individual's sacrifice or work effort. Moreover, people would have an interest in understating their natural talents and abilities. Second, while it would elicit greater work effort and sacrifice, it would do nothing to assure that such effort and sacrifice were expended in a desirable way.[8]

—Thomas Weisskopf

Albert and Hahnel miss the crucial point which is that a society seeking optimum production needs to discourage clumsy effort and encourage proficient effort so as to avoid waste. Otherwise, the less successful have no material incentive to modify bungling methods.[9]

—Mark Hagar

Maximizers would have incentives to perform at less than their best in early stages in order to maximize later effort scores. Albert and Hahnel's appeal to the analogy of rewarding racers according to effort ill-illustrates their point in this respect. A standard strategic move to maximize winnings over a series of handicap races is to intentionally perform badly in early races in order to get a better handicap in later ones.[10]

—John O'Neill

Anyone who has participated in a workplace with more than two or three workers knows the problem of cliques and rivalries that tends to arise. It is not clear how one would prevent cliques and rivalries from intruding into the effort evaluation process—or to prevent a suspicion that such factors had influenced effort evaluations.[11]

—David Kotz

Before addressing these important concerns, I want to dispose of a common misconception about participatory economics and material rewards. Many critics have jumped to the conclusion that there are no material incentives in a participatory economy. This is simply not true. People do not receive equal consumption for unequal efforts in a participatory economy. People's efforts are rated by their coworkers, and people are awarded consumption rights in their neighborhood consumption councils according to those effort ratings. To each according to her effort—the distributive maxim in a participatory economy—means there are material rewards for above-average efforts as well as material penalties for below-average efforts.

However, differences in people's efforts will not lead to the extreme income differentials characteristic of all economies today, nor the degree of income inequality predictable in market socialist economies. So while there *are* material rewards in a participatory economy, it is still legitimate to ask: With no sky to reach for, will people lift their arms? With no hole to fear, will people move their butts? Proponents of participatory economics have also said we believe material incentives will play a smaller role in participatory economies than they do in economies today. Moreover, we have argued that a participatory economy can *eventually* lead to more and more distribution on the basis of need, that is, to a gradual reduction of material incentives. What reasons are there to expect any of this to be the case?

In a society that awards esteem mostly on the basis of conspicuous consumption, it is not surprising that large income differentials are considered necessary to induce effort. But to assume only conspicuous consumption can motivate people because under capitalism we have strained to make this so is unwarranted. There is plenty of evidence that people can be moved to great sacrifices for reasons other than a desire for personal wealth. Family members make sacrifices for one another without the slightest thought of material gain. Patriots die to defend their country's sovereignty for little or no pay. And there is good reason to believe for nonpathological people, wealth is generally coveted only as a *means* of attaining other ends such as economic security, comfort, respect, status, or power. If accumulating disproportionate consumption opportunities is often a means of achieving more fundamental rewards, there is good reason to believe a powerful system of incentives need not be based on widely disparate consumption opportunities when basic needs are guaranteed and fundamental desires are rewarded directly rather than indirectly.

If expertise and excellence are accorded social recognition directly, as they are in participatory economies, there should be less need to employ the intermediary of conspicuous consumption. If economic security is guaranteed, for everyone, as it is in a participatory economy, there should be no need to accumulate out of fear for the future. If the material, medical, and educational needs of one's children are provided for at public expense, as they are in a participatory economy, there should be no need to accumulate to guarantee one's children the opportunities they deserve. Moreover, if people design their own jobs and participate in economic decision making, as they do in a participatory economy, they should carry out their responsibilities with less need for external motivation of any kind. And if the distribution of burdens and benefits is fair, as it is in a participatory economy, people's sense of social duty should be a more powerful incentive than it is today.

In other words, while a participatory economy does have material incentives, it is designed to maximize the motivating potential of certain kinds of nonmaterial incentives as well, and proponents think there are good reasons to believe these nonmaterial incentives can play a more prominent role in a participatory economy than they do today. There is no way to "prove" that material rewards may be less necessary to motivate effort in different social circumstances than we are accustomed to. Nor do I expect to convince skeptics in a few paragraphs. But it is important to pose the question skeptics raise accurately: If medical, retirement, and children's expenses are taken care of at social expense, if valuable contributions are awarded public recognition, if people plan and agree to their tasks themselves, if a fair share of effort and personal sacrifice are demanded by work mates who must otherwise pick up the slack, *and* if effort is rewarded by commensurate increases in consumption opportunities, will people still be insufficiently motivated to do what needs to be done without larger income differentials than are permitted in a participatory economy? In any case, *that* is the relevant question.[12] Now to address critics' specific concerns.

Weisskopf gives voice to the common assumption that effort is difficult, if not impossible to measure, while the value of a worker's contribution can be measured easily. But neither half of this proposition is as
compelling as usually presumed. Assigning responsibility for outcome in
group endeavors is often ambiguous. Sports teams are more suited to such
calibration than production teams. And compared to football, soccer, and
basketball, it is easiest to calibrate the value of individual contribution to
group achievement in baseball. But even in baseball, debates over different
measures of offensive contribution—batting average, on base percentage,
runs batted in, slugging percentage—as well as disagreements over the
relative importance of pitching versus hitting versus fielding, not to speak
of arguments over what are called "intangibles" and "team chemistry,"
testify to the difficulty of assigning individual responsibility for group
outcomes. Moreover, it is usually more difficult, not less, to assign individual responsibility to different workers than to different athletes for the
accomplishments of their "teams."

Nor is measuring effort so impossible. Anyone who has taught and
graded students for long knows there are two different ways to proceed.
Teachers can compare student's performances on tests and papers to some
abstract standard in the teacher's head, or, more realistically, to each other's
performances. Alternatively, teachers can compare a student's performance
to how well we expect the student to be able to do on an assignment. We
can ask: Given the student's level of preparation when she entered the
class, given the student's natural ability, is this an A, B, or C effort on the
assignment *for this student*? This kind of question is not one teachers find
impossible to answer.[13]

Moreover, it should be easier for work mates to judge each other's
efforts than it is for teachers to judge their students' efforts. I can notice
who comes to class, who participates in class discussions, and who comes
to office hours for help on assignments, and who does not. But I have no
idea how many hours my students study per week, nor how hard they
concentrate when studying. By and large I cannot observe my student's
efforts, and I learned long ago that I cannot always rely on their own testimony regarding self-impressions about how hard they worked on assignments. On the other hand, in a participatory economy a worker's effort
is judged by a committee of her workmates. In other words, a worker's
effort is judged by people who by and large do the same kind of work,
people who often work next to and in collaboration with her, and people
who are familiar with how she has worked in the past. For all these reasons

it should be easier for work mates to judge one another's efforts than it is for teachers to judge their student's efforts.

While I believe all worker councils would take the task of effort rating seriously since it affects how much consumption each is entitled to, I would not expect different worker councils to all approach the task of effort rating in the same way. I suspect some groups of workers will decide they only want to make rough distinctions between people's efforts, say, "below average," "average," and "above average." While other groups might want to draw much finer distinctions—perhaps giving everyone a score between zero and a hundred—with fifty the average score. I also think different worker councils will use different procedures to judge one another's efforts. The number of people on the effort-rating committee, their term of office, rules for rotation, the grievance procedure, and the amount of time spent observing others, versus collecting testimony from workmates, versus self-testimony will no doubt vary from worker council to worker council. Presumably one thing people will consider when deciding where they want to work will be if they feel comfortable with the way a worker council goes about rating effort. Do I like the degree of gradation? Do I trust the system? Do I think they spend too much or too little time judging one another's efforts? I suspect these are all questions job applicants will ask about alternative places to work, just as I suspect dissatisfaction with the effort-rating process will be among the reasons people leave employment in one worker council and seek it in another. Ultimately the question is not whether people's efforts, or personal sacrifices in work, will be perfectly estimated, because, of course they will not be. Instead the question is if most people will feel they are being treated fairly most of the time, and if not, if people feel they have reasonable opportunities for redress.

Weisskopf, Hagar, and O'Neill all ask if there are sufficient incentives in a participatory economy to ensure that people will exert themselves in socially useful ways, pointing out that economies that reward the value of people's contributions solve this problem automatically. Because worker councils must win the approval of consumer councils for their proposals by demonstrating that the social benefit of their outputs is at least as great as the social cost of the inputs they propose to use, participatory planning clearly provides powerful incentives for worker councils to exert themselves in socially useful ways. But critics ask if the same holds true for individual workers whose efforts are judged by their peers? I cannot see why one's coworkers would reward clumsy, bungling, or misdirected effort rather than proficient effort. Why would fellow workers have any less incentive to discourage ineffective, and encourage effective effort on the part of coworkers than capitalist employers do? Every effort-rating committee is constrained by a fixed-average effort rating for all workers in their council equal to the council's social benefit-to-social cost ratio. Therefore, rewarding inefficient effort on the part of a coworker is just as detrimental to the interests of other workers in the council as it would be if they deliberately overstated a worker's effort. While those serving on effort-rating committees will surely consider coworkers' contributions as *one piece of evidence* in estimating how hard a work mate is trying to be effective, the difference is that in a participatory economy they will take other factors into account as well because simply rewarding the value of someone's contribution is not fair. Who are better than her coworkers to know if a worker is charging off at breakneck speed without checking to see if her exertions are effectively directed? Who is in a better position to judge if someone habitually engages in "clumsy effort?" Who can better tell if someone only gives the appearance of trying? Not only are coworkers in the best position to make these judgments, fellow workers in a worker council in a participatory economy have just as much incentive to discourage these kinds of behaviors as do capitalist employers or managers of market socialist enterprises.

Weisskopf and O'Neill also worry that people will try to disguise their true abilities to trick work mates into giving them higher effort ratings than they deserve. It is true that competitors in a series of races in which they know they will be handicapped may have an incentive to go slow in early races to inflate their handicap advantages in later ones. But again, remember who is judging effort in a participatory economy. Who is in a better position to know if someone is deliberately underperforming in the beginning than the people working with her in the same kind of task? We should also ask how much damage is done if someone does pull the wool over the eyes of her work mates through this stratagem? There is an efficiency loss from deliberate underperformance in "early races," and there is an injustice because later efforts are overestimated and overrewarded. But rewarding place of finish is much more unfair, and inefficient as well because it provides no incentive to improve performance if an improvement is insufficient to pass a rival. Is it really a fatal flaw if some devious-minded workers in a participatory economy try to underperform early to be overpaid later?

Finally, Kotz worries that cliques and rivalries will lead to inequities and mistrust in participatory workplaces. Of course counterproductive dynamics associated with cliques can arise in many different social situations, but Kotz's point is presumably that problems from cliques would be magnified by the reward system of participatory economics. Why might this be true? Cliques attempt to bias judgments that are the basis for reward. If reward were according to weight, and if all workers were weighed on the same scale, in public view, there would be no reason for cliques to arise because it would be impossible to contest judgments. Or, if reward were according to personal whim, but there was no way to discover the identity of the judge whose whim a clique would have to influence, there would also be no basis for cliques. So the problem with reward according to effort as judged by one's coworkers is that people's efforts *are* subject to question, and everyone knows whose opinion matters. Moreover, if all rotate onto and off of the effort-rating committee, those serving know those they judge now will judge them later. "Payback" and "tit-for-tat" are phrases that spring to mind. Can the problem of cliques be avoided?

I don't think it is possible to eliminate differences of opinion about effort or sacrifice. And, unfortunately, economic justice requires compensating for differences in effort or sacrifice, not differences in weight. So unless we are prepared to forswear attempts to reward people fairly, the best that can be done in this regard is to explore ways to diminish problems that arise due to differences of opinion. Many assume the only way to reduce disagreement about workers' relative efforts is to improve the accuracy of measurement. And this is one strategy: (1) collect more and better evidence, and weigh it more judiciously. However there are two additional strategies that can be pursued as well: (2) improve "due process" so people are less resentful even when they disagree with judgments. Disagreements are only problematic to the degree that they breed resentment. And, (3) reduce the importance of the entire issue relative to other issues. Even if there are disagreements over judgments, and even if there is dissatisfaction over process, if the question of effort rating is farther down on people's list of priorities, the consequences will be less problematic. I am well aware that these are palliatives rather than cures. I began by admitting that perfect measurement is impossible. Moreover, I realize that my second suggestion amounts to searching for ways to make people more accepting of what they believe to be unjust, and my third suggestion amounts to trying to make people care less about economic injustice in general! However, I believe the second and third strategies capture feelings common to proponents of participatory economics that are not misplaced.

An important difference exists between economies that systematically practice injustice and an economy that is organized to distribute the burdens and benefits of economic activity as fairly as is possible. Moreover, there is every reason to believe that people's attitudes about distributive justice would be somewhat different in those very different contexts. If people believe the economic system is fair, might they not be inclined to attach less importance to disagreements over distributive outcomes in general? If workers believe their own council practices due process, might they not be more tolerant when they disagree with their effort-rating committee? More concretely, is there no reason to believe people might be less inclined to form cliques and pursue rivalrous tactics when the overall system is fair, and when workers in every council have it within their power to modify procedures until they are satisfied that at least there is "due process" if not perfect justice? In general, is it unreasonable to hope that the more economic justice people experience, and the longer justice prevails over injustice, the less people will choose to spend their time and energy in invidious comparisons, at least over the distribution of consumption rights over material possessions?

It is possible to immunize judges from pressures coming from those they judge, but I fear the disadvantages of doing so in this context would far outweigh the advantages. Outsiders could be brought in to judge efforts: workers from other worker councils in the same industry federation being obvious candidates. But outside judges reduce self-management for workers in their councils. In other words, the main problem with outside judges is precisely that they are outsiders. Do we want peer review or not? Alternatively, the identity of coworkers serving on the effort ratings committees could be kept secret. While secrecy may appear attractive, I am deeply skeptical that this would minimize rather than maximize the problem of cliques. Public access to information is a terribly important principle. It is one thing to provide consumers the opportunity to submit anonymous consumption requests accompanied by an effort rating to prevent neighbors from knowing what particular items they consume, which we do in a participatory economy. It is another thing entirely to keep me from knowing who decided on my effort rating. For that matter, privacy regarding items of consumption and privacy regarding one's own effort rating are quite different. In the former case one could argue that ignoring the possibility of negative external effects from my consumption—cigarettes, alcohol, and drugs being examples—what I consume is simply not anybody else's business. While the effort rating I receive may well be of legitimate concern to a coworker because she doesn't know whether she agrees with the rating she received without knowing how her rating compared to mine. Besides a host of theoretical reasons that open and easy access to information for all is good policy, there is a major practical reason that secrecy is bad policy. Namely, it doesn't work. More often than not it turns out that what one blithely assumed could be kept secret, actually was not kept secret. So what we usually must choose between is openness and pretense of secrecy, regardless of whether we realize it. In this case, the advantages of openness over pseudo-secrecy *vis á vis* cliques and rivalries are obvious.

David Kotz and I are both all too familiar with rivalries and cliques in noncapitalist settings. We both have decades of experience with professional peer review in university departments where faculty cliques are a ubiquitous problem precisely because "scores" are subject to question, and because judges and plaintiffs not only know one another, but periodically reverse roles! But I should point out that reward in both our departments is supposed to be based on the value of a professor's contribution, not on our effort. Or, at least that is what administration mandates and most faculty accept as the criterion we should be using. Besides the fact that there is nothing fair about pay increases based on the value of contributions if contributions are different from effort and sacrifice, the other problem, of course, is that opinions among faculty about what constitutes a more or less valuable contribution vary greatly. We have debates over the relative importance of teaching, research, and service. We have debates over whether teaching performance should be based on student evaluations, class observations by department chairs, or a review of syllabi and materials covered. We have debates over whether books or journal publications are more valuable, as well as which publishing houses and which journals are more important. And finally, we simply have disagreements over what research programs are more or less promising. Yes, it is possible for tolerance for diversity to be replaced by voting on the accomplishments of others according to one's own personal strengths and weaknesses in different areas of accomplishment. Yes, it is possible for mutual respect to be eroded by rivalrous tactics and the formation of cliques for attacking and defensive purposes, as Professor Kotz and I are well aware. But all this is possible when peers attempt to rate one another according to contribution, not just when we try to rate each other according to effort, which has yet to be tried. And all of the factors I discussed above do contribute toward making matters better or worse. Some departments are better and some are worse in these regards, and there are times when departments are more fractious and times when they are less so.

Kotz expresses a legitimate concern I would not belittle. In the end I can only say: (1) estimating the value of different people's contributions to collaborative outcomes is also subject to question; (2) while proponents of participatory economics *recommend* rewarding effort as an equitable social norm that is compatible with efficiency, in the end we *propose* that individual worker councils rate themselves as they see fit, and expect they will choose to do so in different ways; (3) our critics are right—remuneration according to effort, or sacrifice, as judged by one's coworkers is the worst possible system of compensation—except for all the alternatives!

Incentives to Educate or Train Oneself

Society needs to encourage people to prepare themselves to work where their comparative advantage in contribution is greater. For efficiency, one must reward efforts to improve the success of efforts, and rewarding contribution may be the only feasible way to do so.[14]

—Mark Hagar

Mark Hagar is absolutely correct that efficiency requires that people educate and train themselves in the ways they can be most socially useful. Taken to its logical extreme we could even say there is both an efficient *amount* of education and training each person should receive, and an efficient *distribution* of that training and education over particular programs of study. Of course when put this way the implications of efficiency for education and training might seem a little frightening since most people like the idea that we should be able to *choose* to study what we like. Regarding education and training, how are personal choice and efficiency reconciled in a participatory economy?

All education and training is paid for at public expense, including appropriate living stipends for students. All are free to apply to any educational and training programs they wish. However, applicants are admitted on the basis of merit—using the best predictors available for success in a program—tempered by affirmative action quotas when necessary to correct for racial and gender biases due to historical discrimination. The key questions are how the number of positions in different educational programs are determined, and what the personal consequences of acceptance and rejection are.

Education is both a consumption and investment good, so the number of positions in programs should be determined by how much people enjoy different kinds of education, *and* by how much different kinds of education improve people's social productivity. But how should acceptance or rejection into educational programs affect people? Since education is at public rather than private expense in a participatory economy, it is not fair for those who spend more time in education (while others who were not accepted work) to appropriate the benefits in the form of higher wages due to the higher productivity that results from their extra human capital.[15] But since all remuneration is based on effort rather than productivity in a participatory economy, the expected income of those who spend more time in education will not be higher than the expected income of those with less. In other words, acceptance or rejection into education and training programs beyond those all receive should have no appreciable effect on people's income prospects in a participatory economy. However, this does not mean that acceptance or rejection does not affect people's lives. If I am accepted into a program of study I like, presumably this improves the quality of my life. If I am accepted into an educational program that qualifies me for a job complex I prefer, this improves the quality of my work life. Finally, if I am accepted into an educational program that makes my contributions more valuable this will earn me greater social recognition and appreciation from my fellow workers and the consumers we serve. Since a participatory economy is not an "acquisitive" society where people are judged by their belongings, but rather a society in which esteem and respect are won through "social serviceability," there should be strong social incentives to develop one's most socially useful potentials through education and training. While there are no material incentives in the form of extra consumption privileges to be gained from pursuing socially useful education and training, there are no material *dis*incentives, and there are significant personal benefits.

No doubt some will worry that even under these circumstances the absence of material rewards for human capital in a participatory economy will lead people not to pursue their education and training sufficiently. On the other hand, others may object that those who are rejected by educational programs in a participatory economy are unfairly penalized by nonmaterial losses through no fault of their own. I seriously doubt there would be a dearth of applicants to colleges, graduate programs, or medical schools in participatory economies. When the alternative to education is work—not leisure—education seldom appears so burdensome. And while those who do not qualify for extra education and training may suffer unfairly because they cannot pursue a course of study they would enjoy, or work at a job they prefer, this injustice is much less than occurs in economies where remuneration is based on the value of one's contribution rather than the sacrifices one makes. Moreover, I know of no way to avoid this inequity, and it may be necessary to assure that people do seek to educate themselves in socially useful ways as Hagar reminds us.

Allocative Efficiency

> Apart from their inhibition of personal freedom, balanced job complexes designed to avoid specialization seem likely to deprive society of the benefits of activities performed well only by people who have devoted a disproportionate amount of time and effort to them.[16]
>   —Thomas Weisskopf

> Personal endowments as well as preferences differ greatly. Up to a point, specialization provides important efficiency gains. A certain level of specialization and hierarchy seems necessary and functional to me.[17]
>   —Nancy Folbre

Allocative efficiency requires assigning scarce productive resources where they are most socially useful. In participatory planning worker councils who use scarce productive resources are charged for inputs according to their indicative prices, and consumers of final goods and services are charged according to their indicative prices as well. The indicative prices generated by the planning process are more accurate estimates of true social opportunity costs than market prices because participatory planning eliminates free-rider and transaction-cost problems that plague market systems, and does a better job of internalizing effects that markets externalize. Because consumer federations participate in the planning process on an equal footing with individual worker and consumer councils, there are no free-rider problems, and desires for public goods are as easy to express as desires for private goods. Because federations of residents must give their permission to be polluted in participatory planning, and are compensated when they do so, negative effects of production and consumption on third parties that go unaccounted for as externalities in market economies are accounted for in the indicative prices that emerge from participatory planning. For all these reasons allocative inefficiencies that are prevalent in market systems are avoided in participatory economies.

Participatory economies also avoid the contradiction between fair remuneration and allocative efficiency in market economies. Individuals consume according to their work effort in a participatory economy. But worker councils are charged according to the social opportunity costs of employing different kinds of labor. This neatly avoids the contradiction between equity—wages based on sacrifice, or effort—and allocative efficiency, labor costs that reflect social opportunity costs. But even if participatory planning allocates scarce human and nonhuman resources efficiently to different enterprises—which no critic in the past dozen years has questioned—will balanced job complexes not introduce allocative inefficiencies by failing to economize on scarce talents and costly training and by failing to take advantage of expertise, as Weisskopf and Folbre warn?

BJCs are designed to avoid disparate empowerment and thereby protect the freedom of those who otherwise would not have equal opportunity to participate in economic decision making. BJCs are designed to prevent oppression and class divisions. But BJCs do *not* eliminate specialization. The proposal is not that everyone perform every task. Each person will still perform a very small number of tasks in her particular BJC. Some will still specialize in brain surgery, others in electrical engineering, others in high-voltage welding. But if the specialized tasks in a BJC are more empowering than tasks are on average, those who perform them will also perform some less empowering tasks as well. And if the specialized tasks in a BJC are more desirable than tasks are on average, those who perform them will also perform some less desirable tasks, unless they wish to work more hours or accept a lower-effort rating. Moreover, the tasks each performs only need to be balanced for empowerment and desirability over a reasonable period of time, and the balancing is done in the context of what is practical in particular work situations. Finally, the balancing is all done by committees composed of workers in each workplace, and done as they see fit. BJCs are not designed by an external bureaucracy and imposed on workers. So there is every reason to believe job-balancing committees composed of workers in a workplace will take ample leeway in organizing work to accommodate technological and psychological considerations in their workplace while eliminating large, persistent differences in empowerment and desirability. Nonetheless, critics have repeatedly raised two objections that deserve consideration:

- Talent is scarce and training is socially costly, therefore it is inefficient for talented people or people with training to do menial tasks.
- For everyone to participate equally in economic decisions ignores the importance of expertise.

The "scarce-talent" argument against BJCs makes a valid point that I wish to acknowledge. However, I think the objection is usually overstated. It is true not everyone has the talent to become a brain surgeon, and it is true there are social costs to training brain surgeons. Therefore, there *is* an efficiency loss whenever a skilled brain surgeon does something other than perform brain surgery. Roughly speaking, if brain surgeons spend x percent of their time doing something other than brain surgery, there is an additional social cost of training x percent more brain surgeons. But as noted in the last chapter, virtually every study confirms that participation increases worker productivity. So if BJCs enhance effective participation—as they are intended to—the efficiency loss because they fail to economize on "scarce talent" completely, must be weighed against the productivity gain they bring from greater participation of all workers. Then, if there is still a net efficiency loss, this would have to be weighed against the importance of balancing jobs for empowerment in giving people equal opportunities to exercise self-management in work.

The "expertise" argument against balancing jobs for empowerment fails to distinguish between the legitimate role of expertise and an unwarranted usurpation of decision-making power by experts. In circumstances where the consequences of decisions are complicated and not readily apparent, there is an obvious need for experts. But economic choice entails both determining *and* evaluating consequences. Presumably those with expertise in a matter can predict the consequences of a decision more accurately than nonexperts. But those affected by a choice know best whether they prefer one outcome to another. So, while efficiency requires an important role for experts in predicting consequences of choices in complicated situations, efficiency also requires that those who will be affected determine which consequences they prefer. This means not only is it inefficient to prevent experts from explaining consequences of complicated choices to those who will be affected, it is also inefficient to keep those affected by decisions from making them after considering expert opinion. Self-management, defined as decision-making input in proportion to the degree one is affected by the outcome, does not mean there is no role for experts. Instead it means confining experts to their proper role and keeping them from usurping a role that it is neither fair, democratic, nor efficient for them to assume.

Dynamic Efficiency

Proponents of new models of a socialist economy which seek to combine economic planning with wide participation in decision-making emphasize the potential superiority of their systems over other systems at meeting human needs. However, the claim of superiority has been typically cast in a static framework that largely overlooks the performance of participatory planning in the most important dynamic aspect of economic life: technical change and the process which brings it about—innovation. Does the system provide strong incentives for innovation? Does the system provide substantial means for carrying out innovation? Does the system generate innovative effort that contributes effectively to the improvement of human welfare?[18]

—David Kotz

Even if there are incentives to work hard and smart, even if there are incentives to educate and train oneself to be more socially useful, and even if incentives are compatible with an efficient allocation of scarce productive resources at any point in time, this does not guarantee dynamic efficiency. Do individuals have an incentive to search for innovations, and do worker councils have an incentive and means to implement productive innovations once they are found? These are important questions since even when people come to recognize that environmentally and socially destructive growth is no longer in their interests, raising living standards for today's disadvantaged, reducing everyone's work time, improving the quality of everyone's work lives, and restoring the natural environment will require a great deal of innovation.

Supporters of participatory economics do not support rewarding those who succeed in discovering productive innovations with vastly greater consumption rights than others who make equivalent personal sacrifices in work. Instead we recommend emphasizing social recognition of outstanding achievements for a variety of reasons. First, successful innovation is often the outcome of cumulative human creativity for which a single individual is rarely responsible. Second, an individual's contribution is often the product of genius and luck as much as effort, which implies that recognizing innovation through social esteem rather than material reward is superior on ethical grounds. Third, we are not convinced that social incentives, when tried, will prove less powerful than material ones. It should be recognized that no economy ever has, or could pay innovators the full social value of their innovations. If it did, there would be no benefit left to those who apply them! This means if material compensation is the only reward, innovation will be understimulated in any case. Moreover, often material reward is merely an imperfect substitute for what is truly desired: social esteem. How else can one explain why those who already have more wealth than they, their children, and their children's children can possibly consume continue to strive to accumulate more? In any case, these are the opinions of those who advocate replacing capitalism with participatory economics. Actual policy in a participatory economy would be settled democratically by its members in light of results.

Nor do we see why critics believe there would be insufficient incentives for enterprises to seek and implement innovations, unless they measure a participatory economy against a mythical and misleading image of capitalism. Sometimes supporters of capitalism presume that innovating capitalist enterprises capture the full benefits of their successes, while it is also assumed that innovations spread instantaneously to all enterprises in an industry. When made explicit it is obvious these assumptions are contradictory. Yet only if both assumptions hold can one conclude that capitalism provides maximum material stimulus to innovation *and* achieves technological efficiency throughout the economy. In reality innovative capitalist enterprises temporarily capture "super profits," which are competed away more or less rapidly depending on a host of circumstances including industry structure, barriers to entry, patent laws, and how vigorously intellectual property rights are enforced. This means that in reality there is an unavoidable trade-off in capitalist economies between stimulus to innovation and the rapid spread of innovations, a trade-off between dynamic and static efficiency.

In a participatory economy all innovations will immediately be made available to all enterprises, so there will never be any loss of static efficiency. And while nonmaterial incentives for innovative firms are emphasized, material incentives are available if necessary without sacrificing static efficiency.[19] There are strong incentives for worker councils to search for innovations that increase the social benefits of their outputs, or reduce the social costs of their inputs since this would increase the worker council's social benefit to social cost ratio. Raising the social benefit-to-social cost ratio makes it easier for the council to get its proposals accepted in the participatory-planning process, can allow workers to reduce their efforts, can permit them to improve the quality of their work lives, or can raise the average effort rating the council can award its members. However, it is true that the rapid spread of innovations in a participatory economy will render these advantages temporary. As the innovation spreads to other enterprises, estimates of social opportunity costs will change, job complexes will be rebalanced across enterprises and industries, and the social benefits of innovations as they are realized will be spread to all workers and consumers. So what will curb the incentive to "free ride" on the innovations of others if material benefits to innovating enterprises disappear so quickly in a participatory economy?

First, recognition of "social serviceability" is a more powerful incentive to innovation in a participatory economy where acquisition of personal wealth is both less necessary and less likely to elicit social esteem. Second, a participatory economy is better suited to allocating sufficient resources to research and development because research and development is largely a public good that is predictably undersupplied in market economies but not discriminated against by participatory planning. Third, while we recommend it only as a last resort, there are no reasons in a participatory economy that the recalibration of work complexes for innovative workplaces cannot be delayed, or extra consumption allowances for workers in innovative enterprises cannot be granted for some period of time if members of a participatory economy decide greater material rewards for innovative enterprises are necessary to achieve desirable rates of technical progress.

Too Unfree?

The issue is how much value we should attach to libertarian rights such as freedom of choice, privacy, and the development of one's own specialized talents and abilities—as compared to the more traditional socialist goals of equity, democracy and solidarity. Replacement of markets with a participatory economic system would arguably contribute to a more egalitarian, democratic and solidaristic society, but would appear to do so at a cost in terms of libertarian objectives. Certain libertarian objectives associated with personal freedom of choice can best be satisfied only if individuals have the kind of opportunities for choice and for exit that a market system alone can provide.[20]

—Thomas Weisskopf

Albert and Hahnel underestimate the wide and enduring appeal of traditional American values like individualism, self-reliance, and minding one's own business. Not all individualism, after all, is possessive individualism. Sometimes—a lot of the time—people just want to be left alone.[21]

—George Scialabba

Participatory economics was the result of a self-conscious attempt to design an economy that allows people to control their own economic lives in a system of equitable cooperation with others. Besides putting major economic decisions in the hands of the citizenry rather than in the hands of an elite, freedom of choice of consumption, employment, and career, as well as personal privacy, are fully guaranteed in a participatory economy.

- People in a participatory economy are free to consume whatever goods and services they wish, and consumer preferences determine what will be produced.

An individual's overall consumption is constrained in a participatory economy by her effort or sacrifice, just as an individual's overall consumption is constrained in a market economy, by her income, which is usually *not* the same as her effort or sacrifice. But there is complete freedom of choice in a participatory economy regarding *what* one wishes to consume. Moreover, consumer preferences determine what will be produced in a participatory economy whereas they only do so very imperfectly in market economies. Markets bias consumer choice by overcharging for goods whose production or consumption entail positive external effects, undercharging for goods with negative external effects, and by oversupplying private goods relative to public goods. In this way intrinsic biases in markets influence what will be produced without regard to the true preferences of consumers. Participatory planning is carefully designed to eliminate these biases, which generate inefficiencies and infringe on "consumer sovereignty." People in a participatory economy are also free to choose more consumption and less leisure, or vice versa, simply by working more or fewer hours, and are free to distribute their effort and consumption over their lives as they wish by saving and borrowing. In market economies people deal with banks and loan officers, whereas borrowing and saving is handled by consumer councils and federations in participatory economies.

Critics worry that neighbors' opinions will prove intrusive, that consumers cannot foresee what they will want for a whole year, and that changing consumption orders will prove frustrating. But neighbors can only offer suggestions. They are not permitted to reject consumption requests on grounds of content, only if social cost exceeds effort. And if anyone does not wish to hear her neighbors' opinions, she can submit an anonymous consumption request to a consumption council composed of anonymous members who are not her neighbors. We are well aware that consumers will misestimate what they ask for and need to make changes during the year, and that some will prove more reliable and others more fickle. The easiest way to think about this is to imagine each consumer with a swipe card that records what they consume during the year, and compares their rate of consumption for each item against the amount they asked for. If rates of consumption deviate by, say, 20 percent from the rate implied by the annual request, consumers could be "prompted" and asked if they needed to request a change. If at the end of the year the total social cost of someone's actual consumption differs from the social cost of what they had asked for, they would simply be credited or debited appropriately. One of the functions of consumer councils and federations is to coordinate changes in consumption, if possible, with other consumption federations, and if not with worker federations as well. To whatever extent consumers do foresee their needs, a participatory economy is positioned to capture the efficiency gains of planning over market disequilibria. To the extent that consumers cannot accurately gauge their desires, councils and federations will have to negotiate midcourse adjustments. No doubt there will be less fluctuation in indicative prices than there is in market prices since adjustments in production will be negotiated directly between the national consumer federation and industrial federations. But a participatory economy is certainly not powerless to respond to changes in consumer desires. Is it possible that some consumer may not receive some particular item exactly when they want it if it was not in their original order? Yes. But that should not occur often, and if memory serves, not every child found a Cabbage Patch Doll under her Christmas tree a few years back.

Consumer councils and federations also afford consumers much greater clout *vis á vis* producers over quality and defects than consumers have in market economies. Critics of participatory economics mistakenly assume it is no different from Soviet-style command planning in this regard. It is true consumers were even more disenfranchised in the centrally planned economies than they are in market economies. Soviet, Chinese, Cuban, and Polish consumers not only confronted a huge state-distribution system alone, but faced a "take it or take nothing" proposition. In market economies individual consumers face powerful corporations alone, most of whom devote significant resources to manipulating us. The advantage is we can walk away from one corporate behemoth and buy from another, which mouths the doublespeak mantra "the customer is always right" with equal insincerity. But in a participatory economy neighborhood consumer councils and federations put consumers on an even playing field with producers, *and* each consumer has freedom of exit. Instead of relying on advertisements from profit-seeking producers, consumers in a participatory economy will get information from their consumer councils and federations. It is the difference between getting information about the likelihood of washing machines breaking down from GE or from *Consumer Reports*. It is the difference between GM having to hoodwink Robin Hahnel or Ralph Nader and his research associates about automobile safety. Worker councils don't get credited for goods returned. If a consumer is unsatisfied with a product she only has to refuse it and have it returned as unacceptable by her consumer council. Then the question of whether the product delivered was up to standards is settled between the consumer council, or federation, and the worker council who made it, or their federation.

- People in a participatory economy are free to apply to work wherever they want, free to bid on any job complex at their workplace they want, and free to organize a new enterprise to produce whatever they want, by any means they want, in cooperation with whomever else they want.

Of course, worker councils are also free to hire whomever they want from those who apply, qualified coworkers are also free to bid on any job complex they want, and new worker councils must be certified by their industry federation as "competent" to deliver what they promise, and must submit an acceptable proposal during the participatory planning process. But constraints on individual work choices and certification of competence are necessary in any social division of labor, which is why analogous constraints are present in market economies.

- Students are free to apply to any educational institution and degree program they want, and if accepted, pay no tuition while receiving a living stipend appropriate to their age and needs. Workers are free to bid on any training program offered outside or inside their workplace—all of which are free of charge—and receive their normal compensation while undergoing training.

In a participatory economy educational opportunities are allocated by merit with no chance that a more promising but less affluent applicant will be passed over by one who is less qualified but better able to pay.[22]

But equal educational opportunities will not lead to equal amounts of education for all. Isn't it inequitable if some receive more education at public expense than others? In a market economy it is unfair since those who receive more education will have more human capital and therefore receive higher wages. In market economies public education, in effect, forces poor families to subsidize the extra education of children from wealthier families whenever children from wealthier families qualify for more education than children from poorer families.[23] On the other hand, since consumption is based on effort rather than on marginal-revenue product, consumption opportunities will not be unfairly affected by the fact that some receive more education than others in a participatory economy, just as they will not be unfairly affected by morally arbitrary differences in human capital due to the genetic lottery.

The presumption that "certain libertarian objectives associated with personal freedom of choice can best be satisfied only if individuals have the kind of opportunities for choice and for exit that a market system *alone* can provide" proves to be untrue. Choice of consumption and work, opportunities for exit, and "producer and consumer sovereignty" are as great, or greater in a participatory economy than in market economies. In capitalist economies what can workers do who don't like their boss? In market socialist economies what can workers do who don't like the majority decisions of their work mates? Switching workplaces or starting up a new enterprise is the exit option in those economies. In a participatory economy, workers are free to resign from one worker council and apply for work in another. IFBs in a participatory economy can make finding a more compatible work environment far easier than finding one in capitalism, and at least as easy as finding one in a market socialist economy aided by a Swedish-style labor market board that takes retraining and relocation seriously. As far as starting a new enterprise is concerned, convincing an industry federation of the usefulness of a new enterprise is similar to convincing loan officers at a bank and venture capitalists that a new enterprise will prove profitable. And as we have seen, workers have far more control over how they work, and consumers have greater influence over what is available for them to consume in a participatory economy than they do in market economies where the myth of "producer and consumer sovereignty" is largely a lie.

So why do some persist in believing participatory economies sacrifice libertarian values? Misconceptions about what we have actually proposed aside, the issue reduces to different conceptions of libertarianism. What is a libertarian economy? If people are not free, for example, to buy another human being, is the economy not libertarian? Surely there are circumstances that would lead people knowingly and willingly to sell themselves into slavery, yet few would refuse to call an economy libertarian because slavery was outlawed. If people are not free to hire the services of another human being in return for a wage is the economy not libertarian? There are familiar circumstances that lead people knowingly and willingly to accept what traditional socialists called "wage slavery." Does this mean that market socialism is not libertarian because the employer-employee relation is outlawed? As we discovered in chapter 2, equating "economic democracy" with the freedom of individuals to do whatever they please is a shallow interpretation that is fraught with contradictions. Similarly, equating a libertarian economy with the freedom to buy or sell anything robs libertarianism of the merit it richly deserves.

It is, of course, a good thing for people to be free to do what they please, but only if what they choose to do does not infringe on more important freedoms or rights of others. I should not be free to kill you because that would be robbing you of a more fundamental right to life. I should not be free to own you because that robs you of a more fundamental right to decide how to live your own life. Socialists of all varieties once believed that I should not be free to employ you because my freedom of enterprise, or property right, robs you of a more fundamental human right to manage your own laboring capacities. Socialists and most liberals once believed I should not be free to bequeath substantial inheritance to my children because that robs the children of less wealthy parents of their more fundamental right to an equal economic opportunity in life. We can formulate a general principle: *restrictions on the rights of some individuals are justified when they are necessary to protect more fundamental rights of others,* and since such restrictions do not reduce, but increase individual freedom *in toto,* they are fully consistent with libertarian values. But besides the right to life, the right to manage our own labor, and the right to equal economic opportunity, are there additional rights that others should not be free to violate when choosing to do what they please?

Let's go straight to heart of the matter. Suppose I'm intellectually gifted, score high on standardized tests, do well in my undergraduate studies, attend medical school, followed by a specialty in brain surgery, all paid for at public expense. Should I be free to sell my talents and skills for whatever price I can negotiate? In a free-market economy there would be others willing to pay me a great deal for my services. But the high value of my contribution is not based on my effort alone. It is the joint product of genetic talent and education at public expense, in conjunction with my effort. So if remuneration is according to the value of contribution I will receive more than my sacrifices warrant in free-market exchanges, and other less talented and less educated people will receive less than they deserve based on their sacrifices. Apparently we must decide if people who participate in economic cooperation with others have a right to expect a fair outcome, that is, a right to an equitable distribution of the burdens and benefits of social cooperation. And we must decide if this right is more fundamental than the right of individuals to charge what the market will bear for the exercise of their human capital. Freedom of choice over the different roles people play in the division of labor is not the issue at all. The issue is how people free to choose their economic roles should be compensated. I think a good case can be made that people have a right to equitable compensation when they enter into a system of economic cooperation with others, as argued in chapter 1. On the other hand, I can think of no reason why people have a "right" to the whatever compensation the market would award them. What would be the basis of such a "right?" I believe people should be free to do what they want. But this does not mean they should be free to appropriate more than their fair share from social cooperation. That is why the freedom to pursue education and employment according to one's preferences is protected in a participatory economy, but the freedom to take unfair advantage of morally arbitrary differences in human capital to consume more than others who made equal sacrifices is not.

Or, suppose I'm particularly competent and energetic, and more than willing to spend all my work time analyzing and evaluating different options for my worker council. Should I be free to work in a job complex where I am engaged full time in analytical and decision-making activities? As Weisskopf put it: "Many people are likely to prefer doing more specialized work activities than would be permitted under a balanced job-complex requirement which means that enforcement of the requirement might well involve implicit or explicit coercion."[24] But if I am permitted to work at a job complex significantly more empowering than others, then some of my coworkers must work in job complexes that are less empowering, and before long the fact that my work mates have the same *formal* opportunity to participate in economic self-management as I do will not mean that they have the same *effective* opportunity to participate. Before long I will exert more influence over economic decisions than the degree to which I am affected because my work life is particularly empowering, and my coworkers will exert less influence because their work life disempowered them relative to me.

Supporters of participatory economics think everyone should have the opportunity to participate in making economic decisions in proportion to the degree they are affected by those decisions. We think self-management is a fundamental right of people who enter into economic cooperation with one another. So when people are free to do what they want, this does not mean they should be free to infringe on the self-management rights of others. Therefore, we do not believe when a group of workers design job complexes in their workplace to make sure that all of them have the information and abilities needed to engage effectively in self-management that they are engaging in "implicit or explicit coersion." It is true that when workers balance job complexes for empowerment in their workplace, none of them will be able to "choose" jobs that are significantly more empowering than the jobs of their coworkers. But why should they be able to do so? Why would those who work in more empowering job complexes—if they were available—not be guilty of coercing and oppressing their workmates?

Humanly Unfeasible?

Wouldn't a participatory economic system be viable only if there were a prior transformation of people's basic consciousness from one that is individually oriented to one that is socially oriented? . . . In order for mechanisms to add up to a workable system of motivation which could substitute for individual material incentives, there would surely have to be a wholesale conversion of human behavior patterns from *homo economicus* to what might best be characterized as *homo socialis*—i.e., a person whose very consciousness was socially rather than individually oriented.[25]

—Thomas Weisskopf

Assuming Albert and Hahnel's model of participatory economics is technically feasible, is it humanly feasible? Does it presuppose a degree of solidarity and of indifference to comfort, status, privacy, and mobility that it would be unreasonable to expect?[26]

—George Scialabba

Concerns that a participatory economy assumes people are altruists, or that a participatory economy requires a different set of human motivations than people actually have, are usually the last line of defense against participatory economics. Many who declare that they like the idea, and find it a welcome relief from the cutthroat world of competition and greed, hesitate nonetheless because they think a participatory economy presumes people are more generous than most of us really are, and therefore, while a lovely idea, that it simply won't work.

In chapter 5 of *The Political Economy of Participatory Economics*, we defined a formal model of a participatory economy and asked what individually rational behavior would be. After deducing what individually rational behavior *in that context* would be (i.e., what *homo economicus* would do), we analyzed that behavior to see if it coincided from socially efficient behavior (i.e., Pareto optimality), and equitable behavior (i.e., reward according to effort or sacrifice), and demonstrated that it did. We did *not* engage in the pointless exercise of assuming individuals are "revolutionary saints" who always act in socially responsible ways, and then tautologically proclaim that in a participatory economy the social interest would, indeed, be served, as many critics apparently assume. Instead, we designed institutions, procedures, and rules so when people act out of self-interest their behavior would prove both socially efficient and equitable as well. Jason Pramus, who criticized participatory economics for other reasons, at least acknowledged our very traditional and conservative methodology in this regard:

> *Looking Forward* is not a naïve book. It is not even a utopian book. In its own way it is quite practical. It does not expect people in its hypothetical economy to behave like revolutionary saints. It lays out a system where people's self-interest will very closely coincide with the interests of the larger society they are a part of. It does not expect greed and dishonesty to disappear, but it does present safeguards that should minimize the damage such tendencies would present.[27]

In brief, the principle mechanism that compels a worker council pursuing its own self-interest to behave in a socially responsible way is that it must demonstrate to other worker and consumer councils that its proposal generates an acceptable excess of social benefits over social costs. Consumer councils are induced to behave in socially responsible ways because they must demonstrate to other councils that the social cost of the goods they request is consistent with the average work-effort ratings of their members. The principle mechanism that compels individually responsible behavior are effort ratings by one's coworkers and consumption allocations based on effort ratings. So we most emphatically did not *assume* a "wholesale conversion of human behavior patterns to a person whose very consciousness was socially rather than individualy oriented," nor did we assume people would be motivated by solidarity and indifferent to their individual comfort and status.

However, while in our formal analysis we assumed *homo economicus* and searched for institutions that would lead people to behave in socially responsible ways out of self-interest, we do dare to hope that many years of practicing socially responsible behavior, and observing that others have done likewise, will move people closer to *homo socialis*. There is plenty of evidence that people do behave as *homo socialis* in some matters even today, toward family members, friends, and various communities where members trust and care for one another. So this is not behavior foreign to the human species when we are not mistrustful of one another.[28] But we were very carefull *not* to assume that people in a participatory economy would behave in the social interest if this conflicted with their self interest, for that would have been utopian in the bad sense of the word.

Conclusion

Hopefully I have neither neglected nor misrepresented concerns others have taken the trouble to express about the vision of a participatory economy. I take these concerns seriously. I do not assume my responses are adequate, and I not only expect but hope that debate over the issues and concerns treated in this chapter will continue indefinitely. In any case, I am convinced this kind of debate is an important part of the struggle to achieve the economics of equitable cooperation that is too often neglected.

Part IV:

From Competition and Greed
to Equitable Cooperation

10

From Here to There:

Taking Stock

The idea of a participatory economy described and defended in the last two chapters was first published more than a dozen years ago. If I had a nickel for every person who told me how much they liked the idea, but could not imagine any way to get there from where we are today, I would already be retired. Even those with unshakable faith in the human capacity to cooperate equitably invariably catch my eye and say, in one way or another: "Lovely idea, but you can't be serious!"

I always assure them I am dead serious. This does not mean I believe participatory economics is just around the corner. Quite the contrary, I will consider myself fortunate if I live long enough to see anything remotely resembling a participatory economy operating in even a single country. Nor does it mean I fail to realize how much we will have to change the way people think about their interrelated economic activities. I am painfully aware of the power of capitalist ideological hegemony, and how depressed and cynical most of us have become about the human capacity for equitable economic self-management. On the other hand, I will not be surprised if people in the twenty-second century are discussing how to better balance their jobs for empowerment, how to more effectively compensate one another according to sacrifice and how to make their planning procedures more participatory and efficient, just as we discuss today how to tame the financial sector, how to fine-tune fiscal, monetary, and industrial policies, how to make the tax system more progressive, how to secure workers a living wage, how to shore up holes in the welfare safety net, and how to substitute green taxes on polluters for regressive FICA taxes on workers. That is what I mean when I say I am dead serious about participatory economics, and consider it more than just a lovely idea. If the economics of equitable cooperation does make more headway in this century than it did in the last century—which I believe it will—I feel sure it will lead us in the direction of something resembling participatory economics.

However, as explained in chapter 3, I believe the transition will be a long one, marked more by reform victories than by capitalist breakdowns. I believe overcoming commercial values will take time, but growing awareness of the consequences of relying on competition and greed and the advantages of equitable cooperation will prove decisive. I believe we will have to create imperfect pockets of equitable cooperation in the midst of global capitalism, and learn how to improve them, expand them, and connect them with one another. I believe we must do this even though the deck is stacked against us inside capitalism because it is the only way to test the practicality of our theories, provide evidence of the superiority of equitable cooperation over competition and greed, and sustain and enrich the lives of generations of activists who keep hope alive by living their dream. Unlike most anticapitalists at the beginning of the twentieth century, I fully expect this process to take several generations or more. But it is possible to kick the bad habits of competition and greed over the next hundred years, and failure to do so will surely plunge us into depths of misery, barbarism, and environmental disaster that are hard to imagine.

In any case, a participatory economy may be attractive, and may be both technically and humanly feasible, but it is only of academic interest if there is no way to get there. Besides being technically and humanly feasible, there must be a feasible *transition* from where we are today. Chapter 11 focuses on how reform campaigns already being waged can begin the transition from the economics of competition and greed to the economics of equitable cooperation. Chapter 12 discusses how to better build the mass economic reform movements that will have to tame capitalism over the next decades. But even massive economic reform movements will not be enough. Chapter 13 argues for the importance of expanding living experiments in equitable cooperation that already exist and building new ones as well. The concluding chapter discusses new ways for the progressive economic movement to work with reform movements in other spheres of social life, and explores different ways those committed to fighting for equitable cooperation can work more effectively with people who have doubts about our full agenda and other personal priorities as well.

Taking Stock

Since the movement to replace competition and greed with equitable cooperation is still small and weak, and since the capitalist ruling class shows no signs of relinquishing power as quickly and easily as communist rulers in Eastern Europe and the Soviet Union did, fighting for the economics of equitable cooperation will have to go on inside capitalist economies for the foreseeable future. Fortunately, not all versions of capitalism are equally undemocratic, unjust, inefficient, and environmentally destructive. Just as social democratic reforms made capitalism more stable and equitable during the middle of the twentieth century, there are important reforms dismantled by neoliberals to be restored, and new reforms to be won that can greatly improve the lives of billions of people and retard destruction of the biosphere. So for the time being, most of the heavy lifting to promote the economics of competition and greed will have to take the form of defending and winning reforms that make capitalism less destructive.

Conservative Triumphalism

Many current trends are bleak: (1) Mindless equation of free markets with efficiency and freedom in face of overwhelming evidence to the contrary, callous reductions in minimal programs for the needy and elderly, corporate merger madness, popular worship rather than resentment of power and privilege, and a wholehearted embrace of social Darwinism in racial, class, and gender forms, all make early twenty-first century U.S. capitalism a closer relative to the robber baron capitalism of the late nineteenth century than its "kinder and gentler" post–New Deal cousin. (2) Corporate-sponsored globalization has subordinated the interests of the global majority to the interests of multinational corporations, and financial capital in particular, unmindful of the havoc the neoliberal global economy wreaks on the lesser developed economies and the downward pressure it puts on labor standards, environmental standards, and living standards for the majority of the population in the more developed economies. (3) More than a dozen years after the end of the Cold War it is now clear that the U.S. government has no intention of being a "good neighbor" and paying U.S. taxpayers a "peace dividend." Under Democratic and Republican administrations alike, the U.S. response to the end of the Cold War has been to create thirteen naval task forces to dominate every ocean and sea, to upgrade seven hundred major military installations around the globe, to permanently garrison 120,000 troops in Europe, 92,000 in East Asia and the Pacific, 30,000 in North Africa, the Middle East, and South Asia, and 15,000 in Latin America, to spend as much on defense as the next nine countries in the world combined,[1] to declare a new doctrine of "preventive intervention" that would have served Hitler well in justifying the Nazi invasions of Czechoslovakia, Poland, and the Low Countries, to proclaim a permanent "war on terrorism" against all who resist U.S. hegemony as well as any who attempt to remain neutral, and finally, to assault and occupy a defenseless Iraq in open defiance of international law and the United Nations. As I write this chapter it is clear to all but the blind that under the current Republican administration and Congress that the United States threatens to become the most powerful and belligerent empire the world has ever seen. Moreover, John Kerry, the Democratic Party standard bearer, has made it abundantly clear that he would change only the rhetoric and style used to promote U.S. imperial interests, not the substance of imperial policy.

Obviously, none of this is moving us closer to equitable cooperation. Nor can we expect any other country or alliance of countries to effectively curb U.S. military ambitions in the foreseeable future. U.S. imperial ventures will be opposed abroad by vastly outgunned patriotic movements rejecting the imperial yoke using any and all tactics available to them— including irregular warfare and suicide bombers—until the U.S. anti-imperialist and peace movements grow sufficiently in size, conviction, and power to stop our leaders from turning us into the new Roman Empire.

Finally, as explained in chapter 3, I do not believe those fighting against the economics of competition and greed can take solace in old left doctrines of "capitalist contradictions" leading to economic collapse, or expect capitalism to organize its own replacement. Instead we must focus our efforts on the real crimes of global capitalism and organize for its replacement in its midst. Capitalism will not satisfy the basic economic needs of most who live in the Third World and a growing underclass in the advanced economies. It will not satisfy the need for self-managed, meaningful work that an increasingly educated populace demands. It will not satisfy people's needs for community, dignity, and economic justice. And it cannot keep itself from devouring the natural environment and contributing to an international political environment that fosters war and conflict instead of peace and cooperation. Organizing in response to these problems that capitalism either will not, or cannot solve, is where the movement to replace the economics of competition and greed with the economics of equitable cooperation will largely be built.

Stirrings of Resistance

While regrettable, it is hardly surprising that the demise of communism and decline of social democracy at the close of the twentieth century led to an era of capitalist triumphalism. Emboldened by the defeats of their most powerful twentieth-century opponents, the more greedy and reckless among them prevailed on their fellow capitalists to tear up old compromises and launch all-out class war forcing their victims to defend themselves. One response began in the Third World in the early 1990s where tens of millions demonstrated against IMF, World Bank, and GATT/WTO strong-arm tactics locking them into subservient roles in the brave, new, neoliberal global economy. On November 30, 1999, at the WTO meetings in Seattle the U.S. antiglobalization movement held its belated coming-out party, joining its European counterparts protesting against the race to the bottom effect of corporate-sponsored globalization on First World wages, working conditions, environmental standards, and self-governance. Five years after Seattle there are roughly twenty thousand young, antiglobalization activists in the United States integrated into working collectives, many of whom have expanded their criticisms of IMF, WTO, and World Bank policies to encompass anticorporate and even anticapitalist campaigns.

It is also regrettable that the U.S. anti-imperialist and peace movements, which helped end the war against Vietnam, proved unable to sustain their momentum and "win the peace" twenty years later when Mikhail Gorbachev led the Soviet military off the battlefield to end the Cold War. Instead of leading the world into an era of truly peaceful cooperation in the aftermath of the collapse of the Soviet Union, the U.S. government has proceeded to take advantage of its status as the sole military superpower. Efforts to extend U.S. imperialism began with Bush the Elder, and proceeded without missing a beat for eight years with Clinton in the White House. When the Warsaw Pact was disbanded NATO was strengthened rather than dismantled. The military industrial complex quickly squelched discussion of a peace dividend inside the Democratic as well as the Republican parties. Under Clinton, imperial aggression was disguised as a war on drugs and as humanitarian intervention. Only under Bush the Younger, when strategically positioned neoconservatives in his administration seized on 9/11 as the pretext, was the full imperial agenda was finally launched under the fig leaf of a permanent war on terrorism.

Fortunately, it did not take long for the unabashed imperial arrogance of the Bush administration to provoke both international and domestic opposition. Popular repugnance among foreigners is overwhelming. Britons responded to Blair's support for the war on Iraq with the largest demonstration in their country's history. On the eve of the war opposition ranged from 70 percent in Great Britain whose government became an active participant, to 80 percent in Spain and Italy whose governments provided diplomatic support, to over 85 percent in France and Germany whose governments stood up to U.S. threats in the UN Security Council and condemned the war as unnecessary and illegal. As the occupation has become more expensive and dysfunctional by the day, and as every excuse the administration offered for going to war proved to be a lie, polls revealed that two years after 9/11 the Bush administration had squandered any reservoir of good will for the United States abroad. The Pew Global Attitudes Project reported in the fall of 2003: "In most countries, opinions of the U.S. are markedly lower than they were a year ago. The war has widened the rift between Americans and Western Europeans and further inflamed the Muslim world." Inside the United States, popular opposition to imperial arrogance is less widespread, but impressive in light of circumstances. Despite overwhelming support from both political parties and the entire media establishment, half the American people opposed going to war with Iraq without a UN mandate, and a half million voted with their feet on the eve of war at a hastily organized demonstration on a freezing February day in New York City. Despite everything the media and the Democatic Party establishment have done to channel opposition into questioning the efficacy, rather than the purpose and morality of Bush foreign policy, the percentage of the U.S. population opposed to a U.S. empire is steadily growing. In other words, as I write, opposition to global injustice and militarism outside elite circles has been rekindled in a new generation of activists in the United States, and the prospects for building these movements are promising.[2]

It is possible over the next few years that the young antiglobalization and anti-imperialist movements may help revitalize older movements like the labor movement, civil rights movement, women's movement, gay movement, and environmental movement whose agendas and programs are all under frontal assault by the right. In the United States it is not only capitalists who have launched all-out class war against workers. The campaigns to roll back progress made by the civil rights, women's, gay, and environmental movements are every bit as vicious and brutal.[3] Recognizing that nonclass oppression has escalated alongside class war is crucial for the progressive economic movement to recognize and take seriously.[4] What is discouraging about the present situation is that capitalist, racist, sexist, militarist, and antienvironmental forces are all highly organized and well coordinated, with strong institutional connections that enable them to rally between a quarter and a third of the U.S. populace to their causes. Moreover, this multi-issue, right-wing political force can usually rely on the Republican Party—which currently controls both houses of congress, the White House, and the majority of governorships and state legislatures—to effectively advance its agenda, whereas none of the progressive movements they attack can rely on the Democratic Party to defend our interests, much less to advance our agendas. But despite our disorganization and lack of support inside the political establishment and mainstream media, popular support for progressive agendas and movements in the United States is surprisingly high. Over the past few years polls have consistently revealed that as many, if not more, Americans support progressive agendas in every sphere of social life as those who support conservative agendas. Our immediate problem is that conservatives are well positioned to move their agendas, while we progressives are relatively powerless to move ours, at least for the time being. Over the next few years the main problem will be to avoid defeat at the hands of highly organized, privileged minorities who benefit by perpetuating unjust systems of social cooperation. Over the next decade we must build mass movements to win reforms while simultaneously whetting people's desire for equitable cooperation, always making sure our victories are not Pyrrhic ones that betray the values and causes we fight for.

11

Economic Reform Campaigns

This chapter discusses economic reform campaigns already underway. For each reform I explain why it will significantly improve the lives of the victims of capitalism, but also point out the danger of overexaggerating what can reasonably be expected. The chapter closes with a discussion of how best to work in reform campaigns, and a reminder of why we must move beyond reform work.

Keynesian Reforms

Taming Finance

What's good for the wealthy and the financial companies who serve their interests is *not* necessarily good for the rest of us. If we listen to advice from the financial industry we will never restrict any of their activities, to our detriment. Paul Volcker, who served as chairman of the Board of Governors of the Federal Reserve System from 1979 through 1987, had this to say about financial regulation in a luncheon address to the Overseas Development Council Conference on "Making Globalization Work" on March 18, 1999: "I've been involved in financial supervision and regulation for about 40 of my 70 years, mostly on the regulatory and supervisory side but also on the side of those being regulated. I have to tell you from long experience, bank regulators and supervisors are placed on a pedestal only in the *aftermath* of crises. In benign periods—in periods of boom and exuberance—banking supervision and banking regulations have very little political support and strong industry opposition." Regrettably, disman-

tling prudent regulation of the financial sector is a hallmark of the neoliberal era, in which capital liberalization was pursued as vigorously by
"New" Democrats like Bill Clinton as domestic financial deregulation was
pursued by Republicans like Ronald Reagan. Progressives must participate in campaigns to change the attitude of both the public and elected
officials regarding the need for strong regulation of the financial sector.

Even when there are no crises, an unbridled financial sector will almost
always distribute the lion's share of efficiency gains from extending the
credit system to those who were better off in the first place, and thereby
widens wealth and income inequalities.[1] But financial markets are particularly dangerous and prone to crisis, as people as different as Keynes and
Volcker warn us. In other words, finance not only contains a potential
upside that can improve economic efficiency—the exclusive focus of mainstream finance theory—it also contains a potential downside when financial crises cause efficiency losses.[2] While there is always a downside as
well as an upside potential in the financial sector, an unregulated, or badly
regulated, financial sector is simply an accident waiting to happen. Therefore, the financial industry must be regulated in the public interest to
diminish the likelihood of financial crises of one kind or another, and
when they do occur, to contain their spread and distribute their costs more
equitably.

Robert Pollin, Dean Baker, and Marc Schaberg discuss a minimal step
in the right direction in "Security Transaction Taxes for U.S. Financial
Markets" in the fall 2003 issue of the *Eastern Economic Journal*. Being
careful to point out that security transaction excise taxes (STETS) are by
no means a cure-all, and that other financial regulatory reforms are necessary as well, they rebut neoliberal criticisms of STETS and offer useful
suggestions about how to design them to ameliorate their liabilities. The
Financial Markets Center (www.fmcenter.org) in Philomont, Virginia, is
a small, progressive institute devoted to research about financial reforms
in the United States. Its director of programs, Jane D'Arista, and executive director, Tom Schlesinger, have developed a cornucopia of financial
reform proposals over the decades. Some are modest reforms that reduce
outright corruption and thievery. Others are substantial reforms designed
to protect the real economy from "financial shocks," and ensure that
financial investors, not taxpayers, assume more of the cost of cleaning up
when the financial sector creates a mess. D'Arista and Schlesinger also
propose more ambitious reforms that would dramatically redistribute the
benefits of financial activities from the wealthy to the poor and substantially democratize monetary policy.

In the international arena a tax on international currency transactions—popularly known as a "Tobin tax" after Professor James Tobin who championed the policy in his presidential address given at the 1978 conference of the Eastern Economic Association in Washington, D.C.—is a minimal first step toward taming international finance. Robert Blecker provides an excellent evaluation of this and more far-reaching proposals for international financial reform in *Taming Global Finance* (1999.) John Eatwell and Lance Taylor make a compelling case that the liberalized international financial system is presently an accident waiting to happen in *Global Finance at Risk: The Case for International Regulation* (2000), where they also make useful suggestions about how a lender of last resort for the global economy should be structured and function. Walden Bello, Nicola Bullard, Kamal Malhotra, and others from the ranks of the antiglobalization movement discuss ideas for more far-reaching reforms in *Global Finance: New Thinking on Regulating Speculative Capital Markets* (2000.)

Beside judging if a particular reform is winnable, those who work on financial reforms must judge how the reform will affect efficiency and stability in the real economy, must ask if it will decrease rather than further increase income and wealth inequality, must consider whether it will give ordinary people more or less control over their economic destinies, and most importantly, must evaluate if winning the reform will strengthen the broad movement struggling to replace the economics of competition and greed with the economics of equitable cooperation. But what are the special opportunities and problems associated with campaigns for financial reform?

Because the financial sector is particularly dysfunctional due to so-called neoliberal reforms pushed through over the past two decades by the financial sector and sympathetic politicians in both the Republican and Democratic parties—with an assist from mainstream economists—there is a very large margin for improvement in the performance of both the domestic and international financial sectors. Antireforms like the repeal of the Glass-Steagall regulatory system in the United States in 1999 and various measures that go under the label of international capital liberalization orchestrated by the U.S. Department of theTreasury and the IMF, have eliminated minimal protections and safeguards imposed by legislation and international practices dating back to the New Deal and the Bretton Woods Conference. Not since the roaring twenties have national economies and the global economy been as subject to the destructive effects of financial bubbles and crashes as we are today. Consequently, there is a great deal that can be accomplished to improve the lives of capitalism's victims through financial reform, both domestic and international. Moreover, many of these reforms are not a radical departure from past policies.

While reforms that should be relatively easy to sell can make substantial improvements, unfortunately campaigns for financial reform are particularly difficult for popular progressive forces to work in effectively. Unlike "peace, not war," financial reform is more technically complicated, and therefore harder to educate and mobilize ordinary citizens around. Unlike campaigns against polluters that can often be fought locally, to a great extent financial reform must proceed at the national and international levels through organizations and coalitions that are many steps removed from local constituencies and invariably led by people who are no friends of the economics of equitable cooperation. These are important liabilities to bear in mind for groups deciding whether to prioritize this kind of reform work. There are some exceptions. Anti redlining and community reinvestment campaigns can be fought at the local level. The Financial Markets Center even has a campaign to increase the influence of ordinary citizens over monetary policy by exploiting provisions in the enabling act that created the Federal Reserve Bank for representation of community groups on local boards of the Federal Reserve Bank. But unfortunately, taming domestic and international finance is largely an activity that will appear esoteric and distant to most citizen activists, as much as it affords attractive opportunities to point out how badly the capitalist financial sector misserves the ordinary public.

Full Employment Macropolicies

There is no reason aggregate demand cannot be managed through fiscal and monetary policies to keep actual production close to potential GDP and cyclical unemployment to a minimum. That is, there is no technical, or intellectual reason. Of course there are political reasons that prevent governments from making capitalism as efficient as it can be. Because the wealthy have good reason to fear inflation more than unemployment, they exert political pressure on governments to ignore unemployment problems and prioritize the fight against inflation even when inflation is not a significant danger. Because employee bargaining power increases when labor markets are tight over long time periods, employers pressure governments to permit periodic recessions in the name of fighting inflation. In an increasingly integrated global economy where demand for exports is an important component of aggregate demand in most countries, and where differential interest rates produce large movements of wealth holdings from one country to another, stabilization policies and monetary policies are difficult to conduct unilaterally and must be coordinated internationally. Obviously, when the world's hegemonic superpower persists in behaving unilaterally, international macroeconomic policy coordination is obstructed.[3] However, these are merely some of the political obstacles to winning effective stabilization policies that not only make the economy more efficient, but strengthen the broad movement struggling for equitable cooperation in other ways as well.[4]

Wage increases and improvements in working conditions are easier to win in a full-employment economy. Affirmative action programs designed to redress racial and gender discrimination are easier to win when the economic pie is growing rather than stagnant or shrinking. Union organizing drives are more likely to be successful when labor markets are tight than when unemployment rates are high. The reason privileged sectors in capitalism obstruct efforts to pursue full employment macropolicies—it diminishes their bargaining power—is precisely the reason those fighting for equitable cooperation should campaign for it.[5]

For all these reasons it is crucial to win reforms that move us even closer to "full-employment capitalism" than the Scandinavians achieved during the 1960s and 1970s. Every progressive economic organization should support this reform and work to punish elected officials who fail to do so. But it is important not to overestimate what this will accomplish. Even if everyone had a job, they would not have a job they could support a family on, much less one that paid them fairly for their sacrifices. Low-wage jobs flipping burgers at McDonald's is a poor substitute for better-paid jobs producing farm machinery. Even if everyone had a job, they would not have personally rewarding, socially useful work since most jobs in capitalism are more personally distasteful than necessary, and much work in capitalism is socially useless. Jobs in telemarketing or "temp" services without benefits are poor substitutes for jobs with benefits teaching reasonably sized classes or cleaning up polluted rivers. A full employment economy through military Keynesianism and tax cuts for the wealthy is what the Bush administration is hoping they can pull off just in time for the 2004 elections, which is hardly the kind of full-employment program progressives should support.

So when we fight for full employment stabilization policies we should never forget to point out that what every citizen deserves is a socially useful job with fair compensation. We should never tire of pointing out that while capitalism is incapable of delivering on this, it is just as possible as it is sensible. We must also work to expand opportunities for socially useful, self-managed work for which people are compensated fairly by increasing the number of jobs in worker-owned-and-managed cooperatives so more and more people have an alternative to working for capitalists, as discussed in chapter 13.

Industrial Policy

The French practiced what they called "indicative planning" with such success in the 1950s that the British government tried to copy the policy (unsuccessfully) in the early 1960s.[6] The German model of capitalism dating back to the nineteenth century, the Japanese model in the mid-twentieth century, and what came to be known as "the Asian development model" at the end of the twentieth century all used industrial policy to great advantage. In brief, the policy consists of identifying key economic sectors that are important to prioritize in order to increase overall economic growth rates. In the 1950s, the French Commusariat du Plan identified what they called "bottleneck sectors" whose sluggish growth was holding back the rest of the economy, and arranged with the Finance Ministry and a state-owned development bank for lower business tax rates and interest rates for firms investing in those sectors. During the heyday of the post-World War II Japanese economic miracle, the Ministry of International Trade and Industry (MITI) identified what they called "industries of the future" expected to be crucial to Japanese international economic success, and arranged with the Finance Ministry and Bank of Japan for firms in those industries to be taxed and receive credit on preferential terms. In effect, MITI treated comparative advantage as something to be created rather than meekly accepted as "national fate." As a result Japan became a world powerhouse, first in low-cost light manufactured goods, then in high-quality steel and automobiles, and eventually in electronics and computers.[7] South Korea and Taiwan copied Japan's industrial policies with such success in the 1970s and 1980s that other Asian tigers like Singapore and Thailand followed their examples creating the much-admired group of newly industrializing countries (NICs). While the highly successful Asian development model emphasized export-led growth, it consistently rejected neoliberal laissez-faire advice and embraced a strong interventionist role for government.[8]

Progressive reformers must bear three important things in mind about industrial policy: (1) Real capitalist economies are often plagued by temporary disequilibria among sectors that cause inefficiencies and socially irrational investment priorities. Moreover, most underdeveloped economies are trapped playing a role in the international division of labor that dooms them to produce goods where opportunities to increase wages and profits are minimal. Industrial policies can be used to eliminate short-run imbalances between sectors, establish more socially beneficial investment priorities, or guide an economy out of a vicious cycle of specialization onto a more virtuous long-run development strategy. Since free marketeers like those in power at the IMF, World Bank, and U.S. Department of the Treasury are oblivious to the static and dynamic inefficiencies of markets, they see no purpose to such policies, label them "crony capitalism," and pressure governments to abandon them no matter how successful they may have been. (2) Industrial policies to help create *new* comparative advantages are crucial for less developed economies to break out of their vicious cycle of poverty and forge a path toward more productive economies in the Third World and a more egalitarian global economy.[9] Industrial policy is also crucial to redirect investment in advanced economies away from priorities overvalued by the market, like private luxuries for the affluent, and toward priorities the market neglects, like affordable housing, education, and environmental protection and restoration. (3) However, it is important to realize that industrial policy is highly susceptible to being hijacked by large corporations and high-ranking government bureaucrats. If this occurs, industrial policy can further reduce the power of workers, consumers, farmers, and small businesses if they are excluded from the industrial policy power game. In fact, it can be argued that successful industrial policies in France, Japan, South Korea, and Taiwan often made their economies *less* democratic and weakened popular economic forces.

Industrial policy is a kind of capitalist planning, not to be confused with the kind of democratic, or participatory planning, discussed in Part 3. Corporations with interests at odds with workers and consumers must necessarily play a major role if industrial policy in capitalism is to be successful, and it is possible they may hijack the policy. On the other hand, industrial policy was used effectively without reducing economic democracy in Norway where unions, cooperatives, and organizations representing the interests of consumers, farmers, and small businesses were effectively represented in the planning process. If progressive reformers can win disadvantaged, sectors seats at the planning table, industrial policies can improve investment priorities and increase, rather than diminish, economic democracy in capitalist economies. It is also an ideal place for people to discover the advantages of national economic planning compared to leaving investment priorities and economic development strategy to free-market forces. Finally, it is an important social space for worker and consumer organizations to begin to practice economic democracy at the macro level.

In general, the more powerful the progressive economic movement, the larger and more democratic the organizations representing workers and consumers, and the more sympathetic government is to our cause, the more effective participation in industrial policy can be. When the movement for equitable cooperation is small and without much influence on procorporate government officials, as is presently the case in the United States, little can be gained from calling for, or collaborating with industrial policy initiatives. So when someone like Felix Royhatin proposes to deploy industrial policy to tackle some glaring economic problem in the United States, progressives need not rush to support his initiative—no matter how compelling it is—because it is clear that under present circumstances in the United States corporate interests would dominate any industrial policy if it actually got off the ground. On the other hand, whenever and wherever the movement for equitable cooperation becomes larger and more powerful, fighting for stronger progressive representation in industrial policy, fighting for priorities that better serve human needs, and building confidence in the feasibility and superiority of allocating our scarce productive resources according to a democratically chosen plan, rather than consigning our economic fates to corporate bottom lines and the vagaries of the market, can prove very productive. Powerful progressive movements in places like South Africa, Brazil, and Argentina that have influence with their governments, and an objective interest in keeping those governments from falling victim to reactionary forces, can ill afford to boycott industrial policy initiatives in their countries and thereby allow business interests even greater influence.

It should be recognized that the dangers of co-optation are generally greater with industrial policy than with many other reform campaigns in capitalism. If leaders of progressive organizations trade legitimate aspirations and demands of their members for seats for themselves at the industrial policy-planning table, if progressive organizations are associated with, or even worse, defend woefully inadequate policies to their members, and if participation in industrial policy is not combined with programs like those discussed in chapter 13, industrial policy reform work can be counterproductive. But co-optation is always a danger when embracing reform work of any kind in capitalism. It comes with the territory, and can only be avoided at the price of isolation and irrelevance. In general the answer lies in policies to combat the predictable dangers associated with reform work rather than eschewing reform work itself. Nonetheless, industrial policy-reform work within capitalism is recommended only for movements fighting for equitable cooperation that are already very strong.

Wage-Led Growth

In capitalism the low road growth strategy is to suppress wages to increase profits and hope the wealthy will plow their profits back into productive investments that expand the capital stock so as to increase economic productivity and potential GDP. Beside being highly inequitable, this strategy runs the risk that the wealthy will not invest their profits to expand the domestic capital stock but consume them, save them, or worse yet, send them abroad. In the latter two cases, not only will the profits not be used to add machines to the capital stock, aggregate demand may falter and reduce actual production even further below a stagnant potential GDP.

The high road to growth in capitalism is to raise wages to keep aggregate demand high, trusting that if profitable sales opportunities exist capitalists will find ways to expand capacity to take advantage of them. Besides being more equitable, this strategy minimizes the risk of lost output due to lack of aggregate demand, and reduces unemployment in economies where chronic underemployment is a major social problem. The only risk in this strategy is there will be too little savings to lend to businesses trying to expand their productive capacity, or that capitalists will go on strike demanding higher returns on their investments. If this happens progressive movements must be prepared to demand that the government step in and supply what society requires if capitalists refuse to do so. In other words, the government must be prepared to provide public investment and employment to replace falling private investment and employment if capital goes on strike. Moreover, all the organizations comprising the movement for equitable cooperation must be ready to enthusiastically volunteer their services to help the government determine what the new public investment priorities should be through democratic planning procedures.

Progressives in developing economies need to reject neoliberal, low-road growth programs peddled by the U.S. Treasury, IMF, World Bank, and WTO, and point out that there *is* an alternative: wage-led growth and production oriented toward domestic basic needs. Every developing economy needs some dynamic export industries if for no other reason than to import some cutting-edge technologies. But subordinating the entire economy to export-led, low-road growth is a recipe for disaster.[10] Progressive movements like the ANC in South Africa and the Workers' Party in Brazil made a terrible mistake on coming to power when they imposed fiscal and monetary austerity and prioritize international debt service hoping to placate the IMF and international investors to buy time to consolidate their political power. Nothing is more debilitating to progressive economic movements than to have to read in the *Financial Times* stories like the following: "A year after coming to power Mr. Lula da Silva has reversed the expectations of many Brazilians. Economic orthodoxy during his first year in government has disappointed many on the left but pleasantly surprised much of Brazil's conservative elite. At Daslu, an elite fashion store where the rich drink tea while trying on designer shoes at $1500 a pair, business is flourishing. A customer exits with a half dozen servants carrying her holiday purchases. 'Lula seems to have come to his senses. I thought I was going to have to move to Miami,' she says before disappearing into her air-conditioned limousine."[11] By practicing the very policies they vehemently denounced when they were in the opposition, the ANC and Lula have not only weakened the mass movements for progressive economic change in their countries, they have undermined their own base of political support when push comes to shove, as it eventually will. There *is* an alternative to capitulation to neoliberal capitalism, and when antineoliberal movements are fortunate enough to come to power they must not shy away from pursuing it. But not only must progressive political parties launch aggressive high-road growth programs centered on production for basic needs when elected, the progressive movements behind them need to learn from the bitter experience of François Mitterand and the French Socialist Party. The movements behind progressive political parties must prepare themselves to take over a program of democratically planned public investment if either domestic or international capital goes on strike in response to a wage-led growth program launched by their elected government.

What a Full Keynesian Program Is Not

Subordinating finance to the service of the real economy, rather than the reverse, pursuing full-employment fiscal and monetary policies and intelligent industrial policies, and embracing a wage-led, rather than profit-led growth strategy is nothing more than a full Keynesian program. It may seem radical in an era of free-market triumphalism, but there was a time when the economics of equitable cooperation had made sufficient headway that advocates of this full Keynesian program were considered within the mainstream of the economics profession. In the 1960s, one could even argue that Keynesians had become the dominant faction within the mainstream. But that is no longer the case. Just as capitalism defeated not only communism, but social democracy as well, by the end of the twentieth-century free market neoliberals had vanquished not only radical political economists, but Keynesians as well. Formerly establishment Keynesian economists like Paul Krugman and Joseph Stiglitz have been banished from the mainstream along with those from more radical heterodox schools of economic thought. Since most Keynesian reforms do mitigate the damage caused by the economics of competition and greed, it is important to preserve, win back, and expand on these reforms as part of our strategy to promote the economics of equitable cooperation in the new century.

However, there should be no illusions about what even a full Keynesian program can accomplish. The Keynesian program outlined above falls far short of redressing the fundamental inequities and power imbalances in capitalism. Additional reforms like those below are necessary to make capitalism more just and democratic. Nor will a full Keynesian program establish an institutional framework conducive to equitable cooperation. Only prefigurative experiments in equitable cooperation like those discussed in chapter 13 can begin to accomplish that. Nevertheless, the only golden age capitalism has ever known was during the forty years when the Keynesian program was ascendant, and the only capitalist economies where substantial segments of the workforce ever rose to middle-class status were economies guided by these policies.

Make the Safety Net Safe

The Scandinavian economies in the 1960s and early 1970s were the only capitalist economies to ever provide a safety net for the victims of capitalism worthy of the name. The so-called War on Poverty in the 1960s in the United States created a welfare system that was most noteworthy for how bureaucratic, inefficient, and demeaning it was for those it served, and how miserly it was compared to Scandinavian, German, British, and Canadian welfare programs. But apparently even the pitiful War on Poverty was more than those who were fortunate enough not to need a safety net in the United States could stand. The centerpiece of the 1994 Republican Party "Contract for America"—a.k.a. Contract ON America— was to abolish welfare. Newt Gingrich found in New Democrat Bill Clinton a president willing to collaborate with the same House Republicans who impeached him four years later to "end welfare as we know it" in the president's infamous words. Only because an economic boom prolonged by a stock-market bubble prevented the full consequences of eliminating all economic support for single mothers and their children from becoming visible was Clinton saved the embarrassment of seeing what he had done to our least fortunate fellow citizens until after he was out of office. In *The End of Welfare? Consequences of the Federal Devolution for the Nation* (2000), Max Sawicky and his coauthors explain how welfare reform made tens of millions of Americans vulnerable to the cruel effects of economic recession. Randy Albelda and Ann Withorn, together with a dozen scholars and welfare-rights activists, provide a political analysis that lays bare the cruelty, racism, and misogyny behind the attack on welfare in *Lost Ground: Welfare Reform, Poverty, and Beyond* (2002). Building a safety net for the victims of capitalism that is worthy of the name is the most pressing domestic task facing those who would make U.S. capitalism more equitable and humane.

The reason to fight for an adequate welfare system that treats its clients with respect and dignity is that failure to do so is inhumane. But progressives must never cease to point out that it is capitalism, not the personal failings of its victims, that makes welfare programs necessary. Capitalism *means* there will not be enough jobs for all who need them. Capitalism *means* many jobs will not pay enough to support a family and give one's children the same opportunity to develop their talents and pursue their dreams as children with wealthier parents. Capitalism *means* historically oppressed minorities will be disproportionately represented along with the less able and unlucky, all of whom will be unable to squeeze an acceptable standard of living from an economic system based on competition and greed even when they are willing to sacrifice as much or more than others to do so. In short, welfare is necessary only because capitalism will *not* reward everyone fairly for the work they are able and willing to perform.

Tax Reform

Progressive taxes, that is, taxes that require those with higher income or wealth to pay a higher *percentage* of their income or wealth in taxes, can reduce income and wealth inequality. It is important to note that if those with more income can shield a greater part of their income from a tax by claiming more deductions than those with less income, even if the *rate* on *taxable* income rises with income, the tax will be less progressive than it appears, and may actually be regressive. Federal income taxes in the United States appear to be progressive. In 1998, those with less than seven thousand dollars of taxable income in the United States did not have to pay any income taxes. Those with taxable incomes between seven and thirty thousand dollars had to pay 15 percent of each additional dollar of income. Those with taxable incomes between $30,000 and $65,000 had to pay 28 percent of each additional dollar of income, and the marginal tax rate rose to 39.6 percent for people with taxable incomes in excess of $300,000. However, studies indicate the federal income tax is much less progressive than it appears to be once exclusions of income, deductions, and credits are taken into account. These exceptions to the complete taxation of income, also known as loopholes or preferences, tend to be distributed disproportionately to higher income households. The reason is that most loopholes pertain to savings, home ownership, and capital income of various types, and those with higher-incomes save more, have larger homes, and receive more of their income from capital.[12]

Moreover, many other federal taxes such as Social Security and Medicare, or FICA taxes, are highly regressive, because they require those with lower income to pay a higher *percentage* of their income or wealth in taxes, as are state sales taxes and local property taxes. In an excellent recent article on the oft-neglected subject of fairness in state and local taxes, Rodger Doyle concluded: "State and local governments are shifting away from progressivity. Their revenues from income taxes fell 10% from 2000 to 2003. During the same time period sales taxes rose 6% and property taxes rose 20%. Few realize that state and local taxes are so strongly regressive that they cancel out much of the progressivity of the federal income tax."[13] This is because state and local governments collect most of their revenue from sales and property taxes which are hightly regressive, rather than from taxes on income that are more progressive. But even in states that have an income tax, it is usually far less progressive that the federal income tax. For example, in Maryland where I live and pay state taxes the top tax rate kicks in at a mere three thousand dollars of taxable income, which means that the billionaire owner of the Washington Redskins football team and his chauffeur both pay the same state income tax rate! In any case, it is generally believed that despite progressive income tax schedules, federal taxes as a whole are barely progressive, and the overall tax system including state and local taxes is regressive. In other words, in the United States, taxes are now used to redistribute income from the poor to the rich,[14] whereas equitable cooperation requires exactly the opposite.

A number of organizations support tax-reform proposals that would replace regressive taxes with more progressive ones and make progressive taxes even more progressive. Citizens for Tax Justice (www.ctj.org) and United for a Fair Economy (www.faireconomy.com) not only provide useful critiques of right-wing tax initiatives, but present excellent progressive alternatives for tax reform as well. The unprecedented growth of wealth inequality over the past twenty-five years has also led to calls for new wealth taxes. Yale law professors Bruce Ackerman and Anne Alstott have proposed a 2 percent tax on wealth, law professor Leon Friedman has proposed a 1 percent tax on wealth owned by the top 1 percent, and a number of influential economic reformers including Robert Kuttner and Robert Reich have suggested that wealth taxation should be part of any tax-reform program in the United States. Unfortunately, we have been "progressing" rapidly in reverse in the United States over the past twenty-five years as the wealthy have used their growing influence with politicians they fund to shift the tax burden off themselves, where it belongs, onto the less fortunate, where it does not.[15]

Beside making the tax system more progressive, we need to tax bad behavior not good behavior. Economists since Alfred Pigou have known that efficiency requires taxing pollution emissions an amount equal to the damage suffered by the victims of the pollution. Moreover, if governments did this they would raise a great deal of revenue. But even if the tax is collected from the firms who pollute, the cost of the tax will be distributed between the firms who pollute and the consumers of the products they produce. To the extent that firms pass the pollution tax on in the form of higher prices, consumers pay part of pollution taxes along with producers. There is nothing wrong with this from the perspective of efficienct incentives. Part of the reason pollution taxes improve efficiency in a market economy is they discourage consumption of goods whose production requires pollution precisely by making those products more expensive for consumers.

However, studies of pollution tax incidence—who ultimately bears what part of a tax on pollution—have concluded that lower-income people would bear a great deal of the burden of many pollution, or "green taxes." In other words, many pollution taxes would be highly regressive and therefore aggravate economic injustice. On the other hand, the federal, state, and local governments in the United States already collect many taxes that are even more regressive than pollution taxes would be. In 1998 highly regressive social security taxes were the second greatest source of U.S. federal tax revenues, responsible for more than a third of all federal revenues. If every dollar collected in new federal pollution taxes were paired with a dollar reduction in social security taxes we would substitute taxes on bad behavior—pollution—for taxes on good behavior—productive work—and make the federal tax system more progressive as well. At the state and local level there are even more regressive taxes to choose from that could be replaced with state and local green taxes making state and local taxes less regressive than they are currently. Redefining Progress (www.redefiningprogress.org) is one organization promoting sensible proposals for combining green taxes with reductions in more regressive taxes to achieve accurate prices that reflect environmental costs while making the tax system more, not less, fair.[16]

Contrary to the claims of right-wing ideologues backing antitax initiatives, taxation is not legalized theft just because some people are forced to pay more for a public service than they would honestly be willing to pay. Despite the fact that we do not all have the same preferences for public goods, in the end we must all live with the same public goods, or in economics lingo, we must all "consume" the same "bundle" of public goods. This simple fact of life puts the lie to simplistic conservative arguments that compulsory taxation is an unwarranted infringement on individual economic freedom. In any reasonable system of paying for public goods through taxation most of us inevitably pay more for particular public goods than we would personally be willing to contribute, at the same time that each of us benefits more personally from particular public goods than we are compelled to pay. Nor is charity a substitute for taxation. Because of the free-rider problem, if taxes were voluntary there would be precious little taxes collected at all. Moreover, as explained in chapter 4, one of the fundamental shortcomings of markets is that they are biased against recording preferences for public as compared to private goods. Consequently, what is needed in market economies is *more*, not less, expenditure on public goods, which means efficiency in market economies generally requires *higher*, not lower, levels of taxation. But besides increasing taxes to provide the efficient amount of public goods, and besides spending our taxes on public goods we really want rather than lavishing our hard-earned money on corporate welfare and military overkill, the system of collecting taxes should make the economy more, not less, equitable. One of the great accomplishments of progressives during the twentieth century was convincing the public that fair taxation means progressive rather than proportional taxation, and giving concrete expression to this social norm in the federal income tax code. As conservatives move ever closer to their goal of rolling back this great achievement, it is crucial for progressives to be clear in our thinking about tax justice.

Conservatives try to frame the debate about tax justice in terms of how much individuals benefit from public expenditures, and therefore how much each person should pay for them. From this starting point some conservatives argue that equal "head taxes" are fair on grounds that in the absence of information to the contrary, it is only reasonable to assume that every citizen benefits equally from government expenditures. Other conservatives implicitly concede the likelihood that benefits from government expenditures are likely to be proportionate to one's income or wealth, in which case a proportionate tax, or what is typically called a "flat tax" where all pay the same *percentage* of his or her income or wealth in taxes, is deemed fair. Progressives must reject this conservative framework for debating tax justice, or fall victim to their carefully prepared trap. We must insist that the relevant question about the tax system is whether it makes outcomes *in the economy as a whole* more or less fair. The conservative frame of reference implicitly assumes that the distribution of income and wealth in a capitalist economy before taxes are collected and spent is perfectly fair. Only if that were true would the issue of economic justice reduce to matching the benefits and burdens of public expenditures and their financing fairly. But if we know that labor and capital markets distribute income and wealth unfairly in the first place, the relevant question becomes whether the tax system aggravates or reduces economic injustice. By definition, proportionate taxes do not change the pretax distribution of income or wealth. Therefore, if the distribution of income and wealth in capitalist economies is inequitable in the first place, proportionate taxes merely replicate the degree of inequity that prevails in the economy. The only difference being that the inequitable pretax outcome is the result of market forces over which nobody exercises conscious control, whereas a proportionate tax policy is a matter of conscious, public choice. So in the first instance we merely accept injustice, but in the case of proportionate taxation we consciously impose it.

On the other hand, progressive taxes make economic outcomes more equitable if we accept the proposition that *on average* those with greater wealth and higher incomes in capitalist economies deserve less of what they have than those with less wealth and lower incomes. Once one accepts the value judgment that rewarding effort, or sacrifice, is what is fair (chapter 1), and the factual argument that labor and capital markets tend to reward the value of contribution rather than sacrifice (chapter 4), it follows that *on average* those with more wealth and higher incomes get more than they deserve in capitalist economies, whereas those with less wealth and lower incomes get less than they deserve. It follows immediate from this conclusion that proportionate taxes replicate economic injustice, regressive taxes aggravate injustice, and only progressive taxes ameliorate economic injustice in capitalist economies.

Some justify progressive taxation based on one's "ability to pay." In this view those with more wealth and income are deemed *more able* to pay a higher percentage of their wealth and income than those with less income and wealth for necessary public services. While I do not wish to argue against the norm "from each according to ability," I should point out that this is a different rationale for progressive taxation than the one presented above. The "ability to pay" argument makes no judgment that those who are better off in capitalism *generally* got more than they deserve, while those who are worse off *generally* got less than they deserve. It is a kind of no-fault judgment followed by legislated charity for the rich on grounds of their greater ability to support charity, whereas the alternative argument for progressive taxation in capitalism is based squarely on the proposition that wealth and income are distributed unfairly in capitalism in the first place, and that only progressive taxes reduce these inequities. As long as those in lower tax brackets do not draw the conclusion that they owe thanks to those in higher tax brackets for contributing more both absolutely and relatively, but instead understand that those who are worse off have every moral right to insist that the better off in capitalism contribute more taxes—whether because some of their greater wealth and income was undeserved, or because it is the duty of those with greater ability to contribute more—there is little reason to quibble over the different rationales for progressive taxation.

Living Wages

Since wage-led growth is the best growth strategy in capitalist economies, establishing a minimum wage, and raising it faster than the inflation rate, promotes efficiency as well as economic justice. It is good economics in every sense. Similarly, "living-wage" campaigns in a number of American cities have been important initiatives to make U.S. capitalism more equitable and efficient over the past ten years. Particularly where unions are weak and represent a small fraction of the labor force, minimum- and living-wage programs are important programs to steer capitalism toward the high road to growth.

Opponents invariably argue that minimum-wage laws, and any increase in the minimum wage, hurt the people they are supposed to help by increasing unemployment. Unless the demand for labor is infinitely inelastic raising wages does decrease employment to some extent as simple supply and demand analysis reveals. What opponents of initiatives that raise wages do not want to admit is: (1) The demand for labor is often wage-inelastic in the short run. (2) Even in the short run raising the wage rate, unlike raising other prices, can be expected to shift the demand curve for labor to the right as well as move us up the demand curve for labor. Because workers spend a higher percentage of their income than employers, increases in wage increase the aggregate demand for goods and services in the short run, which will make employers *more* likely to hire workers because they will have less trouble selling the goods those workers make. While moving up a given labor-demand curve reduces employment, shifting the labor-demand curve out—as wage increases do—increases employment. That is also simple supply-and-demand analysis, just not the kind opponents of minimum wages want to engage in. (3) Contrary to the teachings of mainstream economics, in the long run an infinite number of combinations of wage rates and profit rates are technically possible in any capitalist economy.[17] The only difference between combinations where the wage rate is high and profit rate low, and combinations where the profit rate is high and the wage rate is low, is that the former are more equitable and the latter less so! In other words, in the long run increasing the minimum wage just moves us to a more equitable distribution of benefits in capitalist economies, and in the short run expansionary macroeconomic policies can be used to preserve full employment after minimum wage increases.

Not only is the theoretical case that increasing minimum wages reduces employment not compelling, empirical evidence that it does so is also weak. Two distinguished labor economists, David Card and Alan Krueger, argued in *Myth and Measurement* (1997) that a significant increase in the New Jersey minimum wage in 1992 had, in fact, increased rather than decreased employment. In *Raising the Floor* (1994) William Spriggs and Bruce Klein argue that the minimum wage does not aggravate unemployment, and does increase earnings of low-wage workers making more than the minimum. Thomas Palley provided an excellent defense of "the new economics of the minimum wage" as unlikely to significantly increase unemployment in "Building Prosperity from the Bottom Up," in the September/October 1998 issue of *Challenge Magazine*.

Opponents' criticism that living-wage campaigns in a single city will cost jobs in that city as employers move to other locations is more compelling on theoretical grounds. It is the same race-to-the-bottom effect critics of corporate-sponsored globalization are right to worry about. It is no different than the argument that when local governments tighten local environmental standards or raise local business taxes, business will move to where regulations are more lax and business taxes are lower. Anything that raises costs to business in one locale makes it more likely they will move their business and jobs to another locale. But the lessons those working on living-wage campaigns need to draw from this is not to give up, but to expand the living wage into adjoining jurisdictions, and to press for restrictions on the right of businesses to pick up and move. Just as a national minimum wage is better than minimum wages in some states but not others, the more jurisdictions covered by a living wage, the less likely there will be job losses because businesses would have to move farther. And while it is common today to think freedom of enterprise means businesses are free to do whatever they want—including murderous releases of toxic pollutants and life-threatening working conditions—the fact is that corporations are licensed by governments and can be held accountable to community needs. We do not have to permit them to pick up and leave entirely at their own discretion. In the 1980s the Ohio Public Interest Campaign (OPIC) collected enough signatures to get an initiative on the ballot that would have placed serious restrictions on how quickly, and for what reasons, corporations in Ohio could shut down and move out of state. Unfortunately the initiative was defeated when businesses outspent supporters by ten to one.

Theory aside, there is strong empirical evidence that local living wages have *not* led to significant job losses where they have been enacted. Robert Pollin and Stephanie Luce examine evidence regarding job loss and present an excellent analysis of a number of living-wage campaigns in *The Living Wage: Building a Fair Economy* (1998.) An EPI study concluded that one of the longest standing ordinances in Baltimore had not adversely affected employment. As of February 2002, seventy cities and counties in the United States had adopted some form of living wage. By June 2004, the count had risen to 121 and included New York, Los Angeles, Chicago, Boston, Baltimore, Detroit, Denver, Minneapolis, St. Paul, Buffalo, Pittsburg, Cleveland, St. Louis, and Miami.[18] The city of Oakland passed a living-wage ordinance in 1998, but due to the city charter this law did not apply to the Port of Oakland. A local coalition worked for passage of a ballot initiative to force the port authority to pay 1500 low-wage workers at the airport and seaport wages consistent with the living wage established by the city ordinance. No state has yet to pass a living-wage law, although both houses of the Maryland state legislature passed a living-wage bill during their 2004 session, only to have it vetoed by the Republican governor. While generally applicable only to city employees and employers contracting with the city, successful living-wage campaigns also provide opportunities to press private employers not covered by a city ordinance to pay their employees a living wage. The living-wage ordinance in the city of Cambridge helped workers, local unions, students, and progressive faculty at Harvard University win substantial wage concessions from a recalcitrant institution and its neoliberal President, Laurence Summers, in the winter of 2001, highlighted by student occupations of university offices. A much less-publicized campaign at American University in Washington, D.C., where I work, issued a report in February 2002 titled "A Living Wage for Workers at American University: A Question of Fairness and Social Responsibility" recommending an hourly wage of $14.95 in 2001 dollars for a thirty-five-hour work week based on cost-of-living standards for the Washington, D.C., metropolitan region developed by the Economic Policy Institute and Wider Opportunities for Women. United Students Against Sweatshops has made available on their web site, www.usasnet.org, data on a number of campus living-wage campaigns in which they were involved, including campaigns at the University of California at San Diego, Valdosta State University in Georgia, Stanford University, Swarthmore College, and the University of Tennessee at Knoxville. As union power has diminished in the United States, living-wage campaigns have become increasingly important ways for progressive communities to protect their working members against declining living standards.

Strengthen the Public Sector, Curb the Market

Campaigns to protect and strengthen the public sector and tame the destructive effects of free markets are crucial parts of efforts to make life more bearable under capitalism. By strengthening and improving the public sector, and by mitigating damage from market outcomes through public intervention, we also demonstrate the superiority of democratic, social decision making over free-market forces and production for private profit.

Toward a Mixed Economy, not Privatization

The truth is sectors like education, healthcare, transportation, and housing that should deny none what they need, sectors like telecommunications and energy where technology makes monopoly difficult to avoid, and sectors like the banking industry that have a major impact on investment patterns all do *not* perform well in private hands. In Europe and many developing economies during the golden age of capitalism, governments established public enterprises through a variety of means to operate in these sectors producing a *mixed economy*, an economy with a mixture of private and publicly owned firms. Privatization of these public enterprises was a major thrust of the Thatcher governments in Great Britain during the 1980s, and has been a constant theme of neoliberals and the IMF over the past twenty years in developing economies. Fighting to protect public enterprises from privatization, that are often fire sales for the wealthy backers of political rulers and foreign multinationals, is often called for.

Sometimes struggles against privatization are necessary to preserve public services at equitable prices. The sale of the Bolivian water utility to Bechtel Corporation in 1998 led to such dramatic price hikes that it spurred a popular movement that forced the Bolivian government to rescind the deal. In 2003 a similar deal involving natural gas toppled the Bolivian government. In Washington, D.C., a coalition of progressive forces battled the Financial Control Board imposed by the U.S. Congress to oversee city finances to prevent privatization of the city's last public hospital that is required by law to accept any patient in need, D.C. General Hospital. In other situations opposing privatization is necessary to preserve public enterprises that are key allies for governments in their industrial or economic development strategies. Publicly owned banks have played important roles in guiding economies in settings as varied as France in the 1950s and a number of Latin American and African countries in the 1960s and 1970s. While technically private, many banks in Japan and South Korea were so reliant on support from those country's central banks that they could be counted on to cooperate with government industrial policies that brought about the Japanese and Korean economic miracles. Over the past ten years the U.S. government, with a large assist from the IMF in the case of South Korea, has seized on every opportunity to force Korea and Japan to rescind laws barring foreign ownership of their banking sector. Not only does this allow foreign banks to gobble up lucrative assets when crises hit, it eliminates government influence over banking policies that was once an important part of successful industrial policy.

It is often easier to mobilize popular support to oppose privatization than for other reform campaigns, and sometimes a win can be politically empowering for movements fighting the economics of competition and greed, as was the case recently in Bolivia. These campaigns also provide valuable opportunities for activists to explain concretely why production for profit is not a reliable way to meet people's economic needs in contexts where public attention is focused on this issue.

Single-Payer Healthcare

The U.S. healthcare system is in shambles. From both a medical and financial perspective it has been a mushrooming disaster for well over two decades.[19] Healthcare "reform" was the first legislative casualty of the Clinton Administration. But had the Clinton bill not been defeated in Congress, what Clinton proposed would have proved a disaster in any case. In their unsuccessful attempts to buy off the insurance industry, the drug companies, and private hospitals in the early 1990s, Hillary and Bill Clinton squandered the best chance to parlay mounting popular pressure for healthcare reform into meaningful action since 1948. In 2004 the Republican Party tried to get political credit in time for the 2004 elections for fixing a problem Democrats could not. Of course the legislation to reform Medicare that the Bush administration rammed down Congress's throat is an even bigger disaster. On November 21, 2003, the day the Republican-controlled House of Representatives narrowly passed their Medicare Reform bill with a surprise assist from the American Association of Retired People, Paul Krugman warned in his *New York Times* column, "AARP Gone Astray," that the bill "contains several Trojan horse provisions that are clearly intended to undermine Medicare over time—it will allow private insurers to cherry-pick healthy clients in selected cities, and it will heavily subsidize private plans competing with traditional Medicare. Meanwhile, the bill prohibits Medicare from using its bargaining power to cut drug prices; drug company stocks have soared since the bill's details became public." Krugman also pointed out why progressives working in coalitions with mainstream advocacy groups must not be naïve about coalition partners: "Over the years AARP has become much more than an advocacy and service organization for older Americans. It receives more than $150 million each year in commissions on insurance, mutual funds and prescription drugs sold to its members. And this Medicare bill is very friendly to insurance and drug companies." Setting Medicare on the road to privatization combined with more public spending without cost controls in place is corporate welfare, and will only compound America's health-care problems. Instead, the solution begins with expanding government medical insurance to cover all Americans, not privatizing public medical insurance for the elderly who have it, and using the monopsony power of a single government payer to control medical costs.

In all reform campaigns there is always tension between those who want to hold out for more far-reaching, significant changes and those who preach the practical necessity of a more incrementalist approach. Usually the debate reduces to how much better a far-reaching solution is compared to how much more likely incremental changes are to be won. The struggle for healthcare reform in the United States over the past two decades is a rare case where the incremental approach is actually *less* practical than fighting for significant reform because there is simply no way to extend adequate coverage to all and control escalating costs through the private insurance industry. Other than expanding Medicare coverage—for example, to cover those between fifty-five and sixty-four years old—there is no way to even begin to set things right until we have universal coverage and single-payer health insurance in place. At the national level HR676, the Expanded and Improved Medicare for All Bill, introduced by Congressman John Conyers Jr. in 2003, is clearly the reform worth working for. And even if there is no hope for passing national healthcare reform as long as Republicans control the White House and both houses of Congress, and therefore healthcare advocates must pursue reforms at the state level for the time being, efforts at the state level should concentrate on getting state governments to provide universal insurance coverage for all residents with meaningful provisions for cost containment. More incremental strategies at the state level that seek to force businesses or taxpayers to pay for more coverage through private insurers will only prove useless since state legislatures are invariably sensitive to business complaints about cost competitiveness and face serious budget crises of their own.

Only a single-payer, government insurance program can provide universal coverage while containing costs by eliminated the considerable administrative expenses of private-insurance cherry picking. Only a single-payer program can eliminate the paperwork and confusion associated with administering multiple insurance plans, all of which are worse deals than provided through single-payer systems in every other industrialized country in the world. A single-payer system is best suited to use monopsony power to control drug prices and hospital fees. And only a system separated from the workplace and employers' choices about providing insurance can end the strife caused when some companies in an industry who do provide healthcare benefits to their employees must compete against other companies who do not. The fact is that providing health-care through private insurance and managed-care organizations for profit is so inefficient that incremental reforms that leave those institutions in control of the healthcare system simply cannot succeed. Instead, there is a much better deal for healthcare recipients, healthcare professionals, taxpayers, and the business community as a whole: single-payer, govern-ment insurance. The only losers would be private insurance companies, drug companies, and managed-care organizations, in other words, those who are responsible for the crisis in American healthcare today.[20]

While there is a great deal to discuss about how best to run a health-care system so it is effective, fair, responsive and efficient, there is no way a system in the hands of insurers and managed-care organizations trying to maximize profits in a market environment is going to deliver anything other than the mess we have: 43 million uninsured Americans and counting, along with spiraling costs bankrupting families and businesses alike. In this reform struggle settling for anything less than universal, single-payer coverage is not only immoral, it is impractical as well. Once coverage is complete and a singlepayer is controlling costs, progressives can move on to what we do best—make suggestions about how to make healthcare services more user friendly and equitable through regulation of private providers and democratization of public providers—until a fully public, patient-friendly, "well-care" system is finally achieved.

Rebuild Public Education

Progressives must fight for adequate and fair funding for public educa-tion, and for parents, teachers, and students to take control of their schools from corrupt and bloated administrative bureaucracies. However, mandatory standard testing, and linking school funding and teacher's salaries to test results only moves from blaming the victims to punishing the victims. Nor are charter schools and vouchers a program to rebuild the public education system. Instead they are strategies to further destroy it. Proponents of charter schools and vouchers cynically manipulate images of disadvantaged children trapped in overcrowded, ghetto schools with incompetent, tenured teachers to argue for "choice" and "competi-tion" as the solutions. The problem is not that the images fail to accurately represent the educational abuse disadvantaged children do, in fact, suffer. The problem is that competition and choice are not remedies for these problems.

A sufficient reason to oppose these initiatives is that instead of being policies to make sure there will be "no child left behind," vouchers and charter schools are policies designed precisely to "leave the most disadvantaged children behind," so that educational resources can be concentrated on children from advantaged homes who will experience diversity only in the personage of a relatively few poor and minority children from upwardly mobile homes. *What happens to ghetto schools whose children use their vouchers to leave?* When ghetto schools are the predictable losers in school competition, will they be shut down? Will there be no schools in poor neighborhoods? Will all children from poor neighborhoods be bussed out to wealthy areas of cities and the suburbs? Obviously this "solution" is unacceptable because it robs poor children of any chance to enjoy adequate schooling in their own communities and because it places the burden of transportation entirely on their shoulders. But this solution is also unlikely to ever be permitted. Instead, what will happen is ghetto schools will be consolidated and become even more overcrowded. What will happen is that ghetto schools that remain open will be stripped of their better students and more active parents, and become even less able to mount the necessary political pressure to secure their fair share of educational resources. What will happen is the most dysfunctional ghetto schools will be auctioned off to private corporations to run, like jails, for profit, and to be abandoned when opportunities for short-run profit taking have been exhausted, or when outraged parents revolt over the miserable education their children receive in charter schools. *What happens to children who cannot leave their neighborhoods?* Severely disadvantaged families can barely function even when all the children in the family attend local schools. Severely disadvantaged families cannot adequately support children traveling into strange and distant neighborhoods. While proponents of competition and choice don't talk about the schools and the children who will inevitably be left behind, there clearly will be many who are. All one has to do is imagine what conditions will be like in *those* schools for *those* children to understand why competition and choice is not an acceptable strategy for public education.[21]

Instead we must fight for good schools in *all* neighborhoods, and particularly in poor neighborhoods since that is where the least-advantaged students live. Public schools in *all* neighborhoods must be adequately funded and staffed. Scandalous differences in per-pupil expenditures must be eliminated.[22] Appropriate programs and curricula must be available for *all* children in *all* schools. Parents, teachers, and students of schools in *all* neighborhoods must be empowered to participate in the educational process. And as long as housing segregation by race and income is rampant, children and families of all races and incomes must share the burden of integrating schools by participating in a fair lottery whose losers must temporarily forgo the advantages of attending a local school and be bussed to a more distant one. So-called educational reforms that distract us from achieving these formidable goals should be soundly criticized and rejected.

Curb the Market

Since the inefficiencies and inequities generated by market competition are as great as the inefficiencies and inequities caused by corporate power, activists committed to the economics of equitable cooperation must work especially hard in campaigns to replace decision making by market forces with democratic planning. As argued above, this means working to keep education within the purview of democratic decision making, not abandoning it to the ravishes of the marketplace through school vouchers and charter schools. It means fighting to keep Social Security a public pension system, not abandoning old-age insurance to the vagaries of financial markets, which is what creating individual accounts to be managed by mutual funds and brokerage houses amounts to. It means fighting for universal public health insurance, not trying to reform a private medical insurance industry that is incapable of providing universal coverage at minimum cost. It means fighting for green taxes that charge polluters the full cost of the damage they cause, and regulating the use of the environment through democratic, public choice rather than relying on tradable pollution permits polluters receive for free under the "grandfather" system. It means using tax and credit policy to bring private investment closer in line with public priorities, and expanding the role of democratic planning by the citizenry over major investment decisions made today by private financial interests who are *less* accountable to the public than at any point since the Great Depression. And it means making clear that the enemy in all these fights is not only the corporations who benefit while critical public needs go ignored, but also the rule of the market, which must be curbed, tamed, brought to bay—and eventually replaced by democratic decision-making procedures—if victories are to be sustained and expanded.

Local Economic Reform Campaigns

Local citizen groups can demand that governments fund community development corporations, and work to increase the influence of local residents within them. Local groups can build coalitions to fight sprawl and preserve green space. Community development initiatives, antigentrification campaigns, and antisprawl campaigns all afford excellent opportunities to organize locally, win highly visible, concrete victories, and fight against the rule of corporations and market forces.

Community Development Initiatives

When employers, banks, and developers withdraw from areas they consider less profitable than other alternatives, abandoned communities are left without jobs, adequate housing, or a tax base sufficient to provide basic social services. According to the logic of capitalism, when this occurs people should not waste time whining about their fates, but get with the program and move to where the action is. Capitalism tells people they should abandon the neighborhoods they grew up in before they are blighted and move to the suburbs. Capitalism tells people to leave their family and community roots in the "rust belt" and migrate to the "sun belt." According to the logic of capitalism any who fail to move in time are losers and deserve what they get. Community development initiatives are testimony to peoples' unwillingness or inability to follow capitalism's advice.

Many poverty-stricken areas in the United States still have community economic-development projects. Many others have had community-development programs cut back or abandoned. Community development corporations (CDCs), community development banks (CDBs), and community land trusts (CLTs) can all be useful parts of reform efforts to revitalize blighted urban neighborhoods and combat urban unemployment, and should be revived and expanded.[23] These projects also afford excellent opportunities for collaboration between economic reformers and organizations fighting against racism and for minority control over their own communities. Whenever the private economy fails to provide some useful good or service we should demand that the government step in to rectify matters. So when the financial sector fails to provide credit on reasonable terms for rebuilding poor neighborhoods in our cities, we should call for both regulation and intervention. We should insist that the government prevent redlining and require adequate reinvestment of savings from poor communities back into those communities by private banks. But we should also call on the government to create public, or semipublic financial institutions whose mandate is to finance renovation of deteriorated housing stock in city ghettos and help local businesses provide employment opportunities. Particularly when the boards of community-development corporations and banks are dominated by strong community organizations, they are a better way to tackle market failures that create and maintain urban ghettos than free-enterprise zones that buy little development at the cost of large tax breaks for businesses while weakening existing community organizations.

Community-development projects reject the Faustian choice between economic abandonment and gentrification by trying instead to catalyze redevelopment that benefits current residents. Community-development projects do this either by changing incentives to reattract capitalist activity or by substituting noncapitalist means of employment and housing for the capitalist activity that departed. Community-development initiatives that emphasize the latter course are important areas where people are busy meeting needs capitalism leaves unfulfilled. Community land trusts (CLTs) can play an important role in breaking several destructive aspects of capitalist housing markets. Over a hundred CLTs have been formed in communities in the United States in response to disinvestment and gentrification.[24] The CLT acquires land for community use and takes it permanently off the market. A CLT may rehab existing buildings, build new houses or apartment buildings, or use the land in any other way the community wishes. Residents may own the buildings, but the CLT retains ownership of the land. A clause in ground leases enables the CLT to buy back dwellings at a restricted price, allowing the CLT to prevent speculative increases in the housing market from driving working-class families out of area. Finally, there are two classes of membership in CLTs—one for residents who own houses, condos, or shares in co-ops on CLT land—and the other for community members who are not owners. Because the owner and nonowner members typically elect the same number of representatives to the CLT board of directors, it is harder to remove restrictions on resale prices in CLTs than in standalone coops, and the presence of nonowners on the board pressures the CLT to create new affordable housing as well. In a number of ways CLTs generally provide community members greater control than CDCs that are more prone to disenfranchise both tenants and community groups.[25]

More institutional space exists in existing community development projects than progressives presently make good use of. When working in these projects progressives need to reaffirm the right of people to remain in historical communities of their choice, irrespective of the logic of profitability. We need to point out the inefficiency and waste inherent in abandoning perfectly good economic and social infrastructure in existing communities to build socially costly and environmentally damaging new infrastructure in new communities elsewhere. We need to point out the socially destructive effects of speculative real estate bubbles. We need to press for strategies based on noncapitalist employment and housing since this provides more worker, resident, and community security and control than relying on newly courted private capital. And where noncapitalist institutions are not possible or insufficient, progressives should work to maximize community control over employers and developers who benefit from incentives offered by community-development initiatives.

Antisprawl Initiatives

The flip side of capitalist abandonment of poor, inner-city neighborhoods, is environmentally destructive growth, or *sprawl* in outlying areas. But while it is more profitable for developers to spread new homes for upper- and middle-class families indiscriminately over farm land, this is not what is best for either people or the environment. It is an environmental disaster because it needlessly replaces more green space with concrete and asphalt than necessary. It is a fiscal disaster because for every new dollar in local taxes collected from new residents, because they are spread over a large area lacking in existing services, it costs local governments roughly $1.50 to provide new residents with the streets, schools, libraries, and utilities they are entitled to. And it has a disastrous effect on people's life styles as the "rural character of life" in outlying areas is destroyed for older residents, and those moving into bedroom communities spend more and more of their time on gridlocked roads commuting to work and driving to schools and strip malls at a considerable distance from their homes.[26] Nor does sprawl even address the nation's most pressing housing need—a scandalous shortfall of affordable housing.

Instead what is called for is "in growth" and "smart growth." New housing should be built in old, abandoned neighborhoods whose infrastuctures are renovated, and concentrated in new areas that are environmentally less sensitive. Instead of construction patterns dictated by market forces and developers' bottom lines, what is called for is development planning through appropriate changes in zoning, combined with impact fees that distribute costs equitably. Instead of allowing developers to only build the kind of housing they find most profitable, they must be required to build a certain percentage of low-cost units in exchange for permits to build high-cost units. Instead of abandoning farms and green space to the ravishes of market forces, what is needed are preservation trusts, easements, and transfer development rights programs to preserve green space without doing it at farmers' expense.

The battle to replace sprawl with smart growth is a battle to replace the disastrous effects of market forces on local communities with democratic planning by the residents of those communities themselves. It requires democratic determination of community priorities. It requires challenging conservative defenses of individual property rights no matter how damaging to community interests. It requires clever strategies to win farmer approval for downzoning agricultural land so it cannot be developed, by giving farmers transfer development rights and requiring developers to purchase them in order to build in areas designated for concentrated development. It requires withholding construction permits for high-income housing unless accompanied by a sufficient number of affordable units. It requires building coalitions of environmentalists, long-time residents, farmers, and those in need of affordable housing with a package of policies that serve their needs and shields them from shouldering a disproportionate share of the costs of in growth and smart growth. It requires politically isolating and defeating developers, banks, and wealthy newcomers who favor gentrification and sprawl because it serves their interests. It requires running in-growth and smart-growth candidates for local offices who spurn contributions from developers for their election campaigns, and who laugh at developer bluffs to boycott localities who insist on protecting community interests.

Of course the slogan "smart growth" can be misappropriated by clever developers, just as "sustainable development" has been misappropriated by clever corporations seeking to disguise their environmentally destructive growth objectives. What matters are the policies, not the labels put on them for salesmanship. And what matters are whose interests are served by those policies, and which groups and organizations dominate a coalition for smart growth. But antisprawl campaigns, campaigns for slow growth, in growth, and smart growth, and campaigns to protect disappearing green space that are already going on in every major metropolitan area and its surrounding communities afford progressives important organizing opportunities.

How to Work for Reforms

In an era of increasing corporate power, much of our energies must be devoted to reform campaigns like those briefly described in this chapter. These and other reform campaigns must be the major arenas in which progressive activists labor for the time being. But we must make clear that the reason we work in reform campaigns is that we believe *everyone* should control their own economic destiny, and *everyone* should receive economic benefits commensurate with their effort and sacrifice. We must make clear that not only is dictatorship of the capitalists unacceptable, but dictatorship of the educated elite and experts is unacceptable as well. While many of the leaders of reform campaigns we work in will fail to make these points, those fighting to replace the economics of competition and greed with equitable cooperation must never fail to do so.

It is also important for activists working in reform campaigns to make clear that victories can only be partial and temporary as long as economic power is unequally dispersed and economic decisions are based on private gain and market competition. Otherwise, reform efforts give way to disillusionment, and weaken, rather than strengthen the movement for progressive economic change when victories prove partial and erode over time. Not only must activists working for reforms explain why those reforms will be temporary as long as capitalism survives, they must also take time in their reform work to explain concretely how victories can be fuller and more permanent if capitalism is replaced by a system designed to promote equitable economic cooperation in the first place.

While a necessary first step, the reforms outlined in this chapter will suffer the same fate as the best efforts of twentieth-century reformers unless twenty-first century activists never tire of explaining what economic justice and democracy mean, unless we take every opportunity to explain why private enterprise and markets are fundamentally incompatible with equitable cooperation, and unless reforms are accompanied by expanding experiments in equitable cooperation and new safeguards within progressive economic movements discussed in the chapters that follow.

Why Reforms Are Insufficient

Even the most efficient and equitable capitalist economies cannot restore the environment, provide people with economic self-management, distribute the burdens and benefits of economic activity fairly, and promote solidarity and variety while avoiding wastefulness. This is one reason we must go beyond reforming capitalism to build the economics of equitable cooperation. But another reason is that reforms to humanize capitalism are always at risk of being reversed. As long as giant corporations control the bulk of our productive powers, as long as economic survival is determined by market forces, the economics of competition and greed will threaten reforms and lead to renewed attempts to weaken restraints reforms place on corporate freedom of maneuver.

In the United States, the Humphrey-Hawkins Full Employment Act was signed in 1978 after decades of lobbying by organized labor and civil rights groups, only to become a dead letter under a Democratic President, Jimmy Carter, and a Democratic congress as soon as the ink was dry. Financial regulations prompted by the crash of 1929 and the Great Depression were scuttled by the Reagan administration in the early 1980s who invited the financial industry to rewrite rules that had long irked them but protected the rest of us. Welfare reforms dating from the War on Poverty in the 1960s were rolled back when a Democratic President, Bill Clinton, collaborated with Newt Gingrich and a Republican congress in the mid-1990s. Privatization of Social Security was first raised by the Clinton White House, and will be pursued again by whoever occupies the White House when the public has once again forgotten that a stock market that goes up can also go down.[27] In Great Britain in the 1980s, Margaret Thatcher's Tory government systematically dismantled reforms making British capitalism more stable and equitable implemented by Labor Party governments in the aftermath of World War II. Recently the New Labor government of Tony Blair has continued the process of reversing reforms Old Labor and its progressive allies once worked decades to win.

It is invariably the case that critics of hard-won reforms can point to flaws. Reforms are never administered as efficiently and democratically as possible, particularly when administered by governments opposed to them in the first place. Regulatory systems are always subject to being captured by those they were intended to regulate. Reforms are inevitably compromise agreements, and therefore never fully reflect what people wanted and what progressives campaigned for. And even if the reform demands of progressives were fully met and perfectly administered, the results would prove unsatisfying because equitable cooperation cannot be achieved in a system based on the logic of competition and greed. For all these reasons reforms will inevitably be flawed and provide ample grounds for criticism and disappointment. The Humphrey-Hawkins Bill was far from an efficient and flexible system of fiscal and monetary stimulus and restraint. New Deal financial reforms were subject to capture by the financial sector. The U.S. welfare system was seriously flawed from its inception. And British public healthcare was never a first-best well-care system. Nonetheless, when conservatives like Reagan and Thatcher, or more recently "third-way" politicians like Clinton and Blair, harp on failings in order to dismantle imperfect reforms rather than improve and extend reforms, they strengthen the forces of competition and greed and weaken the cause of equitable cooperation.

The most successful attempts to humanize capitalism through reform were in the Scandinavian economies during the 1960s and early 1970s. Norway and Sweden had a full Keynesian program, the most generous welfare system capitalism has ever tolerated, and the Meidner Commission in Sweden had begun to press for significant worker participation in firm ownership and governance. As we saw in chapter 5, starting in the mid-1970s all these reforms came under attack, and all have been dismantled or significantly rolled back. The Scandinavian model is far from dead, *Wall Street Journal* obituaries to the contrary. But as Magnus Ryner explained, thanks in large part to third-way leadership, Scandinavian social democracy has been in retreat for over two decades. Like the triumph of free market over Keynesian capitalism in the United States and Great Britain, the backward trajectory of social democracy in Scandinavia stands as a powerful reminder why we must go beyond reforming capitalism if we expect to sustain progress toward the economics of equitable cooperation.

12

Economic Reform Movements

The last chapter examined various economic reform campaigns combating the pernicious effects of the economics of competition and greed. This chapter critically examines progressive economic-reform movements that those of us seeking to promote equitable cooperation must work to build and strengthen. Some are relatively new, like the antiglobalization movement. Others, like the labor movement have been with us much longer. For each movement I discuss how people can participate in ways that are not only effective at winning important reforms but also build momentum for a fuller program of equitable cooperation.

The Labor Movement

Nothing substitutes for a strong labor movement. In 1998 a new leadership headed by John Sweeney replaced the Cold War leadership of Lane Kirkland and George Meany at the AFL-CIO. The Cold War leadership bequeathed to Sweeney a labor movement greatly reduced in size and power under its fifty-year stewardship, representing only 15 percent of the total workforce and a dismal 11 percent of those employed in the private sector.[1] The new leadership made important changes, but ossification seems to be once again on the rise, and it is clear that much more far-reaching initiatives will be necessary to reverse the decline of organized labor. In "Why Unions Matter," executive director of the Harvard Trade Union Program, outlined an excellent strategy to begin to revitalize the American Labor movement.[2]

Beyond Bread-and-Butter Unionism

Bernard points out that "when the National Labor Relations Act, the cornerstone of U.S. labor law, was adopted by Congress in 1935, its purpose was not simply to provide a procedural mechanism to end industrial strife in the workplace. Rather, this monumental piece of New Deal legislation had a far more ambitious mission: to promote industrial democracy." Bernard goes on to argue that to promote industrial democracy unions must embrace two priorities they largely abandoned during the Cold War era: (1) unions must bring democracy into the workplace by extending constitutional rights like freedom of speech into the autocratic workplace, and by winning their members a say over policies in union shops; and (2) unions must serve the needs of unorganized workers as well their members by winning reforms in the political arena that protect all working people. Bernard argues that failure of unions to return to what she calls their "social movement heritage" will perpetuate their decline. She points out that "American workers are schooled every day at work to believe that democracy stops at the factory or office door. But democracy is not an extracurricular activity that can be relegated to evenings and weekends." She suggests "rather than relegating workplace democracy to an abstract long-term goal, labor today needs to tap this source of wider appeal for unions by placing the extension of democracy into the workplace front and center." Bernard concedes that "there has always been a tension within unions between servicing members and fulfilling the wider social mission of labor to serve the needs of all working people, whether they are organized or not." But she argues "it is becoming increasingly clear in today's political environment that unions need to do both. Unions, like any organization, will not survive if they do not serve the needs of their members. But unions will not survive and grow, if they only serve the needs of their members. The experience of organized labor in the U.S. demonstrates that simply delivering for their own members is not sufficient in the long run."

Jobs with Justice is one organization that learned this lesson well. Founded in 1987, Jobs with Justice had organized coalition chapters in over forty cities by 2003 with impressive records of active support for a variety of labor causes. According to its mission statement Jobs with Justice exists "to improve working people's standard of living, fight for job security, and protect workers' right to organize. A core belief of Jobs with Justice is that in order to be successful, workers' rights struggles have to be part of a larger campaign for economic and social justice. To that end, Jobs with Justice has created a network of local coalitions that connect labor, faith-based, community, and student organizations to work together on workplace and community social justice campaigns." For those who are not fortunate enough to be represented by a union where they work, Jobs with Justice is an organization open to individual as well as organizational membership providing excellent opportunities for people seeking to build the labor movement (www.jwj.org).

Bernard points out that the more successful "bread and butter unionism" is at expanding the "wage premium" unions win their members, compared to unorganized workers in the same industry, "the greater [will be] employer resistance to unionization." She points out that "the sad lesson for U.S. labor is that by failing to extend the gains made by unions to the rest of working people, these gains have come to be threatened. By comparison, in Canada, where unions have been more successful in socializing the gains first achieved through collective bargaining, from healthcare to vacation pay, rates of organization are double what they are in the U.S." She also points out that "management resistance to unionization in Canada is less vigorous than in the U.S. If management busts a union in Canada, it cannot take away Canadian workers' healthcare because this benefit has been socialized and is an entitlement of all Canadian residents. By winning benefits first through collective agreements and then extending them to all working people through political action, labor in Canada has not only assisted all working people, but has made its own victory that much more secure."

As important as it is for union members, activists, and elected officials to move their unions beyond bread and butter, or "business" unionism, Bernard's proposals would only return the U.S. labor movement to its pre-Cold War agenda. This is not a criticism of her proposals, which are a necessary first step. But if American unions are going to promote the economics of equitable cooperation more successfully in the twenty-first century than they did in the twentieth century, they are going to have to change in other ways as well.[3]

Hammer for Justice

Unions must return to their mission of being the hammer for economic justice in capitalism. There is no good reason unions can't do a better job of educating their membership about economic justice. What union today teaches its members that nobody deserves to be paid more than them, unless someone works harder and makes greater personal sacrifices than

they do? What union teaches its members that as long as wages are determined by the law of supply and demand in the marketplace, unions can
only slightly and temporarily reduce the degree of economic injustice?
Yet every union *can* teach these lessons, and grow larger and stronger by
doing so.

Unfortunately most unions have fallen into the ideological trap of justifying wage demands on the basis of the market value of their member's
contributions, their marginal-revenue products. This approach fails to
challenge the legitimacy of capitalist profits and CEO supersalaries, and
creates obstacles to solidarity among workers in different industries and
occupations. If workers should be paid according to their marginal-
revenue products, then why should their employers not receive profits
equal to the marginal-revenue products of the machinery they bring to
the production process, and why should CEOs not be paid according to
their marginal-revenue products as well? If a CEO implements policy
changes that increase the revenues of a firm by 3 million dollars a year,
while an assembly-line worker only increases firm revenues by thirty thousand dollars, why is the CEO *not* entitled to one hundred times more than
the worker? When unions offer no coherent answer to these questions
they cannot serve as a hammer for economic justice.

One of Sweeney's first initiatives after coming to office was a campaign
criticizing outrageous CEO salaries in major U.S. corporations. The
campaign complained that the ratio of CEO salaries to the average salaries
of their employees had risen in U.S. corporations, and provided workers
a way to access the figures for their own companies through the "Executive Pay Watch" program on the AFL-CIO Web site, www.aflcio.org.
As popular as this initiative was, the underlying argument lacked
substance. What if CEO productivity were rising relative to the productivity of average employees? The AFL-CIO also complained that the ratio
of CEO to average employee salary was significantly higher in U.S. corporations than Japanese corporations. But what if U.S. CEOs were more
productive relative to their employees than Japanese CEOs were relative
to their employees? According to the doctrine of reward according to the
value of contribution there would be nothing to complain about if CEO
salary trends merely reflect trends in their marginal-revenue products. Of
course there is no reason to believe the ratio of U.S. CEO productivity to
employee productivity was increasing, any more than there was reason
to think the ratio was higher in U.S. than Japanese corporations. All
evidence points to a dramatic increase in the bargaining power of
American CEOs relative to ordinary U.S. employees as the cause of the

trend, which certainly did make the rapid increases in CEO salaries in U.S. corporations while real wages were falling for their employees during the 1990s particularly egregious. But CEO salary bloat would have been outrageous even if CEO productivity had been rising relative to the productivity of ordinary employees. Larger percentage salary increases for CEOs who enjoy luxurious working conditions and are already making hundreds of times more than a worker toiling on an assembly line is unfair and shameful in any case. It is an outrageous violation of economic justice because it raises the reward to someone who makes less personal sacrifices, and who is already rewarded many times more than people making greater personal sacrifices. But to draw that lesson the AFL-CIO would have to explain that wages and salaries should be determined by people's sacrifices rather than by their contributions.

It is sometimes argued that since unions must convince employers to pay employees more, it is only natural for unions to try to convince employers that their members are worth more to them, that is, that union members' high marginal-revenue products warrants higher pay. But this argument proves weak upon examination. No matter how productive you convince me my employees are, assuming no effect on their effort, I can always get higher profits by paying them less. So the only reason I will pay them more is if I'm convinced that I can't get away with paying them less, or if I fear that paying them less will cause their output to decline. So what matters is not if the employ*er* thinks the employees deserve more, since that has no policy implications for the employer. What matters is if employ*ees* think they deserve more, and therefore are more determined to inconvenience an employer who does not accede to their demands. If a union is really trying to win the maximum wage increase for its members, it should be trying to convince the employ*ees* it represents that they deserve to be paid more, not the employer. In which case the issue reduces to what is the best way for a union to convince its members they are being unfairly compensated: Tell them they are being paid less than their marginal revenue product when they know greater productivity is as often the result of better equipment and machinery as it is from more effort and sacrifice on their part? Or tell them they are being paid less than their sacrifices entitle them to? Showing employees they are compensated less for their sacrifices than those above them in society's wealth and income hierarchy is not only a more logically sound ethical argument, I suspect it is a more powerful motivating strategy as well.

Unions don't have to wait on new organizing successes to teach present members what economic justice is and is not. This is not ground that should be difficult to reconquer. The first step is to clear our own heads of cobwebs and relearn how to preach to the choir. No complicated labor theory of value requiring a graduate degree to master is necessary. The simple logic of reward commensurate with sacrifice defended in chapter 1 is perfectly understandable by ordinary workers, if only union officials would remember how to preach it.

One step in the right direction would be for unions themselves to pay fair wages. As the Wobblies argued long ago, union leaders should get the same wage as the members they represent, never more. The average wage of elected union leaders and staff members should be the same as the average wage of those they represent. And within the union, differences in wages should be based on differences in effort or sacrifice rather than on how high up in the union hierarchy somebody is, or the going wage rate for someone of their skill and experience in the labor market. Instead what has happened is elected union officials have increasingly paid themselves salaries commensurate with salaries of other powerful leaders with whom they hobnob, and salaries for union professional staffs have been increasingly "market determined." Union members have every reason to resent leaders who pay themselves a great deal more than those they represent while generally enjoying better working conditions as well, and every reason to mistrust what such leaders have to say about economic injustice and exploitation.

Democratize Unions

All too often unions are even less democratic than mainstream politics. This is a disgrace for a movement that purports to stand for greater political and economic democracy. Prosecuting attorneys appointed by politicians in the pockets of corporations cannot be trusted to police unions against fraud and corruption. That is one reason progressives must lead reform movements of members to clean up their own unions and tell the government attorneys and judges to butt out. But that is only the beginning of what is necessary to make unions democratic. Electoral systems that stack the deck even more in favor of incumbent union officials than the deck is stacked in favor of incumbent U.S. Congresspeople are an outrage. Yet this is what those who we expect to effectively promote industrial democracy have come up with for themselves. As in the case of economic justice, unions must practice what they preach about democracy. Obviously that means clean elections with no ballot-box stuffing and intimidation. Obviously it means incumbents cannot use union funds to finance their reelection campaigns. But it also means union publications and union-sponsored events must afford challengers the same opportunities to promote their campaigns as afforded incumbents. It also means term limits on union offices. And it means it should be standard practice for union officials to return to their jobs on shop floors when their term of office is over, none of which even speaks to the broader issue of how to promote more active participation by rank-and-file members in determining union strategy and policy. It is not easy to promote union participation among members who are busy earning a living, and who spend their lives in social institutions that teach them to be passive, shut up, and obey. Nor am I suggesting there is any simple panacea. But instead of lagging behind society at large in building a culture of participatory democracy, instead of imitating the hierarchical, authoritarian practices of their corporate foes, unions must search for ways to stimulate participation by their members. For as long as entrenched union leaders dictate policies, and decide when *they* find it convenient to mobilize membership in support of *their* campaigns, member participation will continue to atrophy, and unions will continue to become even less important in the lives of the shrinking minority of U.S. workers who are union members.

Don't Mourn, Organize!

Of course organizing the unorganized is a critical priority for the labor movement. Until unions greatly expand the percentage of the labor force they represent in the United States, what unions can hope to accomplish will remain severely restricted. Not only can unions reduce opposition from employers to unionization drives by extending gains to the workforce at large through government programs and mandates, as Elaine Bernard explained above, progressives working in unions must obviously press for a dramatic reallocation of union resources and energy toward organizing new workers. Just as the federal government can accomplish little in the area of social programs until there is a drastic shift from military spending to domestic spending, union power will not increase until unions dramatically reallocate resources from legislative and political affairs, and from support for contract negotiation, to organizing the unorganized. These are difficult choices for unions. Unlike the preponderance of U.S. military spending that does *not* make U.S. citizens more safe and secure, for the most part lobbying legislatures, get-out-the-vote campaigns for lesser-evil candidates, and support for contract negotiation *does* serve workers' interests. But union dollars spent on these activities are, on average, far less productive than union dollars spent on organizing drives. Besides honest mistakes, two structural problems prevent an efficient real-location of priorities in union budgets: (1) Compared to lobbying, campaign support, and contract negotiation, organizing the unorganized is hard work. Like all of us, unions tend to put off to last the least pleasant and hardest tasks on their "to-do lists." (2) While leading a successful organizing drive can be one way to break into the union hierarchy, for those who are already members of union officialdom, their careers are better served by working on legislative and political affairs as well as contract negotiation. In other words, an emphasis on business unionism rather than organizing is in the personal interests of most union officials. Unless progressives working in unions prioritize efforts to successfully break through the self-defeating misallocation of union resources that results from these structural obstacles, they will not succeed in revital-izing the labor movement.

Beside more resources and a large dose of old-time union religion to rally workers to wage class war, to be successful union organizing drives require rethinking who the most likely recruits will be, and new thinking about how to reach them. In this area the AFL-CIO Organizing Institute has turned over more than one new leaf since the late 1990s, and is busy providing valuable practical training for a new generation of union orga-nizers. For young people aspiring to become labor activists, right now the Organizing Institute is an excellent place to start: www.aflcio.org/aboutunions/oi. Among the national unions, the Service Employees Inter-national Union (SEIU) is setting the best example in organizing drives, and has recently challenged the AFL-CIO to make organizing Wal-Mart the number one priority of the union movement. Mostly we need lots more of what the Organizing Institute is doing, so tripling its budget would be a good place to start. And we also need other unions to answer the wake-up call SEIU issued at its summer 2004 convention, and support the kind of dramatic changes in organizing priorities and methods SEIU is now calling for.

Neither Union Bureaucrat Nor Revolutionary Cadre

Two traditional models exist for leftists going to work in the labor move-ment: join the union establishment, or remain a rank-and-file activist. In the first case a person convinces herself that more can be accomplished by working within the union than against it. She runs for local union office, and tries to proceed up the union ladder in order to promote policies she regards as more effective more widely. The danger with this strategy lies in succumbing to pressure to tow the union line even when it is wrong. Two structural characteristics of modern-day unions increase this danger dramatically: (1) Electoral systems in most unions greatly favor incumbency, so anyone who rises in the union hierarchy necessarily benefits from this antidemocratic bias. The result has been authoritarian union regimes, eventually overthrown by challengers they long repressed, who quickly become new authoritarian regimes once in power. (2) Since there are considerable perks for those who rise in the union hierarchy, it is very tempting to succumb to the temptation to tow the union line irrespective of its merits to keep a salary that is considerably higher than what any official who returned to the shop floor would be paid.

In the case where a labor activist steadfastly remains a rank-and-file worker in the factory, she avoids the corrupting temptations associated with union office and retains her independence to criticize union policy and union officials as well as capitalist employers. But of course she is not really like most of her fellow rank-and-file workers because she is much more political than they are. In the twentieth century, most who pursued this model found it necessary to join a revolutionary sect that provided the psychological and social support necessary to sustain a life of left activism fighting against capitalist exploiters and sell-out union officials alike, all on behalf of fellow rank-and-file workers who were often less than appreciative. One danger in this approach lies in ceding power over issues essential to the labor movement to less principled and talented competitors who covet positions in the union hierarchy. The other danger is becoming isolated from one's fellow workers who do not share one's passion for discussing articles from the latest issue of a revolutionary communist newspaper.

There are unavoidable dilemmas associated with working either inside or outside any reformist organization, and deciding whether to accept or reject a compromise deal any reformist organization negotiates. Whether to work inside or outside unions, and whether to support or reject contracts are not exceptions to the rule, but cases in point. Unfortunately, the traditional models for leftist work in the labor movement exaggerate these dilemmas unnecessarily. The next chapter looks at experiments in equitable cooperation that afford people various ways to live personal lives according to the principles we are fighting for. By implementing the principle "to each according to effort, or sacrifice" within a group of likeminded people, labor activists can begin to enjoy the fruits of living the economics of equitable cooperation even while capitalism denies people that opportunity in general. If activists who believe they can be more effective working as union officials commit to equitable living communities[4] governed by this principle they will be less susceptible to the lure of perks from union office, less fearful of losing office and returning to the shop floor, and therefore more inclined to buck the union line when it is called for. Moreover, their primary peer group—others living in their equitable living communities—will consist of people who accord respect and esteem based on principled behavior rather than material status. Once equitable living communities are available and some union officials commit to them, any who do not will have to explain themselves to those they represent.

If those who remain rank-and-file labor activists live in communities of equitable cooperation they will have the social support needed to sustain them, and they will demonstrate on a daily basis their personal commitment to the principle of economic justice. I also suspect their fellow workers would often be more interested in hearing about how people living in equitable communities deal with the day-to-day housing, healthcare, and educational needs of their families than discussing theoretical articles in the latest issue of a revolutionary newspaper with a miniscule circulation.

Most importantly, when honest differences of opinion arise among labor activists there will be less reason to suspect anyone's sincerity or motives if their own material rewards and social standing are determined independently from positions they take on how best to build the labor movement. In every situation that arises, some people will be tempted to give in too easily, while others will err on the side of holding out for more than can be won. There is no way to prevent people from making these mistakes. But others will no longer have reasons to be suspicious that the mistake of giving in too easily is a self-serving betrayal, or sellout. And taking a rejectionist line will no longer be the only way to demonstrate that one is wholeheartedly commited to labor's cause. Living according to the principles of equitable cooperation should be sufficient to demonstrate one's commitment to labor's cause, so that differences of opinion about the best political strategy to advance labor's cause will come to be seen as honest disagreements.

The Anticorporate Movement

The best thing about Ralph Nader's campaign for President in 2000 was that he never tired of talking about the biggest problem in the world today: unchecked corporate power run amok. Nader was a master at explaining how corporations deceive consumers and manipulate the political system. The best thing about the movement for corporate responsibility is that its campaigns publicize particularly egregious cases of corporate abuse, and provide people who become outraged something concrete to do about it. Corporate power and ideological hegemony has never been greater in the United States than it is today, even surpassing the power of the great trusts during the era of the robber barons over a century ago. Moreover, multinational corporations in general, and U.S. corporations in particular, have never held greater sway over the global economy than they do today.[5] Exposing corporate abuse and fighting corporate power describes a great deal of what those fighting to replace competition and greed with equitable cooperation must do for the foreseeable future. Whereas the labor movement and unions fight corporate power primarily as it adversely affects employees, and the consumer movement (discussed below) seeks to protect consumers from corporate abuse, the anticorporate movement opposes corporate abuse principally from the perspective of citizens. We need to build all three movements to bring corporate power to bay.

Leftists argue that calling for corporations to behave responsibly is like asking tigers to become vegetarians. We point out that modern corporations are designed to maximize profits by any legal means available to them, and corporate officers are subject to legal action by shareholders if they do otherwise. We insist that contrary to the teachings of Adam Smith, many of the most effective ways to increase corporate profits do so at the expense of the public interest and the environment, as well as at the expense of employees and consumers, so it is naïve and foolish to expect corporations to behave in socially responsible ways. Of course we are right when we point all this out. On the other hand, not all corporations behave equally badly. Anyone who thinks so should compare the behavior of Wal-Mart, as described by Bill Quinn in *How Wal-Mart Is Destroying America: And What You Can Do about It* (1998), to the behavior of Malden Mills, whose CEO, after a fire destroyed the factory, kept his entire workforce on salary and paid them their Christmas bonuses while rebuilding the factory in Lawrence, Massachusetts, rather than seizing the opportunity to relocate in the south or overseas as every other mill in New England had already done.[6] Moreover, sometimes even the most socially irresponsible corporations can be forced to abandon harmful practices. Kevin Danaher and Jason Mark provide a useful history of corporations in the United States and the opposition movements they spawned during the nineteenth and early twentieth century in the first chapter of their book, *Insurrection: Citizen Challenges to Corporate Power* (2003).[7] In the five chapters that follow they describe recent, successful campaigns against some of the largest and worst corporate offenders. However, one of the biggest victories for the movement for corporate responsibility came after publication of their book. Aileen Alt Powell, a business writer for the Associated Press, gave the following account of an historic joint press conference held by Citigroup and Rainforest Action Network on the AP wire January 22, 2004:

The nation's largest financial institution announced Thursday that it is adopting a corporate policy to carefully evaluate requests for project financing that could adversely affect the environment and ban any funding for illegal logging operations. It also commits Citigroup "to invest in sustainable forestry and renewable energy." Adoption of the initiatives comes after two years of anti-Citi demonstrations by the Rainforest Action Network aimed at getting the bank to make a commitment to environmental causes. Ilyse Hogue, global finance campaign director for the environmental activist group, which is headquartered in San Francisco, said Citi is the first American bank to adopt such a comprehensive policy. "We think this is the most significant environmental commitment to date in the financial services sector . . . and perhaps in the corporate sector, because of the potential ripple effects," Hogue said. She spoke in a joint announcement of the policy with Pam Flaherty, head of global community relations and environmental affairs for Citigroup. Flaherty said the new initiative builds on voluntary guidelines known as the Equator Principles that 18 global financial institutions have signed since last June. The principles require the banks to adopt procedures to evaluate the social and environmental impacts of infrastructure projects that they finance. "What we've done is moved beyond that, building on it and making it more comprehensive," Flaherty said. The bank said the new policy's main points are: (1) Putting in place additional screening of financing requests for projects "that Citigroup determines could adversely impact a critical natural habitat." Included will be a ban on lending for commercial logging in primary, tropical moist forests. (2) Refusing loans to companies known to be in violation of local or national laws against illegal logging. (3) Developing "a program to invest in sustainable forestry and renewable energy." It will include consumer financing for solar panels, residential wind turbines and fuel cells and other forms of clean energy. (4) Reporting the "greenhouse" gas emissions from power projects in its portfolio. It is not the first time

Citigroup has changed its policies after public protests. The bank adopted reforms to eliminate practices that took advantage of low-income borrowers after community groups bitterly protested its 2000 purchase of Associates First Capital Corp., which specialized in loans to high-risk borrowers. Associates was later merged into CitiFinancial.

Clearly, when anticorporate campaigns succeed in raising the cost sufficiently for corporations who persist in their socially irresponsible behavior, victories can be won. Moreover, the anticorporate movement affords excellent opportunities to reach out to those who are just beginning to see how corporate power undermines political and economic democracy. The anticorporate movement can demonstrate on a case-by-case basis precisely how production for profit differs from production in the public interest in ways that are convincing to ordinary people. The anticorporate movement can provide concrete substance to our anticapitalist message. And perhaps most importantly, the anticorporate movement allows those who are not employees to join fights against corporate abuses through creative tactics and direct action, all of which is important for building the movement for equitable cooperation. In their concluding chapter, Danaher and Mark offer sage advice to fellow anticorporate activists: they argue that the movement for corporate *responsibility* needs to become a movement for corporate *accountability*. In other words, besides continuing to demand responsibility from individual corporations, the movement must also demand that government do its job, namely, *enforce* corporate accountability to the public interest.

However, when leaders of campaigns for corporate responsibility concentrate on changing the consciousness of CEOs, or trying to shame corporations into behaving more responsibly, the movement falls victim to naïve expectations and increases the likelihood that its leaders will be co-opted and their followers will be disappointed and disillusioned. For the most part the personal views and values of corporate officers are irrelevant to corporate policy. Stockholders and competitive financial markets largely dictate choices, and corporate officers understand this even when those in campaigns for corporate responsibility do not. If an anticorporate publicity campaign has a larger negative effect on a company's bottom line than the positive effect of the policy critics oppose, corporate officers may well relent. If campaigners can force elected officials and those they appoint to force corporations to be accountable to community and environmental interests irrespective of the effect on corporate profits, all the better. But the immediate goal should always be to reduce corporate power and expand citizen power. Corporate power should never be accepted as legitimate or inevitable. And because private corporations driven by market competition will continue to try to get away with behavior contrary to the public interest no matter how many battles the movement for corporate responsibility may win, the ultimate goal must be to rid ourselves of corporate power over our lives entirely. For this reason, even though leaders of the movement for corporate accountability may not call for the abolition of corporations altogether themselves for tactical or strategic reasons, they should never criticize those who do, or those who argue for the eventual replacement of capitalism.

The Environmental Movement

The labor movement and the environmental movement evolved as two different movements historically. Each has also given the other good reason to regard it as an enemy rather than an ally. As we have seen, one pillar of the labor movement has been full employment macroeconomic policies. But just as full employment can be pursued through "military Keynesianism," thereby alienating the peace movement, full-employment can be pursued in ways that are environmentally destructive, alienating the environmental movement. Of course full employment macro policies can be pursued in ways that do not strengthen the military industrial complex or aggravate environmental destruction, but unfortunately, this has not always been how organized labor has pursed the goal of full employment. Similarly, when leading organizations in the environmental movement take antigrowth positions that fail to distinguish between growth of economic well-being and growth of material through-put, and when environmental organizations propose policies that foist an unfair share of the burden of the costs of adjusting to environmentally friendly practices on workers and the poor, they alienate the movement fighting for economic justice and make the accusation that the environmental movement is a middle-class, white movement a self-fulfilling prophesy. Again, environmental protection and restoration can be fought for in ways that do not sacrifice jobs and increase poverty,[8] but unfortunately, it has not always been done in this way.

How to better relations not only between the labor and environmental movements, but increase solidarity among all the progressive social movements, will be explored in chapter 14. But a first step in that direction is for each social movement to recognize the others as legitimate, independent social movements, with goals and objectives no less important than its own. No progressive social movement should claim to subsume the goals of another under the umbrella of its own agenda, nor presume to determine priorities for other social movements. So when I discuss economic reform programs to curb the environmentally destructive effects of free markets and production for profit, I do not mean to suggest that campaigns for these reforms should be controlled by the progressive economic movement and its organizations rather than the environmental movement and its organizations. Nor do I mean to suggest that economic reforms should comprise the entire agenda of the environmental movement. Nonetheless, the economic reforms discussed below are one important part of the fight to replace the economics of environmentally destructive competition and greed with a sustainable economics of equitable cooperation. These policies will not protect and preserve the environment, but they can slow the pace of environmental destruction while capitalism persists.

Regulation

The dominant approach to environmental protection in the United States has been what detractors like to call "command and control" (CAC) regulation. This can take the form of requiring use of a particular technology such as catalytic converters in automobiles, or prohibiting the use of a particular technology, such as strip mining, or outlawing use of particular products such as DDT. In other cases, when environmental authorities decide an overall reduction in emissions of a particular pollutant is necessary, the regulatory approach is to require every individual polluter to reduce emissions by whatever percent regulators want to reduce overall emissions.

The principal arguments against this kind of regulation are: (1) they may not minimize the social cost necessary to achieve a particular level of overall reduction, and (2) they offer no incentive for firms to develop new technologies that could reduce emissions by more than the amount mandated. These objections are strongest when it is possible to develop new technologies that are cleaner than mandates require, and when significant differences exist between the costs of pollution reduction for different polluters. For example, if one of two polluters can reduce emissions for half the cost of the other, it is inefficient to have the polluter for whom pollution reduction costs are higher reduce emissions by the same percentage that the polluter with lower pollution-reduction costs does. In this case, equal percentage reductions are achieved at a higher overall cost than if the polluter who can reduce emissions more cheaply did all the cutbacks until its costs of further reduction were no longer lower than those of the other polluter.

There is no denying the fact that when pollution reduction costs differ among polluters, regulations that require equal percentage reductions for all polluters fail to minimize overall reduction costs. But the degree to which such regulations are inefficient depends on the degree to which different polluters face different reduction costs. Where reduction costs are similar, equal percentage reductions are almost as efficient as alternatives such as pollution taxes and tradable pollution permits that allow polluters to reduce emissions by different percentages, and regulations may have significant ideological and political advantages that make them the most attractive policy.

Pollution Taxes and Tradable Pollution Permits

Most economists favor what promarket economists like to call "market-based solutions," or "financial incentives." The new version of financial incentives is tradable pollution permits. The old version is pollution taxes. The logic of pollution taxes is to force producers to take into account the cost to society of their pollution, just as they have to take into account the cost of using scarce labor and raw materials. The market makes them pay for the labor and raw materials they use, but unless the government levies a pollution tax producers don't have to pay for the damage their pollution causes. Consequently, in free markets producers ignore the social cost of pollution in order to maximize their profits. A pollution tax seeks to internalize the otherwise neglected external effect so producers will take it into account.

When all polluters pay the same tax per unit of emission those with lower pollution-reduction costs will find it in their interest to reduce emissions more than those with higher reduction costs. This means pollution taxes distribute pollution reduction among polluters in a way that minimizes the cost of achieving the overall reduction. It also means polluters have an incentive to develop new, less-polluting technologies no matter how much they may already have reduced emissions. Pollution taxes also make the polluter pay, and imply that the polluter does not have a right to pollute unless he pays for the damage he inflicts on others. Unfortunately, as explained in chapter 8, no natural mechanism in a market economy determines how much damage pollution causes. The market generates no quantitative estimate of the damage from pollution, so there is no way to know how high to set the pollution tax. With no objective benchmark, powerful corporations are left to vie with much less powerful environmental groups for the ears of politicians who must decide on a tax rate. The outcome is predictable: pollution taxes are invariably set too low, leading to too much pollution.

The very idea of tradable pollution permits was an outrage to most environmental activists only a short time ago. Yet mainstream environmental groups like the Environmental Defense Fund (EDF) have now endorsed this approach in a number of situations, including the widely studied EPA sulfur dioxide tradable permit program. More surprisingly, some militant environmental activists have voiced a preference for permits over taxes. The policy is simple. If anyone emits x units of a pollutant, they must own x permits for that pollutant. Emissions in excess of the number of permits owned is a violation of the law, just like driving without a driving license, and subject to whatever punishment is established.

In many respects, tradable pollution permits lead polluters to behave in the same way that pollution taxes do. If I want to pollute more I have to have more permits. If I don't own enough permits, I have to buy more in the "pollution permit market"—which is costly. But even if I own enough permits to pollute as much as I want, it is costly for me to pollute because the more I pollute the fewer permits I can sell for a profit to others on the permit market. Either way there is an opportunity cost to polluting more. And if the price of a permit to pollute a ton is the same as the tax on a ton of pollution, the opportunity cost of polluting more is the same in both cases. Once this is recognized, it is easy to see why supporters argue that pollution permits yield the same efficiency advantages as pollution taxes. There is always an incentive to develop cleaner technologies because the business would have to buy fewer (or be able to sell more) pollution permits. And firms with low costs of pollution reduction will reduce more than firms with high costs of pollution reduction since the former will find it cheaper to reduce emissions and avoid having to buy as many permits (or be able to sell more permits), while the latter will find it cheaper to continue polluting and pay for the extra permits (or sell fewer excess permits.)

As a matter of fact, one version of tradable permits yields exactly the same results as a pollution tax. Suppose the EPA decides it wants a 20 percent reduction in emissions of a certain pollutant. They can charge a pollution tax of $x per ton and see if overall pollution drops by more or less than 20 percent. If it drops by less, they can raise the tax until a 20 percent reduction is reached. If a tax of $x lowers pollution by more than

20 percent they can lower the tax until 20 percent is reached. By trial and error the authorities can achieve a 20-percent pollution reduction. Let us say the tax that yields a 20-percent reduction turns out to be y. Alternatively, the authorities can print up pollution permits for 80 percent of the number of tons of pollution that are currently being emitted, and sell these permits at a public auction. If there are no problems caused by market "thinness" or strategic behavior by those with greater market power, permits will end up selling for y at the auction; the public authorities will collect the same amount of revenues as they would from an equivalent pollution tax of y per ton; each polluter will pay as much for pollution permits as they would pay in pollution taxes; each polluter will reduce emissions by exactly the amount they would under a pollution tax of y per ton, low-cost pollution reducers reducing more than high-cost pollution reducers; and, of course, we have the same level of overall reduction, 20 percent, since we only sell permits to pollute 80 percent of previous levels. So why do polluting businesses invariably prefer pollution permits to pollution taxes? Why do most environmental activists hate pollution permits compared to pollution taxes? And why have a few environmentalists recently decided to endorse permit programs?

One reason most environmentalists oppose permit programs is that while marketable permits *could* be auctioned off, they won't be. Instead they will largely be given out free to those who have polluted in the past. As a matter of fact, the most common way to distribute pollution permits known as *grandfathering* is to award permits according to how much a business polluted in the past. For example, if regulatory authorities want a 20-percent reduction in emissions they issue every polluter enough permits to cover 80 percent of the pollution they emitted last year. Under grandfather formulas, not only do polluters as a whole pay nothing, the biggest offenders get the most permits and can resell any they don't use at a profit! In other words, the permit market is a resell market for permits that were handed out free to polluters by the government, and tradable permit programs run on the grandfather basis directly contravene the polluter pays principle.

Another reason environmentalists dislike permit programs is that while the number of permits issued *could* be sufficiently low to achieve significant pollution reduction—ideally reducing pollution up to the point where the marginal social cost of further reduction is equal to the marginal social benefit of further reduction—it won't be. Even if permits are issued free of charge, requiring polluters to own permits will raise production costs above prepermit levels. Therefore, the business community will lobby for free permits over pollution taxes, but they will also lobby for a large number of permits, which legalizes a large amount of pollution. So there is no reason to believe that socially efficient levels of reduction will be obtained through tradable pollution permit programs.

Finally, market thinness and market power are problems in real-world permit markets. It is easy enough for economic theorists to assume away these problems and deduce that if permit markets worked perfectly they could yield the same outcomes as pollution taxes. But if permit markets do not equilibrate instantaneously, or if large players buy and sell strategically—for example, buying up permits to limit entry of new firms into their industry—a permit program will be less efficient than an equivalent pollution tax. So compared to pollution taxes, tradable pollution permits have serious technical disadvantages whenever convenient assumptions about the permit market are unwarranted. With pollution taxes there *is* no permit market where things can go wrong.

I believe the EDF moved to support tradable pollution permit programs precisely because it was more favorable to business than pollution taxes or regulation. The EDF hoped this would reduce corporate opposition to pollution reduction. In effect the EDF decided, "if you can't beat 'em, join 'em." The EDF opted for a policy that shifts the burden of pollution reduction off of business and onto the taxpayer, hoping to thereby maximize the amount of pollution reduction the business community would go along with. No wonder this political strategy drew fire from many in the movement for progressive economic change, as well as from many other environmental organizations and activists. Some from more militant environmental groups have also voiced sympathy for tradable permit programs, but for a different reason. Any who wish to buy permits in the permit (resell) market are free to do so, including environmental organizations with deep pockets. You might ask why anyone who is not planning on polluting would buy a permit to pollute, but permits can be burned—like draft cards—thereby reducing the amount of pollution that can occur below what the program was designed to achieve. In a tax program, after environmentalists have used all their political clout to get the tax set as high as possible there is nothing further they can do. But in a permit program, after using their political clout to get the number of permits issued as low as possible, environmental organizations can use their financial resources to buy and destroy permits to further reduce emissions. While it is tempting to go for a program that gives you two shots at reducing pollution, I, along with most environmentalists, think this strategy is naïve. When the government realizes Green Peace or the

Nature Conservancy is buying and destroying z percent of the permits issued, it will simply issue z percent more permits, and environmental movement money goes into the pockets of polluting corporations who are issued the additional permits free of charge to no avail. Better to buy wetlands and rainforests to put off limits than to purchase pollution permits to destroy when the government can simply print more.

Political Strategy

To turn environmental destruction into environmental restoration two things are necessary: (1) existing incentives to abuse the environment must be replaced by effective incentives to protect and restore it; and (2) a political coalition determined enough and powerful enough to make these changes must be built. As explained in chapter 8, only something like a participatory economy can fully accomplish the first task. However, pollution taxes equal to marginal damages, regulations prohibiting particularly destructive products and technologies, and substituting public stewardship for free access to critical ecosystems can substantially change incentives and outcomes even while production for profit and the market system persist. In a word, beginning to change environmental destruction into restoration requires challenging freedoms corporations take for granted and implementing policies that curb the rule of market forces. Once this is recognized, it should be apparent that tackling the second task by trying to make the coalition attractive to corporations, and adopting a promarket ideology is ultimately self-defeating. While promarket rhetoric may open access to some ears, and concessions to corporations may reduce their opposition somewhat, this approach will never produce a coalition that will protect the environment. Instead, it further empowers the very forces driving environmental destruction in the first place.

The movement to protect the environment must seek to replace market forces with democratic planning for public stewardship. And the coalition to protect the environment must be built from those who are most harmed by environmental destruction, the vast majority of ordinary people, and particularly the poorest among them. Because they are less powerful, poor communities are generally less successful in the political game of not in my backyard (NIMBY). Therefore poor communities are usually the greatest victims of environmental destruction.[9] But poor people and ordinary people need jobs, housing, transportation, and an affordable source of energy—as well as environmental protection and restoration. If the environmental movement makes demands that threaten other vital interests of ordinary people it will never build a sufficiently powerful coalition to protect and restore the environment. And unless the environmental movement supports progressive movements fighting to meet people's other needs, it can hardly expect those movements to rally to its cause and contribute enough political muscle to move the environmental agenda.

The key is recognizing that significant costs as well as benefits are associated with moving from unsustainable to sustainable patterns of work and consumption, and making sure that programs protect ordinary people we need in the environmental coalition from being the ones who have to bear those costs. If coal miners and automobile workers are compensated while being retrained for new jobs that are not environmentally destructive, they will be less likely to oppose carbon taxes. If new affordable housing in old city neighborhoods is available because it is subsidized, young families who need decent housing will not oppose zoning measures preventing suburban sprawl from gobbling up farms and green space surrounding metropolitan areas. If farmers are given transfer development rights in exchange for development rights on their own land, they will be less likely to oppose the downzoning of farm land that smart growth requires because they will not be asked to take a financial loss. If public transportation is convenient and cheap people will be less likely to demand wider highways as the solution to gridlock. If FICA taxes are reduced people will be less likely to oppose raising taxes on automobiles and gasoline to internalize their negative effects on local air and water quality as well as climate change. Environmental protection is efficient not because there are no costs, but because the benefits outweigh the costs. But this means that all who *would* be made worse off by beneficial changes *can* be fully compensated and still leave some positive benefits for others. It is just as important for strategists in the environmental movement to come up with policies that *do* fully compensate different categories of ordinary people who might otherwise be harmed, as it is for them to come up with policies that stop environmental destruction. Otherwise there will never be a coalition strong enough to impose policies that actually stop environmental abuse.

The Consumer Movement

The first anticapitalist reform movement was the labor movement. Unions evolved to protect employees from exploitation at the hands of their employers. The anticorporate reform movement evolved to protect all citizens—irrespective of their work status—from being abused by unchecked corporate power. The environmental movement evolved when people finally realized that profit maximization and market forces were destroying the biosphere that sustains all life. The consumer movement evolved to protect buyers from being taken advantage of by corporate producers. A host of organizations in the United States advocate for consumer interests and try to force government agencies like the Food and Drug Administration to protect consumers from corporate abuses. Two of the most important are the Consumer Federation of America (CFA) and the network of Public Interest Research Groups (PIRGs.)

Organized in 1968, the CFA is composed of more than 285 consumer advocacy and education organizations, credit unions, rural electrical cooperatives, and housing co-ops, with a combined membership exceeding 50 million people. CFA is run by a board of directors elected by a vote of its dues-paying member organizations, who in turn employ a professional staff that collects research; organizes conferences; publishes reports and brochures; disseminates press releases; and lobbies Congress, the White House, and federal and state regulatory agencies on behalf of consumers. It is a cautious, educational and advocacy organization that works to protect the interests of consumers against corporations without being anti-corporate, much less anticapitalist. CFA runs advocacy campaigns seeking to protect consumers of financial services marketed by banks, insurance companies, and real estate brokers. CFA campaigns for greater competition in telephone, electric, and natural-gas markets. CFA lobbies the Consumer Product Safety Commission to improve the safety of household products. CFA advocates improved disclosures in new and used car sales and greater competition among air carriers. And CFA runs campaigns to "protect the integrity and effectiveness of the U.S. Food and Drug Administration," and to protect food products from bacterial contamination in particular.[10]

Beginning in 1971, consumer advocates associated with Ralph Nader and his campaign to force U.S. automobile companies to build safer cars founded Public Citizen and started to create PIRGs in different states. In 1983 the state PIRGs created US-PIRG "to act as watchdog for the public interest in our nation's capital, much as PIRGs have worked to safeguard the public interest in state capitals."[11] Public Citizen and the PIRGs saw themselves as opening a second front against corporate abuse, complimenting the older and more established labor movement. Over the years Public Citizen and PIRGs expanded their focus to include environmental, electoral reform, and healthcare issues as well. Nonetheless, Public Citizen and PIRGs define themselves as "non-profit, consumer advocacy organizations" and continue to work on consumer protection with campaigns to regulate credit card interest rates, ATM charges, and protect consumers from home equity scams, campaigns to require warnings and labels for genetically modified foods, campaigns to advise consumers about effective and ineffective medications and the danger of toxic shock syndrome induced by high-absorbency tampons, campaigns to restrict use of silicone gel breast implants, campaigns to protect airline passengers from overbooking, campaigns to require airbags and head-injury protections in cars and trucks and to make them safe for women and children, campaigns to improve toy safety and strengthen safety regulations for playground equipment, and campaigns to protect consumer privacy and combat identity theft. While CFA is a membership organization financed primarily by dues paid by its member organizations, PIRG chapters raise their funds and recruit individual members by canvassing and soliciting donations door to door. PIRG strategy and campaigns are planned by paid professional staffs, but carried out largely by recent college graduates working as PIRG organizers for a year or two for a "living wage" and health benefits of course.

While organizations like CFA, Public Citizen, and PIRGs for the most part do a competent, professional job of picking campaigns where they have a decent chance of helping consumers, they have much too little to say about the problem of consumerism in general. There is no reason even reformist consumer organizations cannot be a major voice criticizing not only the ways in which the advertising industry promotes consumerism, but underlying biases in the market system itself that channel people's efforts to satisfy themselves into individualistic consumption contrary to their true self-interests. Juliet Schor's books, *The Overspent American*, and *Do Americans Shop Too Much?* should form the centerpiece of a permanent campaign against all the forces that drive people to consumerist lifestyles contrary to their own best interests, and older consumer-advocacy organizations like CFA, Public Citizen, and PIRGs should coordinate their campaigns against consumerism with the Center for a New American Dream (CNAD), a relatively new nonprofit consumer-advocacy organization "dedicated to helping Americans change the way they consume to improve quality of life, protect the environment, and promote social justice."[12] There is no contradiction between protecting consumers from being charged too much, or sold defective products, and protecting them from a systematic consumerist bias in American capitalism that is just as contrary to their interests. When radicals work in the consumer movement this is an important theme we should always emphasize.

While generally more activist than CFA, PIRGs are certainly not anticapitalist organizations, and they can be every bit as hierarchical. While more intellectually ambitious and far-thinking, CNAD is a typical small, nonprofit, educational organization staffed by hardworking, do-good professionals and overseen by well-connected senior members of the do-good NGO community. In all three organizations directors and professional staffs dominate strategic decision making with little involvement of the consumers their organizations serve, while in PIRGs young organizers and fundraisers who go door to door are frequently little more than poorly paid foot soldiers. Why then should anticapitalist activists have anything to do with a reformist consumer movement, or with reformist organizations like CFA, Public Citizen, PIRGs and CNAD? The answer is, for the same reasons we must help build every progressive economic reform movement. Just like the labor movement, the movement for corporate responsibility, and the environmental movement, the consumer movement is a reform movement, dominated by reform organizations with reformist leadership. We must work in all these movements because that is where those who are victims of capitalism go for protection, and where they have every right to expect to see those who claim to oppose capitalist exploitation and oppression to be working effectively. We must work in these movements because the campaigns they wage are where ordinary people can learn how capitalism causes their problems. We must work in these movements because people who become active in them can discover why they must replace the system of competition and greed with a system of equitable cooperation if victories are to be consolidated and expanded. And finally, we must work to build organizations of consumers protecting their own interests at the local, state, and national levels because that is where the human and institutional experience necessary to create consumer councils and federations in a full-fledged system of equitable cooperation must come from. Just as there will never be worker councils who truly control their own work lives without a powerful labor movement, there will never be consumer councils and federations to participate actively in a system of equitable cooperation unless there is a successful consumer movement first.

Of course CFA, Public Citizen, PIRGs, and CNAD do not run their campaigns to highlight anticapitalist lessons. Nor do they tell consumers the only way they can really exert control over what they consume is to have consumer councils and federations who run their own research and development operations and play a powerful role in a participatory planning process. But when anticapitalist activists committed to a full system of equitable cooperation work in the consumer movement we can draw those lessons. The dilemmas anticapitalist activists face when working inside or outside reform organizations in the consumer movement are the same as those faced by activists working inside or outside reform organizations in the labor movement, the anticorporate movement, and the environmental movement. And the best ways to deal with those dilemmas are similar as well.

We must never self-censor our message. Whenever we believe it is important and effective to point out a connection between a consumer problem and capitalism, we must never hesitate to do so. Whenever we believe we can effectively explain why a fuller system of equitable cooperation is necessary to consolidate or extend consumer power, we must do so. Whenever we believe it is necessary to warn consumers of the limitations of what a particular reform campaign can accomplish, we must do so. If certain organizations in the consumer movement won't hire us when we speak our minds, so be it. Then we find or create consumer-advocacy organizations to work in where we can speak our minds. Even if we help create them and speak our minds freely within them, these organizations will still be reform, not anticapitalist organizations. And in many cases to be effective, even organizations we help found may seek to join the CFA as a member organization, or join a coalition organized by PIRG to wage a particular campaign, or participate jointly in an educational project with CNAD, in which case we will find ourselves working with reform organizations even if their leadership discriminates against our anticapitalist message.

Three principles should guide those working in the consumer movement, principles no different from those that should guide how we work in any reform movement: (1) Never allow others to decide when our anticapitalist message is, or is not effective. We must always be the judge of when we can effectively point out that capitalism itself is the root source of a problem, and when we can effectively explain how a system designed to encourage equitable cooperation solves a problem better. Of course others we work with in reformist consumer organizations will sometimes disagree with our analyses, just as we sometimes disagree with theirs. But we cannot allow them to censor our message, any more than they permit us to censor theirs. Since there will always be disagreements in reform movements over what messages are more or less important, we must always fight for democratic procedures to determine allocation of "message time" inside organizations, coalitions, campaigns, and events. This usually reduces to fighting for proportionate representation according to relative numbers of supporters for different messages, rather than representation determined by which groups control more financial resources. (2) Always seek working alliances that are the most effective way to win a reform. We, of course, have other goals and priorities as well, namely, replacing the entire system of competition and greed with a system of equitable cooperation. That is why we engage in activities other than reform campaigns. But we must not expect reform organizations and campaigns to abide by any criterion other than the efficacy of achieving the reform being fought for. To act on any other criterion would be dishonest. (3) Finally, we must take effective measures to counteract the corrupting influence of privileged employment status in reformist consumer organizations when some of us can achieve leadership positions in these organizations and serve the cause of equitable cooperation by doing so. Since some of us who are committed to the cause of replacing the economics of competition and greed with the economics of equitable cooperation will work for decades in the consumer movement, it is pointless to bar talented individuals from rising to more influential positions within this movement when they can be more effective by doing so. Instead, anticapitalists who rise to leadership positions in reformist organizations in the consumer movement must be pressured to personally commit to institutions of equitable cooperation like those discussed next chapter, just as labor activists who rise in the union movement must be pressured to do likewise to avoid sellout and burnout, and to remain above suspicion when they argue that caution is more wise than valor in particular situations.

The Poor People's Movement

Unfortunately, by the end of the twentieth century all of the progressive economic reform movements discussed above had become, to some degree, middle-class movements.[13] I say this not to condemn them, but because I believe this is an important fact activists need to recognize in order to deal with the problems it implies. The labor movement was initially strongest in the skilled crafts, who formed the backbone of the original AFL. When the CIO was formed to organize unskilled workers in mining and manufacturing it did organize poor people and their families. But the greatest achievement of the American labor movement to date was precisely that it lifted tens of millions of unskilled workers in the mining, steel, automobile, manufacturing, and transportation industries out of poverty and into the lower middle class in the decades following World War II. In the post-Vietnam period the greatest union-organizing successes were among government and white-collar employees, which is why SEIU, AFSCEME, and CWA grew relative to the older craft and industrial unions. I am not saying that any who these unions represent do not deserve what their unions have won for them. On the contrary, they deserve a great deal more. I am simply saying that largely to their credit, unions no longer represent the poorest sectors of American society. The middle-class proportion of the constituencies of the other progressive reform movements is even larger. The anticorporate movement has always attracted students and progressive intellectuals in far greater numbers than poor families, and the movement for corporate responsibility continues to do so today. The extent to which the environmental movement has remained a largely white, middle-class movement—despite important campaigns for environmental justice and against environmental racism—is so widely discussed it is commonplace. And no matter how much organizations like CFA, Public Citizen, PIRGs, and CNAD prioritize issues that affect poorer consumers, their main appeal continues to be to middle-class families. In sum, not only are the leaderships of the labor, anticorporate, environmental, and consumer movements largely middle class, so too are a great many who these movements represent.

Which is why a movement representing the interests of poor Americans is an absolute necessity, and should receive the highest priority from activists committed to economic justice. Moreover, it is critical to take whatever measures are necessary to guarantee that the leadership of this movement reflects its base.

In the late 1960s and early 1970s, the National Welfare Rights Organization (NWRO) was the prototype organization in a poor people's movement. In a retrospective Mark Tomey reminds us what an important organization NWRO was.[14]

From 1966 until 1975, the National Welfare Rights Organization made history by organizing tens of thousands of welfare recipients to demand income, clothing, food, and justice for their families. For the first time, U.S. welfare recipients rejected the welfare stigma and organized along class, race, and gender lines to challenge the system that kept them at the bottom of the economic ladder. At its peak in 1969, NWRO membership was estimated at 22,000 families nationwide, mostly black, with local chapters in nearly every state and major city. NWRO's impact extended far beyond money and legal rights. By asserting that the right to welfare is akin to a civil right, and that women and poor people deserve to be treated with dignity and respect, NWRO was the first movement to create a distinct political identity among poor black women, who comprised 90 percent of the organization's membership. It infused thousands with the sense that welfare was an entitlement, not a favor. Its leadership training programs taught women to claim their dignity and respect by insisting that society has a responsibility to care for children, and that women raising children on welfare had the right to determine how to spend their benefit checks on their children's behalf.

After decades of unrelenting right-wing attacks railing against black "welfare queens" driving Cadillacs, and hundreds of thousands of pages written by "progressive" social scientists telling us that *welfare* disempowers people and breeds dependency—instead of telling us that what truly disempowers people and breeds dependency is *poverty*—the Republican Congress, led by Newt Gingrich, and the Democratic White House, in the person of William Jefferson Clinton, combined in 1996 to terminate a sixty-year-old national welfare program. Aid to Families with Dependent Children (AFDC) was created in the 1930s as a program to prevent widows with children from having to go to work and leave their children uncared for. The program was initially sold on the basis of simple cost benefit analysis: the benefit of avoiding the damage children who were not properly reared would wreak on society over their lifetimes was deemed greater than the cost of a meager income support paid to the mother until her children came of age. Of course in the 1930s everyone assumed they were talking about payments to white mothers with white children, since nobody dreamed that blacks would apply. In 1996, the federal government abolished the federally funded and managed AFDC program—which contrary to popular impressions still served more poor white families than poor black and Hispanic families to its dying day— and replaced it with Temporary Assistance to Needy Families (TANF)— a program to be managed by states and local governments. TANF differed from AFDC in three important ways: (1) Assistance for single mothers without income was no longer a "right." To qualify a mother without income had to participate in a program to find herself work, at which time assistance ceased. In other words, whereas AFDC was a welfare program, TANF is a workfare program. TANF is a program to put poor, single mothers to work only providing temporary assistance until they do so. (2) There are strict time limits on how long assistance is provided, as well as strict rules for participation in the program to find work which, if violated, lead to immediate termination of assistance. (3) The responsibility for providing needy families temporary assistance now rests on states and local governments, the federal government having washed its hands of the problem after a short transition period when federal funding was phased out.

The results have been predictable and catastrophic. Gary Delgado first describes and then rebuts highly publicized claims that welfare reform has been overwhelmingly successful:

By all reports, welfare reform is a raging success. And look how quickly it succeeded! The rolls have already been cut in half, and by even more in some states. Everybody is happily and smoothly transitioning from welfare to work. Self-esteem is up and welfare payments are gloriously down. The story is so widely circulated that even some of our so-called "progressive" friends believe it.

The problem with this story is that it's not true. First, many of those being encouraged, pressured, and coerced to move from welfare to work end up with neither. Data from the Department of Health and Human Services suggests that only 21.7% of TANF participants leave the rolls because they got a job. Almost as many (15%) leave because of changes in state policy, while the reason for the greatest number of departures (56%) is "unknown." People disappear from the rolls because they are "sanctioned" for missing appointments or because they can't find childcare, or they are "diverted" from applying in the first place.

Then there are those who *do* find some sort of job and find their circumstances no better, or even worse, than on welfare. Even most of the white "welfare leavers" remain below the poverty line, despite attaining the nirvana of paid employment. And for people of color, of course, the labor market remains discriminatory, as it has always been.

Studies of what happens to women forced off welfare into the low-wage job market are just beginning to come out. Not surprisingly, they show that most of those leaving TANF have found their way into the gender ghettoes of service, sales, and clerical work where, even in northern industrial states, they are earning barely above minimum wage. In New Jersey the average hourly wage of former TANF recipients is $7.31, with more than one-third earning under $6.00. In Illinois the average is $7.17 per hour, with 37% earning below $6.50. Fewer than one-fourth were in jobs that provided health insurance.

A General Accounting Office report on former TANF recipients in seven states found that in five states, average earnings remained below the poverty level. Moreover, one-fourth of those leaving welfare for work soon lost their notoriously unstable low-wage jobs and returned to welfare. This has historically been the "safety net" function of welfare, but with time limits, these women will soon find the net gone and their families in free-fall.[15]

Less than a quarter of those leaving TANF get jobs, and only three quarters of them retain their jobs. Most of the "lucky" 20 percent who find and keep their jobs lost all health benefits and are paid so little they remain below the poverty line, which leaves over 80 percent of the mothers and children who used to be on AFDC either already in free-fall or soon to be so. Welfare reform has been a remarkably successful program to jettison the financial burden of preventing those most victimized by capitalism from falling into conditions reminiscent of Charles Dickens, while salving the public conscience with feel-good tales of triumphant empowerment. It has also put more poor American women and children "at risk" than any event since the Great Depression.

Because localities define the workfare system and distribute funds, local grassroots organizations like Community Voices Heard (New York City), the Contact Center (Cincinnati), Oregon Action, the Kensington Welfare Rights Union (KWRU, Philadelphia), and the Georgia Citizens Hunger Coalition have taken center stage in efforts to fight against cutbacks since 1996. The latter two groups are prime movers in a national Economic Human Rights Campaign asking the United Nations to find the United States in violation of articles 23, 25, and 26 of the United Nations Declaration on Human Rights. KWRU's Executive Director Cheri Honkala explains: "Although we have no great faith in the UN process, the Declaration has begun to shine a light on the fact that poverty really does exist in America. We can monitor human rights violations the same way people do in Latin America, Africa, or China."[16] Article 23 guarantees the right to free choice of employment at a livable wage; Article 25 protects the right to a standard of living that benefits a person's health and welfare; and Article 26 provides the right to a free education. Local organizations use the campaign to challenge public indifference to poverty by pointing out that replacement of AFDC by TANF has left the United States in clear violation of all three UN articles.

The congressional debate on reauthorization of TANF in 2001 provided the impetus for new grassroots welfare rights organizations to come together nationally to challenge misleading TANF success stories and lobby to "reform the reform." The National Campaign for Jobs and Income Support and Grass Roots Organizing for Welfare Leadership (GROWL) initially represented local groups with different approaches to consolidating a political voice for disenfranchised people in the welfare debate. Groups in the National Campaign emphasized work-based approaches to welfare reform, while organizations in GROWL insisted on an income-based strategy. In the end the National Campaign and GROWL agreed to be mutually supportive of each other's demands in order to be able to present a united front against Congress' rush to validate and reauthorize TANF.

The demise of NWRO and the fragmentation of the welfare-rights movement after 1996 when participants in TANF had to battle different state and local government programs, left the Association of Community Organizations for Reform Now, better known as ACORN, as the largest organization in what is a very beleaguered poor people's movement today.[17] ACORN is a direct action organization that chooses campaigns that directly benefit poor communities they work in, like campaigns against slumlords, campaigns for living wages, and campaigns for more investment in poor communities by banks and government. ACORN also acquires and rehabilitates abandoned buildings through a housing corporation it founded that credits buyers for "sweat equity." Founded in 1970, ACORN is now the nation's largest community organization of low- and moderate-income families, with over 160,000 member families organized into 750 neighborhood chapters in more than 68 cities across the country. As ACORN explains on its web site, "these are active members, not just contributors or newsletter readers. Each belongs to one of more than 750 neighborhood chapters working on local, citywide, and national campaigns." Recognizing that if poor people are to control their organization it must be self-funding, ACORN raises more than 80 percent of its budget from member dues, raffles, dinners, etc. ACORN goes on to explain how they see themselves on their Web site:

As we begin the new millenium, the concerns of low and moderate-income people are not on the nation's agenda. Under attack from the right, ignored by the center and many progressives, the poor grow in numbers every day. Yet ACORN stands virtually alone in its dedication to organizing the poor and powerless—a dedication as strong today as it was in 1970 when a group of Arkansas welfare mothers formed ACORN's first membership. ACORN's first priority is building organizations in low-income communities. Because ACORN believes that social change comes from the bottom up, organizers are on the streets every day, knocking on doors and recruiting new members. Major campaigns are designed to reach the unorganized majority of low and moderate-income people. ACORN employs the broadest possible range of tactics. It lobbies, petitions, and files lawsuits. But ACORN's long history proves that confronting decision-makers face-to-face brings the best results. When the situation demands it, ACORN members will march, picket, sit-in, squat, and sometimes go to jail.

Social justice activists need to prioritize work in organizations like ACORN, GROWL, and KWRU over the next decades to rebuild and expand the poor people's movement. We need to support their campaigns because presently they are the most effective ways to improve the situation for America's most desperate families. We need to support their claim that all who work should be paid not only a living wage with benefits, but a wage commensurate with the sacrifices they make, and that child-care is socially valuable work that deserves compensation like any other. We especially need to support efforts to develop and retain indigenous leadership in poor people's organizations and integrate activists into communities supporting equitable lifestyles. Instead of complaining that other progressive economic movements are "too middle class," we need to work to build the poor people's movement into the most dynamic progressive economic movement of all, and make sure that other progressive economic movements support the campaigns of the poor people's movement more fully and consistently than they do at present.

The Antiglobalization Movement

Those opposing corporate-sponsored, neoliberal globalization were labeled the "antiglobalization movement" by an unsympathetic mainstream media. Since our main point was all-out opposition to the kind of globalization that was going on, few of us objected to the name initially. However, the youngest progressive economic movement has never opposed globalization per se, and, contrary to accusations from our detractors, we have become increasingly clear about what we *do* favor, as well as what we oppose. In the words of Jeremy Brecher, we are for "globalization from below" that protects the environment and benefits the vast majority, rather than globalization from above that hastens environmental destruction and benefits those at the top at the expense of those at the bottom.[22] Most of us within the movement now prefer to call ourselves the global justice movement. If I continue to use the term "antiglobalization" it is only because that is the label most know us by.

In the 1980s, corporations were assisted in their efforts to rewrite the rules governing international trade and investment in ways more to their liking by conservative governments like those of Margaret Thatcher, Ronald Reagan, and Helmut Kohl. In the 1990s the "liberal" governments of Bill Clinton, Tony Blair, and Gerhard Schroeder helped corporations press the IMF, World Bank, and GATT/WTO to force capital and trade liberalization down the throats of what they euphemistically called "emerging market economies," no matter how unprepared these economies might be to compete in global goods markets or defend themselves in unregulated global capital markets. While opposition to the disastrous effects of neoliberal globalization has continued to grow in the new millennium, and even though managing directors at the IMF, secretaries at the Department of the Treasury, and occupants of the White House have all changed, the neoliberal global agenda pushed by multinational corporations continues full steam ahead. Like every corporate dominated expansion of the market system before it, this most recent process of corporate-sponsored globalization promises efficiency gains and trickle-down benefits for all, but actually misdirects productive potentials, benefits the few at the expense of the many, and accelerates environmental degradation.

Fortunately, like every previous expansion of capitalism, the neoliberal juggernaut has spawned critics and opponents as victims begin to recognize themselves as such. A full-fledged movement opposed to corporate sponsored globalization finally emerged in the United States with the demonstrations against the WTO in Seattle in November 1999, where U.S. activists joined an international movement that had raised its voice earlier in afflicted Third World countries and Europe. Given the fact that the coalition of victims of corporate sponsored globalization includes workers in different industries and occupations, farmers in very different kinds of economies, environmental organizations with different analyses and priorities, and citizens whose human and political rights have been undermined in different ways, it should come as no surprise that keeping the antiglobalization coalition from fracturing while seeking to deepen and expand it is no easy task. As a participant in this movement my suggestions about how best to proceed are based on the following convictions:

(1) The "real" global economy—production, consumption, and invest-
ment in new plant and equipment—is increasingly held hostage by a
system of global wealth management that is more and more unstable and
prone to crisis. In the early 1990s the IMF and World Bank, at the behest
of the U.S. Department of the Treasury, worked hard to create a disaster
waiting to happen. In country after country IMF delegations used carrots
and sticks to ply amenable governments and force reluctant governments
to eliminate restrictions not only on international business investment,
but on the inflow and outflow of speculative, short-run liquid capital as
well. A mushrooming pool of liquid global wealth, created by record
profits due to stagnant wages, downsizing and megamergers, as well as
rapid increases in technological innovation durring the 1980s and 1990s,
was suddenly free to move wherever and whenever it wished at the click
of a mouse on a computer screen. Moreover, financial liberalization and
deregulation in the advanced economies meant that much of this liquid
global wealth, managed by thirty-year-old recent MBAs knowing little
about the emerging market economies they invested in, was highly leveraged and therefore even more prone to panic and contagion.

There are two rules of behavior in any credit system: Rule #1 is the
rule all participants want all *other* participants to follow: DON'T PANIC!
Rule #2 is the rule each participant must be careful to follow herself:
PANIC FIRST! As the twentieth century came to a close the neoliberal
global managers literally created the financial equivalent of the proverbial nine-hundred-pound gorilla. Question: Where does the nine-hundred-
pound gorilla—global liquid wealth—sit? Answer: Wherever it wants!
And when a derivative tickles, and investors obey Panic Rule #2—Panic
first!—currencies, stock markets, banking systems, and, most importantly
for the rest of us, formerly productive economies all collapse in their
wake. In 1986, $0.2 trillion per day traded on foreign exchange markets.
In 1998, the figure was $1.5 trillion—only 2 percent of which was needed
to finance international trade and productive investment, meaning 98
percent of the $1.5 trillion traded per day in currency markets was for
purely speculative reasons!

Neoliberal capital liberalization over the past twenty years may well
be the most reckless, irresponsible extension of any credit system in
world financial history. Nineteenth-century financial crises that twentieth-century economic historians used to write about as relics of
dangerous bygone days don't hold a candle to the financial crises of the
past decade triggered by an unprecedented pool of liquid global wealth,
new financial products wielded by highly leveraged global hedge funds,

no regulations, no lender of last resort, no monitoring, removal of any and all manner of capital controls governments might use to slow bubbles and panics, and serious regional rivalries that prevent timely emergency interventions. In a word, the global economy is now haunted by the specter Keynes warned against at the Bretton Woods conference over sixty years ago: unregulated international finance.

(2) Liberalization of international trade and investment aggravates inequalties between countries. Whether there is reason to believe capital liberalization or trade liberalization have produced global efficiency gains is highly debatable. Contrary to the claims of proponents that went virtually unquestioned by the mainstream of the economics profession and the mainstream media, empirical evidence suggests that neoliberal policies may well have slowed rather than increased the rate of growth of world GDP per capita.[18] Moreover, contrary to the convictions of most mainstream economists that capital and trade liberalization must, necessarily increase global efficiency, there are many sound theoretical reasons for believing that these policies can do just the opposite.[19] But whether capital and trade liberalization have yielded efficiency gains, there is absolutely no doubt that they have aggravated inequality between more and less developed countries. The empirical evidence that global inequality is widening is so overwhelming that none dispute it. And as long as capital is scarce globally it is predictable that international lending based on free-market rates of interest will distribute more of any efficiency gains from capital liberalization to wealthy lenders than to poor borrowers, and it is also predictable that international trade based on free market prices will distribute more of the efficiency gains to wealthier countries than to poorer countries.[20]

(3) The "race to the bottom effect" is real. Liberalization of international investment does put strong downward pressure on first-world wages, labor standards, and environmental standards as it becomes more easy for companies to relocate or outsource to where wages, labor standards, and environmental standards are lower. Trade liberalization does put downward pressure on wages particularly of unskilled workers in First-World economies, just as mainstream Heckscher-Ohlin trade theory suggests it should. Moreover, as liberalization in agricultural trade destroys the livelihoods of billions of peasant farmers in Third World countries swelling the ranks of the urban unemployed, Third World workers do not enjoy the beneficial effect one might otherwise expect

from increased international investment and specialization in labor intensive manufacturing in their countries. Instead we have seen declining real wages in countries like Mexico as NAFTA displaced more peasants than it created labor-intensive manufacturing jobs. In sum, by strengthening the bargaining power of global capital versus any and all who it negotiates with, liberalization of investment and trade has led to downward pressure on wages, labor standards, and environmental standards in first world and Third World countries alike.

(4) IMF macroeconomic policies prioritize the interests of wealthy international creditors at the expense of citizens of troubled economies, and give rise to unconscionable global asset swindles as well. In exchange for a bail-out loan that allows a country to pay off international loans it would otherwise have defaulted on, IMF conditionality agreements typically demand that recipient governments reduce spending and increase taxes, central banks tighten the money supply, and legislatures remove restrictions on international trade and investment and foreign ownership.

When the IMF team arrives the economy is invariably already in recession. As standard macroeconomic theory predicts, fiscal and monetary austerity further aggravate the recession. Reducing government spending and increasing taxes both decrease aggregate demand, and therefore decrease employment and production. Tightening the money supply raises interest rates, which pushes more financially troubled domestic businesses into bankruptcy and reduces domestic investment demand, and thereby further decreases aggregate demand, employment, and production. This is why IMF structural adjustment programs (SAPs) and conditionality agreements invariably elicit strong opposition from citizens of countries whose economies are already producing far below their meager potentials. But it would be wrong to assume that IMF economists are ignorant of standard macroeconomic theory, or that the IMF is gratuitously sadistic. IMF policies are designed to increase the probability that the country will be better able to repay its international creditors, and makes perfect sense once one realizes this is their goal. If the government is in danger of defaulting on "sovereign" international debt, forcing it to turn budget deficits into surpluses provides funds for repaying its international creditors. If the private sector is in danger of default, anything that reduces imports and increases exports, or increases the inflow of new international investment will provide foreign exchange needed for international debt repayment. By reducing output and therefore income, deflationary fiscal and monetary policies reduce the demand for imports. By raising domestic interest rates tight monetary policy reduces the outflow of domestic financial investment and increases the inflow of new foreign financial investment, providing more foreign exchange to payoff international loans coming due. Finally, since all who owe foreign creditors receive their income in local currency, anything that keeps the local currency from depreciating will allow debtors to buy more dollars with their local currency, which is what they need to pay their international creditors. Reducing imports and raising domestic interest rates both prop up the value of the local currency.

IMF austerity programs are well designed to turn stricken economies into more effective debt-repayment machines as quickly as possible. There is little disagreement among economists about what the short-run effects of fiscal and monetary austerity policies will be. Instead, we have a simple conflict of priorities: if the interests of international creditors are given priority, the IMF programs make perfectly good sense. They are only counterproductive if one cares about employment, output, capital accumulation, and prospects for economic development in economies where the poorest four billion people in the world live and suffer.

Beside causing massive global efficiency losses and unforgivable human suffering for hundreds of millions of Third World residents, IMF programs also create the conditions for what I called the "Great Global Asset Swindle" when writing about it in Z *Magazine* in the aftermath of the Asian financial crisis. It works like this: International investors lose confidence in a Third World economy, and thanks to capital liberalization are free to dump as much of its currency, bonds and stocks as they wish. At the insistence of the IMF, the central bank in the Third World country tightens the money supply to boost domestic interest rates to prevent further capital outflows in an unsuccessful attempt to protect the currency. Even healthy domestic companies can no longer afford loans, so they join the ranks of bankrupted domestic businesses available for purchase. As a precondition for receiving the IMF bailout the government abolishes remaining restrictions on foreign ownership of corporations, banks, and land. With a depreciated local currency, and a long list of bankrupt local businesses, the economy is ready for the acquisition experts from Western multinational corporations and banks who come to the fire sale with a thick wad of almighty dollars in their pockets.

But readers do not have to take my word for it. All one has to do is go back and read the reports filed by Nicholas Kristof who covered Asian economic affairs for the *New York Times* in 1998 and 1999 in which he chronicled foreign asset acquisitions in the Pacific Rim in all its gory details. Or better still, one needs only to listen to Paul Volcker, ex-chairman of the Federal Reserve Bank and honored member of the conservative establishment:

> What is happening in the banking sector is striking. In Argentina today there is only one privately owned bank of any size left that is not owned or substantially controlled by a large foreign bank. We see the same phenomenon at work in Mexico: four out of the five largest Mexican banks are owned by, or have substantial ownership interests, by foreign banks. Mexico is a country that only a few years ago, you will recall, took the position in the NAFTA negotiations that the one thing we want to preserve is Mexican ownership of Mexican banks. That is an essential element of our sovereignty, we must not give it up. Two of the largest banks in Korea, which has had a nationally insulated banking system heretofore, are now in the process of being bought by foreigners. Thailand's financial system is being penetrated by foreign ownership. Surprisingly enough even Japan, not exactly a small emerging economy, in the midst of all this distress is apparently willing to accept some foreign ownership of banks and certainly of other financial institutions.[21]

While U.S. financial corporations have led the charge to buy up attractive assets in lesser-developed economies at bargain-basement prices in the aftermath of financial crises, multinationals in other sectors and from other countries have also participated in bankruptcy auctions and privatization sales, the newest rage in imperial feasting. Based on these four convictions, I offer the advice that follows to my fellow activists in the antiglobalization movement.

The Movement Is Everything

It is more important to build the antiglobalization movement correctly than to have the "correct" analysis or the "correct" set of demands. Organizing opposition to corporate-sponsored globalization from the bottom up is the right approach. Organizing all constituencies negatively affected to fight for their own interests while they learn why their own success necessarily hinges on the successes of other constituencies against whom global corporations will constantly pit them is the right approach. Working closely with Third World organizations in the campaign against the global race to the bottom is the right approach. Basing the movement on grassroots organizations, unions, and independent institutes and coalitions rather than principally on politicians and governments is the right approach. Adopting the Lilliput strategy, where each constituency struggles to tie its own string to contain the Gulliver of global capital knowing (correctly) how weak and vulnerable its own string is without the added strength of tens of thousands of other strings, is the right approach. Our biggest advantage is that the international movement against corporate-sponsored globalization at the turn of the millennium has largely already taken this form. It is noticeably different from the campaign for a New International Economic Order in the 1970s where heads of states from the Global South made grand speeches at conferences only to be ignored by first world powers. It is important to appreciate and nurture our greatest advantage for the moment.[23]

Beware the Trap of Labor and Environmental Standards

No issue is a greater threat to divide the antiglobalization movement along north-south lines than labor and environmental standards. First world workers and environmentalists understandably want to establish meaningful and enforceable universal labor and environmental standards as part of the global economy to avoid the race-to-the-bottom effect unleashed by capital and trade liberalization. On the other hand, many Third World constituencies who desperately want higher Third World labor and environmental standards themselves, resent being dictated to by the governments of wealthier countries regarding how they must achieve higher standards. Moreover, Third World constituencies have good reason to fear that in a global economy where all reasons other than violations of international labor or environmental standards for raising tariffs will have been outlawed by treaty agreement, only the lesser developed countries will be unarmed in the event of possible future trade wars. They have learned from long experience that first world industries all too often manage to convince their governments to resort to protectionist measures when pressured by competition from Third World imports. They fear charging violations of labor or environmental standards could become the new pretext for protectionism in the first world, and they would be left without any means of retaliating since the universal labor and environmental standards would be those already in effect in the first world, and all other reasons for raising tariffs in retaliation would have been outlawed by international treaties. Knowing the international economic playing field is already tilted against them, our southern brothers and sisters in the antiglobalization movement are understandably nervous about any changes that further disadvantage them relative to northerners.

Before Seattle the AFL-CIO was insensitive to this legitimate concern on the part of southern opponents of corporate sponsored globalization. But after Seattle, U.S. labor launched a Campaign for Global Justice and increased ties with southern groups opposing corporate sponsored globalization. Now the AFL-CIO is investigating a number of ways to achieve the goal of raising standards in the Third World to prevent the race-to-the-bottom effect while protecting Third World workers from unfair protectionism in the future. In these negotiations, antiglobalization activists in the United States should never tire of reminding the AFL-CIO that only two things can reduce the race-to-the-bottom effect on first world workers: (1) stop trade and capital liberalization; and (2) increase the bargaining power of Third World workers with their employers. If the U.S. government and the WTO are only willing to accede to some form of labor standards in exchange for further trade and capital liberalization, this is likely to accelerate rather than arrest the race-to-the-bottom effect. On the other hand, if the AFL-CIO focuses on ways to help Third World workers increase their bargaining power with their employers, there are many policies that may do this more effectively than imposing labor standards through an international treaty.

Suppose the WTO gave the United States the right to ban imports from any country where labor standards were lower than those in the United States, and the statute was easy to enforce. That is far beyond the wildest dreams of the AFL-CIO leadership, but how much would it diminish the race to the bottom they fear? If the bargaining power of employees outside the United States remained the same as before, the race-to-the-bottom effect on U.S. wages would be just as great as before. Granted, the internationalization of U.S. labor standards would protect U.S. labor standards (for the time being), and would give workers everywhere else the same labor standards as those workers enjoy here (assuming the standards were actually enforced). But if the new statute did not change the bargaining strength of employees elsewhere, their employers would pass on whatever the higher standards cost them to their employees in the form of lower wages. Presumably if bargaining strength were not changed, the pass through would be 100 percent since what employers and employees bargain over is the wage/standards package. Employees want higher wages and higher standards. Employers want lower wages and lower standards since both are costs to them. So while lower labor standards elsewhere would no longer contribute to the race-to-the-bottom effect in the United States, the *greater* wage gap would produce the same downward pressure as before imposition of the international labor standards!

Only to the extent that universalization of U.S. labor standards increases the bargaining strength of workers elsewhere will it diminish the race-to-the-bottom effect for U.S. workers. But anything that increases the bargaining strength of foreign workers more than a trade treaty with universal labor standards will arrest the race-to-the-bottom effect for first world workers more effectively. What if land reform in the Third World increases the bargaining strength of Third World workers in manufacturing industries by raising the reservation wage and decreasing urban migration more than universal labor standards would? Then land reform in the Third World would be more beneficial to first world workers than universal labor standards. What if stopping U.S. military aid to totalitarian regimes in the Third World improved the bargaining strength of Third World workers more than universal labor standards? Then stopping U.S. military aid would go further to arrest the race-to-the-bottom effect for U.S. workers than universal labor standards. Obviously how much any particular labor standard, land reform, or reduction in military aid affects the bargaining strength of Third World workers depends on the actual reform. But the important point is that the race-to-the-bottom effect depends *only* on how weak labor is elsewhere, and on how free corporations are to move their operations.

I strongly suspect there are other reforms that would better preserve the living standards of first world workers than fighting to achieve some level of universal labor standards, especially if labor standards are achieved only in exchange for further trade and capital liberalization. And if pressing for labor standards in trade treaties threatens to drive a wedge between organizations representing first and Third World workers in the antiglobalization movement while other reforms do not, it is almost surely a counterproductive strategy for slowing the race-to-the-bottom effect. In sum, the AFL-CIO would do well to take their cue from organizations representing Third World workers regarding how the AFL-CIO can best help them improve their bargaining power, because the members of the AFL-CIO will be best served by whatever helps Third World workers most. The AFL-CIO has no reason to insist on labor standards if Third World workers ask for support on some other campaign instead, and no reason to acquiesce to further trade and capital liberalization in exchange for concessions on labor standards that will go largely unenforced in any case.

Do Not Become Isolated

It is critical for the radical wing of the antiglobalization movement not to become isolated from the reform wing. What frightened corporate globalizers most about the demonstration in Seattle in 1999 was not its size but its composition. There were fewer than fifty thousand participants in the permitted rallies, and no more than ten thousand activists who engaged in civil disobedience. I have been to dozens of larger demonstrations over the past thirty years that had far less impact. But the specter of people from mainstream environmental organizations dressed as sea turtles marching together with middle-aged white men from the United Steelworkers, Teamsters, and Longshoremen's unions, as well as with elected officials from small cities and towns—all joining in the chants and songs led by amazing groups of lesbian and anarchist cheerleaders—was a scary sight to the proglobalization establishment, while it was a sight that brought tears to the eyes of activists from my generation who had begun to wonder if we would ever see a vibrant, radical movement in our country again.

But only if the constituencies of mainstream labor, environmental, and civic organizations remain active in the movement, and only if the radical message that a better world is possible continues to infect them can the antiglobalization movement grow enough in size and depth to finally force policy change as well as influence the tenor of public debate. This requires tolerance and patience. This requires respecting others who do not agree with everything we stand for. This requires remembering that we all need each other. Without the organizational skills, dedication, creativity, and courage of radical antiglobalization activists, reformist organizations would not have been nearly as successful as they have been in slowing the globalization juggernaut. Without large numbers of participants at demonstrations, and support from reformist organizations the radical wing of the antiglobalization movement will become isolated and vulnerable to ever more violent repression. Before the anti-WTO demonstrations in Seattle the radical and reformist wings of the movement mistrusted each other, and both were pleasantly surprised, not only by the results, but for the most part by each other's behavior.

Organizing for the anti-IMF/WB demonstrations in April 2000 that began immediately after Seattle built upon the new-found trust and started the process of negotiating working agreements between radical and reformist organizations. In the aftermath of antiglobalization demonstrations in Quebec, Cancun, Winsor, Miami, and Savannah, the danger is that the reform and radical wings of the movement are drifting toward a counterproductive division of labor, where the radical wing only demonstrates and the reformist wing only lobbies. We need to remember that is just how the neoliberal globalizers like to see us, not the specter that frightened them so much in Seattle five years ago.

Conclusion

Until all the economic reform movements discussed in this chapter have attracted more supporters, until all these reform movements have become more politically powerful, until all these reform movements are more clear about what they are fighting for and how to go about it, the goal of replacing capitalism with a system of equitable cooperation will remain beyond our reach. But while nothing can be accomplished until these reform movemens have been greatly stengthened, and activists must therefore prioritize this task, it is not the only work that needs to be tackled. Strong economic reform movements are necessary and in the United States not one of the above movements is nearly strong enough at present. But strong economic reform movemens are not enough. Twenty-first-century activists must also nurture, build, and begin to connect a variety of creative living experiments in equitable cooperation within capitalism if we want to avoid the fate of our twentieth-century social democratic predecessors.

13

Experiments in Equitable Cooperation

The culture of capitalism is firmly rooted among citizens of the advanced economies. Most employees—not just employers—believe that hierarchy and competition are necessary for the economy to run effectively, and that those who contribute more should receive more irrespective of sacrifice. And why should people not believe this? Even if you feel you haven't gotten a fair shake, or that people born with a silver spoon in their mouth don't deserve what they get, few are likely to reject a major linchpin of capitalist culture all on their own. We should not fool ourselves that capitalism teaches people about its failings, or shows them how to live noncapitalistically. Quite the opposite. The only sense in which capitalism serves as midwife for its heir is by forcing people to learn to think and live noncapitalistically in order to meet needs it leaves unfulfilled. It falls to progressives to learn and teach others how to do this. And there can be no mistake about it, this is a monumental task. We can ill afford to repeat the error of our twentieth-century predecessors who failed to face up to the magnitude of this task, looking instead for short cuts and excuses for why it would not be necessary. But where can the culture of equitable cooperation grow in modern capitalism? That is the question this chapter addresses by evaluating various experiments in equitable cooperation that already exist, and by considering ways to create new experiments and link them together to offer an increasingly attractive alterative to capitalism.

The Importance of Prefigurative Experiments

During the twentieth century, one of the most successful strategies of national liberation movements in Asia, Latin America, and Africa was to create "liberated territories" where they began to build the new society while simultaneously fighting guerrilla wars to overthrow procapitalist governments subservient to imperial interests. In Asia, the Chinese Communist Party used this strategy with great success between 1927 and 1949, the Vietminh used it successfully against the French from 1945 to 1954, and the Vietcong used it successfully against the United States from 1960 to 1975. In Latin America, Fidel Castro's 26 of July Movement used it briefly in Cuba from 1956 to 1959, and the Sandinistas used it successfully in Nicaragua during the 1970s. In Africa national liberation movements in Mozambique, Angola, and Zimbabwe all used it successfully during the 1970s. Liberated territories played an important role in the military strategies of national liberation movements as a rear area and staging ground, but they also served an important political function. At the risk of overgeneralizing, the more people who lived in liberated territories, and the longer national liberation movements experimented with new social institutions and campaigns in zones under their control, the more successful these movements proved to be, at least initially, in advancing the cause of equitable cooperation after taking power nationally.

Of course liberated territories could not always be defended, and not all national liberation movements who used the strategy were successful. In Asia, attempts by communist parties to establish and defend liberated territories in Indonesia and India in the 1960s were unsuccessful. In Latin America, Marxist guerilla movements seeking to establish liberated territories in Peru and Bolivia were wiped out in the 1960s, and even larger revolutionary forces lost their liberated zones and the guerrilla war in El Salvador and Guatemala in the 1980s. In South Africa the ANC only succeeded in overthrowing apartheid through urban agitation, strikes, boycotts, mass mobilizations, and civil disobedience after guerrilla struggles in rural areas to establish and defend liberated zones proved largely unsuccessful.

Whether establishing liberated territories will prove as successful a strategy for Third World anticapitalist movements in the century ahead is an important issue for movements in those countries to consider carefully. Even if military circumstances have changed, it is not clear that liberated territories are no longer strategically important for political reasons. Building "base communities" continues to be the centerpiece of the

Zapatistas' political strategy despite unfavorable military circumstances, indicating the importance the EZLN attaches to prefigurative experiments. They provide an important training ground for constructive social activism in a context where most activism is critical and oppositional. Guerrilla warfare teaches its students discipline and bravery, while governing liberated territories teaches its graduates how to be effective midwives of social change. As many revolutionaries have discovered, being willing to die to overthrow a hated tyrant does not necessarily translate into being able to live in ways that advance the cause of equitable cooperation after tyranny is defeated. But my purpose is not to offer unneeded advice to Third World movements, but to point out what anticapitalists in advanced economies should learn from the history of liberated territories in Third World struggles. The lesson for those of us living in "the center" is that living experiments in equitable cooperation are of critical importance. They provide palpable evidence than a better world is possible. They are an invaluable testing ground for ideas about how to achieve equitable cooperation. Living experiments in equitable cooperation begin the process of establishing new norms and expectations among broad segments of the population beyond the core of anticapitalist activists. And experiments in equitable cooperation provide opportunities for activists in anticapitalist reform campaigns suffering from burn out to rejuvenate themselves instead of drifting back into personal lives in the capitalist mainstream. The existence of available opportunities to live—at least to some extent—according to the norms of equitable cooperation also makes it more obvious to all when leaders of reform movements are selling out for personal gain.

Twenty-first-century activists in advanced economies will have to seek different ways to achieve what twentieth-century Third World national liberation movements sometimes accomplished in their liberated territories. However, failure to find ways within advanced capitalist economies to build and sustain noncapitalist networks capable of accommodating the growing numbers who will be drawn to the economics of equitable cooperation can prove just as damaging to our cause as failure to wage successful economic reform campaigns and build mass economic reform movements.

Local Currency Systems

LETS: Local Exchange and Trading Systems

A variety of local currency systems exist in the United States, Canada, the United Kingdom, New Zealand, and Australia. Ithaca Hours and Time

Dollars are two systems in the United States about which much has been written. Most of the local currency systems outside the United States go under the generic label Local Exchange and Trading Systems (LETS).[1] In all local currency systems a person can hire another person from the community to perform a service and pay them in units of a local currency. In some systems there is no money, per se, but simply an account, or ledger, where every "exchange" is recorded as a credit for the person performing the service and a debit for the person receiving it.[2] Other systems use a currency that changes hands when people work for others. Sometimes the alternative currency is pegged to the national currency. For example, one Ithaca Hour can be purchased from the system mangers for ten dollars, or can be sold to the system mangers for ten dollars. Most local currencies, however, are not convertible. Often new members are given some amount of the local currency (or a start up "credit" if there is no physical currency) so they can hire someone to work for them immediately without having to wait until they have been hired to work for someone else. While most exchanges are of labor services among community members, in some systems local merchants participate by agreeing to accept local currency as partial payment for goods they sell.

In the Time Dollar system, labor exchanges on a one-hour-for-one-hour basis. Most Time Dollar systems have facilitated exchanges of services among the elderly. For example, a sixty-five year old may read to an eighty-five year old for x hours. Or an elderly person who can still drive may take one who cannot to the store where the round trip takes x hours. In both cases the person performing the service is credited with x Time Dollars, which they can then use to purchase x hours of whatever services they want from someone else, usually when they are older themselves. So Time Dollars is often a system for the less elderly to bank service hours performed for the more elderly for use when they become older themselves. In all other local currency systems an hour of one kind of labor may be paid more or less local currency than an hour of another kind of labor. In all other systems, how much of the local currency will be paid for an hour of someone's work is negotiated between individual buyers and sellers. In some systems there is a great deal of variation between how much a particular kind of labor is paid in different exchanges, while in other systems a uniform pay rate for each category of labor exchanged evolves depending on supply and demand.

NEITHER MAGIC NOR USELESS

Local currency activists make valid criticisms of the capitalist monetary system and financial markets. They are correct to point out that local regions often remain in recession even when the national economy picks up, and that national and global financial markets often siphon savings out of poor communities to invest it elsewhere. Advocates for local currencies are also right when they sense that we can arrange a division of labor among ourselves that is more fair than the one capitalism arranges for us. On the other hand, local currency activists sometimes espouse misguided theories about money, and become overly enthusiastic about what their local currency systems can and cannot accomplish. While local currencies can bring modest improvements, other reforms are frequently more effective. And while the spirit of anticapitalist independence generated by local currency activists can be empowering, the focus on a new kind of money and market exchange as the antidote to capitalism is unfortunate.

Whenever a capitalist economy fails in any respect, one can respond either by trying to reform the capitalist economy or by creating some new system outside the capitalist economy. A central tenet of this book is that in the long run capitalism must be replaced with a different economic system in order to secure the victory of the economics of equitable cooperation over the economics of competition and greed. A central tenet of this chapter is that creating minialternatives to capitalism before capitalism can be replaced entirely is an important part of a successful strategy to eventually replace capitalism altogether. However, this does not mean it is always better to seek a solution to a problem outside the capitalist economy than it is to address the problem through a reform campaign. Nor does it mean that all minialternatives promote the economics of equitable cooperation effectively. Local currency systems are all attempts to respond to particular failures of capitalist economies by appending a supplementary currency system. What failures do local currency systems respond to, and how effectively do alternative currency systems address these problems?

(1) When local economies are in recession some productive people in the community cannot find gainful employment, and some local businesses suffer for lack of customers. In this situation an obvious deal is begging to be made: hire me, so I can afford to buy from you. Buy from me, so I can afford to hire you. The problem is the capitalist economy is not facilitating these deals. Lacking buyers, local businesses are in no position to hire, and lacking jobs, unemployed locals are in no position to buy from local merchants. Alternative currency systems attempt to redress this failure by creating an alternative system of exchange to jump start mutually beneficial deals that are going unmade in the capitalist economy. Unfortunately, local currencies are unlikely to have more than a marginal impact on local employment, and reform policies can be more effective.

As Keynes pointed out long ago, the government can be a useful catalyst in this situation: government can hire the unemployed, who then will buy from businesses. Government can buy goods from businesses, who then will employ the unemployed. Or government can provide more credit or reduce taxes so somebody will begin to buy more, and thereby break the logjam. Moreover, all these policies can be applied locally in regions where unemployment persists even when it subsides nationally. Social democratic governments in Sweden were particularly adept at devising reforms to combat local unemployment. After approval, local public investment projects in Sweden were put on an *investment shelf* until the local economy was experiencing high unemployment when the projects were taken off the shelf and implemented. Private companies in Sweden were offered incentives to put their profits into an *investment reserve fund* where they were subjected to a lower rate of taxation if they were used when the local *labor market board* indicated that private investment was needed to combat local unemployment. Local labor market boards in Sweden also operated extensive retraining programs for workers in high unemployment areas who received unemployment insurance until they found new jobs. Pressing for reforms such as these may prove more effective at combating regional unemployment than creating a local currency.

(2) The capitalist financial system routinely siphons savings out of poor regions. A bank opens branches in a poor community, accepts deposits from local residents, and then makes loans to businesses outside the community, state, or country, leaving the poor community bereft of the financial capital it needs to facilitate its own economic development. While it is true that local currency systems cannot serve as a mechanism for capital flight, unfortunately local currencies are powerless to prevent capital flight as long as a capitalist financial system continues to operate in the community. Until capitalist banks and financial markets cease to operate inside a community the only effective way to fight against capital flight is through campaigns against red lining, pressing for community reinvestment requirements on banks, and organizing community development initiatives to bring capital into poor areas. Unfortunately, local currencies can do little to affect the outflow or inflow of financial capital as long as capitalist banks and financial institutions function in their communities.

(3) When people exchange labor services with one another, the terms of the trades can be fair or unfair. According to the theory of economic justice espoused in this book, exchanges of labor will be fair when they represent exchanges of equal sacrifices on people's part. If all work were equally undesirable, then trading an hour of one kind of labor for an hour of

another kind of labor would be fair. But if the labor I perform is more dangerous or unpleasant than the labor you perform, then I should only give you what I produce in less than an hour for what you produce in an hour. Of course, this is generally *not* how things work out in exchanges in capitalist economies. In capitalism, goods are generally exchanged in ratios that represent unfair exchanges of labors. The extent to which alternative currency systems rectify this failure of capitalism varies from system to system. To the extent that different kinds of labor are equally unpleasant, Time Dollar exchanges are equitable. And even when different kinds of labor are not equally unpleasant, Time Dollar exchanges are likely to be more fair than exchanges in the capitalist economy. To the extent that individuals from the same community treat each other fairly when agreeing on the terms of payment face-to-face, other local currency systems can also improve on capitalist exchanges. But to the extent that the laws of supply and demand determine the rates of pay for different kinds of labor services in local currency systems, these alternative systems of labor exchange simply mirror the terms of exchange in the capitalist economy at large. Many alternative currency activists are naïve on this point, and fail to see anything wrong with allowing the laws of supply and demand to determine how many hours of lawn mowing labor, for example, exchange for an hour of dentistry labor. Unfortunately, to the extent that the terms of labor exchanges in alternative currency systems are determined by the laws of supply and demand they will not be any more fair than the relative wages and salaries in capitalist labor markets. In this regard, collective bargaining and solidarity wage campaigns carried out by the labor movement will probably do more to promote economic justice than establishing alternative currency systems where the laws of supply and demand are permitted to hold sway.

In conclusion, local currency systems are useful to the extent that they reduce local unemployment, reward people for their labor more fairly than capitalist labor markets, and help people understand that they can—and should—manage their own division of labor equitably. Local currency systems are counterproductive when participants deceive themselves about how much can be accomplished and see nothing wrong with allowing the laws of supply and demand to determine the terms of their labor exchanges.

Worker Participation and Partial Ownership in Capitalist Firms

The essence of capitalism, of course, is that those who own the means of production decide what their employees will produce and how they will go about their work. Capitalism denies workers and consumers *direct* decision making power over how they work and what they consume, and gives them in exchange something mainstream economists call "producer and consumer sovereignty." As explained in chapter 2, producer sovereignty supposedly operates through labor markets where the ability of employees to vote with their feet provides incentives for their employers to take their wishes into account when deciding what they order them to do. Consumer sovereignty supposedly operates through goods markets where the ability of consumers to vote with their pocket books provides incentives for capitalists to take consumer preferences into account when deciding what they order their employees to produce. According to mainstream economists, if labor and goods markets are competitive workers and consumers will exert appropriate influence over issues that concern them *indirectly*. As explained in chapter 4, this indirect influence operates far from perfectly even when markets are more competitive, and less well when markets are not competitive. Contrary to the teachings of mainstream economics, markets do *not* allow workers and consumers to express their preferences in unbiased settings, or to control their economic lives in meaningful ways. The reason it is called "capitalism" is that economic power is concentrated in the hands of *capitalists*. In modern, or monopoly capitalism, power is concentrated in the hands of giant corporations, some of which are larger than entire lesser developed national economies. Modern capitalism *means* corporate power at the expense of worker and consumer power.

But since we humans want control over our lives, and since we work better when we have more control over the economic decisions that affect us, the essence of capitalism—capitalist or corporate power—is problematic, and gives rise to the following dynamic: Employees sometimes try to win some of the direct decision making power capitalism denies them. Employers sometimes pretend to give their employees some direct power because employees work better when they think they have some power. Employee stock ownership plans (ESOPS), total quality programs, joint worker-management committees, and a host of programs that go under the all-embracing label of "autogestion" in Europe, are the outgrowth of this dynamic.[3]

The secret to evaluating different campaigns for worker participation in capitalist firms is to try to distinguish between appearance and reality. Anything that *really* enhances employee power moves us toward the economics of equitable cooperation. Whereas reforms that increase the ability of employers to get more of what they want out of their employees by deceiving them into thinking they have some power when, in fact, they do not, promotes the economics of competition and greed, not the economics of equitable cooperation. Unfortunately it is not always easy to know which is which, or when a concession has been won by employees, rather than bestowed like the Trojan horse by employers. The other problem with ESOP programs is that even when they increase employee power they are invariably ideologically procapitalist. Promoters of ESOPs advertise the promise of a "people's capitalism" which is not only highly unlikely, but if it ever materialized would be just that— people's capitalism—not a system of equitable cooperation.[4]

Worker Ownership

Whereas many programs claiming to offer employees opportunities to participate in decision making in firms they do not own are clever tools of capitalist exploitation, when employees do become their own bosses in worker-owned firms this usually advances the cause of equitable cooperation. Most Americans have no ownership in firms where they work. A small percentage own some shares of stock in the company that employs them, frequently through ESOPs. But in most of these cases the percentage of shares owned by employees is quite small compared to the percentage of shares owned by absentee owners, giving employees little say. However, roughly 10 million Americans are worker-owners in more than ten thousand employee-owned companies with assets of over $400 billion. The National Cooperative Business Association (www.ncba.coop) has served as a trade association for producer cooperatives in all sectors of the American economy since 1916. However, NCBA does not promote worker-ownership as an alternative to capitalism. Grassroots Economic Organizing (GEO), founded in 1988, actively promotes worker-ownership as an alternative to capitalism and has a radical perspective as its mission statement makes clear: "GEOs mission is to build a nation and worldwide movement for a cooperative, social economy based on democratic and responsible production, conscientious consumption, and use of capital to further social and economic justice."[5]

Some employee-owned firms were organized by employees who didn't want to lose their jobs when their capitalist employer no longer found them profitable. In the 1980s, the United Steelworkers of America began helping its members take over troubled companies in Pennsylvania and Ohio, saving thousands of union jobs. The machinists and pilots unions became the majority shareholders of United Airlines when that company faced bankruptcy in the 1990s. Some employee-owned firms were created when idealistic owners relinquished ownership to their employees. Employees, who were just tired of being taken advantage of, initiated others. A temporary employment agency in Baltimore called Solidarity belongs to the same temp workers it sends out every day, the majority of whom are recovering addicts and/or have prison records. In any case, there are now over ten thousand employee-owned enterprises in the United States sprinkled through almost every industry and region of the country, and efforts to increase communication and ties between them have recently accelerated. Several regional conferences were held in preparation for the First National Worker Ownership Conference in Minneapolis on May 24–26, 2004 where the United States Federation of Democratic Workplaces was founded.

While some employee-owned firms are successful, many are not. So far the worker-owners of Solidarity have been able to pay themselves higher wages than other temp agencies in Baltimore, provide themselves with health insurance coverage, and pay themselves a hefty annual bonus check out of profits. United Airlines, however, filed for bankruptcy in 2002, and many of the steel firms saved with help from the steel workers' union in the 1980s survived only a few years. It is important for those working to promote pockets of worker ownership in capitalism to understand the obstacles they face, and be realistic about what they can, and cannot hope to accomplish. Since worker ownership greatly enhances worker participation, it does increase worker productivity. On the other hand, the deck is stacked against labor when it tries to hire capital in capitalist economies in a number of ways. The legal system discriminates against worker-owned companies. Capitalist financial markets discriminate against worker-owned companies. And when worker-owners hesitate to exploit themselves, and refuse to hire workers who are not owners to exploit, they operate at a competitive disadvantage compared to capitalist companies with no such scruples.[6] Moreover, as long as worker-owned companies must compete with capitalist firms in goods, labor, and financial markets they will be under relentless pressure to sacrifice the good of the public to their own bottom line. Markets are not the same as participatory planning. Whereas participatory planning affords worker councils a friendly environment that encourages human values and socially responsible behavior, markets penalize worker-owners who prioritize human values and social responsibility. Nor are capitalist competitors the same as fellow worker-managed enterprises. So while it may be reasonable to expect worker councils to behave in socially responsible ways in a participatory economy, it is not reasonable to expect worker-owned companies competing against capitalist companies in a market economy to always be able to do so.

Which brings us to the major problem employee-owned firms face in capitalism: even if they manage to buck the odds and survive, how can worker-owned firms prevent the dictates of the bottom line from trumping decision making according to human criteria? Most worker-owned firms begin because their members are dissatisfied with capitalism for one reason or another. Sometimes workers rebel against being driven hard and pitted against one another by greedy employers. Sometimes workers despair over lack of control over their work lives. Sometimes workers know they could offer consumers better quality products, and do not want to be prevented from doing so because a cheaper or less safe product is more profitable. Sometimes workers are disgusted with capitalist wage and salary structures that are grossly unjust, and want to reward themselves more fairly for their capitalist employer. Sometimes workers want to escape being silent accomplices in environmentally destructive practices and misleading advertising campaigns pursued by profit maximizing employers. But when worker-owned firms must compete in goods, labor, and financial markets with capitalist firms which adhere to the bottom line, there is relentless pressure on worker-owners to abandon prioritizing the quality of work life and fair systems of compensation, and to succumb to exploitative relations with suppliers, customers, external parties, and the environment. A strong supporter of worker-ownership for over three decades, Gar Alperowitz recently offered these words of caution based on his experiences:

> First, there is little evidence that worker-owned firms significantly alter society's *overall* distribution of income. Within the local or national community, for instance, privileged workers in rich industries do not easily share their advantage with the community as a whole or with workers in other industries, with the elderly, with the poor, or with women and children outside their own families. Second, worker-owned firms tend to develop their own 'interests.' Worker-owned steel mills, for instance, generally seek similar kinds of subsidies (and trade protection) as privately owned mills. Nor, for that matter, do worker-owners have any great interest in expensive pollution controls that may advantage the larger community but cost them money.[7]

For all these reasons, those who work tirelessly to promote the growth of worker-ownership in capitalism should *not* expect their efforts to succeed in replacing capitalism incrementally. The vision of reversing who hires whom—instead of capital hiring labor, labor hires capital—by slowly expanding the employee-owned sector of modern capitalist economies is a utopian pipe dream. The deck is stacked against worker-owned firms, making it very difficult for them to survive, particularly in modern capitalist economies dominated by large multinational firms. And when forced to compete against capitalist firms in a market environment, even the most idealistic worker-owners find it difficult to retain their commitment to decision making according to human values. In short, incrementally increasing the number of worker-owned firms is *not* a feasible transition strategy from the economics of competition and greed to the economics of equitable cooperation.

However, this is not to say that creating employee-owned firms cannot be an important *part* of a feasible transition strategy. The premise of this chapter is that if we are to succeed in the century ahead, building, expanding, and improving imperfect experiments in equitable cooperation within capitalism must occur at the same time that capitalism is being rendered less harmful through various reform campaigns. Worker-owned firms are one kind of partial experiment in equitable cooperation. They afford workers important opportunities to participate in economic decision making unavailable to them in capitalist firms. They train workers to make decisions collectively, together with their coworkers. When they compete successfully against capitalist firms, worker-owned firms challenge the myth that workers cannot govern themselves effectively, and therefore require bosses to decide what they should do and compel them to do it. So the more worker-owned firms there are, and the more successful they are, the stronger the movement for equitable cooperation will become.[8] But until worker-owned firms establish truly equitable systems of compensation, until producer cooperatives coordinate their activities democratically and equitably with *other* producer and consumer cooperatives, until worker-owned firms plan production priorities together with organizations representing consumers, until worker-owned firms embrace constraints on their use of the natural environment placed on them by organizations of citizens, they are only partial and imperfect experiments in equitable cooperation, no better and no worse than other partial experiments discussed in this chapter. After all, many of the most powerful law firms in America who defend the most heinous corporate abuses are owned entirely by their employees, or at least by some of them, the senior partners. So while they can play an important role in a transition to a self-managed system of equitable cooperation, expanding employee ownership in capitalism is no panacea.

Worker Takeovers in Argentina

Because the deck is stacked against them, expanding the employee-owned sector in capitalist economies usually proceeds very slowly. However, when capitalism plunges economies into crises the possibilities for promoting equitable cooperation through worker takeovers multiply, as a review of recent events in Argentina demonstrates. As the predictable consequences of unbridled neoliberal policies unfolded in the late 1990s and the Argentine economy descended into chaos, three popular movements spread quickly: neighborhood assemblies (*asambleas*), organizations of the unemployed (*piqueteros*), and worker takeovers (*fábricas recuperadas*). Soon after the Argentine economy collapsed in December 2001, workers in factories and businesses that had gone bankrupt began the practice of continuing production after their businesses officially closed. A survey by the University of Buenos Aires in October 2003 estimated that about 140 factories had been taken over, or recovered—roughly half in the metal-working industry, and the rest in the printing, food, cleaning services, and hotel industries. By recovering their enterprises over twelve thousand workers have been able to keep their jobs instead of joining the 20 percent of the Argentine labor force who are out of work. Recently these workers have established an organization to represent them, the National Movement of Recovered Enterprises (MNER) whose constitution reads in part: "In the face of the failure of company management, we felt we had to replace individual effort with collective effort, as the crisis demanded. By raising the flag of self-management, we were able to go from a situation of social conflict to a productive consensus."[9] The story of a ceramics factory located in a small city in the south of Argentina reveals a great deal about what is taking place throughout the country. Ginger Gentile, a former activist in Students Against Sweat Shops, provided the following eyewitness account in the March 2004 issue of *Labor Notes*.

Every day, the 330 workers of Zanón Ceramics Factory who both work at and run the largest ceramic floor-tile factory in Argentina are, legally speaking, usurping the factory and its machinery. While an outstanding order to evict these workers has existed for nearly a year, the government will not order the police to fulfill it because the political costs would be too high. Groups ranging from the teachers' union to the petroleum workers' union to the Catholic Church have said that if there is an eviction they will call a general strike throughout the province until the situation is resolved.

The old management structure has been replaced by a group decision-making structure, referred to as an assembly. Each department or work unit elects a representative to convey department concerns during assemblies, which are attended by all the workers. There, workers vote to approve or reject the departments' proposals. There are 30 coordinators elected by their sections. There are also two elected coordinators of the coordinators who perform many managerial functions, with the difference being that all of their decisions have to be reviewed by all workers, and they are recallable. Assemblies are held every week, one per shift, and when there are important decisions to be made a shift is given up to a long assembly, with all workers in attendance. These extraordinary assemblies are not only about the strategy of running the factory and winning their demands, but also about how to work on joint campaigns with other community groups. Zanón has won considerable support from all sectors of the Neuquén community because they are committed to creating a factory that is at the service of the community. Their goal is to get the government to expropriate the factory and let the workers run it, and the workers will prioritize production for state and community institutions. But instead of waiting for the state to act, they are already donating tiles and supporting the struggles of other groups, not just in the street, but having joint political discussions with their allies. Zanón's workers donate tiles to community centers and hospitals. As a result, the nurses union donates a nurse during each shift to supervise the health of the workers. Most importantly, each group that supports Zanón receives jobs as they become available. So far, Zanón has opened 90 new positions. They have turned over security operations (about 30 jobs in total) to members of an unemployed workers group.

The Zanón workers began their struggle to improve conditions within the factory in June 2000 when a worker died there due to employer negligence and their union did not respond strongly enough to the crisis. Despite the inaction of union leadership, Zanón's workers led a nine day strike that ended with workers winning a joint commission of workers and managers to oversee production and safety within the factory. Later, in May 2001, management stopped paying full wages, claiming that the factory was not turning a profit. After a thirty-four day strike (again, an action not supported by the union), the workers won the right to review the accounting books, which clearly showed that the factory was turning a profit. However, on September 5, 2001 the factory's owner locked out the workers, claiming that there was not enough money to pay their salaries due to outstanding debts and that, despite receiving huge state subsidies, the factory was unable to turn a profit. The workers camped outside of the factory in protest and, on the first of October, entered the factory to prevent the owner from removing the machinery. Soon after, a group of twenty workers proposed that they restart production. After a brief discussion, the majority of the workers agreed that it was the only way to continue to earn a living.

On March 2, 2002 the factory began producing again, with only one line of production open. However, by implementing their own ideas to improve production, and with help from engineers from the local university, within a year the workers were producing more than fifty percent of what the factory made before the takeover. Currently, they are looking to exporting tiles once again, and have become recognized as a not-for-profit organization, as all of the profits are used to improve production or make donations to the community. Before the takeover, some workers earned twice as much as others; now everyone earns the same—800 pesos, or about 270 dollars, a good salary in Neuquén.

Clearly, opportunities to expand the worker-owned sector of the economy are far better in a chaotic political situation where capitalist owners cannot always rely on the state to enforce their property rights. Workers who take over factories under these circumstances may also be more inclined to pay themselves equitably, if for no other reason simply because the alternative for more skilled and less skilled alike is unemployment. In these circumstances workers may also be more likely to establish solidaritous relations with others in their community whom they rely on for political support. For these and other reasons the cause of equitable cooperation can often be advanced much more quickly through campaigns for worker control during periods of political and economic crisis than when the capitalist economy and state power are stronger. But this does not mean activists should wait for a crisis to promote worker ownership. The more seeds of worker-ownership that have been planted, the more experience with self-management workers have had, and the stronger the institutional network supporting worker managed firms already in place, the easier it is to spread worker self-management when favorable opportunities arise.

Mondragón

The Mondragón cooperative network is the largest business group in the Basque region of Spain, and the seventh largest in all of Spain.[10] It includes more than 150 cooperative enterprises with sixty thousand workers, and has over 8 billion euros in working capital. It is the largest and most successful example of worker-owned industrial cooperatives in the world. Begun by a visionary Catholic priest in the 1950s during the repressive Franco regime, the Mondragón cooperatives have survived and grown under circumstances that have never been easy, and often been difficult. I will not attempt to review the substantial literature analyzing the Mondragón experiment, except to say that it generally takes the form of describing the glass as half full or as half empty. Compared to capitalist firms, the Mondragón cooperatives provide greater opportunities for workers to participate in decision making and enjoy more equitable pay structures. Compared to cooperatives elsewhere, the Mondragón support network is far more robust and developed. The most important institution in this network is the Caja Laboral, an impressive cooperative bank that provides cooperatives in the network extensive research assistance on technologies, products, and markets, in-depth training in cooperative principles of management, and substantial financial support.

On the other hand, over the years there has been an unmistakable drift toward greater managerial domination of decision making. According to Baleren Bakaikoa, director of the cooperative research institute "Gezki," while the Mondragón cooperatives maintain a representative democratic process, de facto power has become increasingly centralized in the hands of technocratic business managers who manage the cooperatives' money. There is also a significant trend toward greater wage disparities within the cooperatives, and Mondragón's vested members increasingly stand out as a privileged sector in the regional work force. Initially the highest-paid employee in a cooperative could not be paid more than three times as much as the lowest-paid employee. But this "core principle" was suspended repeatedly in what were deemed special circumstances, and has now become a dead letter. While Mondragón cooperatives are better "citizens" than their capitalist counterparts, when profits conflict with community interests, Mondragón cooperatives increasingly favor the former over the latter. Today, well over half of the capital of the Caja Laboral is invested in noncooperative ventures, and many Mondragón cooperatives have entered into partnerships with multinational corporations and opened noncooperative factories in Third World countries. One of the original, ten core principles was "a commitment to create a more just social order." However this radical sentiment has been watered down over the years to mean little more than making "socially conscious investments." What lessons are to be learned from this important experiment in slowly building a network of worker-owned industrial cooperatives in the middle of an advanced capitalist economy?

1. The pressure to shrink rather than expand worker participation is immense, as is the pressure to bring wage differentials more in line with wage rates in capitalist labor markets. The reemergence of class divisions within worker-owned cooperatives, and consolidation of class rule by professionals and managers is a very real danger. The Mondragón experience dramatically confirms what theory predicts in this regard, which implies that tireless efforts to make job complexes more balanced, and to promote the principle of reward according to effort are essential to protect cooperative principles and preserve producer cooperatives as powerful forces for the economics of equitable cooperation.

2. When financial managers control resource allocation the lure of lucrative investment opportunities is difficult, if not impossible to resist, even when investments violate core cooperative principles. Stubborn adherence to the principle that cooperatives lend only to members or to other cooperatives—on terms that can be mutually beneficial but must also be solidaritous—is essential to prevent cooperatives from becoming exploiters of the misery of others in one form or another.

3. Market principles and cooperative principles are contradictory. The first step toward the defeat of cooperative principles is to deny this fact. While cooperatives have limited room for maneuver, unless they can manage to transform the market environment they operate in, the market environment will transform them, and eventually lead them to betray their cooperative principles. The Mondragón experience confirms what theory predicts in this regard. While this is the most difficult task cooperatives face, some practical steps they can take in conjunction with consumer cooperatives to introduce a moral element in their market relations, and eventually transform their market relations altogether are discussed below.

In many ways, the Mondragón cooperative network is a powerful example that workers can manage themselves and compete successfully against capitalist enterprises. But Mondragón also stands as an example of the dangers producer cooperatives face when trying to hold true to their cooperative principles in a capitalist environment.

Consumer Cooperatives

The consumer cooperative movement dates back to 1844 when the people in Rochdale England founded their co-op. It is now widely forgotten that independent, local consumer co-ops flourished and grew in the hundred years after their founding to a dominant position in the European retail industry. But after World War II, large capitalist food chains and retailers expanded rapidly in both Europe and the United States dealing consumer co-ops a serious blow. In the last twenty years, however, co-ops have made something of a comeback. Nobody knows how many consumer cooperatives there are in the United States. A survey in the early 1990s counted more than 40,000, and consumer cooperatives have expanded rapidly since then.[11] Some consumer cooperatives in the United States date back to the early twentieth century, some were organized as part of the countercultural revolt of the 1960s, but most have been organized more recently in response to a growing list of consumer needs unserved by capitalist firms. Some were organized by consumers who couldn't get credit on reasonable terms from capitalist banks, or electricity in rural areas at reasonable rates, or adequate housing in capitalist housing markets. Consumers who wanted to eat food that capitalist supermarkets would not provide created others.

The major problem at this point is not lack of consumer cooperatives, since they are sprouting up faster than we can count them. The major problems are (1) failure to cultivate cooperative principles and practices within the consumer cooperatives that already exist, and (2) failure to develop cooperative relations between producer and consumer cooperatives, leaving individual cooperatives to interact instead with capitalist firms through the marketplace.

Progressives need to help sustain and expand self-management practices and develop more equitable wage structures in consumer cooperatives. We need to devise more creative procedures to help members participate in consumer cooperatives without heavy burdens on their time. We need to develop ways to take advantage of the energy of dedicated staff without the staff usurping member control over cooperative policy. Activists working in consumer cooperatives are already hard at work on these tasks, and are already sharing ideas and experiences with one another through organizations of consumer cooperatives and Internet discussion forums. The Cooperative Grocers Information Network (CGIN, www.cgin.coop) maintains a discussion group for the National Cooperative Grocers Association (NCGA, www.ncga.coop). There is an active discussion group facilitated by Co-op Net (www.co-opnet.coop). And both the University of Wisconsin Center for Cooperatives, UWCC (www.wisc.edu/uwcc) and the International Co-operative Alliance (www.coop.org) provide educational materials on cooperative principles and sponsor information exchanges by topic areas. However, a great deal more educational work must be done inside consumer cooperatives by those who understand how pressure from the bottom line can undermine cooperative principles.

Linking Producer and Consumer Cooperatives

Members of producer and consumer cooperatives also need to learn and teach one another how the competitive market environment limits the capacities of their cooperatives to meet their stated goals. Activists in producer cooperatives need to teach their fellow workers how market relations limit their ability to transform the work process in desirable ways. Activists in consumer cooperatives need to teach their fellow members how market relations limit their ability to secure high quality, safe, environmentally friendly products. And activists in all cooperatives need to explain how market relations prevent them from developing democratic and equitable relations between cooperatives, and undermine economic democracy and justice within their organizations as well.

Once the difference between market and cooperative principles is more clearly understood by more cooperative members, progressives need to try to link cooperatives together in new ways. The first step is to try to help producer and consumer cooperatives buy and sell more from each other, and less from capitalist firms. This would cut down on ways that relationships with capitalist suppliers and buyers undermine cooperative principles. A major effort is now underway to link Community Supported Agriculture (CSA) with local food co-ops. Part of the original aim of CSA was to enlist urban people in support of local agriculture. Some CSA groups go so far as to rent land and hire a farmer. But most CSAs are started as an alternative produce-marketing method by a landowner, with support from local or regional sustainable agriculture organizations. CSAs thrive where small farms can provide a diverse array of consumer-ready products, such as vegetables, fruits, herbs, meats, honey, milk products, and eggs to large urban populations in close proximity to the farm.[12] Local Harvest, an organization supporting CSA, sponsors a program to link local farmers with food co-ops in nearby urban areas (www.local-harvest.org/food-coops/). CSA advocates, like Local Harvest, have recognized that local food co-ops are more reliable partners for local farmers than large national food chains, and now advise farmers in CSA programs to forge links with local food co-ops whenever possible.

A second step could be to establish something like an eBay on the Internet exclusively for producer and consumer cooperatives. Once cooperatives are trading with other cooperatives through a cooperative ebay, a third step could be to classify cooperatives according to their levels of economic development to make it possible to apply the "greater than 50 percent rule" to trades between unequal parties. The idea is to insure that cooperatives in lower categories always get more than 50 percent of the efficiency gain from trades with cooperatives in higher categories. Just as the "fair trade movement" has recently introduced a moral element into international trade, this would bring the cooperative market more in line with the core principles of equitable cooperation. After fair trade between cooperatives became a familiar norm, cooperatives participating in the cooperative eBay market could move toward replacing fair trade exchanges with a rudimentary form of participatory planning, which would facilitate even fairer relationships and allow for greater economic democracy. In this way progressives could eventually connect cooperatives that are both economically and politically solid into a network that functions as a participatory archipelago of worker and consumer self-managed islands. Of course these cooperative islands would not be able to obtain all they need from other cooperatives in the archipelago, nor be able to sell all their output to other cooperatives in the archipelago. But once the participatory archipelago was well established, instead of leaving cooperatives to deal with the capitalist economy individually, the entire archipelago could relate to the capitalist economy as a unit—importing and exporting from the capitalist sector in the same way national participatory economies will eventually relate to the global capitalist economy until capitalism is replaced globally.

A less ambitious example of linking producer cooperatives with a ubiquitous form of public consumption received national attention a few years ago due to the research of an academic nutritionist. The researcher pointed out that the nutritional quality of public school lunch programs could be dramatically increased by replacing processed foods with locally grown vegetables and fruits, provided school cafeteria staffs were taught how to prepare seasonal menus. An economist colleague pointed out that advance contracts can provide local growers much needed economic security especially if they organize into a farmer cooperative for the school system to contract with. Campaigns to link nutritional improvements in public school lunch programs with local farmer cooperatives could be very promising in many rural areas and also revive local and regional cuisines.

Participatory Budgeting

While there are many living experiments in worker-owned firms and consumer owned cooperatives, there are few examples of local jurisdictions deciding how to spend tax revenues through a participatory budgeting process. For that reason, public-good planning by villages in Kerala, India, and participatory budgeting in the city of Porto Alegre in Brazil are particularly important to study and learn from.

Kerala, India

The two states in India where left political parties have had the greatest influence in the half century since independence are West Bengal and Kerala. Despite highly successful programs and widespread popularity, by the mid-1990s the Left United Front (LDF) government in Kerala was losing its electoral advantage. Younger party leaders convinced the older leadership that successful programs like land reform and rice subsidies were no longer sufficient to motivate the electorate to actively support left parties, as neoliberal and right-wing nationalist political forces grew both inside and outside India. In effect younger leaders in the CPI-M, the major party in the LDF, urged the party to move from "serve the people" to "power to the people" by launching an ambitious program to mobilize households at the village level and give them direct control over projects in their villages. Preceded by the "Total Literacy Campaign," the "People's Science Movement," the "People's Resource Mapping Program," and the "Kalliasseri People's Planning Experiment," in 1996 the LDF in Kerala launched one of the world's most extensive experiments in direct, popular democracy. The "Kerala Peoples Campaign for the Ninth Plan" mobilized over 3 million of Kerala's 30 million people in all 1,052 of its villages and urban neighborhoods in a process of bottom-up, participatory planning to decide how to spend 40 percent of state revenues during the period of the ninth plan, 1996 through 2001. The brief description below is excerpted from a presentation by Richard Franke and Barbara Chasin to the International Conference on Democratic Decentralization, held at Kerala University in Thiruvananthapuram, May 23–28, 2000.[13]

The decision of the LDF to send down 35 to 40 percent of the plan funds to the villages and municipal bodies was revolutionary. Ordinary citizens, elected representatives, retired volunteer technical experts, and eventually government departmental bureaucrats talked about problems, studied resources, then drafted, prioritized, appraised, implemented, and monitored projects leading to local development plans in all 990 rural *panchayats*, 152 development blocks, 58 municipalities, and 14 districts.

In the first year of the campaign 373 state-level trainers taught 10,497 district-level resource persons who conducted one-day workshops for over 100,000 local activists who became the backbone of the initial stages of the campaign. The first step in people's participation was the *grama sabhas*, or local assemblies. Two million persons attended the first *grama sabhas* of August-December 1996. In the second set six months later 1.8 million attended, and in the third there were 2.1 million attendees. These numbers equal ten percent of the voting-age population. But people can attend meetings without effectively participating. A major achievement of Kerala's campaign was to devise and implement methods to encourage the involvement of ordinary people. At the *grama sabhas*, speeches by politicians were limited to 30 minutes with another 40 minutes for expert presentations. The next two hours were taken up by small group discussions facilitated by trainers in twelve topic areas where people could voice their needs. The small groups then reassembled in a plenary to hear reports and elect representatives to the next campaign stage.

People's participation continued with a series of data collection activities and the writing of PDRs—local panchayat and urban development reports—that are perhaps unique in the history of decentralization. Running from 75 to 200 pages, the PDRs provided the discussion documents for the development seminars. In this stage of people's participation about twenty persons per ward—elected earlier in the *grama sabhas*—met to make recommendations for projects. The development seminars created task forces charged with drafting actual project proposals that would include any required technical specifications and financial planning. A remarkable innovation was the mobilization of retired experts to assist in the technical and financial appraisal of the projects. The 4000 "Volunteer Technical Corps" (VTC) members included retired engineers, doctors, professors, and other professionals.

People's participation took a new turn when over 200 *panchayats* began forming "Neighborhood Groups" (NHGs). With around 2000 adults, the wards in which the *grama sabhas* are organized were still rather large for effective community interaction. The felt need for greater local involvement led to the formation of groups of 40 to 50 households, represented often by women, who met weekly or biweekly to discuss development issues to bring to the *grama sabhas*.

In the first two years the campaign led to construction of 98,494 houses, 240,307 sanitary latrines, 17,489 public taps, and 50,162 wells, substantially greater numbers than for previous plans. A functional division is emerging among the various levels of local government. The state government keeps plan funds for major electrical power generation projects and certain industrial projects requiring statewide solutions and massive investment. Otherwise, local bodies are supplanting state programs in areas where local plans are more appropriate. In the first year of the campaign, villages and municipalities gave 14.5 percent of service sector finance to build housing, while the previous plan had only 1.4 percent for that purpose. Local bodies spent 13 percent on improvements in sanitation and drinking water compared with 7.5 percent in the eighth 5-year plan.

The Women Component Plan (WCP) is a unique feature of Kerala's democratic decentralization. Requiring a gender-effects evaluation of every project, and a commitment of 10 percent of projects to benefit women only, the WCP has led to projects in vegetable gardening, sewing cooperatives, mobilization of anganawady (preschool) personnel, and construction of new community centers for women. Finally, the campaign has succeeded in delivering a greater percentage than previously of project funds to the Scheduled Caste (untouchables) and Scheduled Tribe communities (SC/ST) that make up 12 percent of Kerala's rural population. Both the WCP and SC/ST elements of the Campaign have the potential of reducing major sources of inequality in Kerala.

The People's Campaign is the latest innovation in the Kerala development model. Not only does the Kerala model as a whole stand as a positive alternative to neoliberalism, the People's Campaign is a powerful testament to the abilities of ordinary people to effectively plan their own programs when creative political leadership creates opportunities for them to do so. It remains to be seen if the Kerala development model can withstand the onslaught of Hindu nationalism and the race to the bottom effect of states in India competing against one another for international and domestic investment by reducing business taxes and lowering labor and environmental standards. It also remains to be seen if popular planning at the village level can be successfully institutionalized and resist bureaucratic inroads. But the Kerala model certainly demonstrates that there *is* another way, and the People's Campaign proves that participatory budgeting is possible and effective.

Porto Alegre, Brazil

In November 1999, the city of Porto Alegre hosted an International Seminar on Participatory Democracy. The Brazilian Workers Party had been in power in the city government for ten years and had pioneered a new way to make decisions about public goods called the "participatory budget." The occasion for the conference was that the Workers Party had won statewide elections in Rio Grande do Sul, and the new state government wanted to expand participatory budgeting to all 10 million inhabitants in Brazil's southernmost state.

For close to a decade the municipal government in Porto Alegre had designated a significant portion of public funds to be used as neighborhoods decided. Vibrant neighborhood organizations evolved to discuss and debate their own priorities, and ask for technical assistance to design projects of their own choosing. Overall the experience was positive. Participatory budgeting reduced citizen apathy and cynicism, tapped citizen creativity and energy in ways that bureaucratic budgeting cannot, and provided local public goods more in line with what those living in different neighborhoods wanted. The participatory budget process also seemed to increase electoral support for the Workers Party in Porto Alegre and build political support for other progressive economic priorities in the city. No wonder the Workers Party called a conference to spread this successful program to the state level when they finally won statewide elections in Rio Grande do Sul in 1999. Now participatory budgeting has spread further since the landslide victory of Ignacio "Lula" da Silva and the Workers Party in the 2002 national elections.

Unfortunately, recent results have not been what activists hoped for. Even before participatory budgeting spread from Porto Alegre to Rio Grande do Sul, the national government under Lula's predecessor, Fernando Cardoza, agreed to crippling IMF conditions for repaying Brazil's 300 billion dollar international debt. Moreover, the Cardoza government assigned specific quotas to state governments, who in turn assigned quotas to municipal governments specifying how much each had to contribute toward international debt repayment from their own revenues. Now the Lula government has agreed not only to honor the Cardoza government commitments to the IMF, but to increase the rate of debt repayment. So now it is Lula and the Workers Party government that is collecting crippling quotas from states and municipalities leaving them to choose which of their budgetary priorities they want to cancel. While those who participate in participatory budgeting are still able to choose and design their own projects with the funds left them, they are not allowed to participate in the much more important decision about how much of their revenues should go to pay off international lenders, and how much is left to satisfy their own needs. The Lula government knows full well that if *this* decision were made through a participatory process, the Brazilian people would never agree to pay as much as the Lula government has agreed to in its attempt to buy favor with the international financial community and the IMF.

Critics point out that the participatory budget process has been reduced to a way to co-opt citizens into deciding how to distribute a budgetary shortfall they never agreed to in the first place, and many Workers Party activists have started calling it "participatory austerity." Activists point out that what participants now must decide is whether to repair the sewers, which break down on a regular basis with deadly consequences in the shantytowns and poor districts, or to pay civil servants, who sometimes go more than six months without pay. They must decide if a district healthcare clinic should be closed, depriving thousands of working class families of minimal healthcare, or if a project to install running water must be cancelled. Critics point out that by enlisting citizens and popular organizations into making these debasing choices, they are manipulated into serving as relays for policies dictated by the IMF and distracted from defending their own interests.

The situation has deteriorated dramatically, and the reputation of participatory budgeting has deteriorated in Brazil as well. The former mayor of Porto Alegre, Tarso Genro, and his former assistant in charge of the participatory budget, Urbitaran de Souza, jointly authored a handbook titled "The Participatory Budget: the Porto Alegre Experience" that was not only widely distributed by the Workers Party nationally, but also printed, translated, and distributed widely by the World Bank, which is now promoting participatory budgeting internationally to minimize social explosions in response to IMF/WB austerity policies. Tarso Genro lost to the conservative candidate in his bid to become governor of Rio Grande do Sul, polling 16 percent less in Porto Alegre than the previous Workers Party candidate. Urbitaran de Souza, who campaigned for the national assembly as the candidate of the participatory budget could not even get enough votes to qualify for the general election. It is widely believed that the electoral defeats of Genro and de Souza resulted directly from their public association with participatory budgeting turned into participatory austerity. Ana, leader of a neighborhood organization in Porto Alegre and member of the Workers Party, had this to say in an inteview reported in the *O Trabalho* newspaper:

> Look. People aren't stupid. At first we believed what they were telling us—that we would finally have a voice in determining the budget priorities of the population. And we were patient, realizing that not everything can change overnight. But then we began to see that the priorities we put forward were never selected for review and implementation by the overseers of the budget process. Little by little, we began to see what was going on. We came to understand that the Workers Party municipalities working under this 'participatory' process were dutifully paying back the debt to the foreign investors—who, we should point out, did not invest a cent to help the Brazilian people. Why should they, the rich and super-rich who have simply speculated on our resources, get paid back when we are hurting so badly? We were told that the issue of the debt could not be discussed or challenged. How democratic is this?

Obviously, people's patience is limited when asked to engage in the time-consuming process of participatory budgeting while being denied the right to make the most important budgetary decisions that affect their lives. It is hard to imagine that millions of people in Kerala would have bothered to attend multiple meetings and planning sessions had they not been deciding how to use a substantial portion of the state budget. In Brazil, people have been quick to recognize when a popular program has been co-opted for a nefarious purpose. Hopefully the reputation of meaningful participatory budgeting, that was given a strong boost during the early 1990s in the city of Porto Alegre, will not be tarnished by its current abuse in Brazil.

Neighborhood Assemblies in Argentina

In Kerala and Brazil, long-established left political parties, during more or less normal economic conditions, initiated the formation of village and neighborhood organizations to manage their own public resources as they saw fit. In both cases the initiative was motivated not only by a desire to spread participatory economic democracy, but also by a desire to consolidate electoral support for the parties in question. In contrast, *asambleas*, or neighborhood assemblies in Buenos Aires, Argentina arose spontaneously in a chaotic economic crisis, motivated by popular disgust with all established political parties.

An economic and political vacuum in which neighborhoods could no longer rely on receiving essential public services, and a complete mistrust for all political figures led to the creation of neighborhood assemblies where, for a time, residents met, discussed, and debated what actions to take on a weekly basis. Among other things, the assemblies had to deal with bank closures and frozen accounts, large hikes in utility bills by foreign owned companies, and residents who were unable to pay their rents and mortgages when they lost their jobs as the unemployment rate soared above 25 percent.

At one point the *asambleas* were the center of political action in Buenos Aires, where, ironically, no politician dared show his or her face. Beside ordinary residents, independent neighborhood activists and members of small left political parties and groups attended weekly neighborhood meetings debating one form of action or another. However, the attempt to form a citywide coordinating council of representatives from all the neighborhood assemblies was short lived, and neighborhood assembly activity had died down considerably even before Kirchner's election. Alan Cibils, an Argentine economist, who participated in the assemblies, offered this succinct explanation for their demise in a private letter: "The main reasons the assemblies declined were: 1) left party interference, not letting the process develop but trying to steer it towards their own goals, 2) lack of political experience on the part of residents and activists who were not members of left sects, and 3) inability to formulate or articulate a clear political project to deal with the local and national governments."

Unlike Kerala and Porto Alegre, no established progressive political party in Argentina was dedicated to expanding the power of assemblies over budgetary matters. And when it became apparent they lacked sufficient political clout to mount a serious campaign for budgetary power on their own, most of the assemblies wilted on the vine. Despite their decline, the rapid rise and scope of neighborhood assemblies in Buenos Aires, and the potential we know they have based on what villages in Kerala and neighborhoods in Porto Alegre have accomplished, make them experiments worth studying.

Egalitarian and Sustainable Intentional Communities

Besides religious communities like the Amish, the Mennonites, the Hutterites, and the Bruderhoff who all live outside the capitalist mainstream to varying degrees, there are close to a thousand secular "intentional communities" in the United States where individuals and families live in ways that are self-consciously different from capitalist life styles. Some of these communities concentrate on living in ways that are environmentally sustainable, including pioneering new environmentally friendly technologies. Others are primarily concerned with building egalitarian relationships. Many intentional communities try to do both, and practice democratic decision making in various forms as well. Donald Pitzer provides an excellent overview of the history of communalism in America with valuable insights for contemporary intentional communities in *America's Communal Past* (1997). *In the Company of Others: Making Community in the Modern World* (1993), edited by Claude Whitmyer, is a collection of insightful articles analyzing successful intentional communities. Richard Fairfield provides an engaging account of countercultural communes in the 1960s and 1970s in *Communes USA: A Personal Tour* (1971). And Geoph Kozeny has produced an excellent video providing an in depth look at eighteen contemporary intentional communities featuring extensive interviews with members in *Utopia 101: Intentional Communities ... the Cooperative Quest to Build a Better World* (2000).

The Fellowship for Intentional Community (FIC) dates back to 1948, but was revitalized in the 1980s, and incorporated as a nonprofit organization in 1986. The FIC today serves as both a membership organization for over 200 communities, and as a clearinghouse for information on more than seven hundred communities appearing in the FIC encyclopedic publication: *Communities Directory: A Guide to Intentional Communities and Cooperative Living* (2000). According to its web site, www.ic.org, the purpose of the FIC is: (1) to embrace the diversity that *exists among communities* and to facilitate increased interaction between communitarians and the wider culture; (2) to build cooperative spirit within and among communities through shared celebrations, joint ventures, and activities that build awareness of our common humanity; (3) to facilitate exchange of information, skills, and economic support among individuals, existing intentional communities, cooperative groups, and newly forming communities; (4) to serve as a reference source for those seeking intentional communities, conferences, and other community building experiences and practices appropriate to their needs; (5) to support education, research, archives, and publishing about contemporary and historic intentional communities; (6) to demonstrate practical applications of communities, cooperatives, and their products and services through seminars, catalogs, demonstration projects, gatherings, and direct sales; and (7) to increase global awareness that intentional communities are pioneers in sustainable living, personal and community transformation, and peaceful social evolution.

A directory of "eco-villages," with information about and links to each one can be found at http://www.ecobusinesslinks.com/sustainable_communities.htm. The primary focus of these communities is changing humans' relations with the natural environment. The proceedings of a conference on sustainable communities held at Findhorn in the mid-1990s were published in *Eco-Villages and Sustainable Communities: Models for 21st Century Living*, edited by Jillian Conrad and Drew Withington (1996.) Two excellent anthologies of essays about alternative city designs and energy systems are *Eco-City Dimensions: Healthy Communities, Healthy Planet*, edited by Mark Roseland (1997), and *Sustainable Communties: A New Design Syhthesis for Cities, Suburbs, and Towns* by Sim Van Der Ryn and Peter Calthorpe (1986.) Diane and Bob Gilman offer excellent suggestions for starting new eco-communities in *Eco-Villages and Sustainable Communities* (1991.)

In 1976 more than a dozen communities focused primarily on changing people's relations with one another formed the Federation of Egalitarian Communities (FEC) to promote egalitarian life styles. Communities in the FEC cooperate on publications, conferences, and recruitment; engage in labor exchanges and skill sharing; and provide joint healthcare coverage. The FEC now has members and affiliate communities spread across North America, ranging in size and emphasis from small agricultural homesteads to villagelike communities with over a hundred members, to urban group houses. The stated aim of these "egalitarian communities" is "not only to help each other, but to help more people discover the advantages of a communal alternative and to promote the evolution of a more egalitarian world."[14] Each of the communities in the federation: (1) holds its land, labor, income, and other resources in common; (2) assumes responsibility for the needs of its members, receiving the products of their labor and distributing these and all other goods equally, or according to need; (3) practices nonviolence; (4) uses a form of decision making in which members have an equal opportunity to participate, either through consensus, direct vote or right of appeal or overrule; (5) works to establish the equality of all people and does not permit discrimination on the basis of race, class, creed, ethnic origin, age, sex, or sexual orientation; (6) acts to conserve natural resources for present and future generations while striving to continually improve ecological awareness and practice; and (7) creates processes for group communication and participation and provides an environment which supports people's development. The FEC has accumulated a library of information they call "systems and structures" available without charge to any who are interested, containing advice on topics as varied as children, conflict resolution, economic planning and budgeting, and taxes.

The number of intentional communities in the United States committed to living in environmentally sustainable and egalitarian ways is truly impressive, as is the longevity and size of some of the communities. Unfortunately, these communities are virtually unknown to most Americans,[15] including most who think of themselves as part of the left. While their lack of visibility in the mainstream is understandable, the disconnect between left activists and those living in intentional communities is surprising since many who live in intentional communities participate faithfully, year in and year out, in various environmental, antiwar, and social justice campaigns. But for the most part, left activists and theoreticians ignore the existence of these experiments in equitable cooperation as both valuable sources of information about how well our visions of alternatives to capitalism work in practice, and as opportunities to practice what they preach themselves. Overcoming this unfortunate "disconnect" is an important priority.

A New World Is Possible

Finally, there are a handful of collectives in the United States and Canada that are not only owned and managed entirely by their members, but organized self-consciously according to the principles of participatory economics. These collectives practice balancing job complexes and remuneration according to effort, promote participatory economic goals, seek to relate to other progressive organizations on a cooperative rather than commercial basis, and explicitly agitate for replacing capitalism with a participatory economy.

Boston: South End Press

The first self-conscious attempt to organize a workplace according to the principles of participatory economics was South End Press (SEP, southend@igc.org). Since 1978 the SEP collective has published close to a thousand titles relevant to social change movements while working in balanced job complexes and paying all members equal salaries. While

SEP has never employed more than a dozen collective members at one time, it has grown and prospered in a very competitive industry for a quarter century while continuing to adhere to participatory economic principles.

Winnipeg: The A-Zone

The first network of collectives operating according to participatory economic principles was organized in Winnipeg, Canada, in the mid-1990s. The Old Market Autonomous Zone is a three-story building and home to many progressive businesses and grassroots organizations. Mondragón Bookstore and Coffee House, (www.a-zone.org/mondragon/) is both a bookstore and a full vegetarian restaurant. Arbeiter Ring Publishing (www.arbeiterring.com/) publishes numerous titles a year. The G-7 Welcoming Committee (www.g7welcomingcommittee.com/) is a recording collective that has released CDs, tapes, and vinyl recordings from political bands, as well as audio lectures by Howard Zinn and Noam Chomsky. Natural Cycle is a bicycle repair and courier company. Each of these enterprises is run by a collective according to participatory economic principles, and the collectives try cooperate with one another according to the principles of participatory economics as well.

Paul Burrows was one of the founders of the Mondragón Bookstore and Coffee House. At the Work after Capitalism panel of the Third World Social Forum held in Porto Alegre, January 23–28, 2003, Burrows offered a supportive but critical appraisal of how the attempt to balance job complexes and reward people according to effort had worked in practice during his five years in the Mondragón collective:[16]

> Informal hierarchies and informal inequities in the division of labor are more difficult to address, and sometimes *more difficult to even see*, than formal ones. Some of these have to do with inevitable differences between experienced and new workers, and worker turn-over usually means losing someone with key skills and "historical memory," and starting from scratch with someone new. Some of these inequities have to do with people becoming too comfortable in their roles, or with a "natural" gravitation towards one's preferences. And some have to do with feeling (rightly or wrongly) that inequities in balancing are too difficult to change, or that even articulating them will lead to personal conflicts. In practice, some people prefer to remain silent about grievances or perceived inequities, for fear of jeopardizing relationships or

friendships with co-workers, or because they feel that the *potential* conflict with a co-worker will create a more negative work environment than the continuation of the inequity or grievance itself.

The point is that structures designed to equalize skills and knowledge do not automatically do so, and even people who agree that this *should* be a goal may find, in practice, that their own preferences or comfort collides with their politics. There is no single answer for overcoming disparities in job complexes, and for rectifying formal or informal hierarchies as they arise. As always, a combination of structural fine-tuning and holding individual co-workers accountable needs to be considered. But even when there are no institutional obstacles blocking access to certain types of work —and even when there is a genuine openness to discussing problems, to listening to alternatives, and to implementing structural or policy changes to address inequities —the goal of achieving fully balanced job complexes is much easier said than done. Ultimately, a "pure" balanced job complex is perhaps best viewed as an endless horizon, towards which we are always moving, always refining our practices, but never quite reaching.

Problems with motivating workers, problems with productivity and accountability, problems with workers taking initiative and setting their own standards and pace of work, have led some of Mondragón's own collective members to question the effectiveness of rewarding work on the basis of effort. They see areas of work that are consistently neglected, they see disparities in terms of the labor that different co-workers are willing to conduct, they see critical tasks getting performed poorly or not at all, they see some people treating the workplace like they are full partners (keeping the "big picture" in mind, doing "extra" tasks, trouble-shooting as needed), while others often act like employees (shirking duties, foot-dragging, remaining silent about business direction and political vision —except insofar as it might affect their immediate work circumstances). In my opinion, these are all serious problems which any collective needs to face and resolve. But they are *not* a consequence of attempting to reward people for effort —as opposed to rewarding people for something seemingly more tangible, such as productivity and desired outcomes. In my opinion, these problems arise in part because Mondragón has failed to actually implement the principle —*not because the principle fails*. Mondragón, strictly speaking, does not reward people on the basis of effort. It tries to approximate such a principle. It pays people equal pay for equal hours shifted, and over time, the kinds of work performed by each worker is roughly balanced with every other worker. But workers' relative efforts are *not* weighed and evaluated in any strict sense. Poor performance or under-average effort is *not* penalized, unless it becomes a systematic pattern and problem that others become unwilling to further tolerate. Paying people equal pay for equal effort would involve holding one's co-workers accountable for, say, getting things done at agreed-upon times. It would involve more systematic judgment and evaluation of effort on and off shift, than actually happens at Mondragón, precisely because many are reluctant to do it. And it would probably involve acknowledging, and attempting to mitigate or correct, some of the class and income disparities among collective members which operate *outside* the workplace.

Based on his personal experience, Burrows offers sobering advice about working in a participatory economics workplace trying to function in a capitalist economy:

> Building alternative institutions and an alternative economy is far more difficult, in my opinion, than organizing speakers and conferences, spiking trees, lying in front of bulldozers, going to rallies, signing petitions, throwing bricks through bank windows, or writing radical, "cutting edge" articles for obscure lefty journals —the kinds of things many people believe constitutes the whole of "activism."

But Burrows also explains why tackling this difficult task is a crucial component of a successful transition strategy from capitalism to the economics of equitable cooperation:

> Part of the motivation behind building participatory economic businesses and organizations today is that we simply want to live in ways consistent with our principles, with dignity, and in solidarity with others, and yes, we want to mitigate the brutality of capitalism, even as we sit in its shadow. But equally important is that we need to learn the skills necessary to govern ourselves, to organize key areas of production, to establish networks of communication and distribution, and to build a culture of resistance and cooperation —all of which will leave us better prepared to fill the political and economic vacuum left by a revolution, and to head off the rise of vanguards, skilled orators, technocrats and goons claiming to rule in "the people's interest."[17]

Vancouver Participatory Economics Collective

This collective does educational work promoting participatory economics. They sponsor community forums, appear on progressive radio and cable TV programs, and maintain an active web site: http://vanparecon.resist.ca. Besides providing a variety of educational materials about participatory economics to any who are interested, the collective is committed to helping establish participatory economics workplaces in the lower mainland of British Columbia.

Syracuse: The New Standard

Peoples NetWorks, which publishes *The New Standard*, is the newest collective organized according to participatory economic principles. *The New Standard* is a noncommercial, independent, professional, twenty-four-hour, hard-news source whose collective members work in balanced job complexes and reward one another according to effort. Information about the news services provided by *The New Standard*, and how the Peoples NetWorks collective functions is available on their Web site, http://newstandardnews.net/.

Partial Commitment to Equitable Cooperation

Most people cannot join a full-scale experiment in equitable cooperation. It is also perfectly understandable why people who could conceivably do so may not be willing to jump whole hog into any of the experiments that already exist, and may not be in a position to organize a new one. Nor is this altogether unfortunate. If all anticapitalists lived in experimental communities the cultural divide between anticapitalists and ordinary people would be more acute than it already is, making it even more difficult to reach people with our criticisms of capitalism and plans for equitable cooperation. However, it is important for people who talk the anticapitalist talk to take some steps toward walking the anticapitalist walk as well. We need to create more ways for people to make partial commitments to live according to the principles of equitable cooperation short of joining full scale intentional communities or working in participatory economics collectives.

However, these programs should not be based on adherence to a particular ideology, political program, or organizing strategy. Activists in the anticapitalist movement fighting for equitable cooperation will continue to have differences of opinions about all these things. Some will be strongly committed to reform campaigns, while others will prioritize anti-capitalist educational work. Some will favor one reform campaign for reasons they find strategic, while others will favor another campaign for reasons they find equally strategic. Some will emphasize electoral work, while others will be committed to grassroots organizing. Not only will people disagree, sometimes strongly, on these matters, many people will change their opinions on political strategy over their lifetimes. But for all who believe in participatory, democratic procedures, and agree that remuneration should be based on effort and sacrifice, tempered by need, and for all who are not going to change their minds on these essential issues, we need to create vehicles to help them begin to live by this creed. People do not have to live together in a full-scale intentional community in order to democratically agree to share income fairly with others. Programs to bring remuneration closer in line with the efforts and sacrifices people make can enroll people from anywhere in the country and need not remove people from their historic living communities.

To a great extent the devil is in the details of working out particular programs people can subscribe to, but the general idea is simple enough: we know that capitalism rewards some less than they deserve and others more than they deserve. This means that among those of us who are fighting to replace capitalism with an equitable system of cooperation—even as we labor as capitalist wage slaves—some of *us* receive less than we deserve, while others *among us* receive more than we deserve *compared to one another*. The idea is to create programs that rectify this injustice among us *now*—even if only in part—rather than postponing steps to achieve economic justice *among ourselves* until after the demise of capitalism. One program could be for people willing to exchange their entire annual income for an income based on their efforts during the year. Other programs could allow people to exchange a percentage of the income they receive in the capitalist economy for the same percentage of an income based on effort. In both cases participants would have to submit self-reports describing their efforts, participate in procedures for evaluating the efforts of other participants, and have a great deal of trust in others in the program.

No one denies that such programs would require more good faith on the part of participants than is required in a fully operational participatory economy, where efforts and sacrifices are monitored by coworkers according to mutually agreeable procedures. And there is no denying that working out procedures to address differences between the tax obligations, dependent expenses, medical expenses, retirement expenses, debts, and assets that different people in the program have would require careful attention to detail if these programs are to provide efficient and practical opportunities for a range of potential participants. However, this is certainly an area where self-selection bias should work in favor of program success. Moreover, existing intentional communities already have a great deal of experience dealing with many of the devilish details to be worked out, and stand ready to provide expertise and ideas. In any case, no matter how imperfect, these programs could provide participants with opportunities to join in a community of people committed to practicing economic justice while working in the capitalist economy and living among neighbors who do likewise. As explained in the last chapter, these programs also provide a way for supporters of progressive economic movements to test their leaders' sincerity and personal commitment to economic justice.

Conclusion

It is important not to put any particular experiment in equitable cooperation on a pedestal and blind oneself to its limitations. It is also important not to focus exclusively on the limitations of a particular experiment and fail to recognize important ways that it advances the cause of equitable cooperation. But it is most important not to underestimate the value of living experiments in equitable cooperation in general.

The glass will always be part full and part empty. All real-world experiments in equitable cooperation in capitalist economies will not only be imperfect because human efforts are always imperfect, more importantly, they will be imperfect because they must survive within a capitalist economy and are subject to the serious limitations and pressures this entails. Of course it is important to evaluate how successfully any particular experiment advances the cause of equitable cooperation and resists pressures emanating from the capitalist economy to compromise principles of economic justice and democracy. But there is little point in either pretending experiments are flawless or vilifying those struggling to create something better. What is called for is to nurture and improve experiments that already exist, to build new ones that can reach out to people who continue to live in their traditional communities, and eventually to link experiments in cooperation together to form a visible alternative to capitalism in its midst.

14

Conclusion

The struggle between competition and greed and equitable cooperation was both fierce and full of surprises during the twentieth century. Unfortunately, by century's end those fighting to replace the economics of competition and greed with the economics of equitable cooperation were in full retreat. What went wrong? What must those struggling to advance the cause of equitable cooperation do differently in the century ahead to achieve better results?

Never Compromise Principles

Agreeing to accept less than what you deserve is not the same as conceding that you do not deserve more than you got. During the course of the twentieth century, too many on the left lost track of this important difference between the necessity of accepting compromise outcomes and compromising our principles. In particular many of us lost sight of what economic justice and economic democracy *mean*, and what is required to achieve them. The difference between recognizing we cannot win full economic justice because the movement for economic justice is not yet strong enough, and modifying our conception of economic justice to rationalize what we can achieve is crucial. In the first case we remind people that we made some progress, but we validate their feeling that things are still unfair and more changes must be made. In the latter case, in one way or another, we tell people who *are* victims of injustice that they are *not* being treated unfairly and they have no right to complain. That is something a movement for economic justice should never do because when it does it becomes an accomplice to injustice and undermines itself as well. Similarly, when we compromise our conception of economic democracy to accommodate what the movement is capable of winning at some point, we become apologists for ways in which people are still being disenfranchised.

Too many on the left in the twentieth century failed to apply the same criteria to analyzing the legitimacy of income deriving from human capital that we applied to income deriving from nonhuman capital. Too many failed to apply the same logic to differences in the desirability of peoples' work lives we applied to differences in peoples' income. As human capital and the quality of work life become more important considerations in the century ahead, failure to be clear on these matters will increasingly undermine the movement for economic justice. Any system of economic cooperation that does not benefit people equally is not treating people as equals. To benefit equally people who sacrifice more must receive extra compensation commensurate with their extra sacrifice. Contribution-based conceptions of economic justice are a philosophical red herring we need to abandon. Similarly, too many of us succumbed to the sleight of hand whereby the reality of undemocratic corporate power was excused on grounds that consumers and workers indirectly influence decisions when they vote with their pocketbooks and their feet in goods and labor markets. And too many of us were willing to substitute "industrial democracy"—worker representation on boards of directors and joint management committees, and partial worker ownership plans—for true economic self-management—where everyone has decision-making power in proportion to the degree they are affected by economic choices. No matter how often reform campaigns and movements must settle for outcomes that are still unfair, no matter how often we must agree to abide by economic decision making procedures that are still undemocratic, it is crucial to remain clear—"crystal clear" in the words of Colonel Jessup in the movie *A Few Good Men*—about what economic justice and economic democracy mean.

Figure out What We Want

No more excuses. No more intellectual laziness. Critics of capitalism have got to think through and explain to others how we propose to do things differently, and why outcomes will be significantly better. Even when people lend an ear to our complaints about capitalism, we have zero credibility with the public when it comes to replacing capitalism with a wholly different economic system. And in the light of history, people have every reason to be skeptical that the left knows how to create a vastly superior economic system. In any case, since the sacrifices people must make on the road to replacing capitalism will often be great, there must be good reasons for people to believe the benefits will be great as well, not necessarily for themselves, but at least for their children. This does not mean we must agree right now on what the best alternative to capitalism looks like, which is fortunate, because at this point we do not agree among ourselves on whether the best alternative is some form of market socialism, community-based economics, or participatory democratic planning. The debate about alternatives to capitalism in the wake of the collapse of communism is still in its infancy. But the quality of the debate over economic vision must inspire confidence that the movement for equitable cooperation is busy tackling this crucial task effectively. How best to organize a system of equitable cooperation is not a trivial intellectual problem. The answers will not be obvious to those who finally jettison capitalism decades from now without a great deal of deliberation, and much of this deliberation must take place before the moment arrives when the answers are needed. The quality of the thinking and discussion about our alternative to capitalism must inspire confidence that we will have good answers when the time comes.

Not only must intellectual and theoretical discussion improve greatly in quality, we must demonstrate to skeptics that we are testing our theories in practice wherever possible, and seriously studying what the results of our experiments in equitable cooperation teach us about our theoretical models and predictions. We have to give concrete answers to serious questions about precisely how choices will be made. We have to demonstrate why there is good reason to believe that new procedures we recommend will provide people with the opportunity to engage in equitable cooperation without undue demands on their time and energy. We have to seriously consider whether or not procedures that are just and democratic will also be efficient, and not prove too cumbersome or demand too much of peoples' time and patience. Finally, we have to be honest and admit when procedures we recommend may still prove problematic, so people will be prepared to deal with problems when they do inevitably arise. If we are not capable of doing all this, if we are not up to this intellectual task, the movement to replace the economics of competition and greed with the economics of equitable cooperation will not succeed in earning people's trust and confidence.

Work Harder in Reform Movements

Unless anticapitalists throw themselves heart and soul into reform movements we will continue to be marginalized. At least for the foreseeable future most victims of capitalism will seek redress through various reform campaigns fighting to ameliorate the damage capitalism causes. We need to understand that people have every right to expect us to be completely dedicated to making reform campaigns as successful as possible, and every right to consider us AWOL if we do not. Moreover, we must work enthusiastically in reform movements knowing full well that we will usually not rise to leadership positions in these movements because our beliefs will not be supported by a majority of those who are attracted to these movements for many years to come.

But this does not mean we must abandon, or play down our politics. When we work in the labor movement we must teach not only that profit income is unfair, but that the salaries of highly paid professionals are unfair as well when they are paid many times more than ordinary workers while making fewer personal sacrifices. And we must be clear that workers in less developed countries deserve incomes commensurate with their efforts, just as workers in the United States do. In other words, when we work in the labor movement we must insist that the labor movement live up to its billing and become the hammer for justice in capitalism. When we work in the anticorporate movement we must never tire of emphasizing that corporations and their unprecedented power are the major problem in the world today. We must make clear that every concession corporations make is because it is rung out of them by activists who convince them that the anticorporate movement will inflict greater losses on their bottom line if they persist in their antisocial and environmentally destructive behavior than if they accede to our demands. When we work for reforms like pollution taxes that modify incentives for private corporations in the market system, we must also make clear that production for profit and market forces are the worst enemies of the environment, and that the environment will never be adequately protected until those economic institutions are replaced. Even while we work to protect consumers from price gouging and defective products we must make clear how the market system inefficiently promotes excessive individual consumption at the expense of social consumption and leisure. And finally, even while antiglobalization activists work to stop the spread of corporate-sponsored, neoliberal globalization, we must explain how a different kind of globalization from below can improve people's lives rather than destroy their livelihoods.

Working in reform campaigns and reform movements *means* working with others who still accept capitalism. Most who are initially attracted to reform campaigns will be neither anticapitalist nor advocates of replacing capitalism with a wholly new system of equitable cooperation. And most of the leadership of reform campaigns and movements will be even more likely to defend capitalism as a system, and argue that correcting a particular abuse is all that is required. We must never allow others to decide how we work in reform movements, or permit others to dictate our politics. We *do* know something most others at this point do not: that capitalism must eventually be replaced altogether with a system of equitable cooperation. Working wholeheartedly in reform campaigns and movements does *not* mean we must adopt reformist politics, which we know will fail to achieve equitable cooperation in the twenty-first century, just as they did in the twentieth century.

Neither Reforms Nor Experiments Alone Will Suffice

Before we will be able to replace competition and greed with equitable cooperation, before we can replace private enterprise and markets with worker and consumer councils and participatory planning, we will have to devise intermediate means to prevent backsliding and regenerate forward momentum. For the foreseeable future most of this must be done by combining reform work with work to establish and expand imperfect experiments in equitable cooperation. A central contention of this book is that work to reform capitalism *and* work to create imperfect experiments in equitable cooperation are both necessary. Neither strategy is effective by itself. Reforms alone cannot achieve equitable cooperation because as long as the institutions of private enterprise and markets are left in place to reinforce antisocial behavior based on greed and fear, progress toward equitable cooperation will be limited, and the danger of retrogression will be everpresent. Moreover, reform campaigns undermine their leaders' commitment to full economic justice and democracy in a number of ways, and do little to demonstrate that equitable cooperation is possible, or establish new norms and expectations. On the other hand, concentrating exclusively on organizing alternative economic institutions within capitalist economies also cannot be successful. First and foremost, exclusive focus on building alternatives to capitalism is too isolating. Until the noncapitalist sector is large, the livelihoods of most people will depend on winning reforms in the capitalist sector, and therefore that is where most people will become engaged. But concentrating exclusively on experiments in equitable cooperation will also not work because the rules of capitalism put alternative institutions at a disadvantage compared to capitalist firms they must compete against, and because market forces drive noncapitalist institutions to abandon cooperative principles.

Unlike liberated territories in Third World countries, in the advanced economies we will have to build our experiments in equitable cooperation inside our capitalist economies. So our experiments will always be fully exposed to competitive pressures and the culture of capitalism. Maintaining cooperative principles in alternative experiments under these conditions requires high levels of political commitment, which it is reasonable to expect from activists committed to building a new world, but not reasonable to expect from everyone. Therefore, concentrating exclusively on reforms, and focusing only on building alternatives within capitalism are both roads that lead to dead ends. Only in combination will reform campaigns and imperfect experiments in equitable cooperation successfully challenge the economics of competition and greed in the decades ahead.

Since both reform work and building alternatives within capitalism are necessary, neither is inherently more crucial or strategic than the other. Neither is more revolutionary or reformist than the other. Campaigns to reform capitalism and building alternative institutions within capitalism are both integral parts of a successful strategy to accomplish in this century what we failed to accomplish in the past century, namely, making this century capitalism's last! Unfortunately, saying we need stronger reform movements and stronger experiments in equitable cooperation does not do justice to the magnitude of the tasks. Particularly in the United States, we are going to need a *lot* more of both before we even reach a point where an odds maker would bother to give odds on our chances of success. While capitalism spins effective enabling myths to spellbind its victims, the left has too often spun consoling myths about mysterious forces that will come to our rescue even if our organizational and political power remains weak. Nothing substitutes for strong organizations and political power, and there are no easy ways to build either. Over the next two decades most of the heavy lifting will have to be done inside various progressive reform movements because that is where the victims of capitalism will be found, and that's where they have every right to expect us to be working our butts off to render capitalism less destructive. But even now it is crucial to build living experiments in equitable cooperation to prove to ourselves as well as to others that equitable cooperation is possible. Expanding and integrating experiments in equitable cooperation to offer opportunities to more and more people whose experiences in reform movements convince them they want to live by cooperative not competitive principles will become ever more important as time goes on.

Live within the Movement

We need to begin to think differently about what the movement is and how it functions. By "the movement" of course I mean all activists devoted to replacing the economics of competition and greed with the economics of equitable cooperation. But whereas in the past anticapitalist activists identified primarily as members of particular radical political organizations—organizations defined by a particular political ideology and strategic program— I suspect in the future activists will more often be identified by their work in particular reform struggles *and* by how they express their willingness to live according to the principles of equitable cooperation. In other words, I suspect movement activists will increasingly come to have two different organizational reference points, instead of a single, all embracing political sect, preparty, party, or group. Which reform struggle, or anticapitalist educational project I work on, and what organization or caucus I belong to when doing that work will be one point of reference. How I choose to live according to the principles of cooperation, and which experiment in equitable cooperation I belong to will be my second point of reference as a movement activist. Of course there will continue to be differences of opinion among activists about the best way to pursue both tasks: anticapitalist reform work and living according to cooperative principles. And since movement activists are human too, different preferences will enter into activists' choices of how and where they work. But I detect a change toward dual allegiances instead of single allegiances among movement activists, and I think this is a fortuitous trend. I think activists who orient and work with a dual orientation and allegiances not only will be more effective, they will be able to sustain themselves longer as activists and enjoy themselves more in the process. Since I have long been of the opinion that it is activists and organizers who make the world go round, anything that improves their effectiveness and increases heir numbers in my opinion greatly improves our chances of success.

In any case, movement activists need to preach what they practice. We must not only fight alongside others for reforms that make capitalism more equitable and democratic and less environmentally destructive, we must prove by personal example that it is possible for people to live in ways that are more democratic, equitable, and sustainable than anything capitalism permits. We must commit to live according to the principles we espouse. We must go beyond arguing theoretically that equitable cooperation is possible and desirable, and begin to show by concrete example that participatory economic decision making and reward accord to sacrifice do not breed laziness or stifle initiative. We must demonstrate that environmentally friendly lifestyles are enjoyable, and that after economic security is assured, sacrificing excessive income for more leisure improves the quality of life. Quite simply, we must show that people will want to choose equitable cooperation when given the chance. When we begin to do this the difference between those who are committed to the cause of equitable cooperation and those who seek only limited reforms of capitalism will no longer be that the former espouse more militant strategies and tactics during reform campaigns than the latter. The measure of dedication to the cause of equitable cooperation will be willingness to enter into arrangements with others as they become available that better express the cooperative principles we espouse.

Participation by activists is also crucial to the success of noncapitalist experiments. Experiments must not only compete successfully to survive, they must also reject competitive principles and remain faithful to cooperative principles to be successful experiments in equitable cooperation. As an examination of experiments like the Mondragon cooperatives in Spain reveals, this is not easy, and requires a high level of political awareness and commitment by participants. Whereas religious convictions can provide the necessary ingredient in Amish, Mennonite, Hutterite, and Bruderhoff intentional communities that coexist with capitalism, political convictions about the superiority of cooperation to competition are necessary for the success of secular intentional communities. Without the presence of committed activists who share this conviction, experiments are less likely to succeed.

Remuneration based on effort, decision making power in proportion to the degree one is affected, making use of expertise while preventing experts from usurping power cannot be demonstrated as viable and desirable within the workings of capitalism. The fact that capitalism makes economic justice and democracy impossible is the reason it must be replaced! But sensible people do not endorse new ideas until they are sure they work. Especially in light of the history of failed alternatives to capitalism that is part of the legacy of the twentieth century, the progressive economic movement must respect people's skepticism. This means testing the principles of equitable cooperation and proving that they *do* work in living experiments in equitable cooperation. Since these experiments cannot succeed without committed activists, and since activists often find it difficult to sustain their commitment to the struggle without the kind of social support these experiments provide, it is important for activists not only to redouble their committment in reform struggles, but also to prioritize finding where and how to live with other like-minded people according to cooperative principles. That is how to keep hope alive, and how the principles of economic justice and economic democracy can successfully challenge the hegemony of "might makes right."

It's Not Just the Economy, Stupid!

This is a book about building the progressive economic movement so we will be more successful in the new century than we were in the century that recently ended. But there should be no illusions that the economics of competition and greed can be replaced by the economics of equitable cooperation unless other progressive social movements succeed as well. Unless the women's and gay movements, the civil rights and antiracist movements, the environmental movement, and the peace movement all make considerable headway in the years ahead, the progressive economic movement will continue to flounder and the economics of competition and greed will continue to reign supreme. There are a number of reasons our fates hang together, and a concluding chapter is not the place to go into them at great length. Suffice it to say that not only do we often face a common political enemy, more importantly, the values these different movements are fighting for, and therefore the kinds of transformations they seek, are very similar. In large part our fates hang together because it is difficult to establish progressive values in one social arena while reactionary values and dynamics hold sway in other spheres of social life.

The movement for progressive economic change must rid itself of economistic biases that adversely affect how it sees and relates to other social movements. The place to start is to recognize that replacing patriarchal with feminist gender relations, replacing racism with real multiculturalism, replacing militarism with real peaceful coexistence, and protecting the environment before it is too late are just as important as replacing the economics of competition and greed with equitable cooperation. The second step is to recognize that independent movements leading the fight for progressive change in different spheres of social life are needed, and none of the movements should be subordinated to any of the others. Those working for progressive economic change need to understand this ourselves, and also let those working in progressive movements in other spheres of social life know that we finally understand this.

The next step is to propose a grand alliance of progressive movements on very different terms than it has been offered in the past. Instead of envisioning the grand progressive alliance centered around the movement for progressive economic change, and around the labor movement in particular, the grand progressive alliance should be an alliance of equals in which no movement is treated as less important than any other. Moreover, the goal of the alliance should not be to hammer out a political program in all areas that all the movements agree on, or even to agree on priorities for the alliance as a whole. Each of the progressive movements must work out priorities and political programs in their own area, and the grand alliance should not assume that this is the order of business for the alliance. The goal of the alliance should be to increase solidarity among the different mass movements while preserving movement autonomy. Each movement should remain responsible for defining its own priorities, strategies, programs, and campaigns, but each should be entitled to support from the other movements as best they can be helpful. Movements can help one another by engaging in mutual educational campaigns responding to reactionary myths that circulate about other movements among members of each movement. All movements share an interest in rebutting misrepresentations. Movements can help one another by emphasizing to their members when other movements are fighting for the same values and kinds of changes as they are. Movements can help one another financially, through list sharing, and by not working at cross purposes when supporting political candidates wherever possible. The progressive alliance should seek to facilitate all these forms of solidarity while recognize the legitimacy and autonomy of each separate progressive movement. The alliance should also recognizing that there are limits to what the leadership of mass movements can commit to when substantial portions of their memberships disagree. Since this is a problem that progressive leadership of progressive movements all face, agreeing on ways to cope with this problem while developing programs to overcome it should also be an important part of alliance work.

Standing Fast

The next century will prove no easy road for progressive organizers in any of the movements in any of the spheres of social life. Unfortunately for those of us working for progressive economic change, capitalism does not dig its own grave. Instead it charges us dearly for the shovels it sells us to dig our own graves. Only when enough of us come to our senses and put our shovels to better use will the increasing human misery and environmental destruction that marked the end of the century that should have been capitalism's last, give way to a sustainable economy of equitable cooperation. Unfortunately, coming to our senses is easier said than done. It will come to pass only after more sweat and tears have flowed in more reform campaigns than we can yet imagine. It will require countless lives devoted to building experiments in equitable cooperation that swim against the current in the increasingly global cauldron of competition and greed. Fortunately, pouring sweat and tears into the cause of economic justice and democracy are at the center of the human spirit and make our lives fuller.

Hasta la Victoria Siempre.

Notes

Introduction

1. My failure to find a satisfactory explanation within the historical profession may stem, in part, from the fact that it never occurs to most historians to start from my premise. Few historians base their research on economic history on the premise that a democratic socialist economy was a feasible and highly desirable alternative to both capitalist and communist economies throughout the twentieth century, no doubt because very few professional economists would tell them this is an accurate premise to start from!

2. Poor leadership and outright betrayals, capitalist encirclement, economic underdevelopment, ethnic conflicts, the negative effects of a totalitarian political system on centralized economic planning—all these and other negative factors—are largely ignored for this reason, not because they did not play a role in the defeat of communism.

Chapter 1: Economic Justice

1. Edward N. Wolff, *Top Heavy: A Study of the Increasing Inequality of Wealth in America* (The Twentieth Century Fund, 1995), 1–2.
2. Chuck Collins and Felice Yeskel with United for a Fair Economy, *Economic Apartheid in America* (The New Press, 2000), 54–57.
3. Nancy Folbre and the Center for Popular Economics, *The New Field Guide to the U.S. Economy* (The New Press, 1995).
4. Lawrence Mishel and Jared Bernstein, *The State of Working America 1994–1995* (ME Sharpe, 1994), 246.
5. *The State of Working America 1998–1999*, 271.
6. *Economic Apartheid in America*, 56.
7. *The State of Working America 1994–1995*, 121.
8. Edward Wolff, *Economics of Poverty, Inequality and Discrimination* (South-Western Publishing, 1997), 75.
9. Walter Park and David Brat, "A Global Kuznets Curve?" *Kylos* 48 (1995): 110.

10. Leaving personal belongings to decedents is unobjectionable and not the issue. The problem is passing on productive property or wealth in quantities that significantly skew the economic opportunities of members of the new generation.

11. In "Exploitation: A Modern Approach," *The Review of Radical Political Economics* (forthcoming, 2005), I develop a simple model that illustrates this moral dilemma nicely. Readers interested in whether profit and interest income are morally justified or exploitative may find this reading insightful.

12. Lester Thurow, *The Future of Capitalism: How Today's Economic Forces Will Shape the Future* (William Morrow, 1996); Daphne Greenwood and Edward Wolff, "Changes in Wealth in the United States 1962–1983," *Journal of Population Economics* 5 (1992); and Laurence Kotlikoff and Lawrence Summers, "The Role of Intergenerational Transfers in Aggregate Capital Accumulation," *Journal of Political Economy* 89 (1981).

13. Milton Friedman argued this point eloquently in chapter 10 of *Capitalism and Freedom* (University of Chicago Press, 1964). However, his conclusion was that since maxim 2 cannot be defended on moral grounds, critics of capitalism—which tends to distribute the burdens and benefits of economic cooperation according to maxim 1—should mute their criticisms. Essentially Friedman reminded critics of capitalism who favor maxim 2 over maxim 1 that those who live in glass houses shouldn't throw stones!

14. John O'Neill, "Participatory Economics: Comment," *Science & Society* 66, 1 (Spring 2002): 24–26.

15. Robert Nozick, *Anarchy, State, and Utopia* (Basic Books, 1974), 259, 260.

16. Unfortunately many interpret the difference principle in the first way, and cite Rawls in support of trickle-down economics. I am convinced they err in their interpretation, and that Rawls intended the second interpretation of the difference principle. I base this belief not only on his other publications on social justice, but also from personal communication during two philosophy classes I had the pleasure of taking with him when he was in the process of writing *A Theory of Justice*.

17. Rawls steadfastly rejected this line of reasoning, no doubt in part because if accepted it would render his theory of economic justice operationally indistinguishable from classical utilitarianism, which he resolutely opposed.

18. It is apparent from his writings that for Rawls being a victim of injustice is unpleasant, to be sure, but discovering oneself to be a victim of injustice with no right to complain—much less do anything about it—because you had foolishly waved those rights in the original position is almost a fate worse than death. For a man who may well be the foremost moral philosopher of the twentieth century to take the right to dispute injustice that seriously is not surprising.

19. In some situations what we mean by prioritizing goals is to list them in order of importance so we can maximize the most important before moving on to the less important. That kind of prioritization is quite different from choosing weights for different priorities. It requires no weights at all. It simply requires us to arrange our goals in order and maximize them sequentially. It eschews any trade-offs between a higher priority and a lower priority.

20. Of course this is not what Rawls thinks the difference principle does. Since Rawls calls the unequal outcome fair and just, he would not see the difference principle as prioritizing efficiency over equity, much less giving complete priority to efficiency and no weight to equity. Yet this is what it does, in effect, when one distinguishes between efficiency and equity as most economists do.

21. Only because Rawls feared this was often likely to prove the case was it necessary for him to go to the great lengths he did to question whether unequal outcomes were always morally unjustified.

22. In the past twenty-five years Don Harris, Stephen Marglin, Lance Taylor, Amitava Dutt, Thomas Palley, and my colleague at American University, Robert Blecker, among others, have elaborated rigorous theoretical models that demonstrate the possibility and advantages of wage-led growth. For an introduction to wage-led versus profit-led growth, see chapters 8 and 9 in my *The ABCs of Political Economy: A Modern Approach* (Pluto Press, 2002.)

23. I am fully aware just how scary this thought is to many of my fellow progressives who tend to have more human than physical capital and who often argue that "dividing workers" only empowers capitalists.

Chapter 2: Economic Democracy

1. I have the greatest respect and admiration for Sen, and recently wrote an essay praising his numerous contributions: "Amartya Sen: The Late Twentieth Century's Greatest Political Economist?" published in *Understanding Capitalism: Critical Analysis from Karl Marx to Amartya Sen*, Doug Dowd, ed. (Pluto Press, 2002).

2. This defense of relations that are exploitative on grounds that people enter into them voluntarily is rebutted in chapter 4 where the major arguments in favor of capitalism are scrutinized. For a more rigorous treatment using models that highlight the crucial issues see Robin Hahnel, "Exploitation: A Modern Approach," *The Review of Radical Political Economics* (forthcoming, 2005).

3. The mainstream economic paradigm effectively mirrors the classical liberal paradigm of John Locke, substituting mathematically sophisticated nonintersecting individual production and consumption possibility sets for Locke's references to independent farmers and artisans.

4. For a theoretical framework that expresses this alternative starting point, see "A Qualitative Model of the Economic Sphere," in Robin Hahnel and Michael Albert, *Quiet Revolution in Welfare Economics* (Princeton University Press, 1990), 133–140.

5. Whereas economic freedom can be criticized as a conception of economic democracy on grounds that it does not provide an operational goal in social circumstances that are realistic, and therefore inevitably requires additional rules that may prove difficult, if not impossible to justify, this criticism does not apply to majority rule. Just as we can always move closer to approximating decision making input in proportion to the extent that different people are affected, we can always move closer to giving everyone an equal say over every economic decision. The problem with majority rule is not that it fails to offer a coherent goal, the problem is that it offers the wrong goal. Why should we strive to give two people equal say over an economic decision when the decision affects one of them more than the other?

Chapter 3: Debilitating Myths

1. Baran's argument was more sophisticated but similar to one Rosa Luxemburg presented during an earlier period of imperialist expansion in *The Accumulation of Capital: A Contribution to an Economic Explanation of Imperialism* (Berlin, 1913).

2. For an accessible presentation, see Robin Hahnel, *The ABCs of Political Economy: A Modern Approach* (Pluto Press, 2002): 231–241.

3. For those familiar with the terminology, much of what I am talking about here was long debated as the difference between "scientific socialism" and "utopian

socialism." After submitting several articles to *Monthly Review* magazine in the 1970s without success, I received a very polite handwritten note from the late Paul Sweezy that I cherish to this day. He wrote that while he appreciated my submissions and found them well written, it was clear to him that my work was firmly based in the "utopian socialist" tradition. He went on to say he had a great deal of respect for many from that tradition, but that he had long pursued his own investigation of capitalism from a different perspective, the tradition of "scientific socialism," and this was the tradition *Monthly Review* was dedicated to developing. He then wrote that he considered it still to be an open question whether scientific or utopian socialism would prove to be more insightful, or correct. He closed by wishing me the best of luck in pursuing my understanding of capitalism and socialism according to the tradition of my choice. In large part what I have expressed in this section is my belief that new evidence from the past thirty years has weakened the case for scientific socialism even further, and greatly strengthened the case for utopian socialism, and it is time for anticapitalists to adjust our thinking accordingly.

4. Barbara and John Ehrenreich, "The Professional-Managerial Class" in *Between Labor and Capital*, Pat Walker, ed. (South End Press, 1979).

5. Michael Albert and Robin Hahnel, *Marxism and Socialist Theory* (South End Press, 1981) and *Socialism Today and Tomorrow* (South End Press, 1981).

6. See Michael Albert, Leslie Cagan, Noam Chomsky, Robin Hahnel, Mel King, Lydia Sargent, and Holly Sklar, *Liberating Theory* (South End Press, 1986) for a social theory written by people from different progressive movements that recognizes the importance of all spheres of social life and avoids the error of economism.

7. Northern forests provide sequestration and other valuable environmental services as well, and their devastation has been much more severe over the past two hundred years and is continuing. According to a "Green Infrastructure Demonstration Project" study, sponsored jointly by the Metropolitan Washington Council of Governments and National Park Service and released in May 2004, between twenty-eight and forty-three acres of green space is lost *per day* in the Washington D.C. metropolitan area due to urban sprawl "produced" by developers.

Chapter 4: Neither Capitalism Nor Communism

1. See John Roemer, *Free to Lose* (Harvard University Press, 1984); or my chapter 3 in *The ABCs of Political Economy: A Modern Approach* (Pluto Press, 2002).

2. In the words of CIA director George Tenet, people will consider their choices "a slam dunk."

3. Milton Friedman, *Capitalism and Freedom* (University of Chicago Press, 1964), 12–13.

4. See E. K. Hunt and R. C. D'Arge, "On Lemmings and Other Acquisitive Animals: Propositions on Consumption," *Journal of Economic Issues* (June, 1973) for an eloquent criticism of the presumption that externalities are exceptions, rather than the rule.

5. Awarding victims a property right not to be victimized without their consent does not solve the incentive problem. As Ronald Coase demonstrated in his famous article "The Problem of Social Cost," published in the *Journal of Law and Economics* (1960), efficiency—or in our case inefficiency—depends solely on incentives, and is unaffected by whether or not victims of external effects possess the property right not to be victimized without their consent.

6. See John Roemer, *Analytical Foundations of Marxian Economic Theory* (Cambridge University Press, 1981), Theorem 4.9; or Robin Hahnel, *The ABCs of Political Economy: A Modern Approach* (Pluto Press, 2002), 112–127.

7. See Michael Reich, *Racial Inequality* (Princeton University Press, 1981), 204–215, for a simple yet powerful model proving that wage discrimination is a necessary condition for profit maximization for individual capitalist employers operating in competitive markets. Reich's model is extended and generalized in chapter 8 of *Quiet Revolution in Welfare Economics* (Princeton University Press, 1990.)

8. See Barbara Bergman, *In Defense of Affirmative Action* (Basic Books, 1996) for persuasive evidence that affirmative action programs do help victims of discrimination, and that discrimination quickly reappears in their absence.

9. Lawrence Mishel and Jared Bernstein, *The State of Working America: 1994–1995* (ME Sharpe, 1994), 187. "Equivalent" means comparing black and white workers with the same level of education, work experience, etc.

10. These constraints are named after Nobel Laureate Wasily Leontiev, who invented input-output theory and was the first to quantify these constraints.

11. See *Quiet Revolution in Welfare Economics*, chapter 9 for a number of incentive compatible procedures that might have improved the truthfulness of enterprise reporting to central planners.

12. Of course market prices deviate systematically and substantially from true social opportunity costs for reasons discussed above, which is of little concern to mainstream critics of central planning.

13. Of course there is a "bad" reason for maintaining excess demand for both necessities and luxuries: it provides opportunities for the politically well connected to gain personal advantage and enrich themselves through graft.

14. I hasten to add that I am convinced that an honest history will credit Gorbachev—not Ronald Reagan—for the crucial diplomatic initiatives leading to the end of the Cold War. But Gorbachev's role as an extraordinary international statesman is *not* the issue here.

15. See David Kotz and Stan Weir, *Revolution from Above: The Demise of the Soviet Union* (Routledge, 1997) for compelling evidence that the economic performance of the centrally planned economies was not nearly as bad as Western experts and journalists claimed.

16. Stalin was by no means the only communist leader to preach the virtues of "one-man management." Lenin and Trotsky campaigned against worker self-management in Soviet enterprises and proclaimed the advantages of "one-man management" long before Stalin. And Mao in China and Che Guevara in Cuba were no less adamant in their support for "one-man management" as opposed to worker councils.

Chapter 5: Social Democracy

1. I use the term social democracy very broadly, in many cases ignoring political pedigree. When I say social democracy I mean not only the Scandinavian and German political parties that go under that name, and all the political parties that are members of what was originally known as the Second Socialist International but is now called the Socialist International, but also the Labor Party in Great Britain, the Socialist Party in France, and even communist parties in Italy, Spain, and France that transformed themselves into "Eurocommunist" parties in the 1970s and 1980s. I also extend the label to the liberal wing of the Democratic Party in the United States and to a number of parties in other

countries that also lack proper social democratic political pedigree but promote social democratic policies in their countries nonetheless.

2. Michael Harrington, *The Next Left: The History of the Future* (Henry Holt & Co., 1986) and *Socialism: Past and Future* (Little, Brown & Co., 1989); Magnus Ryner, "Neoliberal Globalization and the Crisis of Swedish Social Democracy," in *Economic and Industrial Democracy* 20 (February 1999): 39–79 and *Capitalist Restructuring, Globalization and the Third Way: Lessons from the Swedish Model* (Routledge, 2002). Hereafter references to these works are included in the text.

3. At a session on market socialism versus democratic planning at the Allied Social Science Association annual meetings in the early 1990s, David Kotz illustrated the essential difference between the two sides with the following story: One day a frantic market socialist approached a proponent of democratic planning with an urgent plea for help taming the market: "Come help me tame this wild horse I am riding!" The proponent of democratic planning stared at the market socialist in disbelief and answered: "I don't know what horse you're talking about, but if I were you I'd get down off that tiger before it eats you!"

4. The days when mainstream economists preached fiscal responsibility to right-wing and left-wing governments alike are long since past, at least in the United States where the economics establishment preaches the sermon of budget balancing only to Democrats. When Jimmy Carter and Bill Clinton tried to expand or preserve programs for the needy, mainstream economists out did one another advising fiscal responsibility. But when Ronald Reagan and George W. Bush created unprecedented deficits during peacetime with unconscionable tax cuts for the wealthy and irresponsible increases in military spending, most mainstream economists muted their criticisms or fell silent altogether.

5. Since international financial markets are an even more exacting taskmaster in the early twenty-first century than during the 1980s, there is no country, with the possible exception of the United States, where a progressive government could come to power and not quickly face this problem. While there are no miracles, we shall consider what are better rather than worse ways to deal with this crucial problem when it inevitably arises in chapter 11.

6. This and all subsequent quotations are from Magnus Ryner, "Neoliberal Globalization and the Crisis of Swedish Social Democracy" in *Economic and Industrial Democracy* 20 (February 1999): 39–79.

7. Charles Sackrey and Geoffrey Schneider, *Introduction to Political Economy*, 3rd ed., (Economics Affairs Bureau, 2002), 199.

8. Gregg Olsen, "Half Empty or Half Full?" *Canadian Review of Sociology and Anthropology* (May 1999): 241.

Chapter 6: Libertarian Socialism

1. I use the term libertarian socialism more broadly than most people do. Anyone who advocates direct control by workers and consumers over their own economic activities, and believes capitalism must be replaced to achieve the economics of equitable cooperation is a libertarian socialist according to my usage. I include utopian socialists, guild socialists, anarcho-syndicalists, anarcho-communists, and council communists from the nineteenth and early twentieth centuries. More recently I include the new left, socialist feminists, social ecologists, a variety of new anarchist groups, and many in the more radical wings of different new social movements. And of course I include advocates of solidarity economics, libertarian municipalism, and participatory economics.

2. I look forward to reading a definitive history of libertarian socialism in the twentieth century, but to my knowledge none is available at present. Noam Chomsky went to great lengths to point out in his essay, "Objectivity and Liberal Scholarship" (*American Power and the New Mandarins*, Vintage Books, 1967), that even when writing about events like the Spanish Civil War where libertarian socialists unquestionably played a major role, definitive accounts by renowned scholars such as Gabriel Jackson (*The Spanish Republic and the Civil War in Spain*, Princeton University Press, 1965), Gerald Brenan (*The Spanish Labyrinth: An Account of the Social and Political Background of the Civil War*, Cambridge University Press, 1960, 1943 original), and Hugh Thomas (*The Spanish Civil War*, Harper & Row, 1961) either ignore, downplay, or distort the role played by libertarian socialists. Chomsky's point was that the lack of objectivity of liberal, not just conservative scholarship regarding popular, libertarian movements was responsible for a general lack of familiarity with important parts of twentieth-century history. This is not to say that there are not excellent historical accounts, but that because they were ignored by mainstream publishers and neglected by academics, they are relegated to an underground world of hard-to-get pamphlets and out-of-print books known only to a tiny circle of leftists and scholars without influence.

3. I must say that even this change is welcome. I know I am not the only one who greatly prefers working in the antiglobalization and antiwar movements when anarchist groups replace communist sects in attendance at our meetings, teach-ins, and demonstrations. The anarchist sects are no less courageous and dedicated than communist sects, but their principled commitment to democracy and their instinctive aversion to manipulation makes them far less destructive participants in large organizations and coalitions. One can also rely on anarchists never to deny or excuse totalitarian abuses committed by regimes attacked by U.S. imperialism. The propensity of communist sects to defend policies that should never be excused when they were carried out by governments with whom a sect was allied has often made it harder than need be to convince Americans to join the movement against U.S. imperialism.

4. Michael Harrington, *Socialism: Past and Future* (Little, Brown & Co., 1989), 37.

5. These issues are addressed at length in Part 3.

6. Paul Avrich, *The Russian Anarchists* (Princeton University Press, 1967) is a treasure trove of little-known facts about the history of Russian anarchism.

7. We will never know how differently the Russian revolution might have played out had Left Social Revolutionaries and anarchists been allowed to carry out this overwhelmingly popular program in the Russian countryside. Instead: (1) Less than a year after the October Revolution was launched by a coalition of Bolsheviks, Left Social Revolutionaries, and anarchists, the Bolsheviks outlawed the Left Social Revolutionary and anarchist parties and sent armed detachments under the command of Bolshevik commissars to requisition food from villagers loyal to the banned libertarian socialist parties. (2) After the Russian Civil War was over and forced requisitions were suspended, Bolshevik cadre forcibly dismantled the reconstituted *mirs* that were being successfully managed by village committees because Bolshevik ideologues decided the bourgeois revolution must precede collectivization in agriculture. (3) In 1929, Stalin replaced forced privatization with forced collectivization literally over night, and made retention of even the smallest plots a "capital," capitalist crime. When the majority of Russian peasants rejected this alien program imposed by an alien urban-based regime, Stalin responded with collective and state farms that held villagers captives, mass relocations of populations who resisted, and more notoriously, with mass arrests

and deportations to the Gulag prison system and mass executions for the most recalcitrant. The deaths of 10 to 20 million Russian peasants that resulted was not only one of the greatest crimes against humanity in world history, it put the final nail in the coffin of any lingering hopes for democratizing the Russian Revolution.

8. The effect of anarchism on even Bolshevik cadres was so strong that Lenin had trouble convincing the Left Communist opposition inside the Bolshevik Party to go along with his policies to (1) slow the pace of nationalizations, and (2) transfer managerial authority from factory committees to central planning ministry staff. In *The Bolsheviks and Workers Control: 1917–1921* (Solidarity, 1970), Maurice Brinton provides an eye-opening, documentary history of the struggle between anarchist-led factory committees and the Bolshevik government over the pace of nationalization and who would manage nationalized factories. While Brinton is sympathetic to the anarchists, Maurice Dobb who is sympathetic to Lenin and the Bolsheviks and hostile to their anarchist opponents, confirms Brinton's facts in his own historical account *Soviet Economic Development Since 1917* (International Publishers, 1968).

9. See chapter 2 in Michael Albert and Robin Hahnel, *Socialism Today and Tomorrow* (South End Press, 1981) for a fuller but still brief account of this period in Russian history.

10. Sam Dolgoff, *The Anarchist Collectives: Workers Self-Management in the Spanish Revolution 1936–1939* (Free Life, 1974), 143–144.

11. For a comprehensive history of the largest and most important anarchist organization see Jose Peirat's *La CNT en la Revolución España*, in 3 vols. (Toulouse, 1951, 1952, and 1953).

12. Gerald Brenan, *The Spanish Labyrinth: An Account of the Social and Political Background of the Spanish Civil War* (Cambridge University Press, 1950): 227–338.

13. Dolgoff, *The Anarchist Collectives*, 27.

14. Ibid., 27.

15. Brenan, *The Spanish Labyrinth*, 179.

16. Dolgoff, *The Anarchist Collectives*, 28.

Chapter 7: Postcapitalist Visions

1. This is not to say there will not be some programmatic differences. People with different postcapitalist visions will sometimes prioritize different reforms, and argue for a particular reform in somewhat different ways.

2. The experience of awarding citizens coupons in several Eastern European countries and Russia in the early 1990s confirms what theory predicts: inequalities rapidly reemerge when coupon trading takes place.

3. Yugoslavia was a living example of a public-enterprise, employee-managed market economy from 1952 until the collapse of Yugoslavia in the mid-1980s. Benjamin Ward, Branko Horvat, and Jaroslav Vanek elaborated excellent theoretical versions of worker self-managed market socialism the 1960s and 1970s. Michael Howard (*Self-Management and the Crisis of Socialism*, Rowan & Littlefied, 2000) and David Schweickart (*Against Capitalism,* Westview, 1996, and *After Capitalism*, Rowman & Littlefield, 2002) are among the most recent to present and defend theoretical models of employee managed market socialism.

4. It is often assumed by advocates that market socialism entirely eliminates inequities from unequal ownership of productive property. Unfortunately this is usually not the case. In the original Lange/Lerner/Taylor model of state-managed

market socialism everyone did get equal "social dividends" in addition to whatever labor income they received. But as we saw, while everyone begins with the same portfolio in Roemer's coupon economy, coupon trading would soon leave some people with portfolios that paid far greater dividends than received by others. In all employee-managed market socialist models workers fortunate enough to be employed in enterprises with high-profit-per-employee ratios would receive higher dividends than workers who were employed in firms with low-profit-per-employee ratios. To the extent that higher profits are the result of working with more or better capital this awards workers in those enterprises more nonlabor income than workers in less well-endowed enterprises. So it is not the case that nonlabor income is necessarily equalized in market socialist models.

5. Thomas E. Weisskopf, "Toward a Socialism for the Future, in the Wake of the Demise of the Socialism of the Past," *Review of Radical Political Economics* 24, 3 and 4 (Fall and Winter 1992): 8.

6. David Schweickart, "Socialism, Democracy, Market, Planning: Putting the Pieces Together," *Review of Radical Political Economics* 24, 3 and 4 (Fall and Winter 1992): 31.

7. Michael Howard, *Self-Management and the Crisis of Socialism* (Rowman and Littlefield, 2000).

8. This is not to say that I do not fully support fully funded, universal, public education with admission to all programs beyond those all citizens take based on merit. I support this kind of education system wholeheartedly. As a matter of fact, one of the advantages of the participatory economy described in chapter 8 is that the kind of educational system necessary to advance the causes of political democracy, equal opportunity, and efficient training is fully consistent with economic justice because in a participatory economy those who receive more education (and therefore accumulate more human capial) through the publicly funded educational system would reap no greater economic rewards than those who go to school for fewer years.

9. Sam Bowles, "What Markets Can and Cannot Do," *Challenge Magazine* (July 1991): 13.

10. Putnam made this remark at the 1995 annual meeting of the American Association of Political Scientists in Chicago, as quoted in the *Washington Post* (September 3, 1995): A5.

11. Thomas Weisskopf, "Toward a Socialism for the Future in the Wake of the Socialism of the Past," *Review of Radical Political Economics* 24, 3 and 4 (Fall & Winter 1992): 9.

12. Sam Bowles, "What Markets Can and Cannot Do," 15–16.

13. For an excellent survey and defense of community-based economics on ecological grounds, see Fred Curtis, "Eco-localism and Sustainability," *Ecological Economics* 46 (2003):83–102.

14. See Murray Bookchin, *Post Scarcity Anarchism* (Black Rose Books, 1986, original 1970); Murry Bookchin with Janet Biehl, *The Politics of Social Ecology* (Black Rose Books, 1998); and Howard Hawkins, "Community Control, Workers' Controls, and the Cooperative Commonwealth," *Society and Nature* 1, 3 (1993).

15. See David Korten, *The Post-Corporate World: Life after Capitalism* (Kumarian Press, 1999); and Paul Hawken, *The Ecology of Commerce* (HarperCollins, 1993.)

16. E. F. Schumacher, *Small is Beautiful* (Harper and Row, 1973).

17. Kirkpatrick Sale, "Principles of Bioregionalism" in J. Mander and E. Goldsmith, eds., *The Case against the Global Economy* (Sierra Club Books, 1996).

18. Herman Daly and Joshua Farley, *Ecological Economics* (Island Press, 2004).
19. Joel Kovel, *The Enemy of Nature: The End of Capitalism or the End of the World?* (Zed Books, 2002); and Roy Morrison, *Ecological Democracy* (South End Press, 1995).
20. For example, Joel Kovel takes Kirkpatrick Sale to task for thinking he has answered serious questions about the connections between bioregions by simply saying relations "must be nondependent, nonmonetary, and noninjurious." (Kovel, *Enemy of Nature*, 175; Sale, "Principles," 483).
21. Joel Kovel, *Enemy of Nature*, 156.
22. For critical responses from anarchists, see Odessa Steps, "The Sad Conceit of Participatory Economics," *Northeast Anarchist 8*; Jeff Stein, "Review: Looking Forward," *Libertarian Labor Review* (Winter 1992); Jeff Stein, "Review: After Capitalism," *Anarcho Syndicalist Review* 37 (Spring 2003); and Jon Bekken and the editorial collective, "Anarchist Economics," *Anarcho Syndicalist Review* 39 (Spring 2004).
23. See Pat Devine, *Democracy and Economic Planning* (Westview Press, 1988).

Chapter 8: Participatory Economics

1. George Scialabba, "A Participatory Economy," *Dissent* (Spring 1992):280–281.
2. Alec Nove, *The Economics of Feasible Socialism* (George Allen and Unwin, 1983), 44.
3. For an excellent survey of a large literature evaluating the effect of participation on worker productivity, see David I. Levine and Laura D'Andrea Tyson "Participation, Productivity, and the Firm's Environment" in *Paying for Productivity: A Look at the Evidence*, Alan S. Blinder, ed. (Brookings Institution, 1990).
4. Carl Boggs, "A New Economy," *The Progressive* (May 1992):40.
5. Howard Hawkins, "Review of *Looking Forward* and *The Political Economy of Participatory Economics*," *Left Green Notes* (August–September 1991):14.
6. Among those who argue persuasively that local standards under capitalism do create an unfortunate "race-to-the-bottom effect" are Kristen H. Engel, "State Environmental Standard Setting: Is There a 'Race to the Bottom'?" *Hasting Law Journal* 48, 2 (1997); and Barry G. Rabe, "Power to the States: The Promise and Pitfalls of Decentralization" in *Environmental Policy in the 1990s: Reform or Reaction*, 2nd ed., Norman Vig and Michael Kraft, eds. (Congressional Quarterly Press, 1997).
7. There is a fuller discussion of long-run planning in the next chapter where concerns about overtaxing democracy and decision making priorities are addressed.
8. I provide a concise explanation of the predictable effects of international trade and investment when driven by free market forces in chapter 8 of *The ABCs of Political Economy: A Modern Approach* (Pluto Press, 2002).

Chapter 9: Legitimate Concerns

1. Thomas Weisskopf, "Toward a Socialism for the Future, in the Wake of the Demise of the Socialism of the Past," *Review of Radical Political Economics* 24, 3 and 4 (Fall & Winter 1992):14–17.
2. George Scialabba, "A Participatory Economy," *Dissent* (May 1992):282.
3. Pat Devine, *Democracy and Economic Planning* (Westview, 1988), 265.
4. David Levy, "Seeking a Third Way," *Dollars & Sense* (November 1991):19.

5. Formulating and revising proposals is part of the conceptual work of councils and federations. So meetings to decide on proposals and revisions regarding one's own activities are meetings within, not between councils and federations.

6. Weisskopf, "Toward a Socialism," 15.

7. Nancy Folbre, "Looking Forward: A Roundtable on Participatory Economics," *Z Magazine* (August 1991):69.

8. Weisskopf, "Toward a Socialism," 16.

9. Mark Hagar, "Looking Forward: A Roundtable on Participatory Economics," *Z Magazine* (August 1991):71.

10. John O'Neill, "Comment on Participatory Economics," *Science & Society* 66, 1 (Spring 2002):25–26.

11. David Kotz, "Comment on Participatory Economics," *Science & Society* 66, 1 (Spring 2002):22.

12. It is important to remember that a participatory economy will come about only after a lengthy transition period during which the norms of equitable cooperation will have been considerably strengthened thereby changing people's attitudes and expectations to some extent. But there is evidence that both material and nonmaterial incentives can be powerful motivators even today. The editorial in the July 20, 2004 edition of *The Chronicle Herald* of Halifax, Nova Scotia, had this to report about incentives and doctors in their province: "Research opportunities are a magnet for retaining and recruiting the kinds of minds that fuel the knowledge economy. The perfect example of that was in the late 1990s when the number of neurosurgeons in Halifax had dwindled from eight to three, all over the age of 55. An unattractive fee-for-service schedule had contributed to the brain drain. But with provincial government support we were able to build an attractive academic environment where we could provide neurosurgeons with the ability to do research. We developed an academic neurosurgical department that now is in the top three in Canada. Halifax once again has a full complement of neurosurgeons, which proves that money isn't everything and that job satisfaction is a big part of the equation in attracting talent" (A6).

13. Over the past ten years I have prepared two grades for each student in my university classes. One grade is based on the student's performance, and one grade is based on the student's effort. Not to belabor the obvious, but in both cases the grade is clearly my subjective estimate, whether it be of the quality of their performance or how much effort they exerted. I then ask students to indicate whether they agree or disagree with each grade. On average students have agreed no more often with their performance grades than with their effort grades.

14. Hagar, "Looking Forward," 71.

15. If time spent in an educational or training program requires greater personal sacrifices than time spent in work, then those who go through such a program would be eligible for greater remuneration for their extra sacrifice in a participatory economy. But as was pointed out in chapter 1, the relevant question is not if studying is less desirable than leisure, but if studying is less desirable than work, since those who do not qualify for extra education or training are working while those who do qualify are studying.

16. Weisskopf, "Toward a Socialism," 20.

17. Folbre, "Looking Forward," 69.

18. David Kotz, "Socialism and Innovation," *Science & Society* 66, 1 (Spring 1992):94–96.

19. In capitalist economies the only way to permit innovators to capture a larger share of the benefits from their innovations is to permit them to deny others access to the innovation, even if only temporarily. This necessarily entails a loss of static efficiency. A participatory economy can deploy material incentives to

promote dynamic efficiency if deemed necessary with no loss of static efficiency whatsoever.

20. Weisskopf, "Toward a Socialism," 21–22.

21. Scialabba, "A Participatory Economy," 283.

22. "Money counts more than brains in determining who goes to college, a government study said. A private study for the Department of Education found that high school students from low-income families who had high scores on a standard test were less likely to attend college than all students from the top-income groups. Among the low-income students who weren't planning to attend college despite high test scores, 57% said it was because they could not afford it." (*Washington Post*, August 11, 1998: A8) So much for any illusions about an educational meritocracy in the United States!

23. I am not suggesting that winning public funding for the education of all children was not a great victory for economic justice, since prior to this reform only the children of the wealthy received any education at all. But it remains the case that meritocratic education financed at public expense in an economy with a market for labor can be a program that transfers net benefits from the poor to the wealthy.

24. Weisskopf, "Toward a Socialism," 20.

25. Weisskopf, "Toward a Socialism," 17, 18.

26. Scialabba, "A Participatory Economy," 282.

27. Jason Pramus, "Looking Forward: A Roundtable on Participatory Economics," *Z Magazine* (July–August 1991):74.

28. Matt Ridley provides an accessible synthesis of recent developments in mathematical game theory and evolutionary biology that provide a deeper understanding of the genetic and behavioral basis of human instincts and the evolution of cooperation in *The Origins of Virtue* (Penguin Books, 1996).

Chapter 10: From Here to There

1. For a sobering account of how heavily the U.S. military boot weighs on the rest of the world, see Chalmers Johnson, "America's Empire of Bases" on the Common Dreams Web site: www.commondreams.org.

2. For up-to-date information on the extent of opposition to the war and occupation of Iraq see "Paying the Price: The Mounting Costs of the Iraq War," by Phyllis Bennis and the IPS Iraq Task Force, released on June 24, 2004 and available at: www.ips-dc.org/iraq/costsofwar/.

3. For example, according to a Harvard Civil Rights Project study released on Martin Luther King Day 2004, the nation's schools are once again almost as segregated as they were when Dr. King was assassinated in 1969.

4. While many who worked in progressive economic movements during the twentieth century belatedly recognized the importance of the civil rights, women's, gay, and environmental movements, most were affected by an "economistic" bias that led them to presume that the class struggle against capitalism was always of overriding importance. This error adversely affected relations between different progressive movements in the twentieth century. Ways to avoid this error in the future are discussed in chapter 14.

Chapter 11: Economic Reform Campaigns

1. See chapter 3 of *The ABCs of Political Economy: A Modern Approach* (Pluto Press, 2002) for a simple model demonstrating how credit markets increase inequality even when there are no crises and they do increase economic efficiency.

2. See chapter 9 in *The ABCs of Political Economy* for several simple models illustrating the downside as well as the upside potential of banks and financial markets, pp. 209–220.

3. Many have written persuasively about different global imbalances that have plagued economic performance since the breakdown of the Bretton Woods system. Jan Kregel from the United Nations Conference on Trade and Development delivered a poignant address on this subject at a plenary session of the First Triennial Conference of the International Confederation of Associations for Pluralism in Economics held at the University of Missouri at Kansas City in June 2003. The title of his talk was "Global Economic Policy Coordination: Have We Advanced from the Reagan Policies of Telling the Rest of the World, 'You Must Adjust'?" His answer was certainly not.

4. See Jared Bernstein and Dean Baker, *The Benefits of Full Employment* (EPI, 2003) for an excellent rebuttal to the conservative claim that full employment is either impossible or too costly to achieve.

5. Swedish Social Democratic governments developed a number of stabilization policies beyond standard fiscal and monetary policy that helped them achieve remarkable success in combating unemployment for thirty years after World War II. The Swedish Labor Market Board, investment reserve fund, and worker retraining and relocation programs are all reforms the rest of us would do well to fight for in our own countries.

6. Andrew Shonfield provides an excellent evaluation of both the French policy and the failed British attempt to copy it in *Modern Capitalism* (Oxford University Press, 1974).

7. President Nixon created a commission to study The United States in the Global Economy in the early 1970s. Peter Gary Peterson, who headed the commission, was so impressed with the advantages of Japanese industrial policy that he added a special appendix to the commission report published by the GAO called "The Japanese Economic Miracle," in which he urged the U.S. government to imitate Japanese industrial policy.

8. See Alice Amsden, *Asia's Next Giant: South Korea and Late Industrialization* (Oxford University Press, 1989), and more recently *The Rise of "the Rest": Challenges to the West from Late-Industrialization Economies* (Oxford University Press, 2001). For a brief but compelling rebuttal to the claim that NIC successes were caused by elimination of government intervention, see Stephen C. Smith, *Industrial Policy in Developing Countries* (EPI, 1991).

9. See Dean Baker, Gerald Epstein, and Robert Pollin, eds., *Globalization and Progressive Economic Policy* (Cambridge University Press, 1998) for alternatives to neoliberal development strategies. More recently the Development Studies Program in the Faculty of Economics and Politics at Cambridge University has been active in defending the importance of state intervention and industrial policies for success in economic development. See Ha-Joon Chang, *Kicking away the Ladder: Development Strategy in Historical Perspective* (Anthem Press, 2002) and *Globalization, Economic Development and the Role of the State* (Zed Books, 2002), as well as a volume edited by Chang, *Rethinking Development Economics* (Anthem Press, 2003).

10. See Arthur MacEwan, *Neo-Liberalism or Economic Democracy* (Zed Books, 2000) for a comprehensive, wage-led growth program for developing economies emphasizing domestic production for basic needs. MacEwan goes a long way toward rebutting the taunt neoliberals hurl at their critics: TINA—There Is No

Alternative. See Thomas I. Palley, "Does History Repeat? Some Worrying Parallels between Lula Da Silva and Ramsay MacDonald," September 25, 2003, for a critique of Lula's macroeconomic policies during his first nine months, and for specific recommendations for alternative fiscal, monetary, financial, and foreign exchange policies that would be a vast improvement. Published in Mexico in Spanish, available in English from the author at tpalley@uscc.gov.

11. Raymond Colitt, "Wealthy benefit as Brazil's left feels let down by Lula," *The Financial Times*, December 31, 2003, 12.

12. For a readable, up-to-date account of the various ways the wealthy avoid paying their fair share of taxes, leaving the rest of us to shoulder the burden, see David Cay Johnston, *Perfectly Legal: The Secret Campaign to Rig Our Tax System to Benefit the Super Rich—and Cheat Everybody Else* (Portfolio, 2003).

13. Rodger Doyle, "Undercutting Fairness," *Scientific American* 291, 1 (July 2004):35.

14. For an up-to-date analysis of our present tax structure, see "Progressive and Regressive Taxation in the United States: Who's Really Paying (and Not Paying) Their Fair Share?" by Brian Roach, working paper no. 03–10, October 2003, available at the Global Development and Environment Institute of Tufts University Web site: http://ase.tufts.edu/gdae/.

15. In *A Progressive Answer to the Fiscal Deficit* (EPI, 1989), Arne Anderson argued that the burden of paying for the Reagan deficits should have fallen on those who benefited most from those policies: corporations and the wealthy. Instead, the Clinton administration collaborated with the Republican Congress during the mid-1990s to ensure that just the opposite occurred, and Bush the Younger has waged relentless class war pushing through shameless tax cuts for his wealthy campaign contributors.

16. See "A Distributional Analysis of an Environmental Tax Shift" (1999) by Gilbert Metcalf, available on the Redefining Progress Web site.

17. See *The ABCs of Political Economy*, 112–127 for an accessible presentation of the Sraffian theory of wage, price, and profit determination that makes this clear.

18. For up-to-date information on the status of living-wage campaigns visit the web site of the Living Wage Resource Center, www.livingwagecampaign.org.

19. For a brief introduction to healthcare reform see *Seeking Justice in Health Care: A Guide for Advocates*, available from the Universal Health Care Action Network, UHCAN, www.uhcan.org.

20. For a no-nonsense summary of why a single-payer system is in the best interests of all but the private insurers and for-profit providers, see "Time for Single-Payer?" by Ruth Rosen, *The San Francisco Chronicle*, December 29, 2003.

21. In 1993, Edith Rasell and Richard Rothstein edited a large collection of essays in *School Choice: Examining the Evidence* (EPI), which argued that early evidence suggested that choice of schools had neither raised student achievement nor enhanced equal opportunity. Martin Carnoy rebutted new reports purporting to demonstrate that students using vouchers improve their academic performance, and that the threat of vouchers improves performance in public schools in *School Vouchers: Examining the Evidence* (EPI, 2001). And Fred Hiatt reported that a study by Emily Van Dunk and Anneliese Dickman, "School Choice and the Question of Accountability," released in February 2004, "found little evidence that the Milwaukee program, with 10,000 vouchers (about 10 percent of public school enrollment), had spurred improvement in the public schools." ("Limits and Lessons of Vouchers," *Washington Post*, February 23, 2004.)

22. Differences in per-pupil expenditures are largely due to the fact that public education in the United States is provided by local government in a context of large differences of income and wealth between different local jurisdictions. New

Hampshire and Vermont have recently implimented statewide property taxes in order to make school funding more fair.

23. Some organizations that promote and maintain information on community development programs are: the National Association of Development Organizations, www. nado.org; the National Neighborhood Coalition, www.neighbor hoodcoalition.org; the Alliance for National Renewal, National Civic League, www.ncl.org/anr; the Aspen Institute, www.aspeninstitute.org; and the Center for Community Change, www.communitychange.com.

24. In 1967, the Institute for Community Economics (ICE) pioneered the concept of community land trusts as a means to give people with low incomes the opportunity to own their own homes while preserving the affordability of these homes for future residents. In 1979, ICE created a Revolving Loan Fund that has provided communities with more than 370 loans totalling more than $35 million. Besides providing technical and financial assistance to communities with CLTs, ICE has now helped organize the CLT Network, a coalition of CLTs spread across the United States. For more information about ICE and its programs see its Web site: www.iceclt.org.

25. I am grateful to Tom Wetzel, President of the San Francisco Community Land Trust, for explaining to me how it took an uprising of community residents in the Mission District of San Francisco, and a strike by the Mission Housing Development Corporation staff to stop the board of directors of the MHCDC from shifting its priorities to market-rate housing from low-income housing.

26. For an excellent documentary film on the harmful effects of sprawl and what can be done about it, see "Save Our Land Save Our Towns," produced by Thomas Hylton and available from Bullfrog Films.

27. Apparently Karl Rove decided the American attention span is even shorter than most believed. Mike Allen reported in "Bid to Change Social Security is Back: Bush Aides Resurrect Plan for Personal Retirement Accounts" (*Washington Post*, November 21, 2003): "White House advisor Karl Rove is advising President Bush to revive his long-shelved plan to let workers divert some Social Security taxes into stocks as a reelection issue, gambling that market drops have not soured voters on the politically risky idea."

Chapter 12: Economic Reform Movements

1. Nelson Leichtenstein provides an excellent historical overview of the American labor movement in *State of the Union: A Century of American Labor* (Princeton University Press, 2003). It is also important to acknowledge at the outset that real power in the U.S. labor movement resides in individual unions or locals, not in the AFL-CIO. The vast majority of union dues go to locals or regional councils, leaving the AFL-CIO to rely on various enterprises like its credit card business and grants for most of its funds.

2. Available on Elaine Bernard's Web site: www.htup.harvard.edu/eb/whyunion.pdf.

3. Bernard herself suggests more far reaching changes in "Creating Democratic Communities in the Workplace," in *The New Labor Movement for the New Century*, Gregory Mantsios, ed. (Monthly Review Press, 1998), and in "Social Unionism and Restructuring," with Sid Shniad in *New Labor Forum* (Fall 1997). For insightful analyses of recent cases of union alliances with progressive community groups that seek to move beyond business unionism, see *Partnering for Change: Unions and Community Groups Build Coalitions for Economic Justice*, David Reynolds, ed. (M.E. Sharpe, 2004), and *Central Labor Councils and the*

Revival of American Unionism: Organizing for Justice in Our Communities, Immanuel Ness and Stuart Eimer, ed. (M.E. Sharpe, 2001).

4. Equitable living "communities" need not be geographically defined or encompass all aspects of a person's life. While many experiments reviewed in chapter 13 have taken this form, more flexible alternatives are also discussed.

5. *The Corporation* by Mark Achbar, Jennifer Abbott and Joel Bakan is a truly exceptional, must-see documentary film about the modern corporation. David Korten, *When Corporations Rule the World* (Kumarian Press, 1995); Joshua Karliner, *Corporate Planet: Ecology and Politics in the Age of Globalization* (Sierra Club Books, 1997); Naomi Klein, *No Logo: Taking Aim at the Brand Bullies* (Picador, 1999); and Charles Derber, *Corporation Nation* (St. Martins Press, 2000) are some recent books documenting the detrimental effects of the growth of corporate power.

6. Peter Jennings named Malden Mills owner and CEO, Aaron Feurerstein, "Person of the Week," and President Clinton recognized him in his State of the Union Address in January 1996. See Josh Simon, "The Mensch of Malden Mills," *Life* (May 5, 1997), and Susan Vaughn, "Firms Find Long-Term Rewards in Doing Good: A New Breed of Corporation Is Emerging Whose Leaders Place Principles Before Profits," *Los Angeles Times* (November 3, 1997).

7. See chapter 6, "Command and Control," in William Grieder, *The Soul of Capitalism: Opening Paths to a Moral Economy* (Simon and Schuster, 2003) for another excellent introduction to the history of corporations in America.

8. While there are always adjustment costs associated with moving resources out of one industry and into another, if the new pattern of production is more socially useful, and if there is a "conversion" plan to make sure the burdens of adjustment are equitably shared, it is well worthwhile. Seymour Melman was an early pioneer in the field of military conversion. See his *Demilitarized Society: Disarmament and Conversion* (Harvest House, 1988). Ann Markusen and Catherine Hill briefly outline a plan to redeploy human and physical capital from the military sector to the transportation and housing sectors in *Converting the Cold War Economy: Investing in Industries, Workers, and Communities* (EPI, 1992). Similarly, making sure that environmental protection is not done at the expense of jobs is a matter of implementing a good conversion plan. The argument that either converting to peacetime production or environmentally friendly products and technologies must be at the expense of jobs is a political red herring that can be laid to rest by recognizing the need for a conversion plan to minimize transition costs and share them equitably.

9. For an excellent study of struggles against environmental destruction waged by poor communities see Joan Martinez-Alier, *The Environmentalism of the Poor* (Edward Elgar, 2002), especially chapters 5, 6, 7, and 8.

10. For more information about CFA, its publications, and its programs, see www.consumerfed.org.

11. For more information about PIRG, its publications, and its programs see www.pirg.org. For more information about Public Citizen and its campaigns see www.publiccitizen.org.

12. For more information about the programs and publications of the Center for the New American Dream, see www.newdream.org.

13. I am not talking only about the middle-class origins of much of the leadership of these movements, nor the middle-class status their conditions of employment as leaders of these movements secure them personally. I am referring to the middle-class status of a significant portion of the constituencies served by these movements as well.

14. Mark Tomey, "Revisiting the National Welfare Rights Organization," *Color Lines* 3, 3 (Fall 2000).
15. Gary Delgado, "The Truth about Welfare Reform," *Color Lines* 3, 3 (Fall 2000).
16. Quoted by Nicole Davis in "Welfare Organizing at the Grassroots," *Color Line* 3, 3 (Fall 2000).
17. For more information about ACORN and its programs, see www.acorn.org.
18. A report prepared by Angus Maddison for the Organization for Economic Cooperation and Development (OECD) titled *Monitoring the World Economy 1820–1992*, published in 1995, provided an early warning that the popular impression that neoliberal policies had increased world economic growth rates was simply wrong. Maddison compared growth rates in the seven major regions of the world from 1950 to 1973, the Bretton Woods era, to growth rates from 1974 to 1992—the neoliberal era, and found there had been significant *declines* in the annual average rate of growth of GDP per capita in six of the seven regions, and only a slight increase in one region, Asia. Maddison reported that the average annual rate of growth of world GDP per capita during the neoliberal period was only *half* what it had been in the Bretton Woods era. In *Scorecard on Globalization 1980–2000: Twenty Years of Diminished Progress*, available on its web site, www.cepr.net, the Center for Economic Policy Research updated Maddison's work and reconfirmed his conclusion that neoliberal policies continue to be accompanied by a significant *decrease* in the rate of growth of world GDP per capita. If dismantling the Bretton Woods system to promote capital and trade liberalization, combined with macroeconomic structural adjustment policies, had really produced efficiency gains, it is hard to imagine how world growth rates would have been cut by half!
19. See chapters 8 and 9 in *The ABCs of Political Economy*.
20. For simple models that demonstrate why this is the likely result, see "International Investment in a Simple Corn Model," in *The ABCs of Political Economy*, 212–216; and Appendix B in *Panic Rules! Everything You Need to Know about Globalization* (South End Press, 1999).
21. Paul Volcker, Luncheon address to the OECD conference on "Making Globalization Work," March 18, 1999.
22. See *Reclaiming Development: An Alternative Economic Policy Manual* (Zed Books, 2004) by Ha-Joon Chang and Ilene Grabel for an accessible rebuttal of neoliberal myths and a common sense alternative for developing economies.
23. See *We Are Everywhere: The Irresistible Rise of the Global Anti-Capitalism*, by the editorial collective "Notes from Nowhere," (Verso, 2003).

Chapter 13: Experiments in Equitable Cooperation

1. For information on Time Dollars, see www.timedollar.org, and for an enthusiastic account by its creator, see Edgar Cahn, *No More Throw-Away People* (Essential Publishing, 2000). C. George Benello, Robert Swann, Shann Turnbull, and Ward Morehouse provide an overview of alternative currencies and banking systems in *Builiding Sustainable Communities: Tools and Concepts for Self-Reliant Economic Change* (Bootstrap Press, 1997.) The *International Journal of Community Currency Research* is the main journal for information on local currency experiments worldwide.
2. For example, in the Green Dollar LETS program created in 1983 by a self-employed business studies graduate concerned about the 18 percent unemployment rate on Vancouver Island, Canada, participants list what their wants are and what they have to offer along with their phone numbers in a regular monthly

newsletter, and a computer keeps track of account holders' green dollar trading transactions.

3. The ESOP Association in Washington D.C. provides technical assistance, publishes educational materials, and coordinates state chapters of companies with employee stock ownership plans: www.esopassociation.org. American Capital Strategies both promotes and maintains a national directory of ESOPs: www.esops.com. However, by its own admission the Foundation for Enterprise Development is "dedicated to helping entrepreneurs and executives use employee ownership and equity compensation as an effective means of motivating the workforce and improving corporate performance." See: www.fed.org.

4. A famous street poster from the May 1968 uprising in France summarized the problem with many forms of worker participation in capitalist firms. The poster read: "Question: How do you conjugate the verb "to participate?" Answer: I participate. You participate. We participate. They decide."

5. See www.geo.coop. For up-to-date reports on progressive worker-owned firms, see GEO's bimonthly *Newsletter for Democratic Workplaces & Globalization from Below.* For an informative book of testimonies, analyses, and resources about worker-owned cooperatives, see *When Workers Decide: Workplace Democracy Takes Root in America,* Frank Lindenfeld and Len Krimerman, eds. (New Society Publishers, 1990.) For an excellent video about a handful of progressive producer cooperatives in the San Francisco Bay area see *Democracy in the Workplace: Three Worker-Owned Businesses* available at www.ofcenter-video.com. For information about producer cooperatives in the rest of the world, see the International Institute for Self-Management: www.iism.net. For an excellent video about producer cooperatives in the United Kingdom, see *The Co-op Advantage* available from GEO. Finally, for ideas about how producer cooperatives can play an important role in promoting economic development in rural areas in the United States, see *Cooperatives and Local Development: Theory and Applications for the 21st Century,* Christopher Merrett and Norman Walzer, eds. (M.E. Sharpe, 2004).

6. Capitalist firms also discriminate against worker-owned firms without necessarily intending to do so. A visitor studying worker cooperatives in Spain recorded the following sad story in his notebook: "Agustin E. Gonzalez Prado and Luis F. Alonso Ibanez—the current and former manager of Sociedad Cooperativa Ovetense de Mecanización y Maquinaría, a machinist cooperative in the province of Asturias—stated that originally they had difficulties generating business because COVEMYM's nonhierarchical structure made it difficult for the co-op to interface with hierarchical corporations. Business transactions, they explained, are often based on personal relationships between people at the top of the hierarchies who speak for the entire organization. To accommodate these external expectations, a specialized management structure gradually evolved at COVEMYM. Luis stated that this painful process met great internal resistance but was necessary for survival." See Malcolm Harper, *Their Own Ideas: Lessons from Workers' Cooperatives* (Intermediate Technology Publications, 1992) for useful insights into why worker cooperatives have failed more often than not.

7. Gar Alperowitz, "Sustainability and Systemic Issues in a New Era," in *Rethinking Sustainability: Power, Knowledge and Institutions,* Jonathan Harris, ed. (University of Michigan Press, 2003), 19–20.

8. Tim Huet, a cofounder of the Association of Arizmendi Cooperatives in Northern California, provides a compelling rationale for the importance of cooperative development in "A Cooperative Manifesto," *GEO: Grassroots Economic Organizing* 61 (March-April 2004):10–12. I fully concur with his conclusion: "I'm aware that my opening claim of 'There Is No More Important Social Change

Work You Can Do Than Cooperative Development'—TINMISCWYCDTCD—would strike some activists in other social change movements as a bit grandiose and perhaps even offensive. Yet I do not claim that cooperative development is more important than all other forms of social change work. There are various forms of social change work that are just as important, and need to be carried out simultaneously if not in conjunction. I don't think cooperative development in itself will ever solve all the world's problems. Nor do I think worker cooperatives can or should stand apart from other social change movements; for instance, we need to battle the many injustices (racism, sexism, etc.) that pervade our society and will not be barred from our doors by any declaration that 'we're all equal here at our cooperative.' In particular, I think worker cooperators need to think of ourselves and act as part of the larger labor movement, not leaving behind other workers because 'we got ours.' And I can fully understand someone dedicating herself or himself to another form of social change work and never having anything to do with cooperatives. Those who seek to be agents of social change should choose the area(s) in which they can best contribute and find the most fulfillment. For myself, I have found cooperative development to be very fulfilling as well as meaningful, and hope to convince many others to join in."

9. See www.mner.org.ar. For a short article on worker takeovers in Argentina, see Andres Gaudin, "Occupying, Resisting, Producing," *Dollars and Sense* (March/April 2004). For an excellent documentary film about the movement see *The Take* produced and directed by Naomi Klein and Avi Lewis. For an excellent evaluation of a long-lived industrial cooperative in a different Third World setting, see Isaac Thomas, Richard Franke, and Pyaralal Raghavan, *Democracy at work in an Indian industrial cooperative: The story of Kerala Dinesh Beedi* (Cornell University Press, 1998). While not reviewed here, it should be noted there were upsurges in worker takeovers like those in Argentina in South Korea and Brazil in the aftermath of their financial crises in 1997 and 1998, respectively.

10. A great deal of information is available on the Mondragón web site: www. mondragon.mcc.es. Books offering extensive information and analysis are George Cheney, *Values at Work: Employee Participation Meets Market Pressure at Mondragón* (Cornell University Press, 2000); Greg MacLeod, *From Mondragón to America: Experiments in Community Economic Development* (University College of Cape Breton Press, 1998); Roy Morrison, *We Build the Road As We Travel: Mondragón, A Cooperative Social System* (New Society Press, 1991); William Whyte and Kathleen Whyte, *Making Mondragón: The Growth and Dynamics of the Worker Cooperative Complex* (ILR Press, 1988); and Henk Thomas and Chris Logan, *Mondragón: An Economic Analysis* (Allen and Unwin, 1982). For a critical symposium on Mondragón by advocates for worker cooperatives Michael Howard, Holm-Detlev Kohler, William Waterman, Fred Freundlich, and Curtis Haynes Jr. see *GEO*, number 20, January/February 1996.

11. Dawn Nakano, *Community Economic Development: Findings of a Survey of the Field* (National Center for Economic Alternatives, 1994).

12. Just as the University of Wisconsin at Madison maintains an extensive research and support program for consumer cooperatives, the University of Massachusetts at Amherst hosts a useful research and support program for Community Supported Agriculture. See www.umass.edu/umext/csa/.

13. The presentation in its entirety, as well as countless planning documents, numerous other articles, and an extensive bibliography on the "Kerala model" can all be found on the Web site of Richard Franke at Montclair University: http://chss.montclair,edu/anthro/franke.html. For a fascinating account of the People's Campaign by its principle architect, see T. M. Thomas Isaac with

Richard Franke, *Local Democracy and Development: the Kerala People's Campaign for Decentralized Planning* (Rowman & Littlefield, 2002).

14. See the Federation of Egalitarian Communities Web site: www.theFEC.org. The index for this book was done by a founding member of the FEC Twin Oaks International Community. For information about this egalitarian community of 85 adults and 15 children in Louisa Virginia see www.twinoaks.org. For a study of the achievements and failures of a wide variety of cooperative living arrangements see George Melnyk, *The Search for Community* (Black Rose Books, 1985.) Timothy Miller has published the first volume of his exhaustive study of intentional communities in the United States in the twentieth century: *Quest for Utopia in Twentieth Century America: Volume 1: 1900–1960* (Syracuse University Press, 1998). Hopefully the second volume will soon be available as well.

15. "New Standard of Living Blossoms at Eco-Village" published in the *Washington Post,* May 31, 2004, was an exception to the general lack of coverage on intentional communities in the mainstream media. Jason Ukman reports that residents of Eco-Village, located near Lovettsville in Loudon County, Virginia, "have forged an uncommonly tight-knit neighborhood, with covenants designed to foster a sense of community, and promoted an equally remarkable devotion to protecting the environment, with homes and land-use rules that take nature into consideration." Ukman also makes clear that at least in the greater Washington D.C. area, the movement of people seeking an alternative to suburbia through various cohousing projects is growing: "EcoVillage is among the first of several nearby 'co-housing' communities—small-scale neighborhoods that operate on the basis of active resident participation and typically make decisions by consensus. In the District, Maryland and Northern Virginia, at least four such communities now operate, and at least three more are planned, according to Mid-Atlantic Cohousing. The idea behind them is a neighborliness and togetherness not known in the cardboard cutouts of the rest of suburbia."

16. See www.parecon.org/writings/burrows_lac.htm for Burrows' presentation at The World Social Forum III in its entirety.

17. See www.parecon.org/writings/burrows.htm.

Index